HISTORICAL RECORDS OF OLD FREDERICK AND HAMPSHIRE COUNTIES, VIRGINIA

(REVISED)

By

D0869406

Wilmer L. Kerns, Ph.D.

Heritage Books, Inc.
Bowie, Maryland

1992

Published 1992 By

HERITAGE BOOKS, INC.
1540-E Pointer Ridge Place
Bowie, MD 20716
(301) 390-7709

ISBN 1-55613-592-0

Library of Congress Catalog Card Number 92-70412

A Complete Catalog Listing Hundreds of Titles on
History, Genealogy, and Americana
Free on Request

Contents

This book is dedicated to the memory of Ralph L. Triplett, Esquire (1898-1984). He was a backswoodsman, poet, mountain folklorist, musician, genealogist, philosopher, teacher, and author. He is best remembered for his original work in transcribing and publishing graveyard inscriptions, and for authoring a book, A History of Upper Back Creek Valley. Triplett inspired many persons to become interested in genealogy and local history.

Wilmer L. Kerns and Ralph L. Triplett Esq., in 1983, at Gore, Virginia. The family Bible of Bartholomew McKee (1779-1864) is shown in photograph.

Old Frederick County, Virginia

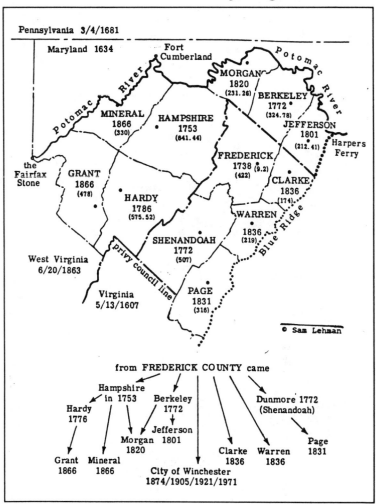

Pennsylvania 3/4/1681

Maryland 1634

Fort Cumberland

Potomac River

MORGAN
1820
(231.26)

BERKELEY
1772
(324.78)

MINERAL
1866
(330)

HAMPSHIRE
1753
(641.44)

JEFFERSON
1801
(212.41)

Harpers
Ferry

FREDERICK
1738
(422) (9.2)

the
Fairfax
Stone

GRANT
1866
(478)

HARDY
1786
(575.52)

CLARKE
1836
(174)

WARREN
1836
(219)

Blue Ridge

West Virginia
6/20/1863

privy council line

SHENANDOAH
1772
(507)

Virginia
5/13/1607

PAGE
1831
(316)

© Sam Lehman

from FREDERICK COUNTY came

Hampshire
in 1753

Berkeley
1772

Dunmore 1772
(Shenandoah)

Hardy
1776

Jefferson
1801

Morgan
1820

Page
1831

Grant
1866

Mineral
1866

Clarke
1836

Warren
1836

City of Winchester
1874/1905/1921/1971

Old Frederick County, Virginia has been subdivided into twelve counties. The map above shows the year of formation and the square-mile area for each county. Seven of the counties are now in the eastern panhandle of West Virginia.

Preface

Vital data in this second revision of historical records have been gleaned from many private and public sources: from the Virginia State Archives, such as death records, jury lists, inquisitions, business licenses, guardian and apprenticeship bonds, ministers' bonds, and constable bonds; courthouse death records; graveyards on private properties; old letters and newspapers; Bible records and prayer books; county histories published in western states during the 19th century; journals and diaries; mortician books; military records (pensions); from notes found on scraps of paper in drawers or in attics; scribblings in old books; denominational or religious periodicals; information found in courthouse deeds, especially the settlement of real estates; chancery and circuit court records; and from individuals who have collected information on their ancestors.

In many cases, a record was established by evaluating conflicting data found in multiple sources. The reader is cautioned that potential errors occur in all sources of information, especially courthouse birth and death records. These should be verified with other references, where possible.

Most of the unpublished and unique records were collected from primary sources during the past two decades, while conducting primary research in Frederick County, Virginia; Hampshire County, West Virginia; and, to a lesser extent, in Morgan, Mineral and Hardy Counties, West Virginia. Priority was given to publishing the older records, especially data on the pioneers and early settlers. This is not a graveyard history, although the authoritative source for many of the records is the graveyard tombstone.

Wilmer L. Kerns, Ph.D.
4715 North 38th Place
Arlington, VA 22207

February 8, 1992

HISTORICAL RECORDS OF OLD FREDERICK AND HAMPSHIRE COUNTIES, VIRGINIA

Introduction

Frederick County came into existence as a political subdivision of Orange County on December 21, 1738. Subsequently, the original geographic area of Old Frederick County was divided into twelve counties; namely Frederick, Shenandoah, Clarke, Warren and Page Counties in Virginia; and Hampshire, Hardy, Morgan, Berkeley, Jefferson, Grant, and Mineral Counties in West Virginia. Good and Ebert have provided a guide for researching records in this general geographic area.[1]

Generally, historic records of present-day Frederick County and Winchester City have been preserved in the respective courts in Winchester, Virginia.[2] A predominant amount of historic data presented in this volume relates to Frederick County, Va., and Old Hampshire County, particularly Hardy, Mineral and Morgan Counties, West Virginia. Hampshire County data are of special value because many of the vital data were lost or destroyed during the Civil War era.

Please refer to the index for a complete list of surnames in this volume, including maiden names. Not all names are presented in alphabetical order. In certain cases, the text contains surnames that are arranged by subject, such as a graveyard, rather than a homogeneous organization of genealogical data.

---

1. Rebecca H. Good and Rebecca A. Ebert, *Finding your People in the Shenandoah Valley of Virginia* (Alexandria, Va.: Hearthside Press, 1988) 104.

2. Certain miscellaneous and loose records have been archived by the county or city court clerks to the Virginia State Library in Richmond, Virginia. Access to these records are available only to researchers who have secured written permission from the clerks of respective local courts.

The Lost Records of Old Hampshire County

Hampshire County was formed from Frederick County, Va., on May 1, 1754. Maxwell and Swisher[3] erroneously stated that Hampshire County was created from Augusta County and this mistake has been propogated by certain researchers.

Because of aggressive Indian attacks during the French and Indian War, and a lack of facilities in Romney, the early Hampshire County Court was held in Winchester, from its inception as a county in 1754, until 1757.

The first resident clerk of court in Hampshire County[4] was Gabriel Jones, who served from 1757 to 1782. Known as "the King's Attorney," he served also as the personal attorney and adminstrator for Lord Fairfax.

During this early period, perhaps no other county in Virginia had a more competent beginning, or a more efficient system for public records management. A review of the early deeds in the county courthouse reveals a high caliber of documentation, written in an artistic form of penmanship.

During the Civil War, many of the Hampshire County court records were either lost or destroyed. All marriage books from the Revolutionary War period to 1865 are missing. Some of the old Will books are gone, as well as order books, and many other valuable records normally preserved by courts.

Researchers should know that Old Virginia county personal property tax lists, 1782-1850, are housed in the Virginia State Library, Archives Division, Richmond, Virginia. Anyone may secure a microfilmed copy of the property tax records through an inter-library loan. Also, real estate tax records for Frederick County are extant, but these same Hampshire County records did not survive.

---

3. Hu Maxwell and H. L. Swisher, *History of Hampshire County, West Virginia*, 1897. Reprint. McClain Printing Company, Parsons, W.Va., 1972, page 82.

4. Archibald Wager was listed as the first clerk, per Maxwell and Swisher, when the court met in Winchester during the 1755-1757 era. He was followed by Gabriel Jones (1757-1782), Andrew Woodrow (1782-1814), Samuel McGuire (1814-1815), and John Baker White (1815-1863). After a break caused by the Civil War, Christian Streit Baker became the next clerk.

Deed books are generally considered to be the most important records in a county courthouse. All of these books were preserved— thanks to both shrewd planning and hustle by local leaders to save the records.

In 1861, two of the most politically influential men in Romney were John Baker White, who had served as clerk of court since 1815, and John Kern, who had served as county commissioner for several decades. When the Civil War started in 1861, the territory was part of the Confederate State of Virginia. On June 20, 1863, West Virginia was formed as the 35th state. Being a border state, it officially changed sides midstream in the war, from Confederate to Union. Most of the servicemen from Hampshire County remained in their Confederate military units.

John Baker White was said to have been sympathetic to the Union when the Civil War began, but he publicly debated both sides of the issues. Because of his frankness and lack of firm committment to either side, during the early stages of the war, White and the Hampshire County courthouse became targets of harrassment by Union armies. In 1861, the Yankees set out to destroy the public records of Hampshire County. Upon learning of these plans, White packed the most important books— primarily the land records— into a wagon and sent them to Winchester. The enemy was thwarted by this action.

Later, White assumed a post in the administration of President Jefferson Davis, in Richmond, Virginia, followed by Kern. Ironically, White died a year later and Kern died the next year, both in Richmond. Before his death, White told his son, Christian Streit White, a captain in the Confederate Army, to preserve the safety of the public records of Hampshire County that were stored in Winchester.

Subsequently, fierce battles were fought throughout Northern Virginia, including Winchester and Frederick County. In fact, during the period of the war, possession of Winchester alternated 78 times between Union armies and Confederate armies.

In 1863, Christian Streit White received intelligence that said the Union army planned to destroy Hampshire County records that were transferred to Winchester for safe keeping. Captain White removed the records and took them to Front Royal, Warren County, Va., with the Yankees in hot pursuit. From Front Royal, the records were taken to a cave near Luray, Va. This cave is believed to have been what is now known as Luray Caverns.

Somehow, during the autumn of 1864, the Yankees learned that the record books were in Luray, and they sought to destroy them. Again, Captain C. S. White learned about the Yankees' planned mission of destruction. He rushed to Luray with a military unit and caught the Yankees in the beginning process of destroying the records.

By the time that he arrived, the soldiers had begun to destroy the records and had already slashed several pages from record books. Engaging the enemy, White and his men fought to preserve the rare and valuable records. After winning the battle, White and his 150-man military unit took the records to a secret hideout in North Carolina.

When the war was over, White went to North Carolina, retrieved the books and hauled them to Staunton, Va. From there, the books were sent back home to Romney, by express coach. These were the deed books and certain will books. In 1872, Christian Streit White— rescuer of the records— became county clerk of court.

The war history of the record books is considered to be accurate because it was based on a first-hand account that White gave to Maxwell and Swisher.[5] The big questions are: What happened to the volumes of records that were left behind in the courthouse in Romney? Where are the marriage records?

A post-war letter from the Frederick County clerk to Rev. Simeon Ward, requested that the record books deposited in Winchester during the War should be reclaimed by Hampshire County. Nothing more is known about the records in that despository.

Many persons have attempted to answer questions about the disappearance of records in Romney, without a knowledge of local history. The courthouse did not burn, nor was it destroyed during the Civil War, as often rumored.

Maxwell and Swisher claimed that Union soldiers used the courthouse as a stable during the war. Records which were left in the building were scattered on the floor and courthouse lawn and

---

5. Maxwell and Swisher, pages 370-372.

were either destroyed or lost over time. Soldiers may have taken record books for souvenirs or to use them for building campfires. Local citizens were said to have retrieved books from the courthouse lawn.

Another possibility is that certain record books were housed in private homes and not returned to the courthouse after the war. One similar incident involved the "burnt records" of Rockingham County, Va., which were rediscovered several decades ago in a private residence in the eastern part of the county and returned to the courthouse. Tradition said that these books had been burned (destroyed) by soldiers who ambushed the records that were being transported to safety in a covered wagon. A private citizen, who lived near the scene, stored the books in a vacant room. Although edges of the books had been burned, many of the records were legible when rediscovered by officials.

One hypothesis is that some of the "lost records" of Hampshire County are in the hands of unsuspecting, private citizens; stored to be rediscovered in dust-filled attics, closets or basements. To test the hypothesis, I wrote an article on this subject in 1984, which was published in a local newspaper.[6] An appeal was made for local citizens to return courthouse record books which their ancestors may have found or taken during the 1860s.

Not surprisingly, a response came almost immediately from a Hampshire County resident, Kenneth Park, who had a record book of Magistrate Philip Fahs, containing a master schedule of court judgments for the 1824-1837 era. The man stated that his ancestor, Benjamin Park, had salvaged the record book from the courthouse lawn during the Civil War. The book was handed down through successive generations of the Park family, and Kenneth Park was relieved and proud to return the volume to county officials.[7] Additional local residents expressed a desire to cooperate on the whereabouts of misplaced public records, but they preferred not to reveal information that would be publicized. Hopefully, more of the "lost records" will find their way back to the courthouse in Romney, W.Va.

---

6. Wilmer L. Kerns, "Hampshire County: The Lost Records." *The West Virginia Advocate* (Capon Bridge, W.Va.), 9 March 1984.

7. See "Historical Lost Records Returned to Hampshire County Courthouse." *The West Virginia Advocate*, 4 June 1984.

1735 Cacapon Valley
Land Order Discovered

Discovery of a 1735 land "grant" record[8], issued by the Virginia Governor and his Council to Charles Chiswell, reveals that Cacapon Valley was known to politicians and land investors in old Virginia at that time.

Chiswell, who served as Clerk of the Hanover County, Virginia Court, invested in lands located in numerous Virginia counties. On April 23, 1734, Chiswell, Vincent Pearse, and William Allen petitioned the Governor for 60,000 acres of land "...on the West side of the River Cohungorooton and bounding Notherly on the East and West lines of the Proprietors of Pensylvania." Cohungorooton was an Indian name for that section the Potomac River which was located above the fork of the Shenandoah River. It appears that land requested in this petition was basically the eastern part of Allegany County, Maryland, as known today.

The Virginia governor deferred action on the petition for land until a better understanding of the boundary of Pennsylvania could be determined. May 5, 1735, Charles Chiswell reported to the Governor and his Council of 10 members that there was not 60,000 acres in that grant. Apparently this was determined after more surveying was accomplished in the mountainous region. One of the first surveyors in that area was named William Mayo.

To complete the quantity of land necessary for the planned settlement, Chiswell petitioned that certain land which was located south of the Potomac River be included, "...a Tract lying between the Rivers little Cacaper and great Cacaper may be assign'd the Petitioners as part of the said Grant."

The plan called for the settlement of foreign Protestants. A study of subsequent land records is being conducted to learn to what extent Chiswell and his two partners developed this land. If true to that era, a plan would have called for the

---

8. Article was first published in the October 9, 1989 issue of *The West Virginia Advocate*. This broad "land grant" was a type of land order issued by the Governor.

settlement of sixty families, with each being assigned 1,000 acres.

In essence, the Chiswell grant included a western portion of what is now Morgan County, W.Va. and that section of northeastern Hampshire County located between the Great Cacapon and Little Cacapon Rivers. This was the first known land grant which was made in Old Hampshire County. Certain families may have settled within the designated geographic area but it is believed that a permanent settlement did not result from this large grant. Although an abundance of land was offered beyond the frontier, it is not certain that Chiswell was able to make a timely marketing appeal of the wilderness land to foreign Protestants.

It is believed that a stream, located in northeastern Hampshire County, was named after Chiswell, which suggests that crude surveys were accomplished as early as the 1730s.

Further research in the land records of Virginia is underway to study the subsequent transactions of land in that region. It is interesting to note that the governor of Virginia, in 1735, considered western Maryland to be a part of the Colony of Virginia during that era.

Local Newspaper Resource

One source of information on the old Frederick County area is a monthly newspaper, *The West Virginia Advocate*, published at Capon Bridge. It is a low-cost method of getting in touch with the culture, heritage, and history of the area. Although the editor does no genealogical research, per se, he is attuned to a need to preserve our heritage.

Newspaper articles have been published from my manuscript collection of historical and genealogical subjects, including over seventy family (surnames) histories published during 1982-1992.

In early 1992, a 1-year subscription was $5.40 per year. For information about the newspaper and subscriptions, write to: Mr. Warren E. Duliere, Editor, *The West Virginia Advocate*, P.O. Box 171, Capon Bridge, W.Va. 26711.

Frederick County Ministerial Bonds

The county court was authorized to license ministers "to celebrate the rights of matrimony." A bond of $1,500 was a statewide requirement. Some of the minister's bonds are missing. Records of all surviving minister's bonds from 1789 through 1860 are reported in this section. The rare, original, bonds are housed in the Virginia State Library, Archives Division, Richmond, Virginia.

Anabaptist. William Northern was licensed on April 4, 1809. Bondsmen: Andrew Turner, John Ramey, and Samuel Drake.

Baptist. (1) William Davis was bonded by the Frederick County Court on Aug. 1, 1814. Bondsman: John Kerfoot. (2) Timothy McMann was licensed in November 1821. Bondsman: Walter Tanquary. (3) George Reynolds was licensed on Nov. 5, 1822. Bondsmen: Walter Tanquary and Jacob McKay. (4) William Marvin was licensed on Oct. 31, 1831. Bondsman: Arthur W. Carter and William O. Bond. (5) John F. Rynoldson was licensed on Feb. 5, 1844. Bondsmen: James W. Mason and David W. Barton. (6) James D. Tabler was licensed on Feb. 28, 1853, as a "German Baptist" minister. Bondsman: William Fahnestock. (7) Joseph D. Strickler was licensed as a "German Baptist" minister, circa 1850s (no date). Bondsman: Daniel Baker. (8) Joshua Hudson, in October 1869. Bondsman: Martin M. Adams. Bond said "Old School Baptist."

Catholic. (1) Charles Duhamel (priest) was licensed to perform marriages, May 1, 1809. Bondsmen were Henry Blacker and Edward Powers. (2) James Redman, licensed by the court on June 2, 1819. Bondsmen were Charles Fitzsimmons and William McFherry.

Christian. (1) Joseph Sidebottom was licensed on July 3, 1809. Bondsmen: Lewis Barnett and Thomas McKewan. (2) Joseph Thomas, in September 1819. Bondsmen: Robert W.

Hamilton and Michael Ritenour. (3) Christy Sine, on May 2, 1825. Bondsmen: John Anderson and William Dunlap.

Episcopal. (1) John Vance Weylie (endorsed by the Rev. Alexander Balmain) was licensed on Dec. 3, 1799. Bondsman: Nathaniel Burwell. (2) William Meade, on Oct. 4, 1813. Bondsman: Richard E. Meade. (3) John Jacob Robertson, on Aug. 6, 1821. Bondsmen: Obed Waite and Thomas Allen Tidball. (4) William H. Pendleton, on Sept. 4, 1823. Bondsmen: David W. Barton and Richard E. Byrd. (5) Jared Rice, on Oct. 31, 1831. Bondsmen: Treadwell Smith and Lewis Glover. (6) Horace Stringfellow, on Nov. 2, 1835. Bondsmen: Thomas F. Nelson and Philip Williams. (7) Richard K. Meade, on Nov. 2, 1835. Bondsmen: Philip N. Meade and Thomas N. Nelson. (8) E.W. Hubard, on Nov. 3, 1868. Bondsman: W.C. Meredith.

German Reformed. (1) Jacob O. Miller was licensed on Nov. 2, 1850. Bondsmen: David W. Barton and Frederick A. Shearer. (2) M.L. Shuford, on Nov. 7, 1867. Bondsmen: L.T. Moore and Richard L. Gray.

Lutheran. (1) David Eyster was licensed on Feb. 6, 1828. Bondsmen: Abraham Lauck and Joseph Slagle. Bond stated that he was "German Lutheran." (2) John Jacob Sumar, on Nov. 6, 1823. Bondsmen: Henry Seevers and Washington G. Singleton. Bond stated that he was an "Evangelical Lutheran." (3) Theophilus T. Stork, on Oct. 2, 1837. Bondsmen: John W. Miller and Thomas B. Campbell. (4) George Diehl, on Nov. 4, 1839. Bondsmen: Joseph Slagle and John Miller. (5) John Thomas Tabler, on March 3, 1834. Bondsmen: William H. Grove and Richard M. Sydnor. (6) Joseph Few Smith, on Nov. 8, 1843. Bondsmen: Jacob Baker and Thomas Allen Tidball. (7) Webster Eichelberger, on July 6, 1870. Bondsman: Godfrey S. Miller.

Methodist. (1) Elisha Phelps was licensed on Oct. 6, 1789. Bondsmen were: John Hite and William Hughes. Phelps was a minister in "Society of the People Called Methodists." The license was delivered "in the presence of Edward Christian."

(2) John B. Tilden, on Jan. 31, 1803. Bondsmen: George Reed and James Chipley. (3) James Sinclair, on April 5, 1808. Bondsmen: George Reed and John B. Tilden. (4) George W. Frye, on April 4, 1809. Bondsmen: Beatty Carson and Simon Lauk. (5) Elic Hinkle, on Aug. 5, 1811. Bondsman: George Ritenour. (6) Nathan Lodge, on Oct. 3, 1814. Bondsmen: Simon Lauk and Beatty Carson. (7) Joseph Dalby, on March 2, 1818. Bondsman: Gabriel Davis. (8) Bennett Dowler, on Aug. 5, 1822. Bondsmen: Beatty Carson and George Lynn. (9) John Miller, on Aug. 5, 1822. Bondsman: Beatty Carson. Josiah William Ware was the cognizant court official. (10) Joseph Dalby Sr., on March 8, 1826. Bondsman: William Wood. (11) William Hamilton, on June 11, 1825. Bondsmen: Sutton Harris and George Reed. (12) Charles A. Davis, on April 6, 1830. Bondsmen: Beatty Carson and William L. Clark. (13) David Steele, on Nov. 11, 1835. Bondsmen: Israel Harrison and Joseph Carson. (14) George A.V. Reed (Rev.), on Dec. 3, 1838. Bondsmen: George Reed and William L. Clark. (15) John Smith, on May 2, 1842. Bondsmen: Thomas Allen Tidball and Daniel Gold. (16) Edward L. Dulin, on May 6, 1844. Bondsmen: Jesse Calvert and Richard Milton. (17) Foushee C. Tabbs, on May 3, 1847. Bondsmen: George Wright and Richard Milton. (18) Henry Farring, on June 1, 1847. Bondsmen: Daniel Gold and Richard Milton. (19) James Turner, on June 6, 1848. Bondsmen: Richard Milton and A.R. Milton. (20) Thomas McGee, on June 2, 1851. Bondsman: Jesse Calvert. (21) William Gibbens, on June 2, 1851. Bondsman: Samuel Sperry. (22) Daniel McCauley, on March 5, 1852. Bondsman: William L. Bent. (23) P. Seibert Davis, on July 5, 1853 (appears to be Methodist). Bondsman: William L. Bent. (24) W. F. Ward, on March 2, 1866. Bondsman: Samuel R. Atwell. (25) David Harris, in March 1866. Bondsman: S.J. Smith. (26) William Hodgson, on April 1, 1867. Bondsman: Lewis M. Forsyth. (27) C.H. Mytinger, on June 2, 1868. Bondsman: Henry B. Pitzer.

Methodist Union Society of Reformers. This organization formed as a splinter to the Methodist Church, circa 1828. (1) George Reed was licensed on Aug. 5, 1828. Bondsman: John B. Tilden. (2) John B. Tilden[9] left the regular Methodists in 1828, and registered under this denominational name.

Presbyterian. (1) Andrew A. Shannon was licensed on Nov. 7, 1809. Bondsmen: Robert L. Wright and William McLeod. (2) Robert Hall, on June 2, 1828. Bondsman: William Hill. (3) Alexander Logan, on March 3, 1828. Bondsmen: John M. Brown and Charles H. Clark. (4) David H. Riddle, on Jan. 6, 1829. Bondsman: John Bell. (5) John D. Matheny, on Sept. 30, 1833. Bondsman: George Lynn. (6) Moses H. Hunter, on March 4, 1840. Bondsmen: Thomas Phillips and Charles H. Clark. (7) Beverly Tucker Lacey, on Aug. 4, 1847. Bondsmen: James C. Baker and A.R. Wood. (8) William Ottinger, on Oct. 2, 1848. Bondsmen: David W. Barton and Thomas S. Sangster.[10]

United Brethren In Christ. (1) Jacob Rinehart was licensed on Dec. 4, 1837. Bondsmen: John Hott and George Swhier. (2) David Spesard, on Sept. 5, 1838. Bondsmen: George Swhier Sr. and David Fries. (3) William Edwards, on April 6, 1846. Bondsmen: Nicholas Perry and John W. Piper. (4) James W. Miles, on Nov. 6, 1848. Bondsmen: Presley Ramey and William Bailey.

---

9. John Bell Tilden was born in Philadelphia on Dec. 9, 1761, and died at Stephen City, Va., July 31, 1838. He was a Revolutionary War veteran, and later became a medical doctor. In 1828, he was expelled from the Methodist church because he advocated lay representation.

10. Biographical information on the Presbyterian ministers is presented by Robert Bell Woodworth, A *History of the Presbytery in Winchester*. The McClure Printing Company, Staunton, Virginia, 1947.

Business Licenses

Licenses for "ordinaries" (taverns, inns, or houses of entertainment) were granted by the Governor through the local courts. These bonds for Winchester and Frederick County are housed in the Virginia State Library, Archives Division.

Most ordinaries were located in private residences, with a rental income in the vicinity of $100 per year. The license fee for a full-service ordinary (lodging, food and stableage for horses) was $18. An ordinary that offered lodging only was classified as a "house of entertainment."

Samuel Kercheval, the Valley historian, operated an ordinary in his Winchester residence during the 1811-1812 era. He also worked as a tax assessor for Frederick County.

In 1813, one year after the death of her husband, Susan Streit was licensed to run an ordinary from her residence in Winchester. Her husband was the Rev. Christian Streit, Lutheran pastor in Winchester.

Ordinaries were popular establishments along the newly constructed turnpikes. For example, after construction began on the Northwest Turnpike in 1832, numerous taverns came into operation along the route. Between Gore, Virginia (Back Creek) and the Hampshire County line, at least four taverns operated during the decade of the 1830s, including George Smith's, Josiah Lockhart's, Thomas Anderson's, and Joseph McKee's.

Anderson's Tavern was established in 1832, in his brick home that is just west of Gore, Va., on a foothill of Little Timber Ridge. The State license cost $18, and the annual tax was about 4½ percent of income. During the first years of operation, the tavern provided a complete range of services, including lodging, food, drink, and facilities for animals. In 1835, the tavern was appraised at $2,000. An income of $110 produced a tax revenue of $5 to Frederick County.

In the same year, in 1835, Josiah Lockhart's Tavern was assessed at the same real value as Anderson's. Lockhart collected $120, and paid $5.50 in taxes. These taverns were in competition during the early operation of the NW Turnpike.

Anderson died in 1836. Records show an income of $100 for that year, and $4.50 paid in taxes. In 1837, Anderson's son, Israel R. , continued the business for a couple of years. Business declined, and Israel paid no taxes before the tavern license expired. By 1840, the tavern was used as a rooming house for boarders. Perhaps overnight guests were entertained, if a room was vacant, but it was primarily a boarding house for local residents. It is believed that the Rev. Christy Sine lived there in 1841. According to an old letter, Benjamin Jackson (1783-1855) was one of the many persons who lived in "the brick house" during the mid-1800s.

Anderson's Tavern

Photograph courtesy of Warren E. Duliere

East end of the Anderson Tavern near Gore, Va., which was licensed during the 1830s as an ordinary by Virginia Governors Floyd and Tazwell. In subsequent years it was called a "house of entertainment," which was equivalent to a place of lodging, without food services or accomodations for domestic animals. It was the first brick house built in Upper Back Creek Valley. The historic house was recently restored by its owners, Mr. and Mrs. Kenneth Elder.

Ordinary Bonds for 1795-1799

Between 1795 and 1800, thirty-four ordinaries received licenses to operate in Winchester, and one in Frederick County. Of these, 26 ordinaries were located along *Loudoun Street* in Winchester; five along *Cameron Street*; and three along *Braddock Street*.

During the administration of Governor James Wood Jr., 1797-1799, thirty-two ordinaries were licensed for operation. Most of the ordinaries were located in the "Corporation of Winchester," from which Wood was a native son.

Isaac Skiles was granted a license to run an ordinary, including "stableage," on Cameron Street in Winchester, on July 6, 1795, under Gov. Robert Brooke. Bondsman: William Secords.

Joseph Britton was granted a license to operate an ordinary on Loudoun Street, Oct. 10, 1795, under Gov. Robert Brooke. Albert Ager was the bondsman.

Isaac Woodrow was granted a license to run an ordinary on Loudoun Street on Oct. 21, 1795, under Gov. Robert Brooke. Bondsman: Conrod Kremer.

Stephen Haines was licensed to operate an ordinary on Braddock Street on Oct. 21, 1795, under Gov. Robert Brooke. Bondsman: John Bowman.

Jacob Poe was licensed to operate an ordinary on Loudoun Street on Jan. 2, 1797, under Gov. James Wood. Bondsman: Jesse Brown.

George Linn was licensed to operate an ordinary on Loudoun Street on Jan. 4, 1797, under Gov. James Wood. Bondsman: Conrod Kremer.

David and Thomas Evans were licensed to operate an ordinary on Loudoun Street on Jan. 9, 1797, under Gov. James Wood.

Andrew Baker was licensed to run an ordinary on Loudoun Street on Feb. 6, 1797, under Gov. James Wood. Bondsman: Peter Windle.

Benjamin Fenton was licensed to operate an ordinary on Braddock Street on March 31, 1797, under Gov. James Wood. Bondsman: John Rynold.

Henry Printz was licensed to operate an ordinary in Winchester on March 31, 1797, under Gov. James Wood.   Bondsman: George Kiger.

James Cochran was licensed to run an ordinary on Loudoun Street on April 4, 1797, under Gov. James Wood. Bondsman: Thomas Keenan.

Thomas Bodkin was licensed to operate an ordinary in Frederick County on April 22, 1797, under Gov. James Wood. Bondsmen were George Wiley and Charles Bodkin.

Jacob Hoffman was licensed to operate an ordinary on Loudoun Street on June 30, 1797, under Gov. James Wood. Bondsman: Conrad Krebs.

Philip Bush was licensed to run an ordinary on Cameron Street on August 4, 1797, under Gov. James Wood. Bondsman: James Edmondson.

James Edmondson was licensed to run an ordinary on Loudoun Street on Aug. 4, 1797, under Gov. James Wood. Bondsman: Philip Bush.

Peter Lauck was licensed to operate an ordinary on Loudoun Street on Aug. 4, 1797, under Gov. James Wood. Bondsman: Conrad Kremer.

Henry Bush was licensed to operate an ordinary on Loudoun Street on Aug. 4, 1797, under Gov. James Wood. Bondsman: William Ball.

Carey Pratt was licensed to run an ordinary at his house on Loudoun Street in Winchester on Aug. 4, 1797, under Gov. James Wood. Bondsman: James Little.

John Butler was licensed to operate an ordinary on Cameron Street on Aug. 5, 1797, under Gov. James Wood. Bondsman: Peter Kehoe.

John Fornwalt was licensed to operate an ordinary on Loudoun Street on Nov. 3, 1797, under Gov. James Wood. Bondsman: Conrad Kremer.

David Osburn was licensed to run an ordinary on Cameron Street in Winchester on Nov. 11, 1797, under Gov. James Wood. Bondsman: Conrad Kremer.

George Lynn was licensed to run an ordinary on Loudoun Street on March 2, 1798, under Gov. James Wood. Bondsman: Conrad Kremer.

Andrew Baker[11] was licensed to operate an ordinary at his residence on Loudoun Street on March 2, 1798, under Gov. James Wood. Bondsman: Samuel Windle.

James H. Davison was licensed to operate an ordinary on Loudoun Street on May 24, 1798, under Gov. James Wood. Bondsman: Conrad Kreemer.

Alexander McConnell was licensed to run an ordinary on Loudoun Street in Winchester on June 1, 1798, under Gov. James Wood. Bondsman: Conrad Kremer.

Jacob Hoffman was licensed to operate an ordinary on Loudoun Street on June 29, 1798, under Gov. James Wood. Bondsman: Conrad Krebs.

Carey Pratt was licensed to run an ordinary on Loudoun Strett on July 19, 1798, under Gov. James Wood. Bondsman: Frederick Hurst.

Henry Printz was licensed to run an ordinary on Loudoun Street on Aug. 20, 1798, under Gov. James Wood. Bondsman: John Prince.

Conrod Kremer was licensed to operate a tavern on Loudoun Street on Nov. 2, 1798, by Gov. James Wood. Bondsman: Daniel Miller.

Henry Bush was licensed to operate an ordinary on Loudoun Street on Nov. 2, 1798, under Gov. James Wood. Bondsman: Philip Bush.

John Linn was licensed to run an ordinary on Loudoun Street on Jan. 10, 1799, under Gov. James Wood. Bondsman: George Linn.

Philip Bower was licensed to run an ordinary on Cameron Street on Feb. 1, 1799 under Gov. James Wood. Bondsman: Conrad Kremer.

---

11. Andrew Baker signed his name in the German language.

William Doster was licensed to run an ordinary on Braddock Street on April 17, 1799, under Gov. James Wood. Bondsman: William Gossett.

Angus McDonald was licensed to run an ordinary on Loudoun Street on April 16, 1799, under Gov. James Wood. Bondsman: John McDonald.

Frederick Haas Jr. was licensed to operate an ordinary on Loudoun Street on July 23, 1799, under Gov. James Wood. Bondsman: Frederick Haas Sr.

Benjamin Fenton was licensed to operate an ordinary on Loudoun Street on Aug. 1, 1799, under Gov. James Wood. Bondsman: John Kinsan.

Ordinary Bonds 1800-1840

Among those who were bonded to operate ordinaries (taverns) in the City of Winchester and in Frederick County[12] during the 1800-1840 era were:

Innkeeper	Bondsman	Date
Rachel Walker	Isaac Littler	1800
Jacob Hoffman	Conrad Kreps	1800
Frederick Haas	Frederick Haas Jr.	1800
William Doster	Benjamin Fenton	1800
George F. Haughman	Peter Kehoe	1801
Thomas Brock	John McDonald	1801
Henry Bush	Philip Bush	1801
Philip Bush	Henry Bush	1801
David Osburn	Adam Anderson	1801
George Lynn[13]	Peter Lauck	1801
John Slate	Enoch Morris	1801
Benjamin Fenton	William Doster	1801
Isaac Heiskell	James Chipley	1801

12. Original, but not all renewal, licenses have been reported on this list of inkeepers.

13. His signature was "George Liner."

Innkeeper	Bondsman	Date
Lewis F. Macholt	Henry Baker[14]	1801
Daniel Thomas	Joel T. Gustine	1802
John Lynn	Adam Young	1802
Jacob Hoffman Jr.	Conrad Crebs	1802
Isaac Heiskell	James Chipley	1802
Peter Lauck	James Chipley	1802
David Osburn	Thomas McKewan	1802
George F. Haughman	Adam Young	1802
George Lynn	John Lynn	1802
John Brady	Thomas M. Kewan	1803
Joseph Passman	Ephraim Fenton	1803
David Osburn	Thomas McKewan	1803
Daniel Linn	Henry Linn	1803
Frederick Haas	Alexander McDonald	1803
Peter Lauck	Philip Bush	1803
Philip Bush	Peter Lauck	1803
Abraham Linde	James Chipley	1803
Jacob Hoffman Jr.	Conrad Crebs	1803
George F. Houghman	Adam Kiger	1803
Rachel Walker	John Kingan	1803
Henry Bush	Obed Waite	1803
Jacob Myers	A. Bajer	1803
Gilbert Meem	Thomas M. Kewan	1803
Benjamin Fenton	William Doster	1804
Henry Printz	Peter Kehoe	1804
George Leps	Charles Brent	1804
John Lynn	John Hoff	1804
Philip Bush	Henry Dangerfield	1804
George Leps	Jacob Anderson	****
**********	and David Osburn	1805
Edward McGuire	John Ball	1805
John Brady	Archibald Magill	1805

---

14. Henry Baker signed his name in the German language.

Innkeeper	Bondsman	Date
James Holliday	Richard Holliday	1805
John Slagle	James Chipley	1805
Peter Lauck	John Ball	1806
Edward McGuire Jr.	John Ball	1806
William Doster	Daniel W. Thomas	1806
William Vanhorn[15]	Lewis Barnett	1807
Philip Bush	John Ball	1807
George Leps	George Osburn	1807
Henry Printz	Peter Printz	1807
John Slagle	Abraham Lauck	1807
John Linn	Daniel Clark	1807
James Holiday	James Holliday Jr.	1807
Peter Lauck	David Osborn	1807
Edward McGuire	John Ball	1807
Gilbert Meem	Christopher Wetzel	1807
John Slagle	Christopher Wetzel	1807
John Brady	Thomas McKewan	1807
Richard Lamon	Henry Canniford	1808
Pendleton Heironimus	Willoughby Morgan	1810
Solomon Myers	Peter Lauck	1810
Jacob Poe	Thomas McKewan	1810
Daniel W. Thomas	Edward Talbott	1810
Samuel Kercheval[16]	Daniel Lee	1811
Thomas Robinson	Daniel Lee	1811
William Van Horn	William Doster	1811
Henry Printz	George Trisler	1811
John Linn	Henry Miller	1811
George Leps	Conrad Kremer	1811
Edward McGuire	John Poe	1811
Daniel W. Thomas	Thomas Robinson	1811
William Pepper	Conrad Kremer	1811

---

15. Vanhorn signed "*his X mark*," being unable to write his name.

16. Kercheval paid a $3.15 tax to the Clerk of Court.

Innkeeper	Bondsman	Date
William Doster	Daniel W. Thomas	1812
Susan Streit	Edward Smith	1813
Thomas Robinson	Samuel Kercheval Jr.	1813
John Hasfeldt	Samuel Brown	1813
Salome Myers	Peter Lauck	1813
George Rice	John Hoff	1813
Margaret Osburn	Charles Grim Jr.	1814
Conrad Kremer	William Van Horn	1814
Edmund Pendleton	Christopher Wetzel	1814
Susan Streit	Edward Smith	1814
Elizabeth Rice	John Hoff	1814
Thomas Rush	William Van Horn	1815
William Van Horn	Thomas M. Rush	1815
William McSherry	Nicholas Fitzsimmons	1815
Elijah Waller	William Sommerville	1815
Lewis Mahaney	William Gore	1816
Isaac Williamson	**********	1816
John Pitman	James Steele	1816
Augustus Green	Gabriel H. Davis	1816
John Talbott	Joseph Long	1816
Ellis Long	Joseph Long	1816
Sanford Bartlett	John C. Clark	1816
Gabriel H. Davis	Lewis McCoole	1816
Mary Hickman	John L. Fout	1816
Charles Negrier	Rezin Duvall	1816
Moses Wilson	George S. Lane	1816
John Grim	Michael Manel	1816
Thomas Hanson	Moses Newbanks	1816
Benjamin Beemer	Thomas M. Rusk	1816
Jacob Thomas	_____ Thomas	1816
Moses Shepherd	Augustine Smith	1816
Jacob Weaver	Jacob Taylor	1817
George Bennett	Jacob Weaver	1817
Patrick Gordon	William Stephenson	1817

Innkeeper	Bondsman	Date
Philip Amick	Benjamin Glass	1817
Peter Babb	John V. Buskirk	1817
James Anderson	Thomas A. Tidball	1817
James Anderson	Dawson McCormick	1817
Moses Shepherd	George S. Lane	1817
George Bennett	Patrick Gordon	1817
Patrick Gordon	George Bennett	1817
George Rust	William Carnagey	1817
Isaac Williamson	Michael Mauck	1817
Peter Babb	John Parrell	1817
Isaac Wood	George Albert	1817
John Pitman	John Talbott	1817
Ellis Long	Joseph Long	1817
Benjamin Beemer	Joseph Long	1817
Samuel Scott	William Vanhorn	1817
Gabriel H. Davis	William H. Harris	1817
Lewis Barnett	George S. Lane	1817
Jacob Weaver	John Weaver	1817
Jacob Thomas	David Castleman Jr.	1817
Augustus Green	**********	1817
Jesse Fawcett	Thomas M. Rusk	1817
John Morgan	**********	1817
Moses Newbanks	Cornelius Gibbons	1817
John Talbut	John B. Tilden	1817
Lewis McHaney	William White	1817
John T. Watters	Lawrence Watters	1817
John Grim[17]	John B. Tilden	1817
John Cryder	James Steel	1817
Frederick Nadenbush	Meredith Darlington	1817
John Rutherford	John Carter	1818
John Carter	John Rutherford	1818
Thomas Derst	James Riley	1818

17. Charles Grim signed his name in the German language.

Innkeeper	Bondsman	Date
John M. Pitman	Michael Mauk	1818
George Rust	Samuel McCormick	1818
William Sommerville	George Leper	1818
Isaac Williamson	James Steel	1818
Patrick Gordon	William Stroup	1818
Gabriel H. Davis	Hiram Neville	1818
James Anderson	Thomas A. Tidball	1818
John Grim	Dawson McCormick	1818
Joseph Shepherd	Dawson McCormick	1818
Samuel Scott	William Vanhorn	1818
Lewis Barnett	William Vanhorn	1818
Jacob Weaver	Lewis McCoole	1818
Ellis Long	Joseph Long	1818
Stephen W. Rowzel	Moses Newbanks	1818
Moses Newbanks	Stephen W. Rowzel	1818
John Beemer	Benjamin Beemer	1818
Frederick S. Shryock	Elisha S. Russell	1818
Jacob Thomas	Robert O. Grayson	1818
Ann Turnbull	Edmund Pendleton	1818
Isaac Wood	Joseph Parrell	1818
Benjamin Langley	Conrod Kremer	1818
John Reed	Henry M. Babb	1818
George Gordon	Adam Kern	1819
Lydia Bennett	George Bennett	1819
Robert Harrison	**********	1819
William Shepherd	Jonathan DeHaven	1819
Moses Newmanks	Lewis Mahaney	1819
Leonard Hiett	Thomas Hiett	1819
Bushrod Taylor[18]	Dawson McCormick	1819
John Rutherford	William Carter	1819
James Anderson	Nathan Anderson	1820
John M. Pitman	John S. Peyton	1820

18. Keeper of Snickers' Ferry

Innkeeper	Bondsman	Date
John Beemer	Philip Hoover	1820
Moses Newbanks	James Newbanks	1820
Isaac Williamson	George Larrick	1821
Jeremiah Reynolds	John Johnston and	****
**********	Leonard Pine	1821
Steed Skinner	Thomas Castleman	1821
Rachel Morgan	Bealis Davis	1821
Thomas C. Lupton	Robert Hodgson	1822
Frederick Nadenboush	Barak Fisher Jr.	1822
David Rinehart	Andrew Kiger	1823
Jacob Baker	Joseph Long	1823
Thomas Dent	George Harris	1823
William Berry	Bealis Davis	1823
Isaac Williamson	George Larrick	1823
Robert H. Little	James Hay	1823
Lewis Fulkison	Joseph W. Carter	1823
Thomas C. Wyndham[19]	Charles C. Byrd	1823
Robert Montgomery	William H. Harris	1823
Samuel Wright	Gabriel H. Davis	1824
John W. Cooper	James Sargent and	****
**********	Joseph Sexton	1825
Abraham Watson	Andrew Kiger	1825
Nelson Green	Richard Green	1825
Leonard Likens	James Carter	1825
Daniel P. Conrad	William Taylor	1825
John Jacobs	Samuel Gardner	1825
Evan Thatcher	James McKenney	1826
William W. Fitzhugh	Samuel H. Davis	1826
William Chapman	William Lynn	1826
Michael H. Reed	Robert Hodgson	1826
Leonard Likens	Gabriel H. Davis	1826
Shepherd B. Grove	Evan Piper	1826
Isaac Wood	Robert Montgomery	1827

19. Keeper of Snickers' Ferry

Innkeeper	Bondsman	Date
Daniel P. Conrad	William Berry	1827
Iver Campbell	Charles Hulet	1827
William Shepherd	Gabriel H. Davis	1827
Leonard Likens	David Likens	1827
Benjamin Glass	Henry Seevers	1828
George W. Kiger	James R. Richards	1828
Andrew Heironimus	Jacob Heironimus	1829
Samuel Price	John Irvin	1829
William Monroe Sr.	Wilford G. Settle	1829
Joseph Seaman	Bushrod Taylor	1830
Jacob Swhiers	Gabriel H. Davis	1830
Daniel Carnell	Michael H. Reed	1830
Gabriel H. Davis	James P. Riley	1830
William Lane	Wilford Settle	1830
Abraham Watson	W.L. Clark	1831
Benjamin Glass	George Heide	1831
Israel Wilkerson	George D. Harrison	1831
George Davis	George McCloud	1831
John Carter	Walter Tanquary	1831
Andrew Heironimus	Gabriel H. Davis	1831
Thomas Anderson	William Adams	1832
Hannah Harris	Peter Shickles	1832
William Denny	Stephen Meyers	1832
John Beemer	Joseph Long	1833
Sarah Chapman	George Smith	1833
Joseph Long	John Beemer	1833
Michael Fisar	George S. Lane	1833
Elias Edmonds	George S. Lane	1833
Joseph B. Lacy	James R. Richards	1833
John Carter	Gabriel H. Davis	1833
Robert Montgomery	Gabriel H. Davis	1833
Thomas Seevers	Isaac Moore	1833
Andrew Heironimus	Gabriel H. Davis	1833
Alexander Catlett	David W. Barton	1833

Innkeeper	Bondsman	Date
Harrison L. Wiatt[20]	James Crop	1833
William Sheppard	George Smith	1834
John W. Morrison	Mordicai B. Cartmell	1834
David Rinehart	David W. Barton	1834
Thomas Anderson	John Piper	1834
John Durney	Benjamin Bushnell	1834
Thomas Seevers	Nathaniel Seevers	1834
Henry Swann	George L. Lane	1834
George Swhier	George Long	1834
Jacob Swhire	John Hott	1834
James Mason	Zachariah Sanks	1835
Leroy P. Williams	William R. Seevers	1835
Alexander Catlett	Joseph Larrick	1835
Joseph Long	Griffin Frost	1835
David Rinehart	William Dooley	1835
Abraham Watson	James R. Richards	1836
David Rinehart	Peter Kremer	1836
Sarah Chapman	William Lynn	1836
John Nisewander Jr.	John Nisewander Sr.	1837
Peter H. Hopwood	Benjamin Bushnell	1837
Joseph Clouser	George R. Long	1837
Joseph Long	John Beemer	1836
Rubin Kile	Thomas M. Rust	1837
Robert Harrison	George D. Harrison	1837
Branch Jordon	George R. Long	1837
Meredith Darlington	Joseph S. Carson	1838
Andrew Ramsey	David Rhodes	1838
George Swhier Jr.	John Griffith III	1838
Sarah Chapman	David W. Barton	1839
William Shepherd	James Robinson	1839
Jonathan Jenkins	John Anderson	1839
George Swhier Jr.	Richard E. Byrd	1840
George Randall	Peter Kremer	1840

20. Keeper of Berry's Ferry

Mahlon Gore Day Book

Mahlon Gore owned a country store in upper Back Creek Valley, at Gore, Frederick County, Va. Names of local residents who obtained credit in 1849 were listed in Gore's *Day Book*, along with lists of items purchased and costs. Persons who established accounts at the country store in 1849 were:

Lewis Carpenter, Sarah Colbert, Thomas Marpole, Gabriel McDonald, Eliza J. Payne, Richard Payne, A.J. Householder, David Hook,

Henry Hanes, Miss Margaret Anderson, John W. Smith, Thomas Murphy, George Anderson, Ellen Garvin, Barton McKee, William Scrivenor, Benjamin McDonald,

Asa Anderson, Simon Marple, Samuel Perry, Rachel Payne, John Oldacre, Joseph Davis, John K. Triplett, Benjamin Marple, John Payne, Thomas Wilcox, Jeremiah Smith, Josiah Lockhart, John Horn,

George Marple, James W. Hackney, David S. Hook, Robert Allen, Joshua Anderson, Samuel Lockhart, Jefferson Murphy, Catherine Howard, James W. Siebert, Ebenezer Jackson,

Harrison Brill, Craven Popkins, John Lonas, Charles J. Rynehart, Jesse Lonas, Beverly Lockhart, Mrs. Giffin, James Cather, Benjamin F. Kerns, Thomas Amick, Moses Hicks, David Kerns, Samuel Hook, Reuben Marker, Benjamin F. Jacobs, Stephen Smith, Mrs. Hannah Muse, Joshua Anderson, John Shuler, James Eaton, Amos Marple,

Cornelius Shuler, Martin B. Muse, Jonathan L. Pugh, Samuel L. Jackson, Samuel Shinholtz, Jeremiah Hix, Benjamin Scrivenor, Joseph D. Davis, Robert V. Lockhart,

Jacob Sirbaugh, Jackson Parish, Jacob Siebert, John W. Muse, Nancy Giffin, John H. Brill, Miss Sarah Evans, Miss Rosey,

William J. Myers, Edwin Triplett, Joseph Seymour, Robert Colbert, William W. Evans, Mahala Marker, Jonathan Lovett, Jesse J. Pugh, Amos Johnson, William Cather, George Slonaker, Newton Furr, Elizabeth Johnson, Israel Anderson,

Miss Cassandra Fletcher, Robert Carlisle, Jefferson Murphy, Washington Whitacre, Nancy Spaid, Elias Keckley, Albert Miller, Wilson Whitacre, James Abrel, Jacob Oates,

Atwell Miller, George R. McKee, Michael M. Anderson, Jesse Colbert, Joshua Anderson, and George F. Dent. Source: Unpublished Mahlon Gore *Day Book*, extracted from the private library of the late Ralph L. Triplett, Gore Va.

J.J. Reid Day Book

Jeremiah J. Reid owned a store in upper Back Creek Valley, during the mid-1800s. He drew customers from Frederick and Hampshire Counties, Virginia, located near the boundary between the counties. It is believed that the store was located in the High View section of Timber Ridge. Entries in the *Reid Day Book* commenced on Oct. 27, 1852, providing proof of residence for customers. These records are important for genealogists who seek proof of residency of ancestors during this time frame.

Store accounts during the 1852-53 era were established for: John D. Good, William Dunlap Jr., Hiram Spaid, John Dunlap, William Ridgeway, N. L. Anderson,

Daniel Anderson, H.S. Eaton, John Racey, Nancy Reid, William W. Hook, Elizabeth Reid, Thomas Anderson, M.F. Hannum, H.W. LaFollette, Elizabeth Newbanks, Jacob Larrick, Jasper McKee, Peter Farmer, John M. Anderson, Amos LaFollette, Aaron Dunlap, Nathan Anderson, James LaFollette, S. Rudolph, Samuel Garvin, Archibald Stephens, Sarah Ridgeway, Aaron Silcot, Michael Brill,

Elias Anderson, P.P. Anderson, John F. Eaton, Nathan L. Anderson, Frederick Sechrist, Elias Milslagle, Martial Anderson, Benjamin Cubbage, Philip LaFollette, Zebulon Eaton, B. F. Anderson, Isaac Lupton, Silas LaFollette, J. Wilson Eaton, William Hart, Samuel Milslagle, Isaiah Anderson, Henry Cump, Lewis Racey, David Wilson and Felix Good.

Country store records, commencing on Jan. 1, 1853, contained written accounts listed under these additional names: William Frank, Rachael Frank, Adam Stephens, William

Davis, N.T. Eaton, C.P.M. Eaton, Archibald Arnold, John Culp, Benjamin F. Anderson, C. Anderson, Abraham Brill, Dorsey Reid, Thomas Pennington, James Anderson, Peter Groves, John Reid, Elisha Spaid, Henry Brill, John Capper,

Jonathan Brill, Cassy Anderson, Flauvius J. Sine, Mary Stephens, James Wilson, Sarah Ridgeway, H. William LaFollette, Mary A. Brill, O.M. Anderson, Susan Frank, A.A. McKee, Anderson McKee, Sarah McGraw, Enos Spaid, Henry Kump, Jacob Kump, John W. Eaton, E.W. Cole, Davis Farmer, Sarah Chamberlain, and M.S. Anderson.

Included in the day book was an account of the Shiloh School for the 1857-58 school term. Source: ***Day Book*** of Jeremiah J. Reid.

Constable Bonds
(1816-1820)

Frederick County constable bonds for the 1816-1850 era are preserved in three volumes.[21]   Constables were bound, along with their bondsmen, to the Governor of the Commonwealth of Virginia, in the sum of $500.   Bonding was important because constables handled money and goods through numerous dealings with public matters.

The bond stated that the constable "...shall well and truly discharge the duties of the said office of Constable, within the said County, and pay and satisfy all sums of money and tobacco by him received, by virtue of any process, to the person or persons to whom the same are due...."

These bonds were discovered while researching for information on Jonas Whitacre. He was a constable in district No. 2, from 1832 until his death in 1835. Historical records contain valuable information for genealogical researchers.

---

21. These Frederick County records are housed in the Virginia State Library, Archives Section, 8/G/24/2/5. Records in Richmond may be inspected with written permission from the Clerk of Court, Frederick County, Va.

Constable	Date	Bond
Patrick Gordon	Feb. 4, 1816	$500
James Scott	Aug. 5, 1816	$500
Joshua Yeo	June 3, 1816	$500
James Steel	Sept. 2, 1816	$500
Andrew Flemming	Sept. 2, 1816	$500
William Dooley	Sept. 2, 1816	$500
Andrew Zigler	Sept. 30, 1816	$500
James Smith	Dec. 2, 1816	$500
Charles Cunningham	March 4, 1817	$500
Townscend McGruder	April 1, 1817	$500
Griffin Haynie	June 2, 1817	$500
Joseph Long	June 2, 1817	$500
Thomas Dann	June 2, 1817	$500
Thomas C. Wyndhaim	June 2, 1817	$500
Michael Brill	Aug. 4, 1817	$500
Jacob Shade Jr.	Aug. 4, 1817	$500
Mager Steel	Aug. 4, 1817	$500
Edward Jennings	June 2, 1818	$500
John L. Johnston	June 2, 1818	$500
John Snyder	Nov. 2, 1818	$500
Enoc Haddox	March 1, 1819	$500
John Crum	April 5, 1819	$500
George Dawson	Sept. 6, 1819	$500
Edward Henry Pendleton	Dec. 6, 1819	$500
James S. Brown	March 6, 1820	$500
Richard D. McGruder	July 5, 1819	$500
Steed Skinner	Jan. 31, 1820	$500
Brawney Gaines	Jan. 31, 1820	$500
John Jacobs	March 6, 1820	$500
Elias Bucker	March 6, 1820	$500
Henry Seevers Jr.	May 15, 1820	$500
John J. Johnston	June 6, 1820	$500
William Dooley	June 6, 1820	$500
Edward Pendleton	June 7, 1820	$500

Persons Receiving Pensions
Under the Act of 1888

A list of pensioners under the *Act of 1888* was maintained by the Frederick County Clerk of the Court. Further information on pensions may be secured by researching Union records in the National Archives, and Confederate records in the Virginia State Library, Archives Division.

The 1894 list. Mary A. Anderson, Cornelius Copenhaver, Jacob Crisman, James Thomas Grubb, H.L. Jewell, Elizabeth Marple (dead), James Jeneta (dead), Elizabeth Ann Padget, Elizabeth Ridenour, Samuel Ritter (dead), Robert S. Robertson (dead), A.B. Rothgeb, Levi Shipe, John W. Simmons, Abrim M. Siebert, B.F. Thompson, Martha A. Willis, Mary L. Beamer, Mrs. S.P.B. Harrison, Susan P. Jones (lived in Washington, D.C.), Charles D. Shoat, Jonathan M. Mason, E.W. Boggs, Job N. Cookus.

The 1900 list. George V. Blake, William B. Crim, George W. Arnold, George B. Lynn, J.P. Crim, Hugh S. Janney, David Kerns, George H. Nokes, Frances Robertson, Mary J. Reed, David E. Boyce, George W. Drake, Joseph H. Dispannett, Charles N. Lambden, Alexander Carlysle, Walter J. Fultz. Elias A. Keckley, Simon N. Orndorff, John B. Guard, Henry W. White, J.A. Grove, George A. Timberlake, George W. Taylor, Sallie Ritter (widow of Harrison D. Ritter).

Mill Owners In Old
Frederick County

An inventory of mills in old Frederick County, Virginia, made during the War of 1812, provides valuable information on the milling industry during that era. Acting under legislative mandate from the Virginia Assembly, county commissioners of revenue identified mills according to: name of county, political district, type of mill, name of owner, tax assessment, and date of assessment.

Rates of taxation for mills were set by individual counties, and the amounts varied from county-to-county. The owner of an average mill in Hampshire County paid a tax of about $2.00 per year, but the larger merchant mills were assessed more, based on the rental value of a mill. For example, Isaac Hollingsworth's mill had an annual rental value of $300, for a $6.00 tax assessment. At the other end of the scale, Peter Larue's mill was assessed $1.00 tax, based on a $10 rental value, per year.

Taxes in Jefferson County appeared to be higher than in surrounding jurisdictions. For example, Thomas Wilson, owner of two large mills, paid $35.34 in taxes, in 1813. On the other end of the scale, Rawleigh Morgan, who owned a small grist mill and a saw mill, paid only $5.00 in taxes for the same period, in the same county.

Counties derived about ten percent of their property tax income from mill operations. For example, Jefferson County collected $2,360.09 during tax year 1813, distributed as follows: taxes on slaves, $1,095; taxes on horses, $588; taxes on coaches, $127.15; taxes on stages (coaches), $2.50; taxes on giggs (carriages), $26.75; taxes on mills, $294.20; taxes on ferries, $13.00; taxes on tanyards, $10.15; and taxes on a printing press, $8.00. These same records for all Virginia counties (for years 1782-1850), including those which later fell into West Virginia, are located in the Virginia State Archives, in Richmond.

Mills were water-powered during this era, including the saw mills. Mill dams were built in the rivers or streams to create a steady water supply. As a general rule, mills were erected on a high bank so that floods would not destroy the structures. A review of numerous mill sites in this region reveals that many foundations were laid on a solid base, such as rock ledges.

All water-powered mills operated under the same principles of physics. The weight of water flowing continuously into compartments of a large wheel (gravity) caused the wheel to rotate which, in turn, drove other wheels to run the mill machinery. Machines were designed to perform operations such as: sawing lumber, grinding grain, manufacturing goods (for example, clothing), or tanning animal hides to make leather.

As shown in the lists of mills below, saw mills were almost as numerous as grist mills during the early 19th century. The population of old Frederick County was expanding rapidly, and lumber was essential to meet the need for both housing and agriculture.

A water-powered saw mill drove an "up-and-down-saw," which sliced through logs that were fed on a crude timber carriage. Rough edges were hand-hewed by an axe. Saw mills were sometimes housed jointly with grist mills, but normally they occupied independent buildings.

Not all of the old mill foundations in this region represent grist mills, but some were saw mills. One such example was a saw mill operated by Peter Mauzy III (1766-1835), on Mill Branch, in eastern Hampshire County. Previously believed to have been the site of a grist mill, recent discovery of archive documents indicates that this was a late 18th century saw mill. Possibly the mill served as both a grist and saw mill at one time.

There were several kinds of grist mills: (1) A custom grist mill was used to grind corn meal, hominy grits, and flour meal. This kind of mill serviced a community, with a radius of about 5-8 miles. Farmers brought their own grain to be ground for their personal use. A typical grist mill operated only one or two days per week, when milling conditions were most favorable.

(2) Merchant's mills purchased wheat to manufacture white flour as a commercial operation. Buckwheat was also a major product in this area, because it could be grown on poor mountainous terrain. This region, the lower Shenandoah Valley, was considered to be "the wheat belt of old Virginia." Some of the mill products were sold locally, but most were exported beyond the communities which produced them.

The grain industry suffered a major setback during the Civil War when farms were burned throughout the Shenandoah Valley. During that same era the Great Plains was establishing itself as a major grain producer. Valley farms never recovered their wheat production after the War, and were replaced with fruit farming. Winchester is sometimes called the "Apple Capital of the United States."

Grist mills utilized a custom-made grindstone. Sometimes chunks of hard quartz were placed within a softer material to form a grindstone. An example of this may be found at the Jack Powell farm, near the Forks of Capon, where "John Largent, Jr." operated a mill in 1813-14, previously belonging to his father, James Largent (1753-1813). Although most of the old mills have vanished from the landscapes, grindstones are still found near former mill sites.

The inventory of mills excluded hand mills and horse-drawn mills. These were two primitive methods for grinding grain, usually for the benefit of one or two families. Excluded, also, were horse-drawn tanyards. Some of the tanyards in old Frederick County were horse drawn during the 1813-14 era, based on descriptions found in journals and diaries. A tanning mill processed animal hides into leather to be used for shoemaking and other domestic purposes, such as harnesses, honing straps, etc.

Another category of mills was "manufacturing mills." A major type of mill within this classification was the woolen mill. As a person who ran a grist mill was called a "miller," a woolen mill operator was called a "fuller." "To full" meant a process of beating newly woven cloth to extract animal grease and soiling; to shrink the cloth; to straighten out knots and uneven weaves; and to stretch the cloth for drying. Such a mill was located in Bloomery, Hampshire County, across the road from the Bloomery Inn (Sherrard's). It appears that sheep raising was one of the early activities in Bloomery.

The mill inventory, made in 1813, listed the owners who paid mill taxes during that year. Age of the mills was not given, but some were very old, while several were in their first year of operation. Many of these mills stayed in one family for several generations, while others changed hands frequently. It is not within the scope of this article to present a history on individual mills.

Berkeley County Mills

The following list includes that part of old Frederick County, Va. which is now Berkeley County, W.Va., plus a western portion of what is present-day Morgan County, W.Va. Names of mill owners are listed.[22]

Saw Mill Owners: James Abernathy, William Ambrose, Jacob Courtney, John Culp, Samuel Hedges, John Hixon, Joseph Henderson, John Johnson, Ephraim Lowman, Zachariah Murry, Nicholas Orrick, Robert Pinkerton, Stephen Snodgrass, Michael Rooney, William Rankins, Abraham Snyder, Jacob and John Shockley (joint), Jane Titus, William Shank, Christopher Tedrick, Thomas Sharp, and Michael Barnes. Edward Beeson, Jonathan Cushwa (?), James Campbell Esq., John C. Cramwell. Robert Daniel, Josiah Flagg, James Foreman, Edward A. Gibbs, Samuel Light, Thomas Lee, James Mendenhall, George Newkirk, James Newcomer, Adam Stephens, Jacob Sybert, Henry Sybert, "John Smith for A.L. Henshaw," Peter Gardner, J. Wickersham, and Joseph Beall.

Grist Mills: William Catlett, Richard Chenoweth, Jacob Coons, Samuel Hedges, William Johnson, John Johnson, Ephraim Lowman, James Lowery, Zachariah Murry, Nicholas

---

22. In certain cases, names of leasees, agents, or heirs were listed instead of "owners."

Orrick, Henry Gore, Stephen Snodgrass, Thomas Robinson, Abraham Snyder, John and Peter Tedrick (joint), and Paul Taylor.

Merchant's Mills: Edward Beeson, Elisha Boyd Esq., George Cunningham, John C. Cramwell, Robert Daniel, Emanuel Eversole, Josiah Flagg, James Foreman, James Hedges, Levi Henshaw, Samuel Light, Thomas Lee, James Mason Jr., James Mendenhall, Joseph Mengheni, George Newkirk, James Newcomer, Hugh Patterson, Peter Riner, Anthony Roseberger, Adam Stephens (3 mills), "John Gregg, guardian of T. Shearer's children," Jacob Sybert, George Tabler, Joel Ward, Thomas Swearington's heirs, Rawleigh Morgan, Henry Sybert, George Keller, and Joseph Beall.

Tanyards: Alburdi Gustine, Valentine Ayle, Joseph Baldwin, Alexander Cooper, and Jacob Snyder.

Ferries: Peter Light & son.

Printing Press: John Alburti

Frederick County Mills

The following mill owners represented not only the area which is still in Frederick County, but also present day Clarke County, Va., plus a portion of Warren County, Va., both of which were formed in 1836. County commissioners did not distinguish between grist and merchant mills. An 1820 map, by John Wood, shows the location of many of these mills. A copy is in the Library of Congress, and in the Handley Library, Archives Section, Winchester, Va. The following list is for the 1813-14 period.

Saw Mill Owners: William Adams, Sr., Henry Babb (two saw mills), Joseph Baker, Thomas Barrett, William Brown, George Bruce, Thomas Bell, Abner Clark, "David Castleman, for heirs of Thomas Shepherd," John Clark in 1813 (and John Clark's heirs in 1814), John Fenton, Joseph Fenton, Martin Freeze, Henry Groves, David Castleman and Charles McCormick, Nathaniel Burrell Sr., William Chipley's heirs, David Carlisle, James Cochran's executors, Philip Earhart, Elias Hickley (free mulatto) Robert Lewright, Jacob Farrow, Benjamin Glascock, Elizabeth G__ (illegible), Henry Franks, William Gore, William Heton,

Hannah Hollingsworth, Isaac Hite, Elias Kackley Sr., Jonathan Lovett, Ninian McGruder, Robert Muse, Jacob Rosenberger, George Shaplar, Notley C. Williams, Thomas Hollingsworth (two saw mills), John Littler, Robert McKee, Jacob Nutt, Thomas Parker, James Smith's heirs, Isaac Pidgeon Sr., Stephen W. Russell, George Shutt, Frederick Snyder, John Smith "gentleman," and William A. Wilson.

Grist Mill Owners: William Adams Sr., Henry M. Babb, Moses Coats, George Bruce, John Clark's heirs (two grist mills), Martin Frees, John Carter, Joseph Hackney Sr., Samuel Littler's heirs, James Hackney, Robert Montgomery, Jacob Null, Castleman and McCormick, Castleman and Garrison, David Carlisle, Philip Earhart, Jacob Farrow, John Hambleton, William Heton, John Hopkins, Robert Hamilton, Hannah Hollingsworth, Isaac Hollingsworth (two mills), John Holker, Ann Kean, Lawrence Lewis, Jonathan Lovett, John Larrick, Ninian McGruder, Robert Muse, John McCallister, Joseph B. Neil's heirs, Jesse O'Rear Jr., John Parkins, Isaac Parkins, James Roberts, Jacob Rosenberger, John Russell, Thomas Shepherd's heirs, Peter Senseny's heirs, George Shaplar, James Smith's heirs, David Tresler, Thomas Hollingsworth, David Lupton, Nathaniel Burrell (two mills), Joseph Glass, Joseph Hotsenpiler, Isaac Hite (two mills), William Helm Sr., Daniel Haines, John Hamilton (two large mills), Edward Smith, Notley C. Williams, John Littler, Jabez Larue, Thomas McIntire, Jacob Nutt, Jacob Null (on Isaac's Creek), Lewis Neil Sr., Joseph Neile's estate, William Pennybaker, Thomas Parker, Daniel Roper (or Royer), David Ridgeway, General John Smith "gentleman," Ebin Taylor, John Wright "the miller," John White (two gristmills), William Wilson, and Joseph Wood.

Court records reveal that Peter Senseny built a mill in 1792. Henry Mercer Babb built a mill on Hog Creek, in 1805. Ninian McGruder built a grist mill on South Fork of Wright's Branch, in 1804. Jonathan Parkins applied to build a mill, in 1803, on Parkin's Run, which was a branch of Abraham's Creek. The Parkins family built numerous mills in the region. Court records show that John McCallister's mill was on Buffalo Marsh, "near the Iron Forge," in 1793.

Ann Kean, mill owner mentioned above, apparently was the widow of John Kean. Kean's Mill was mentioned in a 1795 court record, "...from John Kean's Mill to a Road leading from

Winchester to Marlbrough Iron Works." The Road from Kean's Mill to "the Great Road" was called "Simon Taylor's Road," in 1795.

Thomas McIntyre built a water grist mill on Sleepy Creek, near the Berkeley County line, in 1806. His lands adjoined Francis Titus, Samuel Smith, and Joseph Baker. A court inquisition was held to determine whether it would be proper to build a mill at this site, without infringing upon the rights of other property owners. The inquisition team consisted of: Fielding Luttrell, Henry Burkhimer, Benjamin Jolley, Nathan Littler, Henry Groves, Jacob Groves, John Smith, Samuel Smith, William Smith, Jasper Miller, Jesse Anderson Jr., and Jacob Allemong. McIntyre received court approval for building a mill dam, after much apparent opposition.

Jacob Null applied to erect a water grist mill on North Fork of Isaac's Creek, in 1812, adjoining the lands of Peter Babb and Samuel Wright. This was located in a section of northern Frederick County known today as Cross Junction. It is believed that this was later called "Shanholtz Grist Mill."

Hampshire County Mills

In 1813, Hampshire County included what is now Mineral County, W.Va., plus a western portion of Morgan County, W.Va.

Saw Mills: Peter Bruner, "Reed's executors," "Jeremiah Thompson's executors," Benjamin Foreman, John Largent, Jr., Frederick Buzzard, William Parrill, John Cunningham, Jesse Harland, Thomas Lewis of North River, William and Peter Casey, William Doman, Jonathan Hiett, John and Peter Mauzy, David Shinn, Ebenezer Williams, Joseph Parrill, John Suminez (?), John Parke, Jr., John Stoker, John McBride, Israel Cunningham, Robert Rogers, Francis White, Thomas Edwards, William Wilson of Berkeley County, John Easter, Jr., James Allender, John Iliff, John Casler, William McCanslip (?), Isaac Lupton, and Peter Grove.

Names above were from the "Lower District" of the County, corresponding generally with boundaries of present day

Hampshire County, plus the western part of what later became Morgan County, in 1820.

Saw mills in the western part of old Hampshire County were located approximately in what is now Mineral County. Saw mill owners in that jurisdiction were named: Jacob Bison, William Donaldson, William Fox, Frederick Sheetz, and Moses Thomas.

Grist mills: James Caudy & Co., Peter Bruner, "Reed's executors," Peter Larue, Jesse and Hannah LaRue (joint), John Kidwell, John Largent, Jr., Isaac Hollingsworth, Thomas Lewis of North River, John Thompson of Little Cacapon, Barton Smoot, Frederick Sechrist, Joseph Parrill, John Stoker, John McBride, Francis White, William Wilson of Berkeley County, and Ignatius Russell.

Grist mills in the western part of old Hampshire County (including present day Mineral County) were owned by: Peter Allkyre, John Bardle, James Boseley, Isaac Beall, James Dailey, Jacob Doll, William Donaldson, Benari Goldsmith, Gibson & Gregg, Richard Holliday, Thomas Jones, Isaac Kuykendall, Edward McCarty, Isaac Means, Peter Parker, Frederick Sheetz, John Snyder, John Stewart, Thomas Taylor, and Jacob Vandiver.

As an interesting diversion, the tax list gave the names of the 15 *horse breeders* in Hampshire County. They were: John Hammack, John Loy, Lewis Lumford, William McVicker, John Park Jr., William Pennington, James Shearer, Robert Combs, Benjamin Copsay (?), Felin McNemarron, Frederick Purget, Lewis Vandiver, A. Clary, and Joseph Inskeep. These 15 "studs" serviced a county horse population of 4,800 horses, a ratio of about 320 horses to one stud.

Hardy County Mills

This county was divided into two districts; east and west. It appears that the west district later became Grant County, when it was formed from Hardy County in 1868.

Saw mills in the west district were owned by: Joseph Alfrey, Adam Gilmore, Adam Douglas, Abraham Hutton, James Miles,

Valentine Powers, Abraham Van Meter, and Isaac and Jacob Van Meter (joint).

Saw mills in the east district: Michael Brake, Jonathan Branson, George Claypool, Christian Eyeman, Hannah Fry, Henry Fraville, Jr., Daniel McNeal, Abel Seymour, Conrad Sayger, and Solomon Wilson.

Grist mills (called "merchant manufacturing grist mills" on the inventory) in the west district of Hardy County were owned by: Anthony Baker, Jr., Adam Douglas, Peter Harte (or Harlo?), Martin Hawk, Abraham Hutton, Joseph Nevill, Valentine Powers, John Smith, Abraham Van Meter, and Isaac and Jacob Van Meter (joint ownership).

Grist mills in the east district: Michael Brake, Jacob Burkdole, Jonathan Branson, Christian Dosher, Christian Eyeman, Henry Fraville, Jr., Daniel Harriss, Daniel McNeal, Isaac Oldacre, Abel Seymour, Conrad Sayger, and Solomon Wilson.

Jefferson County Mills

Jefferson was formed from Berkeley County in 1801. The first settlers in Old Frederick County came to this area during the 1720s.[23]

Saw mills. The owners were: Joseph Bond's heirs, Benjamin Heskett, John Lewis, John Haines, John Downey, John Smith, Martin Bilmire, Abraham Shepherd Sr., Rawleigh Morgan, John Line, John Payton's heirs, Adam Wever, and William Roberts.

Grist mills. William Craghill, Joseph Bond's heirs, Daniel Haines, Slusher & Taylor, Samuel McPherson, Benjamin Beeler, John Lewis, Daniel Mussleman, Margaret Muse, John Haines, Thomas Wilson (two mills), John Downey, Benjamin Bell, William Vestall, Robert Worthington, John Yontz, Martin Bilmire, David Hoffman, Abraham Shepherd Sr., Abraham Shepherd Jr., Thomas Shepherd, Rawleigh Morgan, John Payton's heirs, John Hall, Thomas Beall, Isaac Strider, and Adam Wever.

---

23. See Millard K. Bushong, *Historic Jefferson County* (Boyce, Va.: Carr Publishing Co., Inc., 1972), for an excellent local history.

Tanyard mills. Clark & McSherry, David Humphreys, Samuel Howell, Henry Line, John Motter, and John Kearsley.

Richard Williams was taxed $8.00 for the only printing press which operated in Jefferson County, in 1813. Also, Ferdinand Fairfax and John Wager were taxed for the two ferries they operated in the County, the latter being the major ferry.

Shenandoah County Mills

In 1813, Shenandoah County included a major portion of present-day Page County, Va., plus a section of Warren County, Va. Page County was formed in 1831 and Warren County was formed in 1836.

Saw mills. The county was divided into two districts: John Brumback, Jacob Blausser, Arthur Blackford & Co., Spencer N. Calamese, Jacob Copperstone, Samuel Forrer (not legible), Christian Forrer, Hezekiah Freeman, John Fustoe, William Dent, Jacob Keller, Robert Mauk, John Overall, Daniel Strickler, David Seaman, John Smith, John Valentine, Philip Varner, and Benjamin Wood. The above named persons probably lived in that section of Shenandoah County which later became Page County.

Saw mills in the other district were listed under these names: John Arthur & Co., Joseph Arthur & Co., Davis Allen & Sons, Adam Barb Jr., John Buck, Casper Cline, Henry Cagy & Sons, Augustin Coffman, George Cooper of L. Creek, John Cline, Jacob Detwich, Jacob Funkhouser, John Fitzmiers, Joshua Foltz Sr., Philip Granstorf & Sons, Henry Gedich, Henry Holler, John Hamman, Jonathan Harpine, Barnard Koutzman, John Morgan, Godfrey Miller, George Miller Sr., Benjamin Pennybaker, Ephram Rinker, Valentine Roads & Son, Henry Rorer, Francis Reese, John Stover, Michael Seigler, Abraham Sonafrank, Peter Sager, Jacob Sheetz, William Stoner & Son, Jacob Smooker, and John Zirkle (river).

Grist mills. John Brumback, Jacob Burner, Arthur Blackford & Co., Michael Clem Sr., John Koontz (river), Robert Mauk, John Overall, Abner Smith, John Valentine, and Philip Varner.

Merchant mills. Names on the first list were: James Allensworth, John Brumback, John Brewbaker, Jacob Blausser, Jacob Copperstone, Samuel Forner (illegible), John Frederick, William Dent, Lewis Johnstone, Jacob Keller, Adam Kibler, John Mouser Sr., Enos McKay, John Overall, Joseph Rodes, Rowley Smith, Daniel Strickler ("the miller"), John White, and Benjamin Wood. Some of these mills were later redistricted into Page County, Va.

Names on the second list were: Joseph Arthur & Co., John Arthur & Co., Davis Allen & Sons, John Buck, Henry Cagy & Sons, George Cooper ("of L. Creek"), William Dorsey, Joshua Foltz Sr., Jacob Funkhouser (not same man who owned a saw mill), Abraham Funkhouser, Isaac Funk ("the tanner"), Jacob Funk & Sons, Henry Gedick, George Howbert & Sons, Peter Holler & Son, Jacob Hamman, Daniel Hottle, Barnard Koutzman, John Morgan, Joseph More & Sons, Stephen Mahoney & Son, Ephram Rinker, George Rudolph, Francis Reese, John Stover, Peter Sager, Jacob Sheets, Christian Stover Sr., Anthony Spengler, Philip P. Sonner, William Stoner & Son, Ferdinand Smooker, Gabriel Sager, Abraham Smootz, John Wakeman, John Wendle Sr., and John Zircle ("of the Forrest").

Tanyard Mills. Isaac Funk, Isaac Huffman, George Hottle, Ruben Kite, Jacob Ott, Benjamin Pennybaker, and Samuel Watten (or Walten).

There were two *forges* or furnaces operating in Shenandoah County in 1813: Joseph Arthur & Co., and John Arthur & Co.

Fourteen taverns or hotels were licensed to operate in Shenandoah County, in 1813. The tavern keepers were named: John Barbee, John Overall, George Fravel, Alexander Sanford, James Lee, George Rodeffer, Henry Linn, Conrad Hilbert, Gilbert Meem, Jacob Blume, Moses Weeks, Jacob Summers, Philip Hoffman, and Elijah C. Russell.

It is a sad commentary that most of the mills in old Frederick County, Va. have been destroyed. Not one of the old mills is standing in Hampshire County, West Virginia. Possibly the last existing mill in Hardy County has been torn down. We have seen many mills go down during the past two decades.

The July 13, 1988 issue of **The West Virginia Advocate** published a photograph of the ruins of the Taylor Mill on Back Creek, Frederick County, Va. Shortly after the photograph appeared, the ruins were cleared away from the site, leaving no evidence of the mill which was built in 1794. Harrison Taylor built and operated the mill for several years, and sold it to Jonathan Lovett. That historic 18th century mill was part of the environment in Willa Cather's novel, **Sapphira and the Slave Girl.**[24]

Within old Frederick County, I am aware that these mills have been preserved: (1) The Burwell-Morgan Mill, located at Millwood, Clarke County, Va., operates under auspices of the Clarke County Historical Association. It was built during the later years of the Revolutionary War, circa 1783-85, by Hessian soldiers. It is open to the public, but not during mid-winter months. (2) The Thomas Shepherd Mill, located at Shepherdstown, Jefferson County, W.Va., was first built circa 1735. It is listed on The National Register of Historic Places. (3) The well-known Edinburg Mill, located at Edinburg, Shenandoah County, Va., is listed on The National Register of Historic Places. It is situated on the North Fork of the Shenandoah River. (4) The Zirkle Mill, located west of Quicksburg, Shenandoah County, Va., is listed on The National Register of Historic Places. (5) The Springdale Mill, located south of Winchester, is listed in The National Register of Historic Places. Settler Jost Hite had a mill on or near this site. (6) The Bunker Hill Flour Mill is located on Mill Creek, in Berkeley County, W. Va. (7) In Grant County, W.Va. the Lyon Mill (later known as Williamsport Grist Mill), has been restored by its owner, Jim Spicer. It has a 24 foot overshot waterwheel and is located on a tributary of Patterson's Creek.

Mills in varying stages of deterioration may be found in numerous locations, such as a mill at Yellow Spring, Hampshire County, W.Va., or one at Unger's Store, Morgan County, W.Va.

---

24. Records of construction of this mill, which prove its date and origin, are in my possession.

Some mills have been converted to accomodate various kinds of businesses. For example, a mill in Moorefield, Hardy County, W.Va. is being used as an antique shop.

The Green Spring Mill, located in northern Frederick County, Va., has not operated for several decades. It is now being used as a country store at Green Spring. This was an early mill that serviced families in the lower Apple Pie Ridge area. The structure of the mill appears to be sound, and the water supply is still abundant.

Possibly there are other standing mills located within the boundary of old Frederick County, Va. I have come across dozens of mill sites while conducting research in northern Virginia and the eastern panhandle of West Virginia. Mill ruins may be found in every section of old Frederick County.

Acknowledgements: The Honorable George Whitacre, Clerk of the Circuit Court, Frederick County, Va., granted special permission to inspect rare and fragile documents. Don Morecock and Minor Weisiger, Virginia State Archives staff, cooperated and assisted in locating and making available historical documents.

Account Book of Union Mills

Union Mills was a major commercial milling center in Frederick County, near Winchester. An account book that has been preserved in the Virginia State Archives provides details on the operation of the mill during the 1810-1813 era.

A brief abstract of the operation, and names of persons involved in commerce, is presented for the benefit of those who don't know about these records. It presents one facet of who did what in the grain industry during the 1810-1813 years.

The lower Shenandoah Valley was once called the wheat belt of Virginia. The land was a topographical extension of the Cumberland Valley of Pennsylvania. Early Pennsylvania settlers felt at home in the Winchester area, because of the similarity in farming conditions.

During the Civil War, Valley farms were destroyed by Union armies. The area never recovered from the war damage, which happened at the same time that wheat production was coming into its own in the "great plain" states. Farmers converted to fruit husbandry after the Civil War, for which the area is well-known. Winchester claims to be the "Apple Capital of the World," and holds an annual apple blossom festival. Berkeley Springs, W.Va. sponsors an annual apple butter festival.

Milling services were provided for the community at large, with corn, wheat, rye, and buckwheat being mentioned more frequently. Some of the products were destined for Alexandria, Va., but most of the flour was hauled by the barrel to Baltimore.

The account book reveals the names of persons who sold grain to Union Mills, and the transactions. Those who are interested in more detail may study this book in the State Library.[25]

Richard Davis, Isaac Parkins, Adam Bower of Winchester, Samuel Hollingsworth, Nathan Parkins, James Carpenter, Bennett Hall, Joseph Sample, John Manley, Adam Kern, James D. Vance,

John Marpole, Hyram Opea, James Rice, Henry and George Tucker, Thomas Cramer, Joseph Meyers, Vincent Scribner (hauled wheat from Brownley's), Samuel Windle, Joseph Mager, Thomas Henson (hauled flour to Baltimore), Robert McWorter,

William Hill, Cornelius Baldwin, Samuel Baker, John Scragin, Samuel Davison, Jonathan Foster, Nathan Gilbert, John Painter, George Newcomb, Samuel Lane, Peter Smith, Beaty Carson, Thomas Cramer,

John Caudy and Samuel Foreman (64 bushel of wheat transaction), Moses McCoy, Benjamin Welch, Jacob Ward, James

---

25. Written permission to review this book must be secured from The Honorable George Whitacre, Clerk of the Frederick County Court, Winchester, VA 22601. The letter must be signed by Mr. Whitacre, and addressed to the Virginia State Archives. It should specify the original record to be researched, "Union Mills, 1810-1812," 8-G-24-3-3 call number. Research must be conducted in person.

Galaway, William McKee, William Ely, William Mitchell, Jacob Jenkins,

John Racy, William Throckmorton, Joseph Jackson, Peter Allen, John Piper, William Johnson, John Clouser, William Reese, Uriah Cheshire (sold wheat to mill), Michael Blue, Richard Blue, Samuel Vandiver, John Littler, Daniel Clark, Thomas Hinson,

William Adams, William Knight, John Tucker, Christopher Probasco, Richard P. Barton, George Mumma, Henry Hickle, Ezekiel Marple (sold 80 barrels of wheat), Joseph C. Baldwin, Cornelius Baldwin,

Thomas Hook, John Haines, Capt. James Sowers, Henry Bryan, John Lewis, Samuel Jones, Jesse Brown, George Gulick, Swanson Lunsford, William Dunlap, Henry Bayles, Samuel Lane, Alexander Frazier, Samuel Drake,

John Arnold, Samuel Peters, David Darlington, Thomas Pennington, John Baker, Joseph Clutter, Norway Jones, Samuel Lockhart, Amos Parks, Samuel Runnals, John Singleton,

Enoch Marple (sold 39 barrels of wheat), Lewis Wolf, John Smith, Robert Glass, William Marshall, Benjamin Marshall, Philip Miller, Peter Thompson, David Darlington, Mathias Nelson (sold wheat), James Russell,

John Buzzard, Andrew Heironimus, Jonathan Foster, Robert D. Glass, Michael Albert, John Farmer, Abraham Parks (1812), Thomas McCormick, Andrew Albin, Lewis Neil, Joel Nixon, William Stripling, Josiah Jackson, James Bell, Timothy Corn,

Jacob Milslagle, John Horn, Elisha Thompson, John Dutchman, George Athey, Joseph Glass, William Shiplin, John Groves, Henry Surbaugh (Sirbaugh), Joseph McNally, Samuel Rutman (Ruckman), John Mackey (McKay), John Lupton, Ambrose Vasse,

Peter Shoemaker, John Hoover, Richard Davison, John Swisher, Robert Wilson, Charles Brent, George Peters, William Wood, Isaac Hollingsworth, Peter Hansucker, Philip Graybill,

Abraham Shank, David Timberlake, David Brown, Thomas Higgins,

Jonathan Wright, Nicholas Scarff, Joseph Glass, Philip Hoover, Daniel Denver, Jacob Lewis, Joseph Walker, Jonathan Foster, Abraham Shank, Martin Cartmell, Thomas Brown, Jacob Weaver, Joshua Newbraugh (page 127), Thomas Dunn,

David Marple, William Laing, David White, Samuel Windle, William George, William Carr (rye), William Albin, William White, Andrew Allen, John Anderson, John Swats (Swartz), and James Robinson.

Vincent Scrivner hauled wheat and flour for the mill during the 1810-1813 period of time.

Frederick County District Court

Historic *Minute Book 1805-1815* of the Frederick County District Court provides information about the composition of the court[26] in May 1809.

Robert White, Jr., Esquire, a Judge of the General Court and Judge of the Superior Court of Law for the Tenth Judicial Circuit.

Daniel Lee, clerk of the District Court.

Edward Powers, jailor.

Robert White III, sworn attorney-at-law and appointed county prosecutor.

Sworn Attorneys: Charles Magill, Archibald McGill, Mr. Tucker, Alfred H. Powell, Obed Waite, Elisha Boyd, Henry Dangerfield, Lewis Wolfe, Willoughby Morgan, and Joseph Sector.

---

26. *Minute Book 1805-1815* is housed in the Virginia State Library, Archives Division (Call # 8/G/25/1/4).

Frederick County Indentures, Guardian, and Apprentice Bonds

Information on indentures of children and guardian bonds have been gleaned from loose papers in the Virginia State Archives. Children were bound to masters to learn a trade, as well as to learn to "read, write and cypher and to learn the Rule of Three." The children were sometimes indentured because they were orphaned, illegitimate, or living in poverty.

Allen, Henrietta, daughter of Barlet Allen and "a free girl of colour," was born in June 1807. She was bound to James Anderson on Aug. 21, 1821, "to be taught the art of kniting, sewing and spining." Source: Indentured servant records, Frederick County, Va.

Arnold, Solomon, see orphans of, pages 110-111.

Babb, James, was born in Frederick County, Va. on Jan. 17, 1811. He was orphaned and apprenticed to Henry Baker (as house joiner), in 1828. It is believed that his parents were Abner and Susannah (Robinson) Babb. Abner Babb was born in 1768 and died Sept. 7, 1815, in Frederick County. Source: Apprentice bond in Virginia State Archives.

Baker, Austin, born Feb. 3, 1803, was apprenticed to John C. Clark to learn the trades of "skin dresser and breeches maker." Source: Apprentice bond, Frederick County, Va. records, Virginia State Archives.

Baker, George, was born on Oct. 20, 1805. He was bound to William McFee to read, write, cypher, including the Rule of Three, and the trade of a tailor.

Banks, Davenport, free boy, born Dec. 25, 1814, was bound to Stephen Grubbs, Feb. 22, 1822, to learn farming.

Banks, Polly, a free Negro and illegitimate daughter of Caty Banks of Frederick County, Va., was born June 1, 1812. Polly was bound to Stephen Grubs, on Dec. 10, 1821, as an indentured servant. Source: Indentured servant records for Frederick County, Va., located in Virginia State Archives.

Barr, Robert, was deceased before June 3, 1872, which was the date that his widow, Sydney Barr, and James W. Barr took $2,000 guardian bonds for orphans named Virginia R. Barr, Lewis J. Barr, Frank R. Barr, and Robert Barr Jr.   Source: **Guardians' Bonds**, Frederick County, Va.

Bayliss, Vincent, a mulatto, born Sept. 8, 1810, was a son of Elizabeth Vincent. He was bound to John W. Groves, Feb. 17, 1821, as a wagonmaker.

Berry, Jane, was born Jan. 3, 1823. She was bound to James H. White, to learn how to spin, sew and the usual duties of a housewife.

Blair, John, born in April 1739, was orphaned at age 8, in Frederick County, Va. On May 6, 1747, he was apprenticed to David Vance to learn the trade of weaving, by order of Morgan Morgan. On the same day, Margaret Blair, John's sister, was apprenticed to learn spinning and sewing. Margaret was born in September 1735. These indentures are housed in the Virginia State Archives, Frederick County Records.

Butler, Israel, born on Jan. 15, 1804, was bound to John W. Groves, Feb. 17, 1821, to learn wagon-making.

Cain, Betsy, born on Dec. 4, 1839, was bound to Evan Rogers, Nov. 6, 1841.

Campbell, Sophia, was born Feb. 28, 1818. She was bound to Mrs. Elizabeth Bruce, until reaching her 18th birthday. Source: *Apprentice and Guardian Bonds*, Frederick County records, Virginia State Archives.

Carter, Zephania, a base-born child of Lucretia Richards, was born on Feb. 11, 1799. He was bound to George Reed of Winchester on Sept. 4, 1811, to learn the trade of a coppersmith. Mary Carter, another base-born child of Lucretia Richards, was born on Aug. 8, 1801, and bound out.

Clyne, Abraham (Kline), born Oct. 13, 1807, was illegitimate son of Susan S. Kaine. He was given to the Overseers of the Poor to be bound to Joseph C. Poole, to become a shoemaker, Jan. 3, 1823.

Cochran, Edward, son of James Cochran (deceased), was born March 10, 1795. He was bound to David Russell of Winchester, on Aug. 1, 1815.

Cole, Bryant illegitimate child of Rachel Cole, was born June 10, 1807. He was bound to Jacob Newcomer, July 27, 1823.

Davis, William, born in March 1803, was apprenticed to Nathan Parkins, to learn the occupation of milling, per court order dated April 15, 1823.

DeHaven, orphan of David DeHaven, was placed under the guardianship of Jesse DeHaven, June 10, 1856.   Bondsman: John Lamp.

Doyle, George, illegitimate son of Elizabeth Doyle, was born March 10, 1813. He was bound to Armistead Wilson, to become a shoemaker, June 11, 1821.

Enders, Isaac, son of Christina (Enders) Kern, was placed in the care of Mrs. Frances Helm. On Oct. 19, 1802, the Overseers of the Poor levied Christina Kern $30 for support of her son.

Frazier, Louisa illegitimate daughter of Polly Frazier, was born Oct. 8, 1808. She was bound to Batley White, March 10, 1821.

Frazier, Robert, illegitimate son of Polly Frazier, was born on Oct. 1, 1812. He was bound to Robert Widdour, in 1827, to learn the art of boot and shoemaking.

Friend, Charles, "orphan of Israel Friend," came into court to make a choice of John Valentine Howe as his guardian, with John Smith, bondsman. Source: *Minute Book: 1761-63*, page 152, Frederick County records, Virginia State Archives.

Guston, James, a coloured boy, was born Dec. 6, 1832. He was bound to Zachariah Kern, on Aug. 6, 1838, to learn farming.

Hackney, Molly, free girl of color, daughter of Sylva Hackney, born in October 1806, was bound to James Anderson, Aug. 21, 1821, to learn knitting, sewing, and spinning.

Haymaker, Philip, son of John Haymaker, deceased, was born in 1799. Philip was bound to Adam Kurtz, in March 1814, to learn the trade of shoemaker.

Hite, Mary Catherine, orphan of Michael Hite, was placed under the guardianship of James Carper on June 21, 1853. Bondsman was Alfred Hite.

Hoge, Asa was deceased by Sept. 3, 1804, when his three orphan children— Jesse Hoge, Israel Hoge, and Asa Hoge Jr.— were placed under care of Mary Hoge, wife of Asa Sr. A $2,000 bond was taken by Mary Hoge, John Griffith Sr., and Joseph Hackney Jr.

Hott, George and Jacob, sons of Henry Hott Sr., deceased, were to receive a share of their father's estate. Christina Hott, Elizabeth Hott, and Henry Hott Jr., took a $200 bond, Sept. 4, 1809, to assure that these minor children would receive their rightful shares.

Hoyle, Titus, was born on May 15, 1808. At age 13 years, he was bound to Robert Snapp (on Oct. 1, 1821) as an indentured servant. Philip Burwell, overseer of the poor in Frederick County, Va.

Hunter, Solomon, was born on March 11, 1800. He was bound to George Barnhart, Aug. 1, 1816, to learn the trade of carriage-maker.

Johnson, Nancy Pratt, orphan of Stephen Johnson, was born Jan. 27, 1819. She was bound to Henry Payne to learn the art of knitting, sewing, spinning, June 22, 1822.

Johnston, Theresa Jane, orphan of Stephen Johnston, born Aug. 8, 1817, was apprenticed to John Allemong, to learn how to spin, sew and knit. Source: Frederick County, Va. "apprentice bond," dated June 22, 1827.

Lemley, Jacob, orphan of Michael Lemley, was born on Dec. 23, 1809. He was bound to George Ritenour, Nov. 30, 1822, to learn the trade of tanning.

Lewis, David, "orphan of Henry Lewis," was born in Frederick County, July 12, 1806. He was bound to Henry Horner, on Aug. 10, 1821, to learn the trade of coopering. David's mother was Elizabeth Lewis.

Little, William, was born on June 9, 1808. He was bound to Michael Ritenour, March 26, 1819, to learn the trade of coopering.

McVicker, Alfred, was born Jan. 10, 1797. A Frederick County, Va. court document (indenture) shows that Alfred was bound to Goldsmith Chandlee to learn clockmaking, dated Jan. 13, 1814.

Martin, Sydney, daughter of Vincent Martin, was born Dec. 12, 1792. She was bound to David and Mary Lupton, as indentured servant, per Feb. 9, 1805 Frederick County court order.

Mauzy, Henry, orphans listed (Hampshire County) on page 266.

Merchant, Lorenzo Dow, born March 12, 1809, was bound to Jonathan Smith, Oct. 1818, until 21 years old. Was to learn how to read, write and cypher, including the Rule of three, and learn the trade of a miller. Bondsmen: George M. Frye and John Baker.

Murphy, Sylvester, was born on Jan. 24, 1794, in Frederick County, Va. He was bound to William Ball to learn the hat-making trade. His father, John Murphy, was deceased prior to January 24, 1812, when the indenture was dated in the Frederick County, Va. court.

Murphy, Silverton, son of John Murphy, deceased, was born on Jan. 24, 1794. In May 1812, he was bound to William Ball to learn the trade of "hatter."

Noble, William, a free child of color, born in August 1808, was bound to William Rogers, July 1, 1815, to learn farming.

O'Boyle, James Madison, orphan of James O'Boyle, was born Feb. 10, 1810. He was bound to Josiah Lockhart on Feb. 10, 1824, and then bound to Michael Coyle, to apprentice as a hatter.

Owens, John, son of Mary Shivers, was bound to Henry Smith to be taught the blacksmith trade, and to read the Bible, per court record dated March 4, 1786. Bondsmen were George Chick, Argyle Taylor, John Gregory, and Barnaby Rioley. Source: "Indentures and Guardian Bonds," Frederick County, Va. records in the Virginia State Archives.

Parlett, John, son of Joshua Parlett of England, was born on July 27, 1791 and died on April 5, 1837 in Frederick County, Va. He married Elizabeth Yeakley, daughter of John and Mary Ann (Fries) Yeakley. Elizabeth was born on April 23, 1795 and died on July 5, 1880. A guardian bond for $500 was taken from the Frederick County Court by widow Elizabeth Parlett and her father, John Yeakley, on June 7, 1837. The orphans were named: John Parlett, Catherine Jane Parlett, Elizabeth Margaret Parlett, Isaac Thomas Parlett, Henry Joshua Parlett, and James William Parlett. Source: Tombstone inscriptions, Frederick County court "orphan bond," and family records.

Paskel, Madison, illegitimate son of Ruth Mahew, was born on March 21, 1816. He was bound to John S. Rogers, Jan. 7, 1823, to learn the trade of farming. Tilmon Mahew and Ruth Mahew cosigned the indenture. Bondsmen were: Levi Rogers and Andras Showalter.

Reed, Emily, a free Negro woman and daughter of Frances Reed (alias Frances Wills), was bound to George Wright, March 16, 1821, to learn how to spin, knit and sew.

Reed, Rebecca, daughter of John Reed, was to receive a share of Jacob Rinker's estate. Casper Rinker took a $600 bond, Frederick County, on Jan. 1, 1838.

Rosenberry, Mary, orphan of Michael Rosenberry, deceased, to Jacob Kerns and John Rosenberry, $50 bond, Aug. 5, 1823.

Scarff, William C., was born Nov. 28, 1795. He was bound to Job Smith Hendricks, in Sept. 1813, to learn the trade of cabinet-making.

Simmons, Polly, daughter of Thomas and Hannah Simmons, was born on Feb. 6, 1813. She was apprenticed to John Grim Sr., until reaching her 18th birthday. Indenture was between George Lynn and Simon Carson, and John Grim Sr. Frederick County, Va. court indenture was dated March 15, 1815.

Smith, Jeremiah Jr. orphans- see page 343.

Smith, John, born on Dec. 17, 1800, was bound to Adam Kurtz, Aug. 14, 1819, to learn the trade of shoemaking.

Streit, George, born July 21, 1851, was bound to William Peacemaker, March 2, 1859. Bondsman: Martin M. Adams.

Syphert, William, a coloured boy, aged about three years and six months, was an orphan of Susan Syphert, deceased. He was bound to Isaac Groves to learn the art of farming, March 17, 1823.

Vaughn, Susan Elton, illegitimate daughter of Saley Vaughn, was born May 2, 1817. She was bound to Robert McCleave, May 2, 1817, to lear how to sew, knit, spin and weave.

Walsh, Sally, "an orphan child, aged 13 years," was born Aug. 1, 1808. She was "bound" to John White, to learn how to sew, spin and knit, per Frederick County court order dated March 10, 1821.

Webb, Charles, son of Libby Marple, was born June 1, 1813. He was bound to Jonathan Robinson, as a barber, May 6, 1820.

White, Alexander III, married Sarah Gassoway. Son, John White, was orphaned on Aug. 7, 1816, in Frederick County. This John White and one John Heiskell were bound to Thomas Buck, James M. Marshall, Joseph Tidball, Mandly Taylor, and Betsy

Carson, after posting a $4,000 bond. Source: *Frederick County, Virginia Guardians' Bonds*, found in Virginia State Archives, Richmond, Va.

White, Wesley, born on Jan. 8, 1805, was bound by Overseers of the Poor to Jonathan Foster, June 12, 1817, to learn the trade of a printer.

Wilson, Henry, "a free Negro boy," born Dec. 25, 1804, was bound to Stephen Grubb, to apprentice as a farmer, per court order dated Feb. 22, 1822.

Young, Peggy, was born on July 1, 1809. She was bound to Stephen Pritchard when she was 12 years old, "until age 18, when $12 will be given as 'freedom dues.'"

Miscellaneous Public Works Records

"*Payroll of hands employed in repairing the 2nd Eastern section of North Western Road (turnpike), between the 18th day of April and the 30th, 1838.*" The following names were found in Public Works Section, Northwestern Turnpike files, Virginia State Archives. These temporary employees worked on a road gang to repair the turnpike in 1838. This section of the turnpike crossed Timber Ridge, along what is now U.S. Route 50.   A study of the names reveals that employees lived in either Hampshire or Frederick County, Va. These original signatures are preserved in the archives, along with a pay slip signed by each employee: Samuel Hook, Jefferson Keckley, Abraham McDonald, James Slonaker, Michael Slonaker, Benjamin McDonald, Josiah Parish, Joseph Parish, Joshua Kerns, Peter Oats, Christopher Oats, Christopher Parish, Lemuel Pugh, Nathan Kerns, Joseph McKey (McKee), Azariah Pugh, Landon Carlisle, Richard M. Slonaker, Jonathan Oats, John Ferryman, Stephen Ferryman, William Coffman, James Caudy, Joel Ward, and John Fletcher.

Kidwell Genealogy

John Kidwell, progenitor of the surname in Hampshire County, Va., was born circa 1762 in Prince Georges County, Maryland, and immigrated to Hampshire County in 1800, with his wife Eleanor, his children, and a black slave. John Kidwell and Eleanor Hayes were married in Prince Georges County on Jan. 5, 1785. One of her brothers settled in Hardy County, Va.

The Kidwells settled on an eastern slope of Sandy Ridge (Hampshire County), on Fairfax land grants that were previously issued to Thomas Kennedy and John Hiett. He accumulated 343 acres and operated a water-powered grist mill, which was located on a bank of a stream then known as Sandy Lick Run and known today as Cold Stream.

The Kidwells were predominately farmers, although Hampshire County is not known for fertile farmland. Milling and part-time Christian ministries were other occupational choices made by earlier generations. Certain members of the family were interested in various kinds of clocks during the early 19th century, proven by inventories of personal properties in Hampshire County.

John Kidwell died circa 1846, in Hampshire County. A very old graveyard is located on a Sandy Ridge mountainside, marked with field slates, but no engravings. Possibly this contains the burial plot of John and Ellen Kidwell, but it is not known for certain. A local resident calls it "the Hawkins garveyard."

After his death, part of Kidwell's estate, including the water-powered grist mill, was sold to Jacob A. Marker of Frederick County, Va.

Several researchers have attempted to develop an account of the early Kidwell families of Hampshire County, without much success. Based on research in primary records, I have been able to identify 11 children and 60 grandchildren, being the first three generations in Hampshire County.

Children and grandchildren of John and Eleanor Kidwell[27] were:

1. Sophrana Frances "Fannie" Kidwell was born in 1784, and died June 23, 1824. Interment was in the Foreman cemetery at Cold Stream, Hampshire County, W.Va.   Fannie married David Foreman II,   son of David and Catherine Foreman.   David remarried and moved to Logan County, Ohio in 1834.   One unconfirmed source stated that David's second wife was named Rebecca McDonald, a daughter of Benjamin and Margaret (Hiett) McDonald.   Rebecca died before the 1850 census was taken. David Foreman Jr. was born in Hampshire County, Va., March 7, 1785, and died Jan. 21, 1875, in Noble County, Ohio.   Children of David and Fannie (Kidwell) Foreman were:

a. Hiram Foreman was born in Hampshire County, Va., and he immigrated to Senecaville, Guernsey County, Ohio.

b. Ann Foreman married Alexander Morehead, and they settled in Ohio.

c. Henry Foreman was born in Hampshire County in 1809. He married a woman named Julia, and they had several children, including Benjamin, James, Harriett and Rebecca Foreman.

d. Ellen Foreman was born in Hampshire County, Va. in 1810 and died at Keiths, Ohio, in 1895. She did not marry.

e. Austin Foreman was born in Hampshire County, Va. on April 11, 1812 and died Aug. 8, 1884, in Noble County, Ohio.   He married a first-cousin named Joanna Kidwell, who was a daughter of Hawkins and Nancy Kidwell. Joanna Kidwell was born in 1816, in Hampshire County, and died at Sharon Ohio, March 7, 1895.

f. Mary Foreman was born Jan. 15, 1814, and died Dec. 18, 1888. She married Solomon Cooper (1805-1845), on Sept. 10, 1835, in Hampshire County. They immigrated to Noble County, Ohio, where they died.

g. David Foreman III, was born ca. 1815 in Hampshire County. He married a woman named Elizabeth and they were living in Vinton County, Ohio when the 1860 census was taken.

h. Jacob Foreman was born in 1818, in Hampshire County, and died Dec. 17, 1888, in Washington County, Ohio. He married Elizabeth Archibald, daughter of John and Hannah (Reed)

---

27. Proven by many miscellaneous records, especially **Order Book II**, page 336, Sept. 15, 1849; Circuit Court, Romney, W.Va.

Archibald, Aug. 26, 1841, in Noble County, Ohio. Elizabeth was born on June 30, 1825, in Ohio, and died Feb. 5, 1913, at Caldwell, Ohio.

i. John Foreman was born May 12, 1820 in Hampshire County, and died Sept. 27, 1863, in Noble County, Ohio. He married Eliza Wiley, Jan. 4, 1844, in Noble County. She was born on June 22, 1825, and died Aug. 11, 1859. They had seven children.

j. Louisa Foreman was born June 14, 1822 and died May 9, 1898. She was a twin. Louisa married Abraham Miley Jennings, daughter of David D. and Ruth (Wright) Jennings, on April 2, 1840. Abraham was born in Virginia, April 19, 1818, and died in Noble County, Ohio, Feb. 2, 1889. Louisa visited her homeplace in Hampshire County, in 1882, and wrote to a friend about the visit.

k. Lucinda Foreman was born June 14, 1822, in Hampshire County, Va., and died in Noble County, Ohio, on Aug. 13, 1883. Lucinda married Samuel Saylor (1818-1885), Dec. 13, 1839. They lived in Ohio.

2. Hawkins Kidwell was born circa 1786 and died in 1847 in Hampshire County, Va. He owned 200 acres on a west bank of North River, part of an original patent to the Rev. Benjamin Stone. Hawkins Kidwell married Nancy (Hiett?), born in 1797, who survived him. They were poor people— Christians— who lived in the back country. Shortly after his death, Hawkins's estate was sold for $281.63 to pay his debts. George Deaver was the purchaser. Children of Hawkins and Nancy Kidwell were:

a. Evan Kidwell was born in 1814. He married Sally Mercer, who was born in 1820.

b. Malinda Ellen Kidwell married Hugh Slane (1819-1882), a son of Benjamin and Delilah (Poston) Slane. They had four daughters.

c. John Kidwell was born circa 1821 and died in Hampshire County, W.Va., June 30, 1897 (per court death record). John married Mary Ellen Hiett, daughter of John and Anna (Edwards) Hiett. They had no children.

d. Joanna Kidwell married Austin Foreman, son of David and Fannie (Kidwell) Foreman II. They were first cousins, and they settled in Ohio.

e. Lucinda Kidwell married David Critton, who was born in 1820. They lived in Hampshire County, West Virginia.

f. Randolph Hawkins Kidwell, born in 1826, married Betsy Ann Hawkins, March 27, 1882, by The Rev. John A. Corder. She was 44 years old when they were married, and they had no children.

g. Benjamin Franklin Kidwell was born on Jan. 5, 1827 and died in Critton Valley, Hampshire County, W.Va., on Nov. 1, 1867. His wife was Mahala Brelsford, who was a daughter of Jesse and Mary (Jacobs) Brelsford [See Hampshire County *Deed Book 42*, page 518, dated Nov. 10, 1849, for proof of marriage.]

3.   Lucinda Kidwell was born in 1787 and died on Sept. 6, 1870, in Hampshire County. She married Jeremiah Hiett (1783-1861), son of Evan and Sarah (Smith) Hiett. They were buried in unmarked graves in the Evan Hiett graveyard on Sandy Ridge, Hampshire County.   Probably Jeremiah was named after his paternal grandfather, Capt. Jeremiah Smith, who was an early settler in upper Back Creek Valley, Frederick County, Va. Children of Jeremiah and Lucinda (Kidwell) Hiett were:

a. Asa Hiett was born in 1804 and died in 1885. He married Charlotte Arnold, who was born on Oct. 4, 1828 and died on Aug. 25, 1852. I found her grave in the Sloan family graveyard, west of Romney, W.Va., across the road from the "Stone House" on U.S. Route 50. Asa Hiett served in the Virginia House of Delegates during 1845-49 and 1855-56, a total of four terms. Asa left no descendants.

b. Jonathan Hiett was born on April 5, 1808 and died on Sept. 16, 1887.   He first married a Miss Parks, and then, on Jan. 24, 1837, married Margaret McKee, who was a daughter of Joseph and Elizabeth (Reid) McKee. Margaret was born in 1814 and died on Aug. 15, 1872, in Hampshire County. Her brother, Robinson Joseph McKee, who married Maria Sommerville, was a major character in "Early History of Bloomery, W.Va.: A Pioneer's Perspective," published in the Dec. 14, 1987 issue of *The West Virginia Advocate*, Capon Bridge, W.Va. 26711.

c. John Hiett was born on Aug. 11, 1809 and died on Nov. 28, 1896. He married Anna Edwards, daughter of William and Ann (Albin) Edwards, on March 27, 1834. Anna was born on July 15, 1812 and died on Jan. 8, 1895. They lived in Hampshire County. This family possessed many old records which were used to preserve the Hiett history. Who now possesses the original records, or were they destroyed?

d. Elizabeth Hiett was born in 1811 and died in 1889. She married Robert Little (1810-1879). They immigrated to Zenia, Ohio (Greene County in 1830) where they raised six children.

e. Frances "Fannie" Maria Hiett was born Jan. 30, 1813, and died April 24, 1884. She married the Rev. James Alexander Cowgill, son of Ewing and Susannah (Buzzard) Cowgill, on Nov. 24, 1842. He was a preacher in the Disciples Church. James A. was born on April 22, 1818 and died Nov. 18, 1882. Both were buried in the Evan Hiett graveyard on Sandy Ridge. Attractive tombstones were placed at their graves but cattle have knocked over all stones in this historic graveyard.

f. Samuel Patton Hiett was born Oct. 13, 1814 and died Dec. 21, 1902. He first married Elizabeth A. Johnson, born in 1818 and died March 28, 1843. She was buried at Timber Ridge Christian Church graveyard. After Elizabeth's death, he remarried to Susan DeHaven (1827-1908). He and his second wife were buried at Ganotown, Berkeley County, W.Va.

g. Evan Hiett was born in 1816 and died July 22, 1902. He married Frances Hiett, daughter of Samuel S. and Sarah (Parks) Hiett.

h. William Hiett was born circa 1827. He married Rhoda Campbell and they immigrated to Illinois ca 1850. No children.

i. James Sanford Hiett was born circa 1821. He married Susan King, and they moved to Pekin, Illinois in 1869.

j. Sarah Hiett married Levi Hott, son of Conrad and Mary Ann (Stipes) Hott, on Nov. 2, 1845. Levi was born on April 8, 1816, and died Dec. 20, 1901. He served as a Justice of the Peace in Hampshire County. The Hotts resided on Sandy Ridge. See my *Shanholtzer History and Allied Family Roots*, 1980, for extensive information on descendants of Levi and Sarah (Hiett) Hott.

k. Jeremiah Hiett Jr. was born on July 9, 1825 and died on July 2, 1911, at Tomahawk, Berkeley County, W.Va. He married Rachel Shanholtzer, daughter of Jacob and Hannah (Loy) Shanholtz. Rachel was born on June 1, 1834 and died on Aug. 1, 1903. See my book, *Shanholtzer History and Allied Family Roots*.

l. Lucinda Hiett was born Feb. 27, 1827 and died March 10, 1898. Her husband, Capt. George Deaver, was born Nov. 9, 1825, and died Nov. 28, 1907. They were buried in the Hiett graveyard on Sandy Ridge, owned by John Whitacre.

m. Mary Ellen Hiett died unmarried.

4. Elizabeth Kidwell was born on July 17, 1791 and died during the 1820's, in Hampshire County. She married Henry Wolford, son of John and Catherine (Sydner) Wolford. Henry was born Oct. 20, 1789, per family Bible. After Elizabeth's death, he

remarried to Margaret Rinehart.   The children of Henry and Elizabeth (Kidwell) Wolford were:

a. George Wolford (1815-1898) married Nancy Loy, daughter of Adam and Sarah (Hiett, Sarah) Loy. They immigrated to Illinois.

b. Lucinda Wolford married John Stewart.

c. John Wolford.

5. Mariah Kidwell was born in 1796 and died July 16, 1845, in Guernsey County, Ohio.   She married George Bethel II, son of George and Jane Bethel.   George II was born in 1788 and died March 16, 1846. According to a Hampshire County, Va. circuit court document, George and Mariah (Kidwell) Bethel II had these children: John, Joshua, Jane, Ellen, George, James, and Nancy Bethel. Joshua Bethel was mentioned in the document, believed to have been guardian for his brother's children. One descendant who is researching this Bethel family line is: Mr. Roy Bethel, 211 West Street, Groveport, Ohio 43125.

6. John Spaulding Kidwell was born circa 1795 and died in 1861. He married Mary Hiett, daughter of Evan and Sarah (Smith) Hiett. Mary was born on May 15, 1796 and died on July 17, 1882. On May 11, 1868,   James and Joseph Kidwell took a $2,000 executor's bond to administer his estate.   They were buried in the Kidwell private family graveyard near Slanesville, W.Va.   The children of John S. and Mary (Hiett) Kidwell were:

a. Samuel A. Kidwell was born on May 12, 1817, and died on June 25, 1903. He married Nancy Largent, daughter of John and Margaret (Slane) Largent. Nancy was born on Sept. 12, 1821 and died on March 12, 1900. They raised a large family of eleven children.

b. Lorenzo Dow Kidwell was born on July 12, 1818 and died in Wirt County, W.Va., on Feb. 21, 1897. He married Elizabeth Ann Alexander (1841-1921), daughter of William and Elizabeth (Cox) Alexander. [Note: Researching this family branch: Kent Linscott, Access Road Box 38, Williamston, W.Va. 26187.]

c. Jeremiah "Jerry" Kidwell was born in 1820 and allegedly went to California during the gold rush.

d. David Kidwell married Martha Hiett, a daughter of John and Ann (Edwards) Hiett. Martha remarried to Isaac King.

e. James Kidwell was born on Feb. 25, 1823 and died on Jan. 14, 1894. He was first married to Rebecca Slane, a daughter of Benjamin and Delilah (Poston) Slane, on Feb. 21, 1845. Rebecca was born on Feb. 21, 1825 and died in Oct. 1849. They had two children. After Rebecca's death, James remarried to Mary Mencer (spelled Mentzer in the family Bible), on March 7, 1853. Mary was born on Sept. 29, 1831 and died on Sept. 4, 1899. Both were buried in the Kidwell graveyard at Slanesville, W.Va. James Kidwell was the father of six children. Source: The family Bible is a possession of Shirley Ludwick, Mountain Falls Route, Box 163G, Winchester, Va. 22601.

f. Jonathan Kidwell was born on Oct. 11, 1827 and died in 1908. He was buried in the Kidwell graveyard, located near Slanesville, W.Va. He married first to Ann Brelsford. After her death he remarried to Ann Mariah Bennett (1834-1908), daughter of William Bennett, on Jan. 12, 1867.

g. Joseph Kidwell married Lucy Rittenhour.

h. William Kidwell never married, according to Maud Pugh.

i. Evan Kidwell never married.

j. Mary Kidwell was born on June 10, 1830 and died on June 19, 1891. She first married Sylvester Vanorsdale and then Charles Patterson, the latter on March 8, 1858, by the Rev. Christy Sine. Charles was born on Oct. 19, 1833 and died on April 11, 1917. Both were buried in the Kidwell family graveyard, near Slanesville, West Virginia. He served in the Union army, in an Ohio regiment. Source: Tombstone inscriptions in Kidwell graveyard.

7. Nancy Kidwell was born on Oct. 31, 1797 and died on July 12, 1870, in Athens County, Ohio. She married Joshua Bethel, son of George and Jane Bethel I. Joshua was born April 14, 1791, in Parks Valley, Hampshire County, Va., and died May 4, 1873 in Athens County, Ohio. One unconfirmed source stated that Nancy first married a Taylor, but no proof. Names of descendants of Joshua and Nancy Bethel are not known by the compiler at this time.

8. Mary Kidwell married David Hawkins on Oct. 1, 1825 in Hampshire County, Va. She was declared "insane" before 1849. According to *Order Book III*, page 146, Circuit Court of Hampshire County, Va., Mary was awarded a one-eleventh share of her father's estate. The lands of John Kidwell were ordered to be sold. The trustees were Nathaniel Offutt, Eli Beale, Joseph Kackley, and John A. Smith. The latter court document was dated April 19, 1854.

9. James Kidwell was born circa 1800 and died on Sept. 14, 1879, in Hampshire County, Va. An 1839 deed proves that he purchased 160 acres, on which a woolen mill stood. The mill was

previously owned by Daniel and Elizabeth Haines, on land that was granted by Lord Fairfax to Thomas Edwards. On the 1839 deed, James' wife signed her name as Jane, which adds another dimension of mystery about this James Kidwell. He allegedly married: (1) Ann Hiett, daughter of Evan and Sarah (Smith) Hiett, according to tradition, and (2) Elizabeth Ann (Edwards) Largent, widow of William Largent, on July 18, 1871. Elizabeth was a daughter of Anthony Edwards, and she died in Sherman County, Nebraska on Sept. 13, 1887. Apparently researchers have confused the children of Hawkins and James Kidwell. There is no reliable list of James Kidwells' children at this time. One John Kidwell, born circa 1824, was a proven son, according to a tithable list made in 1846, housed in the Virginia State Archives. Are there living descendants of this James Kidwell? Sources: Public records, including Hampshire County marriage and death; Edwards family Bible record; and U.S. census.

10. David Kidwell was listed as an heir, and he was on the personal property tax lists for Hampshire County, Va. No further information is available at this time.

11. William Ashford Kidwell was born in Hampshire County, Va. on Dec. 19, 1808 and died on July 10, 1876. He was buried next to his sister, Nancy (Kidwell) Bethel, in Bethel Ridge Cemetery, Trimble Township, Athens County, Ohio. He was listed as a Reverend on his tombstone. In Hampshire County, he was called Ashford, which was his middle name. Tax records show that he emigrated from Hampshire County in 1835. Apparently, he returned in 1848-49, just after his father's death, but then returned to Ohio. He was listed as a miller on the U.S. Censuses for Athens County, Ohio. He married Susan _____, who was born in Virginia circa 1818. The 1880 census states that her father was born in Germany and her mother in Virginia. Their children, all born in Ohio, were: Peter R. Kidwell, Sarah A. Kidwell, Rebecca Kidwell, Thomas Kidwell, Martha Kidwell, George Kidwell, David Kidwell, James Kidwell, and Austin Kidwell.[28]

---

28. One Fielding Kidwell, born circa 1785, was listed on the U.S. Census for Hampshire County, Va. in 1830. He paid personal property taxes through the year 1833, and then disappeared from the records. A Bazil Kidwell was on the tax list in 1834, possibly one of Fielding Kidwell's sons. Also, an Ellen Kidwell, born during the 1770s, was enumerated on the Hampshire County census for 1830. Presumably these families were related to John Kidwell.

Largent Family History

John Largent II, progenitor of the surname in the Shenandoah, South Branch and Cacapon Valleys, was born about 1720, and died circa 1806 in Hampshire County, Va. Although he went to Kentucky during the mid-1790's, tax records prove that he returned to Hampshire County, Va., where he apparently died. John II was thrice married, according to miscellaneous records and family tradition. His children were listed in sets, viz, "first set, second set, and third set." Lack of proof and clarity of the names and order of his three wives have hampered researchers for decades. [See Maud Pugh's *Capon Valley: It's Pioneers and Their Descendants*.] Two research colleagues on Largent family history have been of tremendous assistance over the years: Mr. Roger A. Stubbs[29] of Long Lake, Minnesota, a Largent researcher for over 50 years; and Mrs. Joanne Eustice of Redlands, Calif., compiler of the *Largent Bulletin*. In 1990, new data were found, which formed the basis for a major revision of this family history. Many errors have been perpetuated on Largent family history. Although this presentation is not the final word, it contains a more accurate account than previously known.   The Largent surname was one of the first to appear in old Orange County, Va. (later Frederick County).   Information below supercedes data published in the first printing of this volume in 1988.

Children of John and Elizabeth Largent (1722-1806)- "first set"– were:

(1) Mary Largent was born April 4, 1746, and no further information is available at this time.

(2) Ann Largent, born March 14, 1749, possibly married a resident of Hampshire County.

(3) John "Big Neck" Largent III was born July 7, 1751 and drowned in the Cacapon River when his boat capsized, circa 1826, in Morgan County, Va. His wife was named Mary. An incomplete list of children of John Largent III (all proven except Catherine):

---

29. Roger Stubbs died on July 30, 1990.

a. Catherine Largent, born in 1785, married John Loy, who died in Hampshire County in 1856. (Catherine not a proven child of John III) Their only child, Dianne Loy, born in 1811, married Joseph Miles.

b. Charity Largent was born circa 1789 and did not marry.

c. Susan A. Largent was born June 11, 1791 and died, unmarried, on July 8, 1854.

d. Elizabeth Largent married a Mr. Henderson, according to a chancery court document in Romney. Elizabeth had two children: (1) Levina Largent married a Mr. Poling, and (2) Betsy Henderson married a Mr. (Alfred?) Iser.

e. Samuel Largent (1798-1879) married twice: Kezziah_____ [4 children], and Mahala Pownall [5 children]. He left many descendants, many of whom lived in Morgan County, W.Va. and in northeastern Hampshire County. Samuel's children were: (1) John K. Largent; (2) Isaac Largent (born in 1828) married Laura Thomas. He went to Missouri and lost contact with the family; (3) Mary Jane Largent, born in 1830, married Richard Moreland, son of John Moreland. (4) Josephine Largent married a Mr. Cowgill. (5) Samuel F. Largent was born March 24, 1854. He married Ann Fischel and they moved to Berkeley County, W.Va. (6) James W. Largent was born on Dec. 11, 1856. He lived near Okonoko, W.Va., in 1909, and was single. (7) Parcena Largent was born in 1856 and died in 1868. (8) Lemuel H. Largent was born in 1858 and died Sept. 17, 1881, unmarried. (9) Eli. A. Largent was born Oct. 28, 1861. He settled in Fulton County, Pennsylvania.

(4) James Largent was born Sept. 1, 1753 and died in 1813, at Forks of Capon. It is believed that he was twice-married: (a) Margaret _____ and (b) Margery Carlin [an heir and legal representative of Andrew Carlin (deceased) according to Hampshire County, Va. **Deed Book 16**, page 379. The 1799 personal property tax list for Hampshire County shows one Margery Carlin, head of household.] Please note this James Largent has often been confused with his uncle (same name) who married Mrs. John (Margaret) Hiett during the late 1760s, or with his step-brother, James Henwood Largent.

a. Margaret "Peggy" Largent was born circa 1769. She married James Slane (ca 1766-1829) son of Daniel and Nancy Slane, Feb. 19, 1786, in Frederick County, Va.

b. Mary Largent was born circa 1770 and probably died after 1812, in Licking County, Ohio. She married Hugh Slane, son of Daniel and Nancy Slane.

c. Major John Largent (War of 1812) was born circa 1772 and died in Hampshire County, before 1831, when his Will was probated. He married Sarah Critton, probably a daughter of John Critton. Sarah survived her husband. Their children were: Mary Largent (1796-1846) married Joseph Largent (of Lewis); William Largent (1798-1862) married Elizabeth Frazier; James T. Largent (1800-1888) married Elizabeth Boxwell; Margaret Largent married William Johnson;   Elizabeth "Betsy" Largent married Edward Frazier, May 7, 1823; John Washington Largent, born ca 1808, married Jane Largent (of Lewis, of Thomas Largent); Sarah Ann Largent married first to Samuel Largent, on Nov. 6, 1830, and secondly to a Mr. Beck; Amelia "Milly" Largent married John Boxwell on Aug. 22, 1832, and they lived in Illinois.

(5) Elizabeth Largent was born April 2, 1755.   No further information is available at this time.

(6) William Largent was born July 29, 1758.   He moved to Kentucky sometime after serving in the Revolutionary War, under Capt. William Vause and Col. James Wood Jr.   William was a tanner, and married a woman named Elizabeth. They raised a family of at least six children. It is believed that William and Elizabeth settled in Champaign County, Ohio, where they died and were buried near Thackeray, Ohio.

Source of birthdates for "first set" above: **Morgan's Chapel Records**, *Norborne Parish, Berkeley County, Va.*

Children of John Largent II, "second set" [possibly second wife was nee Nelson], believed from oral tradition to have been Mrs. Sarah (Nelson) Henwood. A Nelson family settled at Forks of Capon during the 1750s, proven by Fairfax land records and 18th century graves in the Largent-Powell graveyard. Henwood was an early name in Cacapon Valley.

(7) James Henwood Largent, son of Mrs. Sarah Henwood and adopted stepson of John Largent II, was born circa 1755 and died in 1846, in Logan County, Ohio.   He served in the Revolutionary war; then went to Kentucky before settling in Ohio. Certain researchers have confused this man with his stepbrother, by the same name, viz, James Largent (1753-1813).

(8) Thomas Largent was born May 5, 1760 and died in 1830, Hampshire County. He married Eleanor Shivers (See Bible record of Thomas on page 241).

(9) Nelson Largent was born Sept. 27, 1762 and died circa 1846 in Montgomery County, Indiana. He was a Revolutionary War pensioner. After the war he went to Kentucky, but resettled in Ohio in 1806. Nelson was twice-married: (a) Meriam _____ and (2) Sarah ____.

(10) Jane Largent, born circa 1765, married Thomas Johnson, an early-known surname in old Hampshire County. The Johnsons were among the early settlers in the Critton Hollow area of Hampshire County.

(11) Sarah Largent was born circa 1767 in Hampshire County, Va. She married Philip Porter on Feb. 28, 1786, in Frederick County, Va. They immigrated to Champaign County, Ohio, circa 1810.

(12) Lewis Largent was born circa 1770, and died in 1844, in Hampshire County. He married: (a) Kezziah Parrish, daughter of Joseph Parish (4 children) and (b) Betsy Hull, daughter of Benjamin and Elsie Hull (5 children). Children of Lewis Largent:

a. John L. Largent, born in 1793, married Margaret Slane. They lived in the Sandy Ridge area of Hampshire County, and were both alive when the 1860 U.S. census was taken.

b. Joseph Largent (1794-1872) married Mary Largent (of John, of James Largent).

c. William Largent (1796-) married first to Elizabeth Smith and secondly to Elizabeth Ann Edwards, daughter of Anthony Edwards.

d. Thomas Largent (1799-1881) died unmarried.

e. Aaron Largent (1807-) married Catherine Hieronimus.

f. Elizabeth Largent (1809-) married Israel Hardy.

g. Lewis Largent (1810-) never married.

h. Alice Largent (1814-) married Hieronimus Hardy.

i. Samuel L. Largent died young (in 1817).

Children of John Largent II, "third set," were by wife believed to have been Christina Ross, who was born on Nov. 27, 1737 and died June 12, 1838. It is believed that she was from one of two branches of Ross families who settled in old Hampshire County (not descended from Quaker pioneer Alexander Ross of the Hopewell settlement). According to information received from Mr. Roger A. Stubbs of Long Lake, Minnesota, the grave and tombstone of Christina (Ross) Largent is located in Hill Cemetery near St. Paris, Champaign County, Ohio. Their children were:

(13) Randall Largent was born circa 1776 in Hampshire County, and died in Montgomery County, Indiana during the 1840s. He married Sarah Constant, daughter of John Constant, on Feb. 23, 1796, in Mason County, Kentucky. Sarah died in 1831 and Randall remarried to Priscilla Cox during his later years in Montgomery County, IN.

(14) Aaron Largent was born circa 1777. He was living in Hampshire County, Va. until about 1807, when he disappeared from the tax list. Verbal tradition says that he was accidentally shot in a hunting accident by his brother-in-law, Philip Porter, but this story has not been proven. One Aaron Largent was enumerated on the 1840 and 1850 censuses for Morgan County, Ohio.

(15) Abraham Largent was born circa 1778. He married and was the father of children.

(16) Phebe Largent was born June 6, 1781, in Hampshire County, and died April 4, 1866 in Champaign County, Ohio. She married John Fitzpatrick, who was born Jan. 1, 1768 in Delaware, and died July 23, 1852. They raised a family.

(17) Moses Largent, was born in Hampshire County, circa 1783, and died in Morgan County, Ohio in 1860. Moses married Nancy Saville, on Nov. 8, 1804, in Frederick County, Va. They had 15 children.[30]

---

30. Mrs. Joanne Eustice, 1534 Kelly, Redlands, CA 92374, is most knowledgeable about the genealogy of the Largent family. She is compiling Largent records for a publication, and welcomes queries or information. It has been my honor and privilege to assist her with the Hampshire and Frederick County records.

Andrew Emmart Graveyard

These inscriptions were copied from the Andrew Emmart (Emmert) family graveyard located on a hill, between Hanging Rocks and North River, in "Golden Acres," Hampshire County, W. Va. Graveyard has been vandalized during recent years, with tombstones down and broken. One grave has been dug open by curiosity seekers. The following inscriptions were "salvaged" from pieces of stones which were found on Aug. 26, 1986. Dates should be cross-referenced with other sources, where possible.

Emmart, Andrew, born on June 28, 1795 and died on Feb. 16, 1855, aged 59 years, 8 months, 18 days.[31] Buried next to him was his wife, Elizabeth (Pepper) Emmart, daughter of John and Catherine Pepper. Elizabeth died on April 28, 1882, aged 80 years. It is believed that most of the following persons were children of Andrew and Elizabeth Emmart.

Emmart, Catherine, died in 1867, aged 49 years.

Emmart, Eliza, died July 18, 1879, aged 34 (or 54?) years, per tombstone inscription. The Aug. 1, 1879 issue of the *South Branch Intelligencer*, stated that a Mrs. Eliza Emmart died on July 18, 1879, aged 50 years, in Hampshire County. Could this be the same person? Further, a courthouse death record states that Eliza Emmart, unmarried daughter of Andrew and Elizabeth Emmart, died on July 20, 1879, aged 53 years.

Emmart, Elizabeth J., died Sept. 1856, 22 years.

Emmart, George W., died Oct. 4, 1882, aged 67 years. Next to him was his sister, Hannah Emmart, died July 15, 1884, aged about 58 years. [Note: Their deaths were reported to courthouse in Romney, but were "sloppily written"- too inaccurate to report here.]

Emmart, Isaac, died Jan. 1862, aged 24 years.

Emmert, Jacob H., born in 1840, died in 1910. His wife, Elusia V. Heare, daughter of Matthew Heare, was born in 1843 and died in 1923.

---

31. Death date was confirmed by a letter written on March 3, 1855 to a nephew of Andrew Emmart. The letter stated that Jesse Lupton was buried on the same day.

The Jonathan Hiett Graveyard

This graveyard was called "the Jerry Hiett cemetery" in Maud Pugh's book on Capon Valley pioneers, but no tombstone data were published. Located on a high ridge on the west side of North River between Pleasant Dale and North River Mills, this well-planned cemetery cannot be located without the help of a local guide. Access is via a steep mountain path. On my first visit to this site, my guide became exhausted while climbing the steep terrain from the graveyard back to my automobile. Not willing to leave the scene to seek assistance, I pushed the elderly guide up the mountain path (an abandoned 19th century wagon roadbed) to safety. We later joked about the experience.

A metal fence surrounds the graveyard. My guide stated that the fence came from the courthouse grounds in Romney, when the courthouse was rebuilt during the 1920s. All visible tombstone inscriptions are included below:

Hiett, Jonathan, son of Evan and Sarah (Smith) Hiett, was born on Feb. 13, 1781, and died on Dec. 5, 1861, aged 80 years, 9 months, 22 days. His wife, Hannah Harrison, was born in 1789 and died on Oct. 14, 1866.

Hiett, Jane, daughter of Jonathan and Hannah (Harrison) Hiett, born on Dec. 10, 1813 and died on Nov. 5, 1853. She married Wesley Park and, according to Maud Pugh, in *Capon Valley...*, Park died out west and Jane returned to Hampshire County, where she died and was buried in the Jonathan Hiett graveyard on North River, Hampshire County, Va.

Hiett, Jonathan, Jr., was born on Sept. 10, 1822 and died on March 7, 1907, of "old age," according to courthouse death record. He was born in Hampshire County. Dr. E. B. Martin reported his death to the Hampshire County Clerk. (Note: These dates should be checked against other sources.) Maud Pugh, in her *Capon Valley...*, stated that his parents were Jonathan and Hannah (Harrison) Hiett, and that Jonathan, Jr. died on March 7, 1902. Jonathan's tombstone appears to give 1907 as the death year. His wife, Mary M. Arnold of Burlington, W.Va., was born on Dec. 2, 1837 and died in 1921.

Hiett, Sarah, daughter of Jonathan and Hannah (Harrison) Hiett, died on March 4, 1900, aged 83 years and 17 days, "Gone but not forgotten."

Hiett, Margaret, daughter of Jonathan and Hannah (Harrison) Hiett, died on July 27, 1887, aged 74 years, 4 months, 14 days.

Hiett infant, was born and died on Aug. 1, 1831.

Hiett, Jeremiah, son of Jonathan and Hannah (Harrison) Hiett, was born on Nov. 8, 1829 and died on Oct. 9, 1893. His wife, Emily S. Burkett, was born on Sept. 18, 1830 and died on Feb. 21, 1896. The graveyard where they were buried was called "the Jerry Hiett graveyard," by Maud Pugh, local historian.

Hiett, Evan, son of Jonathan and Hannah (Harrison) Hiett, was born on March 5, 1808 and died May 9, 1887. His wife, Barbara Wise, was born on Aug. 15, 1806 and died July 6, 1858. These inscriptions were carved onto the same monument: Hannah J. Hiett, was born on April 12, 1850 and died in Nov. 1861; William Wise Hiett was born on March 15, 1845 and died on Dec. 25, 1861; Elizabeth Hiett was born on May 28, 1838 and died on Jan. 27, 1862 and; Jonathan Hiett was born on June 8, 1838 and died on Sept. 16, 1840. [Note: Miss Maud Pugh did not mention Jonathan, who should have been listed on page 107 in Volume II of *Capon Valley*.]

Delaplane, Eli, was born on Oct. 1, 1792 and died on Nov. 3, 1878, in Hampshire County, W.Va., aged 86 years, 1 month and 2 days. His funeral text was from Isaiah, chapter 10 or 40. According to a military pension record in the National Archives (War of 1812), Eli married: (1) Elizabeth Kurtz and (2) Emily Smith, daughter of Jacob and Rachel (Rhinehart) Smith, on Oct. 27, 1846. She was born on June 15, 1818 and died at Slanesville, W.Va., on Sept. 27, 1905.

Smith, Wesley, son of Jacob and Rachel (Rhinehart) Smith, was born on Oct. 24, 1829 and died on Sept. 8, 1904, aged 74 years, 10 months, 14 days. Mary Moreland, daughter of Basil Moreland, died on Feb. 3, 1899, aged 70 years, 10 months, 17 days. [Note: I believe this Basil Moreland is the one who owned what later became the Frederick Kump place, now owned by the Gilson family. This Basil allegedly fell off a cliff into North River near the mill, about 1846. He left a number of small Moreland surviving children, according to the 1850 census.]

Smith, James W., son of Wesley and Mary (Moreland) Smith, died on April 9, 1891. Miss Maud Pugh stated that he was a young person when he died.

Pugh, Bethuel, was born circa 1740 and died in 1822. His stone is not inscribed. Aaron Malick stated that he dug this grave in 1822, as told to Asa Hiett, according to Miss Maud Pugh. Bethuel married a Miss Tansy, and they were buried together. Miss Pugh believed that Bethuel Pugh was a son of John Pugh I, but proof was not supplied. [Note: I have often wondered whether the name Bethuel was from an old Quaker surname that was more commonly spelled Bethel. One George Bethel died in Park's Valley in 1812, and was buried there in the Quaker graveyard, grave unmarked.]

Roomsburg, Matilda, wife of George W. Roomsburg, 1853-1884, "Gone but not forgotten."

Stewart, John, was born on Jan. 1, 1812, and departed this life A.D. 1862. Probably his wife, Lucinda Wolford, was buried adjacently, marked by an uninscribed fieldstone.

McCool Graveyard

The McCool graveyard is located on Critton Hollow Road, about half way between West Virginia State Route 45 and Great Cacapon River. The graveyard is behind the Eubules Methodist church, which has not been organized for many years. Unlike many of the graveyards reported in this volume, data for this one is being reported as a separate unit, rather than alphabetizing the names and integrating into the text. Maud Pugh's book on Capon Valley pioneers and descendants was consulted.

McCool, James D., son of John and Cassandra (Dent) McCool, was born in 1823 and died in 1903. His wife was Emeline C. Baker, daughter of Joseph S. and Mary Baker. According to her tombstone inscription, she was born in 1834 and died in 1890. James D. McCool served as President of the Board of Education, in the Office of Justice of the Peace, and served as road overseer for thirty years.

McCool, John S., son of James D. and Emeline (Baker) McCool, was born in 1852 and no inscription for his death year was made on his tombstone. His wife, Louisa M. Hardy, daughter of Israel and Elizabeth Hardy, was born in 1850 and died in 1919.

McCool, Thomas W., son of James D. and Emeline G. (Baker) McCool, was born in 1861 and died in 1937. On same tombstone was Mary C. McCool Harley, born in 1856.

McCool, Edgar, son of James D. and Emeline G. McCool, born and died in 1876. Buried next to Edgar was his sister, Florence McCool, born and died in 1870.

Effland, Emmer E., wife of G.I. Effland, and daughter of John S. McCool, was born on March 24, 1885 and died on April 13, 1920. Reva F. Effland, daughter of G.I. and E. Effland, was born on Jan. 14, 1920 and died on Oct. 15, 1920.

Miller, Willie H., died on Jan. 23, 1899, aged one year, 1 month and 17 days. (Note: This inscription was badly eroded.)

Omps Graveyard at Bear Garden

This family graveyard is located on the eastern side of Bear Garden Mountain in Frederick County, Va. The graveyard was enclosed within a cinder-block fence on Aug. 24, 1941. Located on the former farm of German immigrant, Benedictus Omps, it is maintained by descendants. The graveyard is located near the Morgan County, W.Va. line. The Omps farm is still in possession of a descendant, Mrs. Ora Ethel (Omps) Hottle, a great-grandaughter of the immigrant.

Omps, Benedict, born in Germany in 1800 and died in Frederick County, Va., in 1863. Margaret C. (Hovermale) Omps, his wife, was born in 1802 and died in July 1859.

Omps, Clarence E., 1899-1948, and wife Dealie D., 1890-1959.

Omps, George A.J., 1833-1849.

Omps, Harry K., 1907-1908.

Omps, Harry K., son of R.L. and P.C. Omps, died on April 9, 1908, aged 4 months, 8 days.

Omps, James, "infant son of Clarence and Dealie Omps," 1921.

Omps, infant of R.L. and P.C. Omps, 1899. (Note: This infant is not mentioned in the Bible record of Richard L. Omps.)

Omps, James M., was born on Oct. 4, 1841 and died on Jan. 16, 1906. Nearby was: Margaret C. Omps, born on Aug. 25, 1889 (or is it 1839?) and died on March 7, 1906. "Loved in life in death remembered."

Omps, James V., son of Richard L. and Phena C. Omps, was born on March 5, 1906 and died on Feb. 27, 1934. "Gone but not forgotten."

Omps, Joshua G., born on July 27, 1837 and died on July 3, 1910. "God's finger touched him and he slept."

Omps, Lena Fristo, "daughter" born on July 18, 1895 and died on Aug. 1, 1982. This was the last burial in the graveyard.

Omps, Thomas, 1829-1844.

Omps, Richard Lafayette, born in 1864 and died in 1943. His wife, Phena Catherine Dick, was born in 1868 and died in 1955.

Stotler, I.D., born in 1836 and died in 1909.

Stotler, Mary J., born in 1843, died in 1901.

Hottle, infant son of Kiley and Ora (Omps) Hottle, 1919.

There are five unmarked graves in the cemetery.

Henry Pepper Graveyard

This graveyard is located on the east side of North River, on "the Roy Frye farm," now owned by Chalmers R. Souder. It is in fair condition, considering wear and tear due to grazing cattle. A graveyard containing slatestones of Jonathan and Margaret (Wood) Pugh and other first settlers was recently destroyed by farming operations in an adjacent field.

Legible inscriptions in the Pepper graveyard are as follows:

Carter, George W., died March 7, 1914, aged 73 years, 22 days. "May he rest in peace."

Carter, James F., died on Aug. 21, 1910, aged 82 years, 9 months, 20 days.

Carter, Sophia, wife of Robert Carter, was born on June 9, 1809 and died on June 12, 1848. She was a daughter of John and Catherine (Emmart) Pepper. Susan Carter, daughter of Robert and Sophia (Pepper) Carter, was born on Sept. 8, 1848 and died on May 12, 1862.

McCauley, Rachel A.V. daughter of J. and M. McCauley, was born on Dec. 14, 1865 and died on May 17, 1880.

Pepper, Henry, son of John and Catherine (Emmart) Pepper, died on April 23, 1865, aged 70 years, 7 months, 23 days. According to Maud Pugh, Henry's wife was Rachel Tate, born in 1808 and died in 1876.

Pepper, Caleb, died on April 25, 1863, aged 22 years, 2 months, 5 days.

Pepper, Rosa L., wife of Henry D. Pepper, was born on April 14, 1879 and died on March 20, 1897, aged 17 years, 11 months, 6 days.

Pepper, Mary E., daughter of Henry and Rachel Pepper, was born on Oct. 9, 1846 and died Oct. 15, 1851, aged 5 years, 6 days.

Pepper, Rachel J., daughter of Henry and Rachel Pepper, was born on Dec. 3, 1844 and died on Aug. 4, 1882

Pepper, Thomas D., son of Henry and Rachel Pepper, died on April 13, 1863, aged 20 years, 4 months, 3 days.

Pepper, William H., was born on June 25, 1839 and died on March 19, 1920. Sarah E. Dye, daughter of George and Rachel (Offutt) Dye, his wife was born in 1844 and died in 1881. Edna Pepper, their daughter, 1867-1881.

Pepper, Samuel was born on July 3, 1847 and died on Sept. 30, 1850.

Pepper, John T., was born on Oct. 1, 1848 and died on Oct. 7, 1851.

Smith, Jefferson, son of Jacob and Rachel (Rhinehart) Smith, was born on Aug. 13, 1819 and died on July 11, 1870, A.D. His wife, Hannah Pepper, departed this life in May 1852, aged about 40 years. Note: Jefferson Smith's second wife was Susannah Arnold.

Capt. Jonathan Pugh Graveyard

Located on a farm formerly owned by pioneer Jonathan Pugh, this very old family graveyard is in reasonably good condition because it stayed in the family. It is now owned by Mrs. Marie (Pugh) Brill.

During her later years, Miss Maud Pugh moved back into the Jonathan Pugh ancestral log house which was probably built during the late 18th century. The log house is still standing on the west side of North River, but very persons are aware of this structure. Entrance to the Pugh estate is via Hickory Corner Road. The graveyard is on an elevated section of a ridge, located several hundred yards south of the house.

Pugh, Capt. Jonathan, son of Jonathan and Margaret (Wood) Pugh, was born on Aug. 26, 1757, and died on Aug. 21, 1834. The inscriptions on natural stone are still readable. Buried next to him was wife Mary Ellen Tansy. Her uninscribed headstone and footstone survives. On the opposite side of Capt. Jonathan Pugh was buried his son Daniel Pugh. Only a natural stone in his honor survives.

Pugh, Jonathan, was born in 1835 and died in 1914.

Maria (Pugh) Smith, wife of William Smith, was born in 1802 and died in 1875. Maria was a daughter of Jonathan and Mary E. (Tansy) Pugh.

Yost, Elizabeth (Pugh), wife of Peter Youst (Yost), was born on April 16, 1837, and died on Oct. 7, 1925. John W. Youst was born on March 19, 1876, and died on Dec. 3, 1909. His twin-sister, Lucy M. Youst, was born on March 19, 1876, and died on April 11, 1892.

Monroe, Lucy, daughter of Capt. Jonathan and Mary Ellen (Tansy) Pugh, was born in 1803 and died in 1880.

Monroe, Euphema (Pugh), was born in 1828 and died in 1913. Her husband was Alexander Monroe.

History of Little Cacapon
Primitive Baptist Church

Little Cacapon Primitive Baptist Church, in Hampshire County, was formed by residents in the Levels community, about 1810.   Worship services were conducted by lay persons in private homes for about five years before land was secured from Peter Stump and a building was erected.

The church at Little Cacapon was influenced by the Rev. Dr. John Monroe, pioneer Baptist preacher in Hampshire County, who settled along lower North River of the Cacapon, in 1796. He was a medical doctor who placed a high priority and calling was to preach the Gospel and build the church. Dr. Monroe was associated with the Ketocton Association of Baptists. That particular association of the Baptist church was founded in 1766, in Loudoun County, Va.[32] The Little Cacapon church was formally connected to this association in 1814, when it met at Broad Run Meeting in Fauquier County, Va. Baptist doctrine was based on Calvinistic theology, sometimes referred to as TULIP: **T**otal depravity, **U**nlimited grace, **L**imited atonement, **I**rresistable grace, and **P**erserverance of the saints.

Many early members of Little Cacapon Baptist Church were former residents of Loudoun and Fauquier Counties.

In August 1828, Little Cacapon Baptist Church joined the Patterson's Creek Association, apparently an organization of churches that formed west of Great North Mountain.

The first written, official, record of the Little Cacapon Primitive Baptist Church described a worship service and a business meeting that followed, on Saturday, October 2, 1813.[33] Worship services were held once a month, on

---

32. Robert Baylor Semple, *History of the Baptists in Virginia*, 1810. Reprint. Church History Research and Archives, Lafayette, Tennessee, 1976.

33. *Church Record Book I*, Little Cacapon Baptist Church, in possession of Mrs. Joan Shambaugh, clerk. This fragile volume will be placed in an archives. All vital records were extracted and printed on these pages, so that casual public inspection and further deterioration of the book will not be necessary.

Saturdays, preceeding the first Lord's Day (Sunday) of each month. Abraham Pennington was the first Clerk. The Rev. John Arnold served as the first pastor, from 1813 until 1855.

A statement of the local church creed was handwritten on page one of *Church Record Book I*. It is reproduced, unedited, as follows:

> Forasmuch as almighty god by his grace has been pleased to call us whose names are underneath subscribed out of darkness into his marvelous light and all of us have been baptised on profession of our faith in Christ Jesus we do profess to believe the docturn of the trinity three persons in one god the father son and holy Spirit and these three are one the same in Spirit equal in power and glory we also believe in particular election and effectual calling and the final perserverance of the Saints in grace we also believe that the Scriptural mod of Baptism is immersion only and the only proper Subject to be one that has been Regenerated or born again and having agreed to give our selves to the lord and to one annother in A gospel Church way which branch Shall be known and distinguished by the name of little cacapon church to be governed and guided by A proper discipline agreeable to the word of god we do therefore by his assistance agree to keep up the discipline of the church we are members of in the most brotherly affection towards each other while we endeavor punctually to observe the following rules Viz. 1st in brotherly love to pray for each other to watch over one annother and if needs be in the most tender and affectionate manner to reprove one annother that is if we see anything amiss in our brother to go and tell him his faults according to the direction given by our lord in the 18th of St Mathews gospel and not to be whispering and backbiting we also agree with gods assistance to pray in our family attend our church meetings observe the lords day and keep it holy and not absent our selves from the communion of the lord supper without lawfull excuse to be ready to contribute to the defraying of the church expenses and for the support of the Ministry not irregularly to depart from the fellowship of the church nor remove to distant churches without A regular dismysion Signed by the mutual consent of the members whose names are underneath Subscribed.

These names were written below the creed (no dates): Abraham Penington, Jacob Penington, Catharine Penington (Pennington), John Johnson, Lety Critton, Ann Colvin, Ann

Chinwith, Sarah Perry, Isaac Pownell, Margret Doman, Marthy Pownell, Nathaniel Huddleston, Iby Huddleston, Mathias Ginevan, Catharin Ginevan, James Higins, David Tracy, Jonathan Pownell, Mary Pownell, Thomas Pownell, Elizabeth Pownell, Catharine Smoot, Samuel Sutton, Margret Sutton, Ann Hagerty,   Susy Bacon of Culler,

Salvenis Warfield, Jemima McDonald, Joseph Stump, Elizabeth Stump, Isaac Pownell, Jr., John J. Pownell, John Reignor, Elizabeth Newman, George Saunders, Jacob Huff, Catharine Huff, Isarel Hardy, Elizabeth Hardy, Richard Vanasdal (Vanarsdal), Rhody Vanasdal, William Alderton, Mary Alderton, Isaac Hutchinson, Margaret Hutchinson, William Henderson, Catharine Henderson,

Robert Monroe, Mary Johnson, James Moreland, Catherine (Stump) Shinholtzer, Margaret Stump, Sarah Moore, Catherine Easter, Luther Ginevan, Margery Moreland, Jacob Stump, Rody A. Stump, Sarah Ulary, Sarah Stump, Benjamin Williamson,

Martha Williamson, Malinda Pownell, Elenor Vanasdal, Elizabeth Alderton, Mary Alderton, Catharine J. Hiett, Catherine Ginevan, Elder John A. Carder, Thomas Alderton, Ann Alderton, Elizabeth Ginevan, and Aaron Simmons. Additional names are given with a date notation of 1878 and later.

The first pastor of the church was the Rev. Dr. John Arnold, whose tenure was from 1813 to 1850.   Arnold was a pioneer Baptist preacher in Hampshire County, possibly descended from Richard Arnold who died in 1757, near what is known as Kale's Ford.

John Arnold resided on a mountain west of the Little Cacapon River, along the Great Wagon Road from Winchester to Romney. The Arnold house is now owned by Paul Roomsburg, who is a school teacher, horiculturalist, and well-known bluegrass and mountain musician of Augusta, W.Va.

The Arnold family graveyard is located near the old house. A tombstone inscription shows that John Arnold was born Aug. 10, 1777, and died Oct. 14, 1850. Rosanna Shaffer, his wife, was buried at his side, no inscriptions.

The second pastor at Little Cacapon Baptist was the Rev. Jesse Monroe, son of the Rev. Dr. John and Eleanor (Asberry) Monroe. He assumed that pastorate in 1850, and continued until 1856. Jesse, who also farmed and practiced law, was born Jan. 9, 1785, and died May 11, 1857. Jesse and wife, Eleanor Blue, were buried in the cemetery at Three Churches, located on Branch Mountain, in Hampshire County.

The third pastor of the Little Cacapon Church was the Rev. George Loy, from 1856 through 1860, followed by Benjamin Cornwell, who served from 1860 through May 1871. Then came Elder John A. Carder, who served from 1871 until his death on March 2, 1883. Elder P. McInturff was the pastor from 1883 to 1885, followed by Elder B.W. Power, who was ordained in 1886 and served until his death in 1927.

Abraham Pennington was the first clerk at Little Cacapon. He attended faithfully and kept the church records through August 5, 1826. Pennington received a letter of transfer, the place not specified. After Pennington's departure, no minutes were recorded for one year, until James Higgins replaced him as clerk, in September 1827.

Jacob Pennington was an early supporter of the church, who opened his home for religious services. He was appointed to prepare the communion elements for the first Sunday in November (7th) 1813. He related his experience on Saturday, April 30, 1814 and was scheduled to be baptized on the following Lord's day.

Catherine Pennington was a charter member. A letter of transfer was given to Catherine when she moved (probably in late 1820s), but no date or place was recorded.

Marthy Pownell related her experience and was to be baptised on the following day, Sunday, Nov. 7, 1813.

Nancy Chenoweth transfered her membership to Little Cacapon, by letter dated Sept. 11, 1813.[34] A "letter of dismission" was given to sister Nancy Chenoweth, on Saturday, March 5,

---

34. It is believed that this Nancy was married to Elias Chenoweth, son of John Chenoweth (1735-1835), of Hampshire County, Va. Elias was born on Oct. 10, 1781 and Nancy (nee Carleton) was born July 2, 1784, both in Hampshire County. They moved to Ohio and raised eight children.

1814. Such letters were given to persons in good standing, who moved to another location.

Joseph Stump related his experience on Saturday, Dec. 4, 1813 and was baptized on the following Lord's day. A church record stated that Stump died on June 30, 1856. His wife, Elizabeth Boggess died on Nov. 25, 1849. See pages 352-354 for a more detailed account of the Stump family.

Abraham Pennington, Jonathan Pownal, John Johnson and Joseph Stump were to confer with old Mr. (Peter) Stump, New Years's day, 1814, regarding a piece of ground to build a meeting house.

Elizabeth (Boggess) Stump, baptized at last meeting, was received into membership on Feb. 5, 1814. Elizabeth Pownall was baptized and received into the church on same day as Mrs. Stump. It was reported that Peter Stump was willing to donate a lot for building a Baptist meeting house.

Money ($3.00) was raised for Elder John Monroe "...for attending to assist in constructing the church on the Levels and put into the hands of Elder John Arnold to (deliver to) said Monroe," March 5, 1814.

John Johnson was elected moderator and the church decided, on Saturday June 4, 1814, that he should be a deacon.

"The church constituted on the Levels is removed to the new meeting house and is now known by the name Little Capon Church," dated Saturday, July 2, 1814. Same date, Elder John Arnold wrote a corresponding letter to the Ketocton Baptist Association to be held at Broad Run Meeting House in Fauquier County, Va. Elder John Arnold and Jacob Pennington were elected trustees for the Little Capon church and were instructed to convey the meeting house lot from old Mr. Stump to the trustees. Brother John Johnson was to be ordained to the office of deacon on Lord's day, July 3, 1814, but the ordination was postponed because Elder Jesse Monroe failed to appear at the service.

Brother Richard Anderson was dismissed from the Union Church to join the Little Capon Church. He received the right hand of fellowship on Saturday, October 1, 1814. Brother Joseph Stump was appointed to serve as superintendent for completing the new meeting house, as soon as money is furnished. On same day, "old sister Mary Critton being about to remove, a letter of Dismission is granted to her."

Brother John Johnson was ordained a Deacon on Saturday, Nov. 5, 1814.

A day of fasting and prayer was held in the home of Joseph Stump, on Saturday, Dec. 31, 1814. ("Saturday before first Lord's day in January 1815").

On Saturday before the first Lord's day in Feb. 1814, the church appointed Jacob Pennington to visit Richard Anderson to find out why he was absent from church services. Charges of drinking alcohol and "unfavorable reports respecting the moral character of Mr. Anderson, plus continued non-attendance of worship services, resulted in excommunication from fellowship, on Saturday, May 1, 1815.

Joseph Stump was ordained deacon, by the Rev. John Arnold on Saturday, June 6, 1815.

Saturday, July 1, 1815, Elder John Arnold was appointed to be a messenger from Little Capon Church to Happy Creek Church, at Front Royal, Va. to commence on Thursday, Aug. 13, 1815. Other business included a collection taken to raise money to furnish the meeting house, with contributions as follows: Joseph Stump and Abraham Pennington, $1.00 each; Jacob Pennington and Jonathan Pownall $.75 each; John Pownall and Martha Pownall, $.50 each; and Sarah Perry, $25.

Saturday, Aug. 5, 1815, the church met in the meeting house to discuss subscriptions to raise money. At the September meeting, Joseph Stump was elected treasurer, to account for all monies received and to make a quarterly report to the church on money received and money expended. Elder John Arnold, the church pastor, was appointed the Trustee to whom the deed of conveyance should be made.

Saturday, Sept. 30, 1815, sister Mary Calvin was received by letter from Union Church. Brother Jonathan Pownall was asked to confer with John Higgins regarding the deed for the meeting house lot and to secure a plat.

Saturday, Nov. 4, 1815, the church chose Brother Joseph Stump to be moderator for the day. An offering of $1.07 was received.

Saturday, Dec. 2, 1815, the church met at Jacob Pennington's, with singing and prayer, but no business to conduct.

Saturday, Feb. 3, 1816, the church met at Jacob Pennington's house. Deed will be brought to next meeting for examination. Communion Sunday will follow on Lord's day.

Saturday, March 2, 1816, the church met at Jacob Pennington's house. After singing and prayer, a deed was presented for examination by congregation and approved.

Serious business was conducted on Saturday, June 1, 1816. "Whereas Sarah Perry has removed to another part without complying with our Discipline, we therefore excommunicate her from the communion of this church."

Saturday July 6, 1816, Brother Joseph Stump and Elder John Arnold were appointed as messengers to the Ketocton Baptist Association. Brother Arnold was instructed to prepare the letter. Abraham and Jacob Pennington and Jonathan Pownall each contributed $1.00 and Martha and Elizabeth Pownall contributed $.50 each, for a total of $4.00.

Saturday, Aug. 31, 1816, Brother Stump was instructed to employ a workman to complete the inside of the meeting house.

Saturday, Nov. 2, 1816, Sarah Perry requested a letter of dismission. The church ordered that she be answered by letter.

Nov. 30, 1816, an announcement was made that the (Branch) Mountain meeting house will hold a service on every 3rd Saturday of each month "for purposes of hearing experiences and other matters that may concern this body."

On Saturday before the 3rd Lord's day in December 1816, the church met on the mountain at the house of Nathan Huddleston. Martha Shingleton related her experience and was scheduled to be baptized on Saturday before the first Lord's day in Feb. 1817. George Saunders was received into membership, by authority of letter from the Pleasant Valley Church.

Saturday, May 3, 1817, the church met at the meeting house. "The church is to take into consideration Cate Errate's (Herrity?) application for a letter of recommendation to Sideling Hill Church."

Saturday, May 17, 1817, Cate Errate's request for transfer to Sideling Hill Church was approved. Martha Shingleton was received into the church by giving her the right hand of fellowship.

Saturday, July 5, 1817, "The missionary business laid over at our last meeting we think it not expedient to consider at this time." Catherine Smoot came forward to relate her experience and was received into membership. John Pownall related his experience and was received. He is to be baptized on the Lord's Day. Brother Jonathan Pownall and Abraham Pennington were chosen as messengers to the Ketocton Baptist Association. Contributions were as follows: Mathias Ginevan, $1.00; John Pownall and Cate Errate, $.50 each; Martha and Eleanor Pownall, $.25 each; and George Sanders, $.18. It was ordered that Brother Pennington get a church book, and the church agreed to pay the same.

Saturday, August 2, 1817, Mathias Ginevan was received into the church by giving a right hand of fellowship. Also, Mrs. Catherine Ginevan gave her experience at the mountain and was received and baptized on August 3, 1817. Also Thomas and Isaac Pownall were baptised on the same day and the four were received into membership on 1st Lord's Day.

Saturday, Sept. 6, 1817, the church negotiated with John Fouke, a hired workman, to finish the church, at following prices: $12.00 for the pulpit; $15.00 for the windows; $4.00 for the stairs; $2.50 for the shutters; and floor per square, at $1.00.

Saturday, Jan. 31, 1818 the church met at Jacob Pennington's house. Margaret Doman was received in to membership and given the right hand of fellowship.

Saturday, Feb. 28, 1818, the church met at Jonathan Pownall's house. As always, there was singing and prayer. No business was conducted after the service.

Saturday, July 4, 1818, Brother Sylvester Warfield was appointed to write a letter and bring or send it to the Baptist association. In the future, Little Cacapon Church services shall commence at 12:00 on Saturday (before the first Lord's day of each month.

Saturday, August 1, 1818, Brother John Arnold was appointed to be messenger to the association. The following contributions were made: Mathias Ginevan $1.00; Joseph Stump and Abraham Pennington, $.75 each; Jonathan Pownall, $.56; Isaac Pownall, John Pownall, Thomas Pownall, $.20 each; Margaret Doman, Martha Pownall, Catherine Ginevan, Nancy Calvin and Sylvester

Warfield, $.25 each. The church decided to discontinue church meetings "at the mountain" for the time being.

Saturday, Oct. 3, 1818, Brother John Arnold was appointed to procure a stove for the church, and Mathias Ginevan will furnish the sheet iron for the stove pipe.

Saturday, March 6, 1819, Brother John Pownall is appointed to visit Brother Sanders to inform him that the church is uneasy about him, and to request that he attend the next meeting. In the following meeting, held Saturday, April 3, 1819, Brother Sanders attended and gave a satisfactory answer regarding his absence.

Saturday, July 3, 1819, Brother Arnold is to write a letter to the association and Brother Ginevan and Brother Stump are to "bear" the letter to the association.   The collection was itemized, by amount given: Abraham Pennington, $.75; Jonathan, John and Thomas Pownall, $.50 each; and Margaret Doman, $.18 and three-fourths cent.   The church agreed to dismiss Martha Shingleton to the Union Church.

Saturday, July 31, 1819, "The Covenant is to be read to the church every Saturday before communion." The annual letter for the association was prepared and read by Brother Arnold and approved by the church.

Saturday, Sept. 4, 1819, Nathan Huddleson and wife related their experience and were received. Both were baptized on next Lord's day and were given the right hand of fellowship, Saturday, Oct. 2, 1819.

Business was conducted after singing and prayer, on Saturday, March 4, 1820.   Regarding the excommunication of Sister Sarah Perry, a letter was received from the Eden Church in Sandy Creek Settlement in Preston County, Va., which satified the Little Capon Church. She was restored to her former standing and a letter of dismission to the Eden Church was approved.

Saturday, August 5, 1820, Jacob Pennington and George Sanders were appointed as messengers to the association, with Elder John Arnold to be an as an alternate. Contributions were collected as follows: Joseph Stump and Mathias Ginevan $.50 each; Jonathan Pownall, Sylvester Warfield, and Nathan Huddleston, $.25 each; and Thomas Pownall, $.12 and one-half cent; and Margaret Doman, $0.5. Brother Warfield was appointed to write the annual letter to the association.

Saturday, June 30, 1821, Brother George Sanders was appointed as a messenger to the association. Brother Arnold was appointed to write the letter and bring it to the next meeting.

Saturday, April 6, 1822, Abraham Pennington and Joseph Stump were appointed to attend the Union Meeting on April 26-28, 1822, for purpose of joining in a union meeting.

Saturday, Aug. 3, 1822, the constitution of the association was examined and approved by the church. Brother Joseph Stump was selected as messenger to the association. John Pownall applied for dismission in order to join the Union Church, due to convenience.

Saturday, March 1, 1823: "Business respecting Sister Calvin the church deferred the matter until next meeting." Brother Jacob Pennington was appointed to visit Brother Sanders and request him to attend the next meeting. Unfavorable reports have been received about him.

Saturday, May 3, 1823, Brother Sanders attended church and gave a satisfactory answer for his absence.

Saturday, August 2, 1823: Brethren Sanders and Ginevan were appointed as messengers to the association. A matter regarding Sister Colvin was deferred. "The business respecting the General Association but not having received the minutes, we are not able to give an answer." "The business respecting the plan of the Association meeting on Wednesday instead of Thursday is approved."

Saturday, October 4, 1823: The case of sister Calvin was deferred.

Saturday, Jan. 31, 1824: "The case of sister Calvin going away in a disorderly manner and the same being considered by the church, is excluded from the privileges until she shall come under satisfaction."

Saturday, July 31, 1824, Brother Jacob Pennington's letter to the association was read and approved by the church. Joseph Stump and Jacob Pennington were appointed messengers to the association.

Saturday, August 6, 1825: Brother John Arnold was appointed to write and "bear" the annual letter to the association. Brother and sister Huddleston applied for dismission to the Union Church, to be handled by the clerk.

Saturday, June 3, 1826, David Tracy and Elizabeth Newman came forward and gave their experiences. They are to be baptized "tomorrow."

Saturday, August 5, 1826: The clerk reported that David Tracy and Elizabeth Newman were baptized. Brother Tracy is appointed messenger to the association and "Brother Arnold (will write) the letter to the Association."[35]

Saturday, Sept. 1, 1827: The church advised Joseph Stump, Jonathan Pownall, and James Higgins to attend as delegates at the Union meeting house on Friday, October 5, 1827, for the purpose of forming and establishing a constitution for an association west of the North Mountain. A copy of the order is to be certified by the church and sent by delegates.

Saturday Nov. 3, 1827: Brother Sanders was given approval for a letter of dismission. "He is about to remove (emigrate)."

Saturday, Aug. 2, 1828: Joseph Stump, David Tracy and Brother Pownall were selected as messengers to attend the Pattersons Creek Association.

Saturday, May 1, 1830: "A letter having been received and read from the Union Church gallery on this church to send delegates to the Union Church on Tuesday next (May 4, 1830) for the purpose of settling a matter of grievance or dealing among the preachers belonging to Patterson's Creek Association. We have therefore appointed Brethren Joseph Stump and James Higgins to assist you in your deliberations."

Saturday, July 31, 1830: Brother James Higgins was appointed to write a letter to the association, to be held at the Timber Ridge Church in Frederick County, Va. Thomas Pownall, Joseph Stump and James Higgins were to attend as messengers.

Saturday, Sept. 4, 1830: Jonathan Pownall was appointed as messenger to the association, replacing Thomas Pownall. Thomas Pownall and wife have asked for a letter of dismission, as they are moving west.

---

35. This was the last entry made by Abraham Pennington, first Clerk. No minutes were recorded until a year later, when James Higgins became the next Clerk.

Saturday Sept. 4, 1831:   Jonathan Pownall, Isaac Pownall, Joseph Stump, and James Higgins were appointed as messengers to the next association to be held at Union. The letter was to be prepared by the clerk and forwarded to the association.

Saturday, Sept. 1, 1832:   Letitia Critton and Anna Haggerty related their experience and were received by the church. "Susan Parker, a coloured woman having given in her expression first Sabbath in August be also admitted to baptism."

Saturday, August 3, 1833:   The church ordered that Joseph Stump, Isaac Pownall, and James Higgins attend as messengers to the association.

Saturday, Aug. 31, 1833:   James Haggerty applied to become a member of the church. He was baptized by Elder Herbert Cool (previously), and was unanamously received by the church. Brother Higgins is to write the letter to the association. Brother Arnold moved that a letter of dismission be given to Jemima McDonald, a member of this church.

Saturday, March 1, 1834, it was ordered that communion be held in May, August, November and February of each year. The clerk was ordered to draw a subscription to raise money for Elder John Arnold, for his services as a preacher.

Saturday, July 5, 1834:   Samuel Sutton and Margaret his wife related their experience and were unanamously received by the church.[36] This was the last entry made by Clerk James Higgins.

Saturday, August 2, 1834:   James Higgins, James Haggerty and Samuel Sutton were appointed messengers to the association, to be held at Georges Creek, Allegany County, Maryland, commencing on Friday, Sept. 12, 1834.[37]

Saturday, June 5, 1841:   Brother Henry Foreman presented a letter of dismission from the Lower North River Church and was received into the Cacapon church by the right hand of fellowship.

Saturday, July 31, 1841:   Ordered that Brethren Pownall, Moreland,   Henderson,   Monroe and Foreman serve as

36. Samuel Sutton married Margaret Critton in 1824, according to Ms. Marilyn Robinson, 325 South Batavia Ave., Batavia, IL 60510.

37. This entry was signed by John Arnold M.D. A seven year gap (blank pages reserved, but not recorded) occurred from 1834-1841, after which Robert Monroe became the new clerk.

messengers to the next association meeting. Robert Monroe was instructed to write the corresponding letter, and to raise $1.50 to be used by the association. Communion will be served at the next meeting. Finally, the case of brother Theodorus Prather was continued until the next meeting.

Saturday, Sept. 4, 1841: Letter to the association was read and approved by the church. $1.10 was received for the church fund. Brother Prather's case was continued.

Saturday, Oct. 2, 1841: Sister Martha McDonald presented a letter of dismission from the Lower North River Church and was received by the Little Cacapon Church.

Saturday, Feb. 1842, the church raised $3.00 to pay for reprinting the Baptist Confession of Faith. The case of Brother T. Prather was continued. Communion was served on the first Lord's day in February.

Saturday, May 1842: Brethren Moreland and Monroe reported that they had not seen brother Prather. Brethren Henderson and Moreland were ordered to visit Prather and notify him to attend the next meeting so that he could answer charges against him.

Saturday, July 2, 1842: The case of brother Prather was continued until the next meeting. Brethren James Higgins, James Moreland, Isaac Pownall and Robert Monroe were appointed to serve as messengers at the next association. It was ordered that the church raise $1.50 for printing the minutes.

Saturday, August 6, 1842: After singing and prayer, John Remer related his experience and was received by the church. Baptism was scheduled for the next day. Theodorus Prather was excommunicated from the fellowship of the Little Cacapon Church.

Friday, Sept. 2, 1842 was devoted to preparing the grounds of the church for the association meeting.[38] James Higgins, James Moreland and Isaac Pownall were appointed to superintend the grounds.

---

38. It appears that the Pattersons Creek Baptist Association conducted its annual meeting at the Little Cacapon Church, in September 1842.

Saturday, Sept. 3, 1842, Brethren Moreland and Monroe were appointed as a committee to examine the stove. Two stove-pipe joints were defective.

Saturday, June 4, 1843: The church voted to establish a branch of the Little Cacapon Baptist Church on the Big Cacapon, at Enon, Morgan County.

Saturday, July 1, 1843: After singing and prayer it was ordered that $2.00 be raised to send to the association. James Moreland, John Remer and Robert Monroe were appointed to attend the association, as messengers. The offering amounted to $.30.

Saturday, April 6, 1844, Brother Jacob Huff and sister Catherine Huff presented letters of dismission from the Timber Ridge Baptist Church and their membership will be in the Enon branch, on the Big Cacapon. The church record shows that Jacob died on April 19, 1859 and Catherine (nee Dinham) died on July 1, 1865.

Saturday, June 1, 1844, brother Robert Monroe reported on his visit with Henry Foreman to find out why he had not been attending the meeting. Foreman stated that he had no horse to transport him to church. Also, when he joined the Lower North River Baptist Church, he objected to the doctrine of election and predestination, as held by some Baptists. Apart from that doctrinal difference, Foreman was very friendly and sympathetic to the church. He promised to attend more regularly. In the same meeting, Mary Johnson presented a letter of dismission from the Regular Baptist Church at Sugar Creek, and was received by the church as a member.

Saturday, Aug. 31, 1844, Brother Robert Monroe wrote the corresponding letter (report) to the association. $1.50 was authorized for printing the minutes of the association, and a church collection amounted to $1.91.   The trustees were appointed to superintend the repairs of the meeting house.

Saturday, Nov. 2, 1844: ordered that James Moreland and Robert Monroe visit brother Henry Foreman and make a report at the next meeting.

Saturday, May 3, 1845 Brother John Remer requested a letter of dismission. The letter was granted, but lost. A replacement letter was written on July 5th.

Saturday, July 5, 1845, the church met and discussed the case of brother Henry Foreman. It was continued until the next meeting. Brother Huff wrote the annual letter to the association. Messengers were apponted: Israel Hardy, brother Vanarsdale, James Moreland and Robert Monroe. The church voted to raise $2.50 for the association.

Saturday, August 2, 1845, Henry Foreman was excluded from the fellowship of the church. The church offering amounted to $.81.

At the August 1846 meeting, brethren Huff, Hardy, Vanarsdale, Moreland, and Monroe were appointed as messengers to the association. Robert Monroe wrote the annual corresponding letter.

Pages in the church book were blank for several years until Sept 1, 1849. At that meeting, brethren Vanarsdale, Hardy, Moreland, and Monroe were appointed messengers to the association. The corresponding letter to the association was written by brother Moreland.

Nov. 30, 1850, Elder Jesse Monroe was received as the new pastor of Cacapon Baptist Church. Trustees were appointed: brethren Pownall, Huff and Moreland.

Records were kept by Jesse Monroe for several years. The 1852 association meeting was held at Cacapon Baptist Church. James McDonald, Jacob Stump, William Stump, and James Moreland were members of the building and grounds committee, with Isaac Pownall serving as foreman.

Catherine Easter was baptized Sept. 5, 1852 and was received into the church by the right hand of fellowship, Oct. 2, 1852.

Jan. 1, 1853, brother Vanarsdale and Isaac Hutchinson informed the church of John Hardy's unfair dealing with brother Butterson. Also, the church nominated brother William Alderton to see brother Slady and tell him to come to the next meeting.

April 30, 1853, The church excluded brother John Hardy from the fellowship of the Baptist church. Luther Ginevan came forward and gave his experience. Baptism was to follow on the Lord's day.

June 4, 1853, Ivy Ginevan and Margery Moreland related their experiences and were to be baptized the next day.

Dec. 3, 1853, Jacob Stump related his experience and was to be baptized the next day. He was given the right hand of fellowship and received into the church.

April 1, 1854, Luther Ginevan was appointed clerk. Elder George Loy filled in several times. In 1858, he was replaced by Jacob Stump.

Robert Monroe was excluded for misconduct.

March 1871, Luther Ginevan was ordained a Deacon in the church. Church records state that he died on June 5, 1882.

August 1871, Evan McDonald applied for a letter of dismission and it was granted.

October 1871, Elder John A. Corder was appointed pastor.

Jonas Kerns died on March 24, 1899 and his wife, Eliza A. (Whitacre) Kerns, died on Nov. 11, 1898.

Records for this congregation have been kept to present day, and services are held on the first Sunday of each month. Elder Douglas W. Heare is pastor of the church and Mrs. Joan Shambaugh is the current clerk.

Crooked Run Baptist Church

The Crooked Run Baptist congregation was established on Saturday, Dec. 19, 1789, with 44 members, according to a church record book. The newly organized church adopted the principles contained in the Baptist confession of Faith that were "...adopted by the association at Philadelphia in the year 1742."

The Rev. Benjamin Stone organized Crooked Run Church, and served as its first pastor. The church was built on a mountain site along the Great Wagon Road from Winchester to Romney, several hundred yards east of the residence of the Rev. John Arnold, overlooking Little Cacapon Valley. The first church building burned in 1861. Ruins of a metal churchyard fence are still visible on the old site.

Crooked Run Church was renamed Union Primitive Baptist Church, circa 1814. Today the congregation meets in a sanctuary located near the fire station in Augusta, W.Va. Pastor of the church is Elder Douglas Heare.

Minutes of Crooked Run Baptist Church list members of the church, including 44 charter members of 1790. The following names are presented in the same order as found in the church record book: Benjamin Stone, William Laingore, Joseph Asbury, William Corbin, Tunis Peters, Michael Blue, Isaac Newman, Nathaniel Foster, Thomas Rogers, Jonas Combs, Reason Howard, John Chenowith, Andrew Corbin, Thomas Haley, Jesse Laingon, Thomas Williamson, Samuel Williamson, George Martin, Marjoram Brelsford, James Peters, Mary Ann Ruckman, Jesse Monroe,

Margaret Newman, Ann Newman, Elizabeth Pownell, Barbara Gorden, Ann Stone, Francy Combs, Bathsheeba Corbin, Francinah Peters, Jane Martin, Esther Howard, Esther Laingore, Priscilla Howard, Jane Day, Mary Asbury, Hannah Asbury, Rhoda Stone, Jemima Howell, Mary Stone, Hannah Williamson,

Margaret Williamson, Margaret Haggerty, Sarah Parker, Samuel Peters, James Cunningham, Charity Garrison, Rebecca Colvin, Mary Blue, Martha Williamson, David Potts, Elizabeth Belsford,

Samuel Peters, Robert Poland, MosesPoland, Richard Blue, John Arnold, Peter Bier, John Persall, Rebecca Colvin, Permelia Potts, Jane Newman,

Nancy Peters, Lucretia Smoot, Catherine Lee, Mary Blue (wife of Garret Blue), Jude ("a woman of colour"), Hannah Persall, Ann Colvin, Aaron Ashbrook, Eli Ashbrook, Eleanor Grayham, Mahlon Peters, Peter Ruckman, James Peters (son of John Peters), Philip Peters, Joseph Ruckman, Richard Anderson, Tunis Peters, James Monroe, John Pownall, John Pownall Sr., Elisha Gulick, Mary Baldwin, Absalom Shingleton, Martha Shingleton, Elizabeth Mills, Mary Pownall, Abigail Heare,

George ("a man of colour"), Abigail Pownall, Robert Slocum, Permelia Peters, Ann Patterson, Deborah Blue, Catherine Ashbrook, Hannah Blue, Sarah Colvin, Elizabeth Timbrook, Sarah Ruckman, Agnes Pownall, Elizabeth Pettit, Malinda Monroe, Mary Queen, Margaret Pownall, Eleanor French, Ann

Martin, John Monroe (of James Monroe), George Carder Sr., John Peters, John Carder, John J. Pownall, Philip Fahs, Rebecca Fahs, Mary Stewart, James Carter, Margret Shank, Amos Poland, Margret Doman, Sarah Pownall, Becknall Alverson, Tacy A. McFarling, Precious Powell, Elizabeth Powell, Aaron Malick, James B. Watkins, Nancy Watkins, Letty Carder, Elizabeth Poland, Elisha Pownall, Judy Carder, George Carder Jr., John P. Blue,

Leviny Carder, Elizabeth Ambler, Cinthy Cooper, Hannah Thornton, Dyner ("a woman of colour"), Charity Wills, Catherine Smoot, Benjamin B. Thornton, James Stewart, Peter ("a man of colour"), Charlotty ("a woman of colour"), Elizabeth Foster, Elizabeth Ruckman, John Myres, Milly Berry ("a woman of color"), William Monroe, Nelson Wilson ("a man of color"), Elenor Martin, Nelson Howard ("a man of color"), George Loy, John Ambler,

Abraham Saville, Samuel C. Ruckman, Eleanor Patten, James W. Albin, David Malick, Dorothy Albin, Mary Carter, Sarah Malick, Rebecca A. Malick, Walker B. Pepper, Martha V. Pepper, James Jefferson Carter, John B. Thornton, Jacob Pepper, Frances Pepper, J. W. Carter, John Hott, and Mary McBride (wife of Robert McBride).

In 1833, Aaron Malick was church clerk for Union Baptist Church and Elisha Gulick served as moderator. Malick was a good clerk. However, in 1838 he was excommunicated for "intemperance" (alcohol abuse). A hearing was held by the pastor, the Rev. John Arnold, to prove a charge of drunkeness. A key witness was Philip Fahs. After being inactive for a couple of decades, Malick returned during the early 1860s and was fully restored to the church where he served as clerk until his death in 1895.

Selected entries from the Union Church are presented:

Officials of the church counseled with Mr. and Mrs. James B. Watkins, who were experiencing "unhappy differences," in April 1833. Sister Watkins was visited by Sisters Hannah Thornton, Hannah Blue, and Leviny Carder.

July 27, 1833, Joseph Ruckman, Richard Blue, and Aaron Malick were chosen as Messengers to the Association meeting.

Oct. 26, 1833, Cinthy Cooper related an experience of salvation and grace, and was scheduled to be baptized the next day, before the sermon.

Oct. 26, 1833, Tacy A. Patterson requested a letter of dismission, which was granted. (She went to Perry County, Ohio.) Sister Sarah Thompson was also granted a letter of dismission.

Jan. 25, 1834, Rebecca Fahs and Elizabeth Kidner were transferred to the Mount Zion Church, which was also in the Patterson's Creek Association.

Feb. 22, 1834, George W. Arnold was paid $2.50 for maintaining the church for the past two years. The church collection amounted to $4.67 at that meeting.

May 24, 1834, Sister Ann Patterson came forward in the church; made a confession about her immoral conduct; and she was restored to grace in the church.

June 28, 1834, Joseph Ruckman, John Carder, and Aaron Malick were appointed as messengers to the Association meeting that was to be held at Georges Creek Meeting House in Allegany County, Maryland.

Aug. 23, 1834, the church ordered that William Poland be dealt with for "Quarling," and Brother George, a man of colour, for fighting. These charges were investigated and the issues were resolved.

Jan. 24, 1835, John P. Blue asked why the church did not practice footwashing. The Rev. John Arnold replied that Christ did it only as an example of love and humility, and that an ordinance was not required today.

June 27, 1835, after singing and prayer by the Rev. John Arnold, Catherine Smoot transferred her membership from the Little Cacapon Church to Union Church. In the same meeting, Dyann, a woman of colour, related her experience of grace, and was to be baptized the next day.

July 25, 1835, Elisha Gulick, Aaron Malick, and Richard Blue were appointed to attend the Patterson's Creek Association meeting to be held at the Little Cacapon Church.

Jan. 23, 1836, James B. Watkins was fired from the office of "singing Clerk," and replaced by George Carder.

Aug. 27, 1836, Brother John Carder was appointed by the church to visit Sister Wills, Abigail Pownall, Margaret Doman, and Letty Carder, because of irregular church attendance. All three ladies stated that they wanted to attend, but they were advanced in age.

Feb. 25, 1837, Abigail Pownall transferred her membership to the Mount Zion Church.

June 24, 1837, "James B. Watkins was excommunicated from the fellowship of this church until God be pleased to restore him again by humble repentance." at the same meeting, Nancy Watkins was cited for poor church attendance ("immoral conduct"), as Abigail Heare was aggigned to deal with her.

June 24, 1837, John Meyers related his experience of salvation, and was scheduled for baptism the next day, before the sermon was preached.

Aug. 26, 1837, Joseph Ruckman asked permission to preach while he travelled and visited in the west. Permission was granted.

On Sunday, the Lord's Day, Aug. 27, 1837, a special meeting was called to hear the testimony of salvation and grace related by Milly Berry. She was baptized the same day, after the sermon.

Oct. 28, 1837, Robert Poland transferred his membership from the North River Church to Union Church. James Stewart was baptized on the 4th Lord's Day, Sept. 24, 1837. This was the last entry by Aaron Malick, after which the minutes were handwritten by the Rev. John Arnold.

June 23, 1838, Tacy Patterson transferred back to Union Church, from Perry County, Ohio.

Aug. 25, 1838, Elisha Gulick requested a transfer of membership, which was granted.

Dec. 22, 1838, The Rev. John Arnold was paid a salary of $5.00 per year to pastor the Union Baptist Church.

May 25, 1839, James Stewart was appointed Church Clerk, and the Rev. John Arnold was appointed Moderator. This was a time of turmoil, according to the minutes. The church was in the process of confronting Aaron Malick with his drinking problem, and the church was also moderating a squabble that was disrupting the congregation at North River Primitive Baptist Church.

Sept. 28, 1839. John and Mary Meyers immigrated to the west and were given a letter of transfer.

Dec. 28, 1839, the church approved the ordination of Brother Joseph Ruckman, to be done at Mt. Zion Church.

Aug. 12 1840. William Monroe Sr., formerly of North River Church, was granted a letter of transfer, Sat. before the 2nd Lord's day.

Aug. 26, 1840, the Patterson's Creek Association met in 1840 at Union Baptist Church.

May 22, 1841, received Mary Furr from the North River Church. Her letter is dismission was dated Aug. 7, 1840.

A day of fasting and prayer was declared Saturday, July 17, 1841, on behalf of John Blue and William Monroe. They were ordained to the office of Deacon on July 24, 1841.

Sept. 25, 1841, Delilah Blue, wife of John Blue, related her experience of grace, and was ordered to be baptized on the following day.

Nov. 27, 1841, sent a letter of transfer to Sister Precious "Pressa" Powell, who has already gone to the State of Ohio.

June 25, 1842, Brother George Carder transferred to the North River Church. William Shanks was given $1.96 to keep the meeting house.

July 22, 1843, Robert Poland, John Pownall, James Carter, and William Monroe were chosen as messengers to the Association meeting to be held at the Granwell Church.

Oct. 28, 1843, received from the Lower North River Church, Eleanor Martin, and Nelson Wilson ("a man of colour")

July 27, 1844, James Carter, William Monroe, and John J. Pownell were chosen as messengers to attend the Association meeting at the Lower North River Church.

No records were kept between August 1844 and May 1859. In March of the latter year, James B. Watkins was restored in good standing. Abraham Saville was the Clerk in 1859.

In the Fall of 1861, the church building burned to the ground. The church was inactive for several years.

On Nov. 6, 1869, a reorganization meeting was held at Hopewell School House near Pleasant Dale, under the pastoral care of Elders Jacob Walters (of Pennsylvania) and George Loy. The first item of business in that meeting was, "Our beloved Sister and Mother in Israel, Elenor Patterson, was received by letter." These persons were baptized: James W. Albin, David Malick, Dorothy Albin, Mary Carter, Sarah Malick, and Rebecca A. Malick. Aaron Malick was restored to his former standing, prior to being excommunicated.

Nov. 7, 1869, Walker B. and Martha Virginia Pepper were baptized. James Jefferson Carter, son of James Carter, was baptized on the Saturday, Nov. 27th.

Jan. 29, 1870, John William Carter became a member of the church. David Malick was ordained a Deacon.

April 23, 1870, John Hott and Mary McBride, wife of Robert McBride, related their experiences of salvation before the church.

June 25, 1870, John Trenton gave his experience of grace, and was ordered to be baptized the next day.

Aug. 27, 1870, Jacob and Frances Pepper related their experience of salvation.

Sept. 24, 1870, Abraham Saville, expecting to travel west, asked for a letter of transfer, which was granted. In August 1871, Saville returned to the church and they received him with brotherly love and joy.

Jan. 25, 1873, the Rev. William D. Rees was called to pastor the Union Baptist Church.

Aug. 23, 1873, sister Mary J. Albin, gave her testimony of grace, and was ordered to be baptized the next day.

The Union Baptist Church is still an active congregation, located in Augusta, Hampshire County, W.Va. Current pastor is Elder Douglas Heare.

Historical and Genealogical Records

Abernathy, David, was born April 3, 1792 and died on May 24, 1825. He was buried in a cemetery on a high hill which overlooks the town of Springfield, Hampshire County, W.Va. Most of the tombstones in this large graveyard have not been copied. Source: Tombstone inscriptions.

Abernathy, Eliza, was born on March 23, 1793, and died on Aug. 23, 1830. Source: Tombstone inscription, Springfield, W.Va.

Abernathy, Harriett, died on May 4, 18__, aged 80 years, 1 month. Source: Tombstone inscription, Springfield, W.Va., on top of hill overlooking the town.

Abernathy, Mariah, died in Hampshire County, December 1869, aged 67 years, "of paralysis." Source: 1870 Mortality Schedule for Hampshire County, W.Va.

Abernathy, Nancy, was born on Aug. 4, 1794 and died on June 22, 1859: Source: Tombstone inscription, Springfield, W.Va.

Abernathy, William, died on Sept. 9, 1804. Nancy, wife of William Abernathy, was born on June 2, 1761 and died Feb. 3, 1842. Next to William was a gravestone with the inscription, "Agnes Hopkins our grandmother," no dates given. Source: Tombstone inscription, Springfield, W.Va.

Abernathy, William, born Sept. 2, 1786 and died Jan. 10, 1855 at Springfield, W.Va. Source: Tombstone inscription in graveyard on hill overlooking the town of Springfield, W.Va.

Abrell, Charles, died on Aug. 20, 1899, at 32 years of age. Courthouse death record stated that he was married but the name of his wife was not given. Residence: Slanesville, W.Va.

Abrell, Lemuel, son of Joseph and Lucinda (Oates) Abrell, was born in Hampshire County, Va., March 11, 1845, and died Jan. 27, 1927. He was buried at Three Churches, W.Va. Served in Union Army. Married Sarah Elizabeth Whitacre, daughter of Aquilla and Rachel (Kerns) Whitacre, Oct. 22, 1866, by the Rev. John S. Kidwell, at Cold Stream, Hampshire County. She was born in eastern Hampshire County, in August, 1848. Their children: (1) George William Abrell, born Nov. 20, 1867, and died March 31, 1948, at Mason, Michigan. He married Sallie Virginia Thompson, daughter of Robert James and Martha (Shanholtzer) Thompson.

She was born Aug. 20, 1871 and died July 8, 1907, in Hampshire County. (2) Kirgus Abrell was born May 10, 1869 and died May 11, 1869. (3) John E. Abrell was born Jan. 2, 1871 and died Jan. 4, 1871. (4) Charles F. Abrell was born April 25, 1872. (5) Nannie M. Abrell was born Aug. 28, 1874. (6) Edith Virginia Abrell was born July 8, 1876. (7) Ollie E. Abrell was born Aug. 6, 1878. (8) a male child was born Aug. 6, 1882 and died Nov. 11, 1883. (9) Joseph Franklin Abrell was born Oct. 20, 1883. (10) Herman A. Abrell was born Aug. 30, 1886, and (11) Emmett W. Abrell was born Aug. 30, 1890. Sources: Bible record and family data from private sources.

Abrell, Sarah Ann, daughter of Joseph and Lucinda (Oates) Abrell, was born May 25, 1843 and died on June 21, 1917. On Dec. 6, 1860, she married William Cornelius Shuler, son of Cornelius and Harriett (Kerns) Shuler. Possibly he died in the war, because she became a widow within a few years. Sarah Ann then married Walter Jefferson Leith, son of William P. and Mary (Powell) Leith, on Oct. 23, 1866. He was born on Sept. 25, 1823 and died on Sept. 7, 1903. They were buried in the Bloomery Presbyterian Graveyard. A marriage record, established in Frederick County, Virginia, showed that he was previously married. They lived near Leith Mountain in the Bloomery District of Hampshire County, W.Va.

Abrell, Richard, was one of the early settlers in old Frederick County in "the Opekin settlement." He died circa 1759. Richard had a son named John Abrell who died in 1770, whose wife was named Elizabeth. After John's death, his widow Elizabeth remarried to Joseph Edwards. Fairfax grants made to the Edwards and Abrells were adjoining properties on Opequon Creek near the four-county intersection of Frederick-Clarke-Jefferson and Berkeley counties. These two men were patriarchs of the Abrell family in this area, sometimes spelled Abell or Abrill surname. One researcher of the Abrell family is: Mr. Robert A. White, 8610 Dovedale Road, Randallstown, MD 21133.

Abrell, Thomas J., son of Joseph and Margaret (Reed) Abrell Sr., was born in 1821 and died on May 13, 1863, at Chancellorsville, Va. He served in the 82nd Ohio Infantry. Thomas married Mary Miller, daughter of Hiram Miller, on May 18, 1857. She was born circa 1834 and died on March 6, 1867. Source: Robert A. White, whose address is in previous entry.

Abrell, Willliam E., son of Joseph and Lucinda (Oates)Abrell, was born Feb. 14, 1840 and died April 12, 1914. He served in the Union Army, in Company B, 2nd Maryland Regiment, USA. His wife, Angelina (or Jemima Ann) Whitacre, was born April 14, 1847 and died June 13, 1915. Her parents were Aquilla and Rachel (Kerns) Whitacre. They lived in the Bloomery District of Hampshire County, and were buried in the Bloomery Presbyterian Church graveyard.

Adams, Jonathan Wright, son of Joseph and Mary (Wright) Thatcher Adams, was born Jan. 1, 1800 and died Oct. 2, 1839.[39] He married Ann Mariah Hamilton, daughter of James and Rachel Hamilton, April 14, 1831. Ann Mariah was born Dec. 15, 1806. Children of Jonathan W. and Ann M. (Hamilton) Adams were: (1) Joseph Hamilton Adams was born Aug. 20, 1832. (2) James William Adams was born April 10, 1834. (3) Rachel Ann Adams was born May 21, 1835 and died May 31, 1907. She married Josiah G. Boxwell. (4) John Henry Adams was born Dec. 27, 1836 and died Aug. 13, 1837. (5) Mary Elizabeth Adams was born Jan. 30, 1838 and died Jan. 11, 1912, in Hampshire County, W.Va. She married Joseph F. Smith, Sept. 27, 1860, in Frederick County, Va. Source: Family Bible of Jonathan Wright Adams, in hands of Robert N. Smith of Paw Paw, W.Va.

Adams, Sarah "Ann," was born in Frederick County, Va. on Oct. 20, 1777, and died in Clinton County, Ohio. She married Jacob Files. Sources: *Clinton Republican*, and Michael Pollock, who is editor of *Frederick Findings*. Michael is researching the Adams family and his address is: Lineage Search Associates, 6419 Colt's Neck Road, Mechanicsville, Va. 23111-4233.

Albin, Elizabeth, wife of James Albin, was born in Frederick County, Va. in 1807 and died in Hardy County, Va. on May 1, 1860, aged 52 years, 7 months, "of pneumonia." Her parents were George and Sarah Reid. Source: Hardy County death record in courthouse in Moorefield, W.Va.

Albin, John, son of William and Mary (Bruce) Albin, was born ca. 1739 in Frederick County, Virginia and died on April 16, 1820 in Green Township, Clark County, Ohio. He married Ann McNeill.

---

39. The Bible record did not state where Jonathan W. Adams died, but it is believed by Michael Pollock to have been in Warren County, Ohio. Adams' widow was listed on the 1850 and 1860 censuses for Frederick County, Va.

Source: Ms. Ethel Albin, Sabetha, KS. 66534, who cited the dates from a tombstone inscription.

Albin, Rachel, daughter of James and Barbara Albin, was born April 24, 1791. She married Peter Jordon, Jan. 25, 1810, Muskingham County, Ohio. Source: Hebron Lutheran Church Record, 1784-1850, Hampshire County, Va., and Ms. Ethel Albin.

Albin, Robert, was born circa 1743 and died in Frederick County, Va. in April 1814. It is believed that his parents were William and Mary (Bruce) Albin. Robert's wives were named Anne and Elizabeth _____ (maiden names not now established). Robert Albin's children were: (1) Andrew Albin (ca 1769-1843) married Martha Sutton (2) William Albin (ca 1771-June 1842) married Catherine Ritenour, daughter of Michael Ritenour. (3) Anna Albin married William Edwards, Aug. 23, 1796, in Frederick County, Va. (4) Robert Albin Jr. (ca 1771-March 14, 1857), married Jane _____ and they lived in Monroe County, Michigan. (5) Rebecca Albin (1782-April 14, 1847) married Luke Blacker. They lived in Clinton County, Indiana. (6) Jane Albin married Alexander McWhorter on July 7, 1803. (7) Samuel Albin (Jan. 12, 1785-Oct. 30, 1844) married Sarah Smith, daughter of Jeremiah Smith Jr. They first went to Pickaway County, Ohio and then to Vermillion County, Indiana. (8) James Albin married Ann Ellis, who was a daughter of Morris Ellis (9) Susannah Albin was mentioned in her father's will. (10) Elizabeth Albin married John S. Crumly on Jan. 25, 1815. (11) Elijah Albin (1793-1870) married: (a) Susan Dalby, daughter of Joseph and Hannah (Stonebridge) Dalby (b) Nancy Peters, and (c) Rebecca Lee. (12) Name of 12th child not proven. Source: According to Miss Ethel Albin, 307 Harrison Street, Sabetha, KS 66534, who has published a book, *The Virginia Albins* (1989), the above list of children is very likely the case, but not proven and developed to her satisfaction. Miss Albin's caliber of research is excellent, and her book is highly recommended.

Albin, William, son of James and Barbara (Hoover) Albin, was born in Hardy County, Va. on Oct. 4, 1793 and moved with his parents to Guernsey County, Ohio, circa 1804. He was one of ten children, and he had two half-brothers from his father's previous marriage. William Albin married Nancy Clark in 1814. She was born in Greene County, Pennsylvania on Aug. 13, 1799. They moved to Vinton County, Ohio in 1852. William's father, James

Albin, died in Guernsey County, Ohio in 1813, aged 60 years. His wife, Barbara Hoover, died in the same county at age 86 years. Source: *History of Hocking Valley*, page 1311.

Albin, William, died in August 1869, aged 19 years. He died of a heat stroke while serving as an apprenticed carpenter. Source: 1870 Mortality Schedule for Frederick County, Va.

Alderton, Anna, died in May 1870 (born circa 1789), aged 82 years, in Morgan County, W.Va. Cause of death was pneumonia. Source: 1870 Mortality Schedule for Morgan County, W.Va.

Alderton, Daniel, son of Thomas and Ann (Vanorsdall) Alderton, was born in Hampshire County, Va. on Nov. 13, 1816 and died on Aug. 21, 1875 in Lewis County, Missouri. His wife, Nancy Haggerty, was born in Hampshire County, Va. on Aug. 11, 1820 and died in Lewis County, MO. on Oct. 20, 1877.

Alderton, David, was born in 1859, and no death date was inscribed on his stone. On same tombstone are these inscriptions: Alice Alderton (1870-1927), wife of David; and Ira L. Alderton (1896-1924). Source: Tombstone inscriptions in Jacob Alderton Graveyard, Bower's Run, Hampshire County.

Alderton, Isaac P., was born March 30, 1843 and died April 22, 1920. His wife, Lucinda Kidwell, was born Feb. 21, 1848 and died April 25, 1911. Source: Tombstone inscriptions in Kidwell family graveyard, Slanesville, W.Va.

Alderton, Mariah, died on May 29, 1889, aged 66 years, 7 months, 8 days. It is believed that her maiden name was Hardy, and that she was the second wife of Jacob Alderton. Source: Tombstone inscription in Jacob Alderton Graveyard, near Critton Hollow, Hampshire County, W.Va.

Alderton, Peter, died on March 16, 1873 (or 1878?), aged 21 years. Source: Tombstone inscription in Jacob Alderton Graveyard, near Bower's Run, Hampshire County, W.Va.

Alderton, Margaret, daughter of William and Margaret (Edwards) Alderton, died on June 6, 1883, aged 81 years, in Morgan County, W.Va. Her husband was Richard Vanorsdall who died on Aug. 18, 1889, aged 89 years. Source: Morgan County, W.Va. courthouse death records.

Alderton, Martha, was born in 1793 and died of pneumonia in March 1870 in Morgan County, W.Va., according to the 1870 Mortality census for the County.

Alderton, Mary, daughter of William and Mary Alderton, was born circa 1797 and died in Hampshire County, W.Va., on Dec. 6, 1875, per courthouse death record.

Alderton, Sarah (nee Largent), daughter of Thomas and Eleanor (Shivers) Largent, was born on Nov. 6, 1807, in Hampshire County. She married Jacob Alderton. According to a tombstone inscription in the Alderton Graveyard, near Bower's Run, Hampshire County, Jacob Alderton died on Jan. 19, 1877, aged 74 years. Sources: Bible record and tombstone inscription.

Alderton, Thomas, son of William and Margaret (Edwards) Alderton, was born in 1787 in Hampshire County, Va., and was alive when the 1850 census was taken in Morgan County, Va. His wife was Ann Vanorsdall, daughter of Peter and Ellen Vanorsdall. According to the 1870 mortality census for Morgan County, W.Va., Ann died in May 1869 (or in 1870?), aged 82 years.

Alderton, Thomas, died in January 1870, of consumption, aged 38 years. He was a farmer, according to the 1870 Mortality Schedule for Morgan County, W.Va. A bible record shows that Thomas Alderton [probably a son of Jacob and Sarah (Largent) Alderton] was born on Jan. 23, 1832 and died Jan. 24, 1870. His wife, Barbara Swaney, was born in Nov. 1838, in Baltimore, Md., and died in 1929. Their children were: (1) Sarah Catherine Alderton was born May 31, 1856 in Morgan Co., Va. and died March 13, 1920, at Aliquippa, Beaver Co., PA. She married Edward Trickle Largent, son of John H. and Elizabeth (McAtee) Largent. He was born on Sept. 5, 1845, at Bloomery, Va., and died Dec. 16, 1932, at Harrison, Alleghney Co., PA. (2) Jacob Sanford Alderton was born Aug. 16, 1858 and died Dec. 27, 1934. He married Catherine Effland, who was born on Dec. 27, 1855 and died Aug. 12, 1925. (3) Selina Lear Alderton was born Nov. 30, 1860 and died Aug. 31, 1949. She married a Mr. Dunn. (4) Aron Alderton was born Sept. 22, 1864, in Morgan County, W.Va., and did not marry. (5) Lemuel Melroy Alderton was born on April 21, 1867, in Morgan County, W.Va., married twice. (6) Anna Maria Alderton was born on Oct. 10, 1869, in Morgan County, W.Va.

Alderton, William, was born on March 15, 1808 and died on June 15, 1883. His wife Margaret was born on April 7, 1812 and died on April 21, 1876. Source: Tombstone inscriptions in Powell Cemetery, Forks of Capon, Hampshire County, West Virginia.

Alderton, William C., husband of Mary M. Alderton, died on Oct. 5, 1885, aged 32 years, 6 months, 5 days. Source: Tombstone inscription in the Jacob Alderton graveyard, located in wooded terrain near Bower's Run, Hampshire County, W.Va.

Alkire, Mrs. Belle, died on Sept. 21, 1896, age 42 years. Source: Hampshire County Courthouse death record.

Alkire/Alguire, Harmonus was born in 1700 and died in 1796 in Mercer County, Kentucky. His wife was Mary Craymore (sometimes spelled Kramer?). They were among the earliest settlers on the South Branch of the Potomac River during the late 1740's. See "Family History: The Alkire Family," *The West Virginia Advocate*, December 1982 issue; Capon Bridge, W.Va. 26711.

Alkire, Peter Sr., was born on March 10, 1773 and died on Sept. 30, 1850 at Fort Ashby, Hampshire County, Va. He married Sarah Stump, daughter of George and Elizabeth (Wilson) Stump, on April 27, 1796 in Hardy County, Va. She was born on June 5, 1777 and died in 1853. Their children were: (1) Elizabeth Alkire was born Aug. 19, 1798 and died in 1850. (2) Solomon Alkire was born on Sept. 9, 1800 and died in 1881. He married Jemima Arnold. (3) John Alkire was born Jan. 19, 1802. He married Elizabeth Neff on Aug. 23, 1823. (4) Magdalene Alkire was born Aug. 19, 1804. (5) Sarah Alkire was born Jan. 24, 1808. She married Jacob Daniel. (6) Peter Alkire, Jr. was born Aug. 26, 1810. See entry below. (7) Nimrod Alkire was born April 13, 1813 and died Feb. 11, 1900. He married a Miss Taylor and Mary (Fox) Reese. (8) Hiram Alkire was born May 27, 1816 and died Jan. 21, 1893. He married Mary Ann Marker, a widow. (9) Mahalia Ann Alkire was born Dec. 22, 1820 and died in 1878. She married Thompson Neff, Nov. 15, 1839. (10) Elmire Alkire was born Oct. 15, 1823. She married Thomas S. Wheeler, who was born Jan. 12, 1821. Source: Bible records.

Alkire, Peter, Jr., was born on Aug. 26, 1810 and died on Jan. 20, 1903. He was buried at Three Churches, W.Va. His wives were: (1) Alcinda Howard and (2) Harriett Rebecca Smoot, daughter of Silas Smoot. She died Feb. 18, 1883, aged 56 years, in Hampshire County. See an article on the history of the Alkire family in *The West Virginia Advocate*, December 1982 issue.

Alkire, Solomon, son of Peter and Sarah (Stump) Alkire, Sr., was born on Sept. 9, 1800 and died in 1881. He married Jemima Arnold. Source: Carl S. Alkire, Weatherford, TX.

Allemong, Casper, son of Jacob and Elizabeth (Rinker) Allamong, was born on Nov. 29, 1789 in Frederick County, Va.; died on Nov. 11, 1871 in Frederick County, Va. He married Christine Dick on Jan. 21, 1818. She was born on April 30, 1790 and died on Oct. 30, 1855. Source: Tombstone inscriptions in Heironimus graveyard, Whitacre, Virginia.

Allemong, Jacob, was born in Northampton County, Penn. in 1754 and died in Frederick County, Va. on March 8, 1808. His wife was Elizabeth Rinker, daughter of Casper and Maria (Schultz) Rinker. She was born on Nov. 6, 1761 in Penn.; died in 1848. A record located in the Virginia State Archives, in Frederick County, Va. "Inquisition of Dead Bodies," stated that Jacob Allemong was found dead along a roadside on Timber Ridge in March 1808, "in the 32 year of the Commonwealth." A jury, composed of neighbors, was appointed to study the cause of death and they determined that it was by natural causes, "died by the visitation of God." The presiding Justice of the Peace was John McCoole, and the jurors were: Patrick Reynolds, Henry Heironimus, Thomas Collins, Reason Mason, Jacob Grove, Henry Grove, John Newland, Jacob Null, Patrick Reynolds, William Dawson, Joseph Ware, Samuel Wright, and Jacob Heironimus. The inquisition was held on March 23, 1808. [Comment: The above should be verified because of a possible "mix-up" on notes taken hurriedly.]

Allemong, William, son of Jacob and Elizabeth (Rinker) Allamong, was born July 27, 1783 in Frederick County, Va. and died on March 2, 1862 in Champaign County, Illinois. He married Charity Lewis in Frederick County, Va. on April 12, 1808. Sources: Courthouse record and cemetery inscription.

Allen, Robert, died on Aug. 2, 1878, in Mineral County, W.Va., aged 70 years. Source: Aug. 9, 1878 issue of the *South Branch Intelligencer*, published in Romney, W.Va.

Allen, Ruth, (wife of Joseph Allen) of Frederick County, Virginia, was born in 1732 and died on Oct. 15, 1781. Source: Hopewell Meeting (Quaker) records.

Allen, Sarah "wife of William Allen," died on April 18, 1859, in 58th year of her life.   Source: Tombstone inscription at Three Churches, Hampshire County, W.Va.

Allen, Thomas, died on March 16, 1879, aged 94 years, 7 months, 14 days, in Hampshire County. Source: The *South Branch Intelligencer*.

Allender, George, son of James and Sarah (Alderton) Allender, was born in Dec. 1808 in Hampshire County; died on April 5, 1890. He married Mary Allender, daughter of Alexander Allender, born in May 1809 and died on Feb. 11, 1887.   The 1850 U.S. Census for Hampshire County, Va. shows that James Allender was born in Maryland in 1783 and his wife Sarah was born in Virginia in 1786. Source: Archive Record, Mormon Library, Salt Lake City, Utah.

Allender, the Rev. James, son of James and Sarah (Alderton) Allender, was born at Okonoko, W.Va., on Feb. 21, 1823 and died on Sept. 1, 1899. He married: (1) Malinda Allender on June 6, 1844. She was born on July 6, 1818 and died on May 4, 1849. (2) Mary Shuttleworth, on May 30, 1850. Source: Church Archives, Mormon Library, Salt Lake City, Utah.

Allender, Mary Ellen, daughter of Thomas and Eleanor (Largent) Allender, died Oct. 31, 1934, aged 71 years, 7 months, 14 days. Her married name was Powell, and she was buried in the Ginevan graveyard at Little Cacapon, Hampshire County, W.Va.

Amick, Robert E., (1867-1941) and wife, Fannie Y., (1878-1941), were buried in the Saville section of the Ginevan graveyard, Okonoko, Hampshire County, W.Va.

Anderson, Asa, born Feb. 10, 1807 and died Oct. 30, 1861. His wife, Mary Ann Marple, was born April 13, 1820 and died April 3, 1902. She was a daughter of Thomas Marple. Asa and Mary Ann were buried in Bethel Methodist Cemetery on Timber Ridge, located on the Frederick-Hampshire County line. Source: Records of Ralph L. Triplett, Gore, Va.

Anderson, Daniel, filed a chancery court suit, Circuit Court, Hampshire County, Va., on Sept. 18, 1843. It was against a number of relatives but their relationships were not stated. They were: (1) John Anderson and Sarah   (2) James Anderson married Christina Spaid   (3) Jonathan Anderson   (4) Nathan

Anderson   (5) Rachel Anderson married John Triplett (6) Maria Anderson (7) Thomas Anderson (8) Hannah Anderson married John Spaid (9) Margaret Anderson married James Cogle(?) (10) Mary Anderson (11) James Anderson (12) Joseph Anderson (13) Benjamin Anderson (14) David Anderson (15) Isaac Anderson (16) Rachel Anderson married Isaac Miller, and Jesse Anderson, deceased, had a daughter named Mary Anderson. Source: *Order Book II*, page 34, Circuit Court, Hampshire County, Va., dated Sept. 18, 1843.

Anderson, Christina, wife of James Anderson, died Oct. 11, 1881, aged 85 years. Born in Hampshire County. Death reported to courthouse by George N. Anderson, grandson.

Anderson, Daniel, was born Aug. 17, 1797 and died Oct. 9, 1884. His wife, Mary Kelso, was born March 15, 1797, and died May 23, 1862. Source: Tombstone inscriptions in Shiloh Cemetery, LeHew, W.Va.

Anderson, Daniel, was born Oct. 6, 1811 and died Feb. 25, 1885. Source: Tombstone inscription in Bloomery Presbyterian graveyard, Hampshire County. The 1860 census for Hampshire County states that he was born in Pennsylvania.

Anderson, Daniel A., died of "dropsy" in 1856, aged 70 years. Source: Hampshire County, Va. death record in Virginia State Archives.

Anderson, Henry (and his wife named Susan), were members of the Reformed Church of Winchester, Va. On Aug. 25, 1840, four of his children were baptized, sponsored by Mary Grim and Susan Anderson. The children were: Mary Jane Anderson, Sophia Ann Anderson, George Montgomery Anderson, and John Henry Anderson. Source: German Reformed Church Records, Winchester, Va.

Anderson, Jacob, born on July 5, 1758 and died in Pulaski County, Va., on Feb. 21, 1842. He was living in Frederick County, Va. when he enlisted in the Revolutionary War, in 1777. He married Christina Wysor (Wiser) on March 24, 1779, in Frederick County, Va. Source: DAR Records, submitted by descendant.

Anderson, Capt. James, born Jan. 3, 1797 and died Jan. 18, 1884. He married Christina Spaid. Source: Tombstone inscriptions in Timber Ridge Christian Church, Hampshire County, W.Va.

Anderson, John, was born in Pennsylvania in 1770 and died in Morgan County, Va. in April 1850. Source: 1850 Mortality Schedule of U.S. Census.

Anderson, John L., was born Jan. 27, 1801, and died May 17, 1877. His wife, Margaret Groves, daughter of Peter Groves, died on Sept. 1, 1850. Source: Tombstone inscriptions in Timber Ridge Christian Church Graveyard, Hampshire County, W.Va.

Anderson, John M., died July 28, 1875, aged 52 years, "of consumption." Wife was named Rebecca. Occupation was farmer. Source: Hampshire County courthouse death record.

Anderson, Otway M., was born in 1832, probably in Frederick County, Va., and died in 1879, at Boston, KY. Possibly he was a son of John L. and Margaret (Groves) Anderson. He married Amanda Virginia Sine, daughter of the Rev. Christy Sine. She was born Feb. 9, 1834 and died Dec. 15, 1900. They were buried in Kirby cemetery, Boston Station, KY.

Anderson, Paul Pierce, was born Nov. 29, 1809 and died Dec. 11, 1880. His wife, Mariah Garvin, was born Dec. 27, 1811, and died Feb. 1, 1897. Joseph Anderson (brother of Paul P.) was born June 13, 1803 and died July 2, 1878. Source: Tombstone inscriptions in Timber Ridge Christian Church Cemetery, Hampshire County, W.Va.

Anderson, Thomas, and wife Jane, came to "old Frederick County, Va." from New York, in 1734; filed a Will on Dec. 11, 1747. He was a blacksmith. Oldest son was named James Anderson (who died in South Carolina during the 1770s), and another son was Colbert Anderson. One daughter, Mary, married a Mr. Yates. Thomas took a 1,000-acre land grant along Opequon Creek, from Morgan and Bryan. Colbert Anderson died and his wife remarried to Francis Lilburn.

Anderson, Thomas, born in "Hampshire County, Va." (Note: Then it was in Orange County, Va..), ca 1735, and died in Fairfield County, Ohio, in 1806. He married Elizabeth Bruce. Thomas' parents were William and Rachel Anderson, among first settlers along the Potomac, Hampshire County. Source: Records submitted to DAR Library, by descendants.

Anderson, Thomas, II, was born on Oct. 9, 1777 and died on Sept. 29, 1836, in Frederick County, Va. His second wife, Margaret Bruner, daughter of George and Polly Bruner, was born on Aug. 24, 1794 and died on Aug. 9, 1883. According to the **Undertaker Book**, by John W. Mellon, she was buried on Aug. 11, 1883. They lived on Timber Ridge, near High View, Frederick County, Va. (near the W.Va. line). Source: Mrs. Cheryl (Jackson) Malone, 140 Jackson Street, Morgantown, W.Va. 26505.

Anderson, Thomas Ewel, son of Isaiah and Margaret (LaFollette) Anderson, eas born on Sept. 13, 1853, and died April 11, 1931. He married Laura Virginia Dunlap, daughter of Archibald and Mary C. (Griffith) Dunlap, March 4, 1879. Laura was born Oct. 9, 1859, and died April 4, 1945. Interment was in the Timber Ridge Christian Church, Hampshire County, W.Va. Their children were: (1) Bertie Blanch Anderson was born Feb. 12, 1880. She married Henry Barrett. (2) Vergie Anderson was born Oct. 11, 1882 and died Feb. 4, 1953. She married Thomas Davis of Yellow Springs, who died April 20, 1973. (3) Oscar Riley Anderson was born Oct. 21, 1884 and died Nov. 30, 1884. (4) Franklin B. Anderson was born Sept. 13, 1886 and died Feb. 2, 1945. He married Bessie LaFollette, who died on Nov. 23, 1918. He remarried to Anna Mary Beaver. (5) Willie Lorah Anderson was born on Sept. 13, 1888, and died April 22, 1967. He did not marry, but left a son, Thomas Eugene Good (Anderson), who was born on June 11, 1935. (6) Ernest Pitman Anderson, born June 15, 1892 and died on Oct. 6, 1966. He married Leone Jackson, born March 29, 1901, and died July 14, 1971. (7) Harry Anderson was born April 5, 1895 and died May 1, 1974. He first married Ina C. Whitlock, who died on Aug. 3, 1923. He remarried to Eleanor Cain. (8) Thomas F. Anderson was born May 1, 1901, and died Aug. 28, 1901. Source: Copied from Bible of Thomas E. and Lula (Dunlap) Anderson, now possessed by Mrs. Isabelle (Anderson) Kump, of Timber Ridge, Gore, Va.

Anderson, William, was born in Scotland in 1693 and died in Hampshire County in 1797. He was 104 years old, and a copy of his Will is on file in the courthouse at Romney. He married Rachel _____; became one of the first settlers along the North Branch, in an area sometimes known as "Anderson's Bottom." Source: DAR records.

Armstrong, David, native of Ireland, died on April 29, 1838. His wife, Eleanor Baxter, died on Sept. 15, 1826. Source: Tombstone inscriptions in the Indian Mound cemetery, Romney, W.Va. Other information, such as the town and County in Ireland, is written on the tombstone, now almost illegible.

Armstrong, William, born in Lisburn, Ireland on Dec. 23, 1782 and died on May 10, 1865, in Hampshire County. His wife, Elizabeth, died on July 4, 1843, aged 57 years. They were Presbyterians. Source: Tombstone inscriptions in the Indian Mound Cemetery, Romney, West Virginia.

Arnold, The Rev. Daniel, son of Samuel and Abigail Arnold, was born in 1768 and died on June 16, 1849. He married: (1) Elizabeth Thomas in 1792. She was born on March 4, 1774 and died on July 5, 1820. (2) Elizabeth Wine, born in May 1761 and died on Oct. 13, 1853. He was buried in the Beaver Run cemetery.

Arnold, Eliza, daughter of the Rev. Dr. John and Mrs. Eleanor (Asberry) Monroe, was born in Hampshire County, Va. on March 11, 1798 and died on Sept. 15, 1843, in Pendleton County, Kentucky. She married Elias Arnold, son of Andrew and Mary Arnold of Hampshire County, Va. Elias and Eliza were married on Sept. 26, 1816, in Hampshire County. Elias Arnold was born circa 1791 and died in Feb. 1872, aged 82 years, in Kentucky. After Eliza's death, he remarried to Polly Williams, on Jan. 24, 1845. Source: Family Bible record; information provided by Mrs. Sue Schneider (deceased), P.O. Box 343, Benson, Illinois 61516.

Arnold, Frances, died in December 1849, aged 75 years. She was born in Virginia. Cause of death was "pleuresy," after a 6-day illness. Source: 1850 Mortality Schedule for Frederick County, Va.

Arnold, the Rev. John, was born on Aug. 10, 1777, and died on Oct. 14, 1850 near Mouser's Ridge, at Little Capon. He was buried in the Arnold family cemetery near his residence. His wife was Rosanna Shaffer. The Rev. Arnold was a preacher in Primitive Baptist Churches of Hampshire County. Source: Tombstone inscription in Arnold family graveyard.

Arnold, John, son of Zachariah and Catherine or Abigail (Miller) Arnold, died on Aug. 20, 1854, aged 64. His wife was Catherine Buckly. Source: Death record in Virginia State Archives.

Arnold, John, son of Richard and Christina (Davis) Arnold, pioneers to Hampshire County, was born on Sept. 6, 1735 and died in 1819 in Hampshire County. He married Hannah Parks, daughter of Roger and Hannah Parks. John's father, Richard

Arnold, died in Hampshire County in 1758. He helped George Washington survey several of the lots along the Cacapon River. Source: Court deposition re Nixon case, et al.

Arnold, John James, son of George William and Sarah Ann (Powell) Arnold, was born in Hampshire County on Aug. 25, 1839 and died in the Civil War on July 18, 1863. He was buried at Winchester, Va.

Arnold, The Rev. Joseph, aged 78 years, died on Oct. 13, 1878, in Mineral County, W.Va., according to the Oct. 18, 1878 issue of the *South Branch Intelligencer*. He was born on Feb. 3, 1799, to Zachariah and Abigail (Miller) Arnold. Joseph married Elizabeth Sloan on Jan. 25, 1827. She was born on Nov. 25, 1805 and died in 1880. They lived on Patterson's Creek.

Arnold, Kesiah, wife of Jesse Arnold, was born in Maryland in 1784, and died in Frederick County, Va. in July 1869, "of pneumonia." Source: 1870 Mortality Schedule for Frederick County, Va.

Arnold, Michael, aged 74 (sic), son of the Rev. Daniel and Elizabeth (Thomas) Arnold, of Hampshire County, died May 19, 1873 in Philadelphia, according to the May 30, 1873 issue of the *South Branch Intelligencer*. His birthdate was Dec. 17, 1804. Michael married Sarah Sloan, and he served as a lawyer and Judge in Philadelphia, Penn.

Arnold, Peter, died at the home of Zachariah and Elizabeth (Arnold) Arnold, II, on Oct. 23, 1875. He was 80 years, 1 month and 3 days old (born on Sept. 20, 1795). Peter was an unmarried son of Zachariah and Abigail (Miller) Arnold. Source: *South Branch Intelligencer*, Nov. 1, 1875 issue.

Arnold, Richard, Jr., son of Richard and Sarah (Chamberlain) Arnold, was born circa 1694 at Thornbury, Chester County, Pennsylvania, and died on Dec. 12, 1758 in Hampshire County, Va. He was one of the first pioneers in Capon Valley, settling south of Capon Bridge. His wife was Christiana Davis. Source: Harold McBride, Clovis, CA.

Arnold, Solomon, son of Daniel and Elizabeth (Thomas) Arnold, was born on April 26, 1801 and died on Nov. 11, 1851. He married Susan Wine of Rockingham County, Virginia. After his death, his orphan children were bound out to Zachariah Arnold (bond signed by Peter Arnold on Feb. 23, 1852.) The children named in the orphans bond book in the Hampshire County courthouse were: Mary, Samuel, Daniel, Benjamin, Margaret, John and Elizabeth Arnold.

Arnold, Zachariah, was born on Dec. 5, 1767 and died on June 5, 1829 at Beaver Run, Hampshire County. His parents were Samuel and Abigail Arnold (German Baptist Brethren) who came to Hampshire County in 1784-85 from Frederick County, Md. Zachariah Arnold's wife was Abigail Miller, born on Jan. 8, 1776 and died on Oct. 24, 1850. Note: This German branch of the Arnold family was not the same as the Arnold branch which settled at Capon Bridge circa 1740. Dr. Emmert Bittinger, professor at Bridgewater College (Va.) has collected extensive data on the "Beaver Run" Arnold families.

Arnold, Zachariah, Jr., son of Zachariah and Abigail (Miller) Arnold, Sr., was born on March 3, 1805 and died on Nov. 26, 1887. He married Elizabeth Arnold, daughter of Daniel and Elizabeth (Thomas) Arnold. Elizabeth was born on Sept. 3, 1812 and died on Nov. 28, 1893.

Asbury/Asberry, Joseph, Sr., son of George and Hannah (Hardwick) Asbury, was born in Westmoreland County, Va. about 1743 and died in Hampshire County in 1823. He was a slave-owner, and property owner in the Cacapon Valley. Wife was named Mary. Joseph's sister, Anna Asbury, settled in Hampshire County, too. Born on Oct. 6, 1747, she married the Rev. Benjamin Stone, one of the early Baptist preachers in Hampshire County. Sources: Multiple— public records, Mrs. Sue Schneider, Benson, IL.

Ashbrook, Aaron, son of Levi and Mary (Chenoweth) Ashbrook, was born in Hampshire County, Va. on Jan. 7, 1780 and died on April 12, 1865 in Fairfield County, Ohio. He married Abigail Peters, daughter of Tunis and Francina (Adams) Peters, on Dec. 22, 1800, in Hampshire County, Va. Abigail was born on June 7, 1782 and died on Nov. 4, 1876. Source: Information from Bible records.

Ashbrook, Levi, was born circa 1738 and died on Oct. 15, 1794 in Hampshire County, Va. He married: (1) Mary Pentecost, and (2) In 1779 he married Mary Chenoweth, who was born on Oct. 14, 1748 and died on July 27, 1830 in Hampshire County. Ashbrook was a census taken for Hampshire County in 1784. Major source:

"Grandfather Papers" in D.A.R. Library, 1776 D. St., N.W., Washington, D.C.

Ashbrook, Rev. Eli, son of Levi and Mary (Chenoweth) Ashbrook, was born in Hampshire County, Va. on Sept. 23, 1781 and died at Johnstown, Ohio on Jan. 24, 1877. He married Catherine Peters, daughter of Tunis and Francina (Adams) Peters, on Jan. 5, 1802 in Hampshire County. She was born on April 6, 1784 and died on Jan. 1, 1871 at Johnstown, Ohio. Source: "Grandfather Papers," DAR Library, Washington, D.C.

Ashbrook, Levi, Jr., son of Levi and Mary (Pentecost) Ashbrook, Sr., was born circa 1771. He married Ellender Chenoweth, daughter of John Chenoweth, Clark County, Kentucky. Source: "Grandfather Papers," DAR Library, Washington, D.C.

Ashbrook, Thomas, son of Levi and Mary (Chenoweth) Ashbrook, was born in Hampshire County, Va. on June 28, 1793 and died in Coles County, Illinois on Nov. 27, 1855. He married Nancy Wells. Source: "Grandfather Papers" in DAR Library, Washington, D.C.

Ashbrook, Thomas, was born in 1758 and died on Aug. 24, 1848. His wife was named Agnes. Thomas lived in Hampshire County, Va., according to *Colonial Lineages*, Volume II, pp. 454-456. It is believed that he was a brother of Levi Ashbrook.

Ashbrook, William, son of Levi and Mary (Chenoweth) Ashbrook, was born in Hampshire County, Va. on Oct. 17, 1790. He married Parmelia Peters, daughter of Tunis and Francina (Adams) Peters. She was born on Oct. 1, 1793 and died on Sept. 27, 1885. One Bible record states that Parmelia emigrated from Hampshire County on April 1, 1812. Source: Bible records.

Austin, Mrs. W.A., born on July 18, 1827 and died on Nov. 26, 1879. Source: Tombstone inscription on grave in the woods below the Indian Mound cemetery in Romney, W.Va.

Babb, Harriett, daughter of Abner and Susannah (Robinson) Babb, was born in Frederick County, Virginia in 1801 and died in 1883 in Greene County, Ohio. She married Benjamin Keiter, son of George and Esther (Buzzard) Keiter, on Jan. 27, 1818. He was born on June 27, 1798 and died on Aug. 7, 1885 in Greene County, where he was buried in the Maple Corner churchyard.

One source says that they immigrated to Ohio in 1840 and another says it was in 1872.

Babb, Henry, died on April 13, 1820, in Frederick County, Virginia. Source: Tombstone inscription in Quaker Graveyard (Back Creek Meeting), Gainsboro Va.

Babb, Henry, died on Nov. 2, 1821, aged 55 years. He was from Frederick County, Va. Probably this was the Henry Babb who married Elizabeth Walker, Jan. 31, 1793. If so, his parents were Peter and Mary (Bowen) Babb of Frederick County. Source: Tombstone inscription in Center Friends Burying Ground, Clinton County, Ohio.

Babb, Peter, son of Abner and Susannah (Robinson) Babb, was born in Frederick County, Virginia on Feb. 13, 1796 and died on Oct. 25, 1865 in Greene County, Ohio. He was buried at Woodland, Ohio. His wife was Jane Scharff, daughter of James and Mary (Hollingshead) Scharff. Jane was born on April 8, 1795 and died on Feb. 14, 1889. Her mother, Mary Hollingshead, was born on Dec. 5, 1761 in Virginia and died on July 30, 1853 in Ohio. One source: *History of Greene County, Ohio*, page 269, by George F. Robinson, published in 1902.

Bageant, Alice (Miss), died at home of Ves Bageant, Nov. 11, 1900 and was buried on Nov. 13th. Source: *Diary of George Edwards*, Cross Junction, Frederick County, Va.

Bageant, Abner Clark, son of John and Mary "Polly" (Clark) Bageant Jr., was born on Feb. 17, 1830, in Frederick County, Va. and died on May 29, 1868. He married Mary Ann Bohrer, daughter of Peter and Elizabeth (Shade) Bohrer. An old account book in my possession states" "This is to show that Abner C. Bageant Departed this life on the twenty-ninth of May 1868 and was thirty eight years three months and twelve days when he died." Another entry in the same book says, "Susan Bageant departed this life the third day of May 1907." Source: *Bageant Account Book*, in possession of Wilmer L. Kerns.

Bageant, Andrew Jackson, son of William and Elizabeth (Dick) Bageant, was born in Frederick County, Va. on Aug. 9, 1824 and died on July 2, 1902. He married Mary Ann (Hook) Mauzy, daughter of Samuel Hook and widow of Henry Mauzy. Source: A.J. Bageant was buried in the Bageant Family Graveyard in

Northern Frederick County, Va. Also, Mrs. Kathleen Fletcher of Littleton, CO, contributed data from her family files.

Bageant, Henry Jackson, son of Andrew Jackson and Mary Ann (Hook) Bageant, was born on March 10, 1859 and died on Aug. 21, 1939. He married Louisa Jane "Jennie" Kerns, daughter of Joseph and Lucy Margaret (Shuler) Kerns, on March 10, 1887. She was born on Feb. 24, 1864 and died on Dec. 15, 1937. Source: Tombstone inscriptions in Mt. Hebron (United Brethren in Christ) cemetery at Cross Junction, Frederick County, Va.

Bageant, Homer, was born in 1877 and died in 1928. His wife was Laura Estelle Sirbaugh, daughter of George Lemuel and Mary (Keiter) Sirbaugh. She was born on Sept. 12, 1878 in Smokey Hollow, Hampshire County, W.Va., and died on April 19, 1921. They had two children— Cleo and Estella Bageant— and they lived in the Timber Ridge area. Source: Sirbaugh family record maintained by Roger Sirbaugh of Paw Paw, W.Va.

Bageant, John, son of William and Eleanor Bageant, was born on Aug. 10, 1761 and died in 1832 in the northern "tip" of Frederick County, Va. Bageant moved to Frederick County, Va. from Frederick County, Md., in 1808. He married: (1) Catherine Whitnak on June 17, 1783 and (2) Catherine Lewis (1786-1855). Source: DAR records.

Bageant, John Jr., son of John and Catherine (Lewis) Bageant, was born in 1797 and died in July 1855, in Frederick County, Va. He married Mary "Polly" Clark, daughter of Abner and Isabel Clark, on Aug. 30, 1823. Polly was born in 1807 and died in 1857. Source: Tombstone inscriptions in Primitive Baptist Cemetery, Timber Ridge, Frederick County, Virginia and courthouse records.

Bageant, John W., was born on Dec. 23, 1819 and died on March 28, 1849, aged 32 years, 3 months, 5 days. Source: Tombstone inscription in Bageant family graveyard on Timber Ridge, Frederick County, Virginia.

Bageant, John Washington, was born in Frederick County, Va. on Dec. 23, 1816 and died on March 28, 1849. He married: (1) Isabella Ann Ware on Dec. 20, 1838 and (2) Sarah Ann Heironimus, on July 1, 1843. Source: Mrs. Kathleen Fletcher, Littleton, CO.

Bageant, John William, son of John W. and Mary "Polly" (Clark) Bageant, was born Oct. 14, 1843, and died Dec. 2, 1923. He married Harriett Jane Bohrer, Aug. 20, 1867. She was born May 2, 1842 and died March 5, 1922. They had five children: (1) Minnie V. Bageant married Offutt Peacemaker, son of Adam and Elizabeth C. (Johnson) Peacemaker. (2) Annie Luray Bageant married Edward Stine. (3) Dora Belle Bageant married Robert Eugene Borden. (4) Lilly Tamson Bageant married Eldon Luttrell. (5) Tenna Lee Bageant married Dustin Fearnow. Source: Bohrer papers of Frederick T. Newbraugh, Berkeley Springs, W.Va.

Bageant, Mary, daughter of John and Catherine (Lewis) Bageant, was born on Sept. 29, 1792 and died on April 30, 1875. She married Jacob Miller who died in 1873. According to Kathleen Fletcher of Littleton, CO, they emigrated from Frederick County, Va. to Kansas, and later settled in Van Buren County, Iowa.

Bageant, Mary Isabella, daughter of John W. and Mary "Polly" (Clark) Bageant, was born in 1837 and died in Frederick County, Va., Aug. 18, 1865. Her husband was John W. Heironimus.

Bageant, Mary Marie, daughter of William and Elizabeth (Dick) Bageant, was born on July 6, 1820 and died on Feb. 11, 1911. She married Michael M. Dolan on July 21, 1840. Source: Tombstone inscription in the Bageant family graveyard, on Timber Ridge, in northern Frederick County, Va., located in a field near an apple orchard operated by George Whitacre (1991).

Bageant, Sampson Clark, son of John and Mary "Polly" (Clark) Bageant, was born in Frederick County, Va. on April 20, 1827 and died on Sept. 13, 1869, aged 42 years, 4 months, 23 days. He married Susannah Hart on March 4, 1848. She was born on June 18, 1817 and died on May 3, 1907, aged 89 years, 10 months, 15 days. Source: Tombstone inscriptions in the Primitive Baptist Church Graveyard on Timber Ridge, Frederick County, Virginia, and *Bageant Account Book*, in possession of Wilmer L. Kerns.

Bageant, William, son of John and Catherine (Whitnak) Bageant, was born on Aug. 15, 1784 and died on Sept. 23, 1863. He married Elizabeth Dick on Nov. 19, 1813. She was born in 1789, and died in February 1860. The 1850 Mortality Schedule for Frederick County shows that she died of "dropsy," after a 120-day illness. Source: Tombstone inscriptions in Bageant family graveyard in northern Frederick County, Va.

Bajent (Bageant), William was "...an apprentice bound to Merback Sexton, being drafted in the militia for the span of 6 months to march against the Indians, ordered that the said Bajent do return to his said Master's Services as soon as the draft is expired, and that the said term be allowed in his service. At a court held for Frederick County, Va., Sept. 2, 1777. Heard by John Smith, Joseph Holmes, William Gibbs, Edward McGuire, and Thomas Helm (presiding), Gentlemen Justices." Source: *Minute Book 1773-1780*, Frederick County, Va. records in the Virginia State Archives.

Baker, Aaron Levi, married Mary Parrish, aged 54 years, Sept. 8, 1879. On Oct. 28, 1887, Aaron L., aged 72 years, remarried to Ann Hahn, aged 54 years, She was born in Shenandoah County, Va. Source: Marriage records in Hampshire County courthouse.

Baker, Asberry L., died in Mineral County, W.Va., aged seven years, in June 1870, of "measles." Source: 1870 Mortality Schedule for Mineral County, W.Va. (U.S. Census)

Baker, Benjamin F., was born on Jan. 1, 1812 and died May 25, 1896. His wife, Elizabeth, was born April 16, 1814 and died June 12, 1882. Source: Tombstone inscriptions in town cemetery, Wardensville, Hardy County, W.Va.

Baker, Cornelius, son of Jacob and Jemima (Ashbrook) Baker, was born in Hardy County, June 18, 1793, and died Oct. 13, 1865 in Richfield Township, _____ County, Illinois. His first wife, Phebe Switzer (Swisher), was born June 14, 1795 and died Nov. 29, 1829. They were married Dec. 19, 1815. His second wife was Lydia Arnett, born May 7, 1808 and died July 7, 1843, in Hampshire County. Source: Jim Welton, 12 Mill Stream Road, Upper Saddle River, NJ 07458

Baker, Eliza J., daughter of Isaac N. Wilson, was born on April 1, 1835 and died on Feb. 11, 1894. She was buried in the Baker private graveyard near Delray, Hampshire County, W.Va., and it is believed that she married one of the sons of Aaron and Malinda Baker.

Baker, Elizabeth, was born in Delaware in 1779, and died in Hardy County, Va. in January 1850, aged 70 years, "of dropsy." Source: 1850 Mortality Schedule for Hampshire County, Va.

Baker, Elizabeth, "widow," died in December 1859, aged 78 years. She suffered a 7-week illness before succumbing to "dropsy." Born in Virginia. Source: 1860 Mortality Schedule for Shenandoah County, Va.

Baker, Harriett C., was born Jan. 17, 1819 and died on Sept. 14, 1866. She was the first wife of John Cram Edwards (born on March 26, 1819). Sources: Tombstone inscription at the Cold Stream Episcopal Cemetery, Capon Bridge, W.Va., and from family records.

Baker, Jacob, son of John Baker, of Hampshire County, was born on March 14, 1805 and died April 25, 1856, in Adams County, Illinois. He married Sarah E. Rhinehart, daughter of Abraham and Mary (Ward) Rhinehart Jr. Sarah was born in 1813 and died in 1891. Source: Mrs. Janice Butler, 6708 North 31st Street, Arlington, Va. 22213.

Baker, Jacob V., son of Aaron L. and Malinda Baker, was born on Jan. 17, 1841. He was buried in the Baker graveyard south of Delray Post Office, on a bank of North River. His family Bible provides this information: His first wife, Hannah M. Perrill was born on May 15, 1851. His second wife, Elizabeth B. Strawderman was born on March 1, 1859. The children of Jacob V. Baker by both marriages were: John T.L. Jackson Baker was born on Oct. 3, 1871, and he married Alberta Combs; Mary Margaret L.R.L. Baker was born on May 11, 1873; James A.M. Baker was born on July 27, 1875; Joseph F. Baker was born on March 17, 1877; Charles H.S. Baker was born in March 1878; Harvey E. Baker was born on April 10, 1883 and died on Dec. 19, 1969; George Washington Baker was born on Dec. 5, 1878; Hezekiah Baker was born on June 22, 1884; Julias A. Baker was born in Nov. 1885; Grover Cleveland Baker was born on Nov. 15, 1887; Jesse Garn Baker was born on Nov. 27, 1889; Liza Virginia Baker was born on March 4, 1893 and she married James Croston; Jacob Washington Baker was born on May 18, 1895. Source: Copied from the Baker family Bible in the hands of Mrs. Otis B. Baker, Capon Bridge, W.Va. 26711.

Baker, James, was born on Dec. 7, 1808 and died on Jan. 17, 1858. Rebecca, his wife, was born on Jan. 7, 1811 and died on June 18, 1890. Buried nearby were: Henry F. Baker, born on Sept. 10, 1834 and died on Sept. 9, 1863; John W. Baker was born on Feb. 23, 1836 and died on Aug. 9, 1862; Isaac N. Baker was born on May 10, 1842 and died on July 22, 1926. His wife, Catherine, was born on Dec. 20, 1844 and died on Feb. 1, 1907 and; Joseph M. Smith, born on April 4, 1838 and died on Oct. 30, 1924. His wife, Sarah E., was born on Oct. 26, 1839 and died on

Jan. 1, 1920. Source: Graveyard inscriptions in a Baker cemetery located on Gilbert Park's place on North River Road, at Sedan, W.Va.

Baker, John,   died in Hampshire County in Jan. 1860, of bronchitus, aged 48 years. Source: 1860 Mortality Schedule for Hampshire County, Va.

Baker, Julian, died in Hampshire County, Va., May 1850, aged 18 years, of "consumption." Source: Mortality Schedule of 1850 U.S. Census.

Baker, Malinda, "consort of Aaron L. Baker," was born on Oct. 2, 1812 and died on Feb. 19, 1879. Next to Malinda's grave is her husband's, Aaron L. Baker, with uninscribed river stones for head-and-foot-markers. The private graveyard is located in isolated brush and briars, south of Delray, W.Va. on the bank of North River.

Baker, Otis B., was born in Romney, W.Va. on Feb. 21, 1910 and died May 24, 1987, at Capon Bridge, W.Va. He married Audrey (Sine) Baker. Otis was buried in the Ebenezer Cemetery on Branch Mountain, along U.S. Route 50. His wife, Audrey, has assisted this compiler in collecting genealogical records for more than a decade.

Baker, Phebe, wife of Cornelius Baker, was born on June 14, 1795 and died on Dec. 15, 1829. Buried nearby: Jacob N. Baker was born on Sept. 18, 1826 and died on Sept. 12, 1830 and; Rebecca Wilson, Sept. 1841. According to Mrs. Eldora Park, who lives near Sedan, W.Va., on the Delray Road, tombstones were removed some years ago and Denny's Garage now sets on the old graveyard site.

Baldwin, David, was born in Chester County, PA on Aug. 1, 1748. His second wife, Sarah, was born June 7, 1751. David's third wife was Margaret (Rees) Ellis, widow of Thomas Ellis. They were married in Frederick County, Va. on June 26, 1802, by John Newbraugh. David Baldwin served in the Revolutionary War, in a Chester County militia. It is believed that he came to Frederick or Berkeley County, Va. circa 1786. Contact: Mrs. Pauline Allen, Route 4, Box 62, Scottsburg, IN 47170.

Baldwin, William, son of David and Sarah Baldwin, was born in PA on April 16, 1782 and died in Scott County, IN on March 6, 1842. William married Elizabeth Mann, Nov. 28, 1805, in Frederick

County, Va. Elizabeth died circa 1838, in Tuscarawas County, Ohio. They emigrated from Frederick County to Ohio, about 1813. They had at least nine children. Source: Mrs. Pauline Allen, same as last entry above.

Baldwin, William, and his wife Mary were early settlers in old Frederick County, Va. Their children were: William Baldwin Jr., born Oct. 8, 1744; Thomas Baldwin, born Sept. 2, 1746; John Baldwin, born Feb. 21, 1749; Rebecca Baldwin, born Sept. 3, 1751; Mary Baldwin, born April 16, 1754; Francis Baldwin, born Nov. 27, 1756; and Benjamin Baldwin, born May 21, 1759. Source: Morgan Chapel Register, 1741-1838, Norborne Parish (now Berkeley County, W.Va.)

Banks, Patsy, died on Feb. 14, 1873, aged 66 years. Source: Tombstone inscription found in woods, below (outside) the Indian Mound cemetery, Romney, W.Va. Patsy was obviously a black American.

Barnes, Rebecca, was born in Maryland in 1809 and died in Sept. 1859, in Hampshire County, "of typhoid fever." Source: 1860 Mortality Schedule for Hampshire County, Va.

Barnes, Mrs. Susan, widow of William Barnes, died on March 12, 1877, aged 83 years. Source: March 23, 1877 issue of the *South Branch Intelligencer*, Romney, W.Va.

Barr, Peter, died in Grant County, W.Va. on Sept. 18, 1870, aged 74 years. Source: Sept. 30, 1874 issue of the *South Branch Intelligencer* newspaper.

Barrett, Mrs., died in Capon Valley on June 29, 1855. Joseph Barrett ordered a coffin to be made for her by William Meade Edwards, a coffin-maker from Cold Stream, Hampshire County, Va. (Question: Could this have been Hester (Newbanks) Barrett?)

Barton, Richard W., died in January 1860, aged 61 years. He was survived by his wife. Born in Virginia, his occupation was listed as a farmer. Cause of death was "inflammation of the bowels," and the duration of his illness was one-half day. It is believed that this is the same as an "intestinal obstruction," in contemporary medical classification. Source: 1860 Mortality Schedule for Frederick County, Va.

Batt, Sarah, was born in Virginia in 1766 and died in Frederick County in March 1850, of "old age." She was ill for three days prior to her death, according to her attending physician. Source: 1850 Mortality Schedule for Frederick County, Va.

Beale, Eli, son of Elisha and Ann (Parrill) Beale, died at Capon Bridge on Nov. 14, 1870, aged 81 years, according to a courthouse death record. His wife was Margaret Caudy, daughter of James and Elizabeth (Lyons) Caudy. She was born on Nov. 11, 1799 and died on June 1, 1873. His tombstone inscription shows a birthdate of March 25, 1789 and deathdate of Nov. 14, 1870. Sources: Courthouse death record and tombstone inscription at Capon Chapel, Capon Bridge, W.Va.

Beale, Sarah, daughter of William and Rachel (Parry) Beale, was born on Sept. 14, 1784 and died on Jan. 6, 1818. She was the first wife of John Keiter, son of George and Esther (Buzzard) Keiter. They were married on Oct. 27, 1816 and one child was born to this union. Sarah was buried in the Buckwalter cemetery in the Bloomery District of Hampshire County. Source: Keiter family Bible record provided by Mrs. Gladys Crouse, Paw Paw, W.Va.

Beale, William, son of William and Grace (Gill) Beale, Sr., of Bucks County, Pennsylvania, was born on Aug. 12, 1752. He married Rachel Parry on Jan. 30, 1779. After her death, William, Jr. remarried to Mary McClun, daughter of Thomas and Hannah McClun, on Aug. 15, 1798. They resided in northern Frederick County, Virginia. Source: Mr. Terry C. Thompson, 140 Woodberry Road, N.W., Leesburg, Va. 22075.

Beall, Octavio, "widowed," died in June 1860, aged 86 years, after an illness of 365 days. Born in Maryland. Source: 1860 Mortality Schedule for Frederick County, Va.

Bean, Ann, died in Hardy County, Va. in September 1849, aged 58 years. Cause of death was "opium usage." She was born in Maryland. Source: 1850 U.S. Mortality Census.

Bean, Thomas, died March 3, 1758. Source: Records of Morgan's Chapel, Norborne Parish (now Berkeley County, W.Va.)

Beard, George, was born in 1732 and died in Hampshire County on March 10, 1820. He served in the Revolutionary War. Sources: DAR record and tombstone inscription in Thompson cemetery near Three Churches, Hampshire County, W.Va.

Beery, David, son of Abraham and Barbara (Good) Beery, was born in Rockingham County, Va. on Oct. 8, 1808 and died at Augusta, W.Va. on March 7, 1883. He had just started west in 1847 but his first wife became ill and died enroute, at Levels, Va., in Hampshire County. She was nee Elizabeth NISWANDER, born on Sept. 18, 1808 and died on June 18, 1848. After her death, David remarried to Susannah ROHRBAUGH in March 1849. She was born in Rockingham County, Va. on March 24, 1808 and died on Nov. 9, 1892. David and Susannah were buried on the Jacob D. Beery farm near Augusta, W.Va., in a family plot. As you approach this farm, you will sense the Mennonite heritage in as expressed through the design of the house, barn and outbuildings. Source: Dorothy Beery, SR 2 Box 171, Augusta, W.Va. 26704.

Bennett, Cornelius B., born on July 8, 1824 and died on March 26, 1890, aged 60 years, 8 months, 18 days. Source: Tombstone inscriptions in Park's Graveyard, Parke's Valley, Hampshire County, W.Va.

Bennett, Isaac Newton, died on Nov. 9, 1869, age 45 years and 7 months. He married Margaret Oates, daughter of George Oates. Source: His death was announced in the *South Branch Intelligencer*, Romney, W.Va.

Bennett, James, born on June 25, 1787 and died on Feb. 2, 1852. His wife, Mary D., was born on Oct. 18, 1795 and died on Jan. 20, 1868. Source: Tombstone inscriptions in Park's Graveyard, Parke's Valley, Hampshire County, W.Va.

Berry, George, died on June 6, 1873, at Bentonville, Clinton County, Ohio. He married Sally Floyd on April 15, 1815, in Hampshire County, Va. She died on April 14, 1880. Source: War of 1812 Pension Application Records, National Archives, Washington, D.C.

Berry, William, was born in 1753 and died in Hampshire County on May 22, 1836. According to his Revolutionary War pension record, he married Elizabeth Watkins on May 22, 1793, in Loudoun County, Va. She was still alive in May 1855, aged 96 years, living with her son, George Berry, in Butler County, Ohio. Source: Military pension record of William Berry in National Archives, Washington, D.C.

Bethel, Joshua, son of George and Jane Bethel, was born on April 14, 1791 and died on May 4, 1873, in Trimble Township, Athens County, Ohio. He married Nancy Kidwell, daughter of John and Ellen Kidwell. One source hints that Nancy was twice-married (first to a Mr. Taylor) but this is an allegation rather than a proven fact. Nancy was born on Oct. 31, 1797 and died on July 12, 1870. Joshua and Nancy were buried in the Bethel Ridge cemetery, in Trimble Township. Joshua's father, George Bethel, died in Hampshire County, Va. on May 5, 1810, and was buried in the Quaker Cemetery near Dillon Run, in unmarked grave. It is believed that the Bethel family came from Loudoun County, Va. [Note: The Bethel research is ongoing, and you are urged to get in touch with a family researcher and descendant: Roy Bethel, 211 West Street, Groveport, Ohio 43125.]

Biser, Nicholas, (born in 1784), died on April 23, 1880, in Mineral County, aged 95 and one-half years, according to the March 5, 1880 issue of the *South Branch Intelligencer*. His wife was Susan Arnold, daughter of the Rev. Samuel Arnold, Jr. She died on Sept. 27, 1878, aged 89 years, 6 months, 29 days, at the home of Peter Biser, In Mineral County, W.Va.

Blaker, Fenton D., son of John Blaker, was born in Loudoun County, Va. in 1822 and died in Bloomery District, Hampshire County, W.Va., on Sept. 11, 1886. He married Eveline Grove on Oct. 26, 1841. Source: Family records maintained by descendants.

Blue, Charles, was born on Dec. 28, 1801 and died on March 21, 1863. His wife, Mary C., was born on Feb. 3, 1811 and died on Jan. 31, 1870. Source: Tombstone inscriptions in Indian Mound Cemetery in Romney, W.Va.

Blue, Capt. Garrett I., aged 78, died on June 21, 1872, at his home on the South Branch. Source: The June 28, 1872 issue of the *South Branch Intelligencer*, Romney, W.Va.

Blue, Garrett W., died "last Tuesday," aged 81 years. He was an uncle of Mrs. Susan Parsons. Source: The June 21, 1872 issue of the *South Branch Intelligencer*, Romney, W.Va.

Blue, Scotia, wife of Uriah Blue, and daughter of Abraham and Annie Inskeep, died in Springfield, W.Va., April 3, 1874, in her 58th year. Source: *South Branch Intelligencer*, issue of April 10, 1874.

Blue, Uriah, died on May 3, 1854, aged 74 years. His wife, Elizabeth, died Oct. 30, 1857, aged 80 years.

Blue, Uriah L., born on Dec. 9, 1807 and died on April 15, 1864. Source: Tombstone inscription in Indian Mound cemetery in Romney, W.Va.

Bohrer, Augustus, died on March 30, 1894, aged 73 years, 2 months, 1 day, according to a tombstone inscription in the Timber Ridge Primitive Baptist Church, Frederick County, Va.

Bohrer, John Adam, was born on March 12, 1758 and died in Morgan County, Va., after his Will was filed on March 18, 1829 and before it was probated in 1831. Bondsmen to the writing of his Will were: Benedict Omps, Joshua Tyson, and John Stotler. Adam Bohrer's wife was named Lucinda, and these were their children: (1) Isaac Bohrer was born on March 13, 1780 and his Will was filed in Morgan County, Va. on March 30, 1848. Isaac married Elizabeth Dick, daughter of Peter Dick. (2) Abraham Bohrer was born in Oct. 9, 1785 and married Elizabeth ____. (3) Elizabeth Bohrer was born on Jan. 19, 1787. She married George Widmyer. (4) Barbara Bohrer was born on Feb. 6, 1790, and died in Morgan County in 1865. She married her cousin, George Bohrer (1783-1860), on May 29, 1818, in Berkeley County, Va. George was a practicing physician in Morgan County, Va. (5) Druella Bohrer was born on July 15, 1791. She married William Bailey and they were living in Ross County, Ohio in 1831 (6) Rosannah Bohrer was born on Sept. 2, 1792. She married Philip Walters and they were living in Tippacanoe County, Indiana in 1831. (7) Jacob Bohrer was born on Jan. 2, 1794. He married Elizabeth Marple, daughter of Enoch Marple, Jr. (8) Mary "Polly" Bohrer was born on April 7, 1795, and married a Mr. Gray. Source: Based on information provided to me by Mr. Frederick T. Newbraugh, historian of Morgan County, W.Va., who is also a Bohrer descendant.

Boseley, Jacob, son of James Boseley, was born in Pennsylvania in 1778 and died in Grant County, W.Va., December 1869, aged 91 years. Source: 1870 Mortality Schedule for Grant County, W.Va.

Boseley, James, was born circa 1744 and died in 1834 in Hampshire County, Va. (probably in present-day Mineral County, W.Va.). His wife was named Elizabeth. Some of their descendants were listed as mulattoes on the U.S. censuses. Prior to settling in Hampshire County, they lived in Frederick County, Maryland, and probably in Pennsylvania.

Bosley, Eleanor, died Nov. 1849, of chlorea, in Hampshire County, aged 77 years. (Her parents were James and ElizabethBosley.) Source: 1850 Mortality Schedule for Hampshire County, Va.

Bowen, Priscilla, dau. of Henry and Jean (Carter) Bowen, was born in 1718, possibly in Chester County, Pennsylvania and died on Feb. 17, 1796 near Uniontown, Fayette County, PA. It has been said that her marked grave is the oldest in the County. She married William Gaddis. They lived along the Opequon Creek in Frederick County, Va. during the 1740's and early 1750's, before taking up a Fairfax grant in Hampshire County, Va. Gaddis died in 1773 and was buried on his 421 acre farm, on the foothill of Bear Garden Mountain, Hampshire County. Ironically, his grave is probably the oldest inscribed tombstone in Hampshire County. See stories and pictures of this old grave, published in the Oct. and Nov., 1986 issues of *The West Virginia Advocate*, Capon Bridge, W.Va. 26711.

Bowman, Eleanor, daughter of John and Rose Arnold, was born in Hampshire County in 1806 and died on Aug. 17, 1879. Her husband was Andrew Bowman, according to a death record in the Hampshire County, W.Va. Courthouse.

Bowman, Mary, died on March 25, 1831, two years after her marriage. She was 24 years old at the time of death. Source: An old cemetery at Highview, on Timber Ridge. It is believed this was the first cemetery of the Timber Ridge Christian Church. Inscriptions were copied by Dan P. Oates of Romney, W.Va.

Boxwell, Winny Ann, died on May 23, 1876, aged 48 years, 6 months, 16 days. On the 1850 census, she was living with the Jacob and Elizabeth Critton family. Source: Tombstone inscription in the Bethel Methodist Graveyard, Okonoko, Hampshire County, W.Va.

Brady, Hannah, wife of John Brady, was born Oct. 5, 1795 and died Dec. 12, 1881. Source: Tombstone inscription, Springfield, W.Va.

Brady, John, was born in 1789 and died on Dec. 30, 1857 at Springfield. Source: Tombstone inscription.

Brady, John, was born in 1806 in Hardy County, Va. and died in Braxton County, W.Va., Aug. 27, 1874. His wife, Elizabeth, was born in 1805. They had these children: James, Christena, Solomon, William, Edmond, Andrew, Sarah, and Catherine Brady. Source: Evan H. Brady, 412 Everett Place, Romney, W.Va. 26757.

Brady, James M., was born on Oct. 20, 1816 and died in April 1902. Source: Tombstone inscription, Springfield, W.Va.

Brady, William, son of Joshua and Mary Brady, died on July 12, 1866, aged 59 years. He was born "in Berkeley County, Va.," and worked as a miller. William's wife was Catherine Fresett.

Braithwaite- I have extensive, unpublished records on this family name and will exchange data. Write to: Wilmer L. Kerns, 4715 North 38th Place, Arlington, Va. 22207.

Braithwaite, John A., son of John and Susan (Farmer) Braithwaite, was born on Janaury 23, 1832 and died in 1925. He married: (1) Sidney Ann Grove, daughter of Henry and Phebe Grove, in 1865. She was born on Jan. 1, 1842 and died on Jan. 12, 1875, aged 33 years and 11 days. (2) Rhoda A. Hughes, born on Feb. 17, 1858 and died on March 23, 1903. Source: Tombstone inscriptions in the Primitive Baptist Church graveyard, Frederick County, Va.

Braithwaite, Martha, wife of Henry Sylvester Braithwaite, was born on Jan. 9, 1835 in Frederick County, Va. and died in Bloom Township, Richland County, Wisconsin, on Nov. 19, 1871. They resided in Fayette County or Madison County, Ohio during the Civil War. Her parents were Elisha and Rachel (Whitacre) Kerns. Henry was a son of William and Alena (King) Braithwaite Jr. William Jr. was born in Frederick County, Va., Dec. 25, 1787 and died in Ohio, circa 1865. Source: Wayne Braithwaite, 508 South Central Ave., Richland Center, WI 53581.

Braithwaite, William Farmer, son of John and Susan (Farmer) Braithwaite, was born on May 1, 1830 and died on April 12, 1904. His wife, Mary Sophia Grove, was born on Nov. 19, 1834 and died on Feb. 6, 1910. His obituary in the Winchester paper, dated April 15, 1904, stated that he was well-known as a school trustee and magistrate, gaining the title of Squire. He was a prominent person in the sawmilling industry.. Burial was at the Timber Ridge Primitive Baptist Church in Frederick County, Va., where the tombstones are inscribed. [Comment: My grandfather, Robert R. Kerns, was very fond of Will Braithwaite, and used to talk about him when I was young. Grandpa claimed that Mr. Braithwaite influenced him to go into the teaching profession, and gave him a position at the Railroad Union School at Cross Junction, Va., in 1896-97.]

Branson, Lionel, was born circa 1752 and died in Hardy County, Va. on March 21, 1810, in his 58th year. His wife, Rebecca Branson, was born on Feb. 19, 1753 and died Aug. 25, 1825. They were buried in the Wood-Branson cemetery at Lost River, Hardy County, W.Va.   Source: Information provided by Wendell F. Inskeep, 3223 Bobwhite Place, Beavercreek, OH 45431.

Brelsford, Bernard, was born circa 1755 and died in 1843 in Hampshire County. His wife (possibly a second marriage?) was Naomi (Edwards) Owens, a daughter of Thomas and Sarah (Hiett) Edwards. Source: Courthouse records.

Brelsford, David, died in Hampshire County in May 1850, aged 86 years. This would place his birth year circa 1764. His place of birth not stated, although some researchers have speculated in Pennsylvania. His exact relationship with Bernard, Marjoram and other Brelsfords is not known. Source: Mortality Schedule of the 1850 Census, Hampshire County, Va.

Brelsford, Elizabeth, wife of Thomas Brelsford, was born in Loudoun County, Va. in 1808 and died in Hampshire County on Oct. 18, 1875. Her parents were Spencer and Nancy Walker, according to her death record which is in the Hampshire County courthouse.

Brelsford, Jesse, died on Oct. 9, 1882, aged 74 years. He was an unmarried son of David and M. Brelsford. His death was reported to the County Clerk by Eliza J. Braman, niece.   The *Undertaker Book* of John W. Mellon shows a journal date of Oct. 31, 1882 (which was possibly the date of burial). Jesse's brother Thomas Brelsford paid $12.00 for the funeral costs.

Brelsford, Jesse, was deceased before Sept. 16, 1847, according to *Order Book II*, page 235, Circuit Court of Hampshire County, W.Va. His wife, Mary, was left to raise these children: Mahala Brelsford; George Washington Brelsford; Jesse Lewis Brelsford; John Francis Edward Brelsford; James William

Brelsford; Ann Maria Brelsford; Margaret Ellen Brelsford; Mary Ann Brelsford. See, also, Deed Book 42, page 518, Hampshire County Court, dated Nov. 10, 1849. Lands were sold to Christopher Slonaker, which adjoined Charles Gill, Abrell heirs, et. al. Jesse was a veteran of the War of 1812. According to records in the National Archives (War of 1812 pension), Jesse died on Nov. 29, 1845. He married Mary Jacobs on Jan. 14, 1814.

Brelsford, Marjoram, was born circa 1762 and died in 1841. He married Eve Horn, daughter of George Horn. Sources: Courthouse Wills by Brelsford and Horn; U.S. Census.

Brelsford, Margaret (female), was 86 years old when the 1850 census was taken, meaning a birthyear of circa 1764. In the household was Mary Brelsford, age 41 and Milly Brelsford, age 37. Source: 1850 U.S. Census for Hampshire County, Va., Family # 535.

Brelsford, Nathan, was born in Hampshire County, Va. and died on July 29, 1839. He married Elizabeth Ann Garner, daughter of Henry Garner of Frederick County, Va. They emigrated to Kentucky during the latter part of 18th century, and later lived in Ohio. His eldest son was named Marjoram, an old family name which suggests a close relationship with the Hampshire County Brelsfords.

Brelsford, James, W., son of Nathan and Peggy (McDonald) Brelsford, was born on Sept. 4, 1840 and died on Nov. 9, 1916. He served in Civil War, Co. K, 15th Va. Regiment. Source: Tombstone inscription in old Benjamin McDonald's graveyard, North River, below Ice Mountain, Hampshire County, W.Va.

Brelsford, Zebedee, was born on April 12, 1812 and died in Morgan County, W.Va. in Aug. 1871. He was employed as a guard on the railroad, and "was shot." Zebedee was a widower. Source: Morgan County, W.Va. courthouse death record.

Brill, Alice May, wife of L.H. Brill, died on May 7, 1891, aged 23 years, 3 months. Source: Tombstone inscription in the Evan Hiett graveyard on Sandy Ridge, Hampshire County, now owned by Mr. John Whitacre.

Brill, Henry, of Lowman's Branch, Hampshire County, Va., was born circa 1765 and died in 1834. Occupation was farming. He married Elizabeth Orndorff, daughter of Johannes and Elizabeth (Mentz) Orndorff, on Dec. 11, 1796. According to the *South*

Branch Intelligencer, issue of May 31, 1867, Elizabeth died on April 12, 1867, in Hampshire County, W.Va. The paper stated that she had 14 children, 89 grandchildren and 133 great-grandchildren. The number of great-great grandchildren was not reported.

Brill, Henry, was born in 1765 and died in Frederick County, Va., July 1849. Occupation was farming. Henry was paralyzed, and he was ill for 300 days prior to his death. His wife survived him. Source: 1850 Mortality Schedule for Frederick County, Va.

Brill, Magdalene, died in March 1850, aged 85 years. She was ill for 70 days, and was listed as a widow. She was born in Virginia. Source: 1850 Mortality Schedule for Frederick County, Va.

Broughton, William, was born circa 1732 and died in 1797 in Hardy County, Va. His wife was named Hannah, and they raised at least six children. Source: Mrs. Richard Arnold, 1600 Beaucaire Drive, St. Louis, MO 63122.

Brown, Adam, was born Aug. 16, 1767 and died in Frederick County, March 18, 1831. He was superintendent of the Frederick County Poor Farm. Adam married Christina Zuber, daughter of Martin and Catherine Zuber, June 6, 1799. Source: Bible record.

Bruce, John, was one of the early "Opeckin settlers" in old Frederick County, Va. He was born circa 1690, probably in Scotland, and came to Chester County, Penn. circa 1730 or earlier. He settled along Opequon Creek during the early 1730's and died there. His Will, filed on Nov. 1, 1748, mentioned his wife Sarah. Brucetown, a community known for its flour mills, was named after this Bruce family. A book was recently published on the Bruce family. Contact: Ms. Violet Bruce, 1520 La Sierra Road, Fort Worth, Texas 76134.

Brumbeck, George, "a mullatto," died in June 1860, aged 91 years, of "consumption." He was born in Virginia, and the duration of his illness was 365 days. Source: 1860 Mortality Schedule for Frederick County, Va.

Bruner, Henry, was born in Frederick County, Va. on May 27, 1803 and died on Aug. 26, 1882, in LaSalle County, Illinois. His wife was Mary Ann Matthews, born in 1801 in Loudoun County, Va. and died on Dec. 20, 1873, in LaSalle County, Ill. Her parents were Richard and Elizabeth (Wolfcale) Matthews, of Loudoun

County, Va. Source: Mrs. Nancy Jane Cotton, 1704 Leawood Drive, Edmond, OK 73034.

Bryan, Jonathan (son of Thomas), was born June 30, 1818 and died Oct. 29, 1854. Source: Tombstone inscription, Springfield, Hampshire County, W.Va.

Bryan, Massa ("wife of Thomas," "our mother"), was born on May 4, 1782 and died Dec. 31, 1854. Source: Tombstone inscription, Springfield, W. Va.

Bryan, Morgan, was born circa 1671 and died in the Yadkin Valley of North Carolina on April 3, 1763. His wife was Martha Strode, born circa 1697 and died on Aug. 24, 1762, according to a tombstone inscription. Morgan Bryan was listed on the Tax Roll for Birmingham Township, Chester County, PA in 1719. During the 1720's he appeared on the tax lists of Marlboro Township, Chester County, PA. Morgan is believed to have been a trader which brought him to old Frederick County, Va. during the 1720's. In 1730, he and Alexander Ross presented a colonization plan to Governor William Gooch for a 100,000 acre grant, provided that 100 families would be brought in within two years. The new settlement was on the basin of Opequon Creek, bounded by North Mountain to the west and the Potomac River to the north. At that time "old Frederick County, Va." was still a part of Spotsylvania County, Virginia. I am currently researching this settlement. By-and-large, the new settlement was successfully made by Quakers, although Morgan Bryan was probably not a Quaker. In 1748, with the development completed, Bryan and his family moved to the Forks of the Yadkin, in what is now Anson County, North Carolina.

Buck, Thomas, son of Charles Buck, of Mt. Pleasant, Warren County, Va., was born Nov. 15, 1780, according to a letter that he wrote to the editor of *Zion's Advocate*, dated July 15, 1854. This periodical was published by John Clark at Front Royal, Va. Buck was a preacher in the Old School (anti-missionary) Baptist Church.

Buckwalter, Anthony, son of Jacob and Mary Magdalene (Acre) Buckwalter, was born at Phoenixville, Pennsylvania on Dec. 29, 1786 and died at Bloomery, Hampshire County, W.Va. on Aug. 10, 1868. He married Mary Buzzard, daughter of John and Mary (High) Buzzard, on June 18, 1818 in Berkeley County, Virginia. She was born on Sept. 11, 1797 and died on Sept. 1, 1874. He lived to be 82 years old. They had 13 children: Mary, Sarah, George, David, Elizabeth, Jacob, John, Susan, Daniel, Maria, Esther Ann, Virginia and Joseph Buckwalter.

Buckwalter, David H., was born in 1824 and died on July 20, 1905. Source: Tombstone inscriptions in the Gaddis graveyard in Bloomery District in Hampshire County, W.Va.

Buckwalter, John B., was born in 1831 and died on Feb. 15, 1918. Source: Tombstone inscription in Gaddis graveyard on Bear Garden Mountain, Hampshire County, W.Va.

Buckwalter, Joseph, son of Anthony and Mary (Buzzard) Buckwalter, was born at Bloomery, Virginia on July 19, 1841. In 1872 he immigrated to Greene County, Ohio. On May 26, 1874, he married Esther Jane Keiter, daughter of Frederick and Mary (Weaver) Keiter. She was the ninth of twelve children born in herKeiter family unit. Source: *History of Greene County, Ohio*.

Buckwalter, Sarah, was born on Aug. 4, 1770 and died on July 30, 1851. She was buried near Anthony Buckwalter in the family graveyard at Bloomery, Hampshire County.

Burke, Malachi, was born in Maryland in 1783 and died in Hampshire County in 1870, according to the 1870 Mortality Schedule for Hampshire County, W.Va. The *South Branch Intelligencer*, issue of June 17, 1870, stated that "Malcijah Burke," aged 87 years, died on June 6, 1870. He was a Veteran of the War of 1812.

Burkett, Isaiah, a former resident of Hampshire County, died recently in Peoria County, Illinois, according to the Oct. 10, 1879 issue of the *South Branch Intelligencer*. His wife, Margaret, nee Patterson, died on March 16, 1878, in Peoria County, aged 75 years, 5 months, 13 days. She was born in Hampshire County, Va. on Aug. 29, 1804, according to the April 12, 1878 issue of the *South Branch Intelligencer*.

Burkett, Thomas A., died on Sept. 26, 1892; aged 77 yrs., 10 mo, 1 day. Source: Tombstone inscriptions in graveyard at Three Churches, Hampshire County, W.Va.

Burner, Isaac, of Shendandoah County, Va., died in Frederick County, Va., "of a waggon wheel running over his head," on Jan. 26, 1822. A hearing was held at the home of Ellis Long in

Stephensburg, Va., to obtain details of the accident. Source: Frederick County, Va., "Inquisition of Dead Bodies," Virginia State Archives, Richmond, Va.

Burton, Jane, drowned in Brush Creek, Frederick County, Va., on Oct. 8, 1854. Source: "Inquisition of Dead Bodies," Virginia State Archives.

Butler, Thomas Sr., was born in old Frederick County, Va. on May 6, 1747 and died in Wayne County, OH, Sept. 22, 1825. He married Rebecca Daugherty. Their children were: Elizabeth, Sarah, Mary, Jonathan, Elijah, Thomas, Priscilla, Rachel, and Rebecca Butler. Contact: Roberta E. Johnson, 1510 NW Menlo Drive, Corvallis, OR 97330.

Buzzard, David, son of John and Mary (High) Buzzard, was born in Hampshire County on April 16, 1796 and died in Indiana in 1870. He married Louisa Baker (1800-1869), a daughter of Jacob H. and Maria Barbara (Heironimus) Baker, on Feb. 1, 1822. Jacob H. Baker was born on April 29, 1770 and Maria Barbara (Heironimus) Baker was born on June 16, 1777. Source: Family records.

Buzzard, Elizabeth, daughter of Frederick and Susannah (Buckwalter) Buzzard, was born in 1765-66 at Phoenixville, PA and died on April 18, 1840, aged 74 years, in Smokey Hollow, Hampshire County, Va. She married Peter Mauzy Sr., Source: Tombstone inscription in Mauzy graveyard, Hampshire County, W.Va.

Buzzard, Elizabeth, was deceased before 1848, according to *Order Book II*, page 309, Circuit Court of Hampshire County, W.Va.

B(uzzard), I. or F., died May 3, 1853 at Bloomery, Va. Buried in the old German cemetery known as "Buckwalter's," but was a colonial cemetery of the Gaddis family.

Buzzard, Jasper N., 1842-1919, was buried at Mt. Bethel, Three Churches, W.Va.

Buzzard, John, son of Frederick and Susannah (Buckwalter) Buzzard, Sr., was born in 1761 in Phoenixville, Pennsylvania; died in Hampshire County, Va. in 1811. He served in the Revolutionary War, then married Mary High circa 1786.

Buzzard, William, of Hampshire County, had these children: Jacob N. Buzzard died during the Civil War. Carlton J. Buzzard, William G. Buzzard, Henry Buzzard, John Buzzard, Slyvester Buzzard, and George Buzzard died intestate during the Civil War. Source: Circuit Court of Hampshire County, W.Va., Box 238, in chancery suit dated Oct. 9, 1873.

C., H., is inscribed on a stone in the Thomas Edwards, graveyard at Cold Stream, Hampshire County, Va. The year of death is not legible, but it says, "H.C. died March 31st, ____, 56 years old." This is a very old stone, in an old cemetery where burials were commenced during the late 1700's. Could it be, Cram, Caudy, Cheshire, Cooper, Capper....?

Caldwell, Andrew, died July 4, 1758. Source: Records in Morgan's Chapel, Norborne Parish (now Bunker Hill, Berkeley County, W.Va.)

Calvert, Jesse, was born on Aug. 31, 1804 and died on April 21, 1863. His wife was Sarah Ann McKee, born on Dec. 16, 1805. They lived in Frederick County, Va. Source: Records maintained by Ralph L. Triplett Esq.

Cann, Jacob, was born on Jan. 27, 1805 and died on Aug. 5, 1881, in the Cacapon District of Morgan County, W.Va. His wife, Susan Spohr, died on Aug. 15, 1889, aged 77 years, "of rheumatism," according to a death record in the Morgan County, W.Va. courthouse. Jacob Cann's estate sale bill was filed in the Morgan County courthouse, *Inventory and Estate Settlement Book # 1*, page 503, dated Oct. 25, 1881. The Cann family resided in the Great Cacapon area of Morgan County.

Capper, Gabriel, died on March 21, 1873, in Deerville, Harrison County, Ohio. He married Malinda Chamberlin on Oct. 13, 1819 in Hampshire County, Va. She died on March 9, 1886 in Harrison County, Ohio. Source: War of 1812 Pension Application, National Archives, Washington, D.C.

Capper, Michael, allegedly born in Ireland, in 1756 and died near Timber Ridge, June 15, 1804. His wife, Sarah Stewart, was born circa 1760 and died in April 1808. They were early settlers in western Frederick and eastern Hampshire Counties, Va. Source: Adele Kail Loudermilk, 1067 Concord, Costa Mesa, CA 92626.

Capper, William, "Michael Capper's son (William) died about one year ago, with the fevers, aged about twenty years old."

Source: Letter from Simeon and Sarah Ward, High View, Va., to John Bruner, LaSalle County, Illinois, dated May 22, 1844.

Carder, J.F., died on March 3, 1920, aged 76 years. Source: Tombstone inscription in Benjamin McDonald's old graveyard, on North River, downstream from Ice Mountain, Hampshire County, W.Va.

Carder, John, aged 80 years, died in Hampshire County on July 17, 1879. Source: July 25, 1879 issue of the *South Branch Intelligencer*.

Carder, John, died on July 24, 1879, aged 88 (or 80) years. Source: Tombstone inscription at Three Churches, Hampshire County, W.Va.

Carder, William, died in Hampshire County in September 1849, aged 78 years. Letty Carder, aged 75 years, died in Hampshire County in July 1849, of paralysis. Both were born in Virginia. Source: 1850 Mortality Census of U.S. Census.

Carlyle, Ann was born on July 22, 1746 and died on April 22, 1831. She was buried in the Carlyle cemetery near Capon Bridge. Her husband, William Carlyle, was buried next to her, with only an unmarked, high-quality, stone to identify the place. It is believed that his vital years were 1730-1831. Samuel Kercheval interviewed William Carlyle for his history book which was later published, in 1833. Source: Tombstone inscription in Carlyle graveyard, Capon Bridge, W.Va.

Carlyle, Benjamin F., was born on April 2, 1832 and died on Feb. 12, 1913. His wife, Bettie (Haines) Carlyle, was born on March 6, 1840 and died on Nov. 16, 1918. Source: Tombstone inscriptions in the Green Lane cemetery located near Delray, W.Va.

Carlyle, Charles, was born in 1773; died on April 7, 1849. Buried in the Carlyle cemetery at Capon Bridge. Believe his wife was buried next to him, but the stone is no longer there. Source: Cemetery inscription.

Carlyle, Charles died at Cold Stream in Hampshire County, on Jan. 31, 1862. His mother ordered his coffin, but did not give his age. Source: *Coffin Book* kept by William Meade Edwards, undertaker at Cold Stream, Hampshire County, Va.

Carlyle, David, married Mary Edwards, daughter of Thomas and Martha (Keener) Edwards, II. Source: Hampshire County courthouse deed, Book 23, page 472, dated in the year 1823.

Carlyle, Elizabeth, was born in Hampshire County, Va. on Feb. 22, 1792 and died at Lexington, Missouri on Jan. 12, 1892. Her husband, Henry Wallace, was born on March 24, 1792 and died on May 27, 1875. Source: Tombstone inscriptions, Lafayette County, Missouri.

Carlyle, "Jack" (John), was dead by 1844. In a letter from the Rev. Simion and Sarah Ward, of High View, W.Va., to John Bruner, Ottoway, LaSalle County, Illinois, dated May 23, 1844, he stated: "Old Jack Carlyle is dead, he died very suddenly." A copy of the letter was submitted to me by Nancy J. Cotton of Edmond, Oklahoma. [Comment: see entry for Elizabeth Oates]

Carlyle, Jonathan, married Elizabeth Snyder, daughter of Dr. John and Letitia Snyder, of Hampshire County. Jonathan was deceased by Sept. 15, 1845.

Carlyle, Robert A., was born in Hampshire County, Va. in 1790 and died on Sept. 16, 1850, in Lafayette County, Missouri. His wife was Elizabeth (nee McCauley), born also in Hampshire County, died on May 12, 1851, in her 49th year. Source: Tombstone inscriptions in Lafayette County, Missouri.

Carter, Benjamin, son of James and Susannah (Griffith) Carter, was born in Pa. circa 1705, and died in 1748, in Frederick County, Va. He married Margaret Hollingsworth, daughter of Abraham Hollingsworth. See *Carter Cousins, 1681-1989*, by Marie Thompson Eberle and Margaret Shipp Henley, 1989.

Carter, James II, son of James and Susannah (Griffith) Carter, was born circa 1709, in Bucks County, Pa., and died in Frederick County, Va., in November or December 1758. He married Hannah Chenoweth, daughter of John and Mary Chenoweth. See *Carter Cousins, 1681-1989*, by Marie Thompson Eberle and Margaret Shipp Henley, 1989

Cartmell, Nathaniel, died on Aug. 4, 1826, aged 73 years, according to a tombstone inscription in St. John's Lutheran Church graveyard, near Hayfield, Frederick County, Virginia. According to T.K. Cartmell, the historian, Nathaniel was born on Nov. 20, 1753, and his second wife was named Sarah Bean, born on Sept. 19, 1781 and died on Feb. 7, 1830.

Casey, Nicholas, son of Peter and Magdalena (DuPuy) Casey, was born on Nov. 17, 1745 and died on May 14, 1833. His wife was Grace Foreman, daughter of William and Catherine (Parker) Foreman. See "Foreman History" in May 1989 issue of *The West Virginia Advocate*.

Cather, David, son of Jasper Cather, Sr., died during the night of Jan. 29, 1835, of a fall from his horse into Back Creek. A jury was appointed to investigate the cause of death, and the coroner ruled that he died of drowning. His birth year was not given, but estimated to be circa 1790. David served in the War of 1812. On May 2, 1824, he married Delilah Williams. She died on Nov. 22, 1834. They had five children. Source: "Inquisitions of Dead Bodies: Frederick County, Va.," in Virginia State Archives.

Cather, Jane, daughter of Jasper Cather Sr., was born on Nov. 12, 1773, and died on Aug. 31, 1853 in Frederick County. She married Robert McKee Jr. on Sept. 15, 1795, in Frederick County, Va.

Cather, Jasper was born in Ireland in 1740 and died on July 30, 1812. Source: Tombstone inscription in Quaker graveyard, Gainsboro, Frederick County, Va.

Cather, Mary, daughter of Jasper Cather Sr., was born in Virginia on June 15, 1775 and died on Aug. 1, 1803, in Harrison County, Virginia. She married James McDonald, son of Benjamin and Massie McDonald, on March 12, 1795. James remarried to Tabitha Husted on Sept. 19, 1805. Source: Mrs. Eleanor M. White, Rockledge, Florida.

Catlett, Jacob, son of John Catlett, was born on June 25, 1850. His wife, Martha D. Hinkle, was born on May 8, 1855. Their children were: (1) Robert W. Catlett was born on Sept. 5, 1874. He married Laura Unger, daughter of Beverly and Eliza (Stotler) Unger. (2) Hilary J. Catlett was born on July 19, 1877 and married Melva Cline, daughter of John Cline. (3) Denver E. Catlett was born on Aug. 11, 1888 and died on Aug. 13, 1983. He married Arzona Puffenberger. Source: Family Bible in possession of Oakley Catlett of Smokey Hollow, Hampshire County, W.Va., which I copied during a visit to his home in Oct. 1983.

Catlett, Mary, daughter of William and Margaret Catlett, died on May 1, 1866, aged 70 years, "of typhoid fever." Her husband was Elias Trotter or Troten. Source: Courthouse death record in Morgan County, W.Va.

Catlett, Phebe (nee Finch), wife of John Catlett, died on Feb. 5, 1877, aged 83 years, 1 month, and 17 days, per tombstone inscription in Timber Ridge Primitive Baptist Church Cemetery, Frederick County, Va. Her husband, John Catlett, son of William and Ursula (Bailey) Catlett, was born Nov. 20, 1797.

Catlett, Susan, daughter of William and Margaret Catlett, was born on Jan. 6, 1784 and died on May 30, 1871. Her husband was Lewis Shockey. These exact dates are given in the Morgan County, W.Va. courthouse death records.

Caudy, James, pioneer settler in the Cacapon Valley of Hampshire County, and Indian fighter, remarried circa 1761 to the widow of James McCoy of Timber Ridge. Source: Notes in Fairfax land grant dispute.

Caudy, John, son of David and Martha (Hiett) Caudy, was born on Jan. 22, 1770 and died on March 23, 1826. His wife, Rebecca McDonald, is believed to have been buried nearby, in the same plot, grave unmarked. According to Grace K. Garner, Rebecca died in January 1866. The Caudy farm was located off State Route 45, down Hickory Corner Road, near North River. John Caudy purchased this land in Sept. 1796, upon which the graveyard was established. According to Mrs. Garner, the property is now owned by a Mr. and Mrs. Frane of Washington, D.C. (in 1986). In same graveyard are: Benjamin Caudy, son of John and Rebecca Caudy, died in Sept. 1804, age 8 years, and members of the Short and Stump families. Source: Tombstone inscriptions in Caudy graveyard near North River, Hampshire County, W.Va.

Caudy, John, aged 60 years, "died yesterday." (Note: "Yesterday" was possibly July 13, 1867.) Source: July 21, 1867 issue of the *South Branch Intelligencer*.

Caudy, John B., born Oct. 15, 1849 and died Oct. 5, 1898. Source: Tombstone inscription, Indian Mound Cemetery, Romney, W.Va.

Caudy, Margaret E., born March 3, 1817 and died July 4, 1902, "At Rest." Source: Indian Mound Cemetery, Romney, W.Va.

Caudy, Maria C., born March 19, 1838, and died June 29, 1916. Source: Tombstone inscriptions, Indian Mound Cemetery, Romney, W.Va.

Chenoweth, John Jr., was born in 1735, probably in Baltimore County, Maryland, and died in Sept. 1812 in Hampshire County. He married Eleanor _____, according to a court document. A published Chenoweth history, states that John's father was also named John Chenoweth, born in 1706 in Baltimore County, Maryland and died in Frederick County, Va. in March 1771. John Sr. married Mary Smith on Nov. 26, 1730. They were among the early settlers in old Frederick County, Va. This entry was corrected by Ms. Marie T. Eberle, #5 Brookside Court, Edwardsville, IL 62025. Ms. Eberle is a leading authority on the Chenoweth family history.

Chenoweth, John, son of William and Ruth (Calvert) Chenoweth, was born in Hampshire County, Va. on Nov. 15, 1755 and died in Randolph County, Va. on Jan. 16, 1831. On Jan. 7, 1779, he married Mary Pugh, daughter of Robert and Mary (Edwards) Pugh. Mary was born Jan. 29, 1762 in the Cacapon Valley and died on Feb. 1, 1849. Source: From a Bible record.

Chenoweth, Richard, died intestate in Frederick County, Va., Dec. 17, 1827. He left these orphan children: John Chenoweth, William Chenoweth, Hannah Chenoweth, Mary Chenoweth, Eleanor Chenoweth, Juliet Ann Chenoweth, Eliza Chenoweth, Richard Chenoweth, Rachel Chenoweth, and Joseph Chenoweth. Source: Frederick County *Superior Court Book 1825-1827*, page 463.

Chenoweth, William, son of John and Mary (Smith) Chenoweth Sr., was born Jan. 8, 1832 in Baltimore County, Md. and died in 1772 in Frederick County, Va. He married Ruth Calvert and their children were: (1) John Chenoweth (1755-1731) married Mary Pugh. (2) Jonathan Chenoweth (1757-1820) married Chloe Aitchison. (3) Mary Chenoweth was born in 1759. (4) Major William Chenoweth (1760-1828) married Mary (Van Meter) Henton, daughter of Jacob Van Meter.

Cheshire, Delilah, daughter of Obediah and Sallie Cheshire, was born March 16, 1807, in Hampshire County, Va. and died Jan. 5, 1885, in Hardy County, W.Va. She married James

Herbaugh. Her death was reported to the courthouse in Moorefield by William F. Bean, her son-in-law.

Cheshire, Perry, aged 59 years, "died last Wednesday," in Hampshire County, according to the Sept. 19, 1879 issue of the *South Branch Intelligencer*. According to the research of Mrs. Gladys C. Stubbs of Johnson City, Texas, Perry Cheshire married Mary Delaplane on July 29, 1866. His father was Uriah Cheshire (1785- ca 1857), of Hampshire County, Va.

Cheshire, Samuel, died on the Mississippi River, on June 1, 1848. His second marriage was to Sarah Godlove, in Hampshire County, Va., on Feb. 15, 1816. She was in Hocking County, Ohio during the 1870's. It is believed that Samuel was a son of Samuel and Christina Barbara (Emmart) Cheshire, of Hampshire County, Virginia. Source: War of 1812 Pension Records in The National Archives.

Cheshire, Uriah, son of Samuel and Christina Barbara (Emmart) Cheshire, Jr., was born in 1785 and died circa 1857 (date of probation of his Will). He first married Taney Emmart, daughter of Jacob and Eve Barbara (Rupp) Emmart. Their children were: (1) John Cheshire, (2) Samuel Cheshire, (3) Elias Cheshire, (4) William Cheshire, (5) Nancy Cheshire married Washington Cross. After the death of Taney, Uriah remarried to Mary Ann _____, and had another set of children, named as follows: (1) Mary Cheshire married Jacob McCauley, (2) Delilah Cheshire married John Swartz, (3) Rachel Cheshire married Mr. Messick, (4) Catherine Cheshire married James Powelson, and (5) James F. Cheshire married Sarah Ann Davis. Source: The above information was taken from handwritten notes made in 1880, by a niece of Uriah and Taney (Emmart) Cheshire.

Cheshire, Uriah B., son of Uriah and Mary Ann Cheshire, aged 37 years, died on Jan. 23, 1879, in Hampshire County. He left a widow, Emma Cheshire, and one child, according to the *South Branch Intelligencer*, issue of Jan. 31, 1879.

Cheshire, William, was born in 1820 and died on Feb. 14, 1900, of "dropsy." Source: Hampshire County, W.Va. death record.

Chilcott, Amos, was born on Jan. 25, 1827 and died on Dec. 20, 1903. His wife, Eliza A. (Abrell) Chilcott, was born on March 15, 1837 and died on March 13, 1908, according to tombstone inscriptions. They were buried in the Frederick Kump graveyard at North River Mills, Hampshire County. The property is now owned by Mr. and Mrs. Paul Gilson.

Chilcott, Mrs. Priscilla, died on Jan. 5, 1867, aged 78 years, 3 months, 21 days. Source: *South Branch Intelligencer*.

Clark, Abraham, son of Henry Clark, was born on May 11, 1731 in Essex County, New Jersey and his Will was probated in Hardy County, Va. on April 13, 1808. He married Sarah Badgley, born on Jan. 17, 1731. They raised six children. Source: Mrs. Richard Arnold, 1600 Beaucaire Drive, St. Louis, MO 63122.

Clark, Elias, son of Henry and Mary (Valentine) Clark, was born at Westfield, Essex County, N.J., and died circa 1806 at Uniontown, Fayette County, PA. He married Hannah Broughton, daughter of William and Hannah Broughton. She was born at "Lost River," Hardy County, Va. on June 17, 1773. Elias was a nephew of the Abraham Clark, who was mentioned above. Both resided in Hardy County, Va. Source: Mrs. Richard Arnold, St. Louis, MO.

Clark, Henry, son of Abraham and Sarah (Badgley) Clark, was born on Aug. 31, 1752 in Essex County, New Jersey. He married Mary Ward and they lived in Hardy County, Va. where he died in 1818. Source: Mrs. Richard Arnold, St. Louis, MO.

Clark, Isabel (nee Ware), was born in Ireland in 1780 and died in Frederick County, Va. in October 1869. Her husband, Abner Clark, preceded her in death. Source: 1870 Mortality Schedule for Frederick County, Va.

Clark, Joseph T., son of Sampson Clark, was born in 1841 and died at age 56, on Oct. 10, 1897, in an accident. His wife was named Margaret Clark. Source: Hampshire County death record in Romney courthouse.

Clark, Margaret (nee Lewis), widow of William Clark, died in October 1859, aged 72 years, of "jaundice," after a 14-day illness. She was born in Virginia.

Clark, Sampson B., son of Abner and Isabel (Ware) Clark, was born on March 28, 1810 in Frederick County, Va. and died at Isaac's Creek, near Cross Junction, Va., on June 11, 1886. This graveyard is in danger of being destroyed, based on actions of recent owners. Sampson descends from Abner Clark, a Quaker immigrant to Back Creek during the 18th century. Sampson married: (1) Mary Null/Noel, and (2) Sarah E. Peacemaker (born in 1834), daughter of Jacob and Margaret (Smith) Peacemaker, on Oct. 31, 1865, in Frederick County, Va. Source: Courthouse marriage record in Winchester, Va., and Tombstone inscription in Clark graveyard, Cross Junction, Va.

Claypool, James, was born Feb. 14, 1701 and died Oct. 7, 1789. Jane Claypool, his wife, was born in 1701 and died in 1788. James Claypool Jr. was born in 1730 and died in 1811. John Claypool was born in 1733 and died in 1823. Margaret Dunbar was born in 1736 and died in 1813. Source: Gravestone inscriptions in family plot, Hardy County, W.Va.

Clayton, Dr. Townscend, age 71, died on March 11, 1874 in Hampshire County. He was born in Loudoun County, but lived in Hampshire County for fifty years, where he served as Justice of the Peace, and as Superintendent of Schools. Source: March 13, 1874 issue of the *South Branch Intelligencer*. A death record in the Hampshire County courthouse states that he died on March 11, 1874, aged 73 years, 5 months, 22 years; that his parents were Amos and Elizabeth Clayton; that he was a physician. The Heiskell genealogy shows that he was born on Sept. 16, 1800 and died on March 11, 1874. His wife was Susan O'Hara Heiskell, daughter of Christopher and Eleanor (Abernathy) Heiskell. Susan was born on Sept. 6, 1809. They were married on April 13, 1830.

Cline, Henry, died in November 1859. Cause of death was consumption. His wife, Catherine Cline, died in March 1860, of dropsy. She was ill for 19 days prior to her death. Both were born in Virginia. Source: 1860 Mortality Schedule for Shenandoah County, Va.

Clutter, Ann, wife of Joseph Clutter, died In Hardy County, Va. on March 29, 1855, aged 67 years, of pneumonia. She was born in Hampshire County. Death was reported to courthouse in Moorefield by R. L. Davis, son-in-law. Source: *West Virginia Vital Statistics: Hardy County Death Records*, Reel # 3, Virginia State Archives, Richmond, Va.

Coe, Abraham, son of William and Elizabeth (Gore) Coe, was born on Timber Ridge, Frederick County, Va., on Dec. 23, 1806 and died in 1900. He moved to Mt. Gilead, Morrow County, Ohio in 1827. Abraham married: (1) Margaret Nichols, daughter of

Nathan and Sarah (Thomas) Nichols, of Round Hill, Loudoun County, Va. Margaret was born on Oct. 4, 1813 and died on Sept. 21, 1849, and (2) Elizabeth (Wallace) Sellers, widow of Joseph Sellers, of Perry County, Ohio.

Coe, Craven, son of William and Elizabeth (Gore) Coe, was born on May 27, 1814, according to one family source. His tombstone inscription says that he died on Feb. 16, 1892, aged 76 years, 2 months, 26 days. Craven was a shoemaker. His wife, Sarah Miller (daughter of Ephrium Miller) died on Aug. 24, 1882, aged 64 years, 4 months, 24 days. Source: Tombstone inscriptions in Primitive Baptist Church Graveyard, on Timber Ridge, in Frederick County, Virginia. Craven lived on the William Coe homeplace on Timber Ridge.

Coe, Henry, son of William and Mary Coe, II, was born on Timber Ridge, on Oct. 26, 1825, and died on April 6, 1873. He married Mary Ann Omps, daughter of Benedict and Margaret (Hovermale) Omps, of Frederick County, Va., on Dec. 8, 1847. She was born on Jan. 18, 1823 and died on Jan. 18, 1873. They moved to Fayette County, Ohio in 1867, where they died and were buried in the Bookwalter Cemetery.

Coe, Henry, died near High View, Timber Ridge, Frederick County, Va., in May 1829. It is believed that he came from Loudoun County, Virginia. His relationship with William Coe, who settled farther north on Timber Ridge, has not been established. This Henry Coe married Sarah Anderson on Dec. 27, 1787, in Frederick County, Va. According to Henry's Will, some of his children were: Wesley Coe (ca 1800-1836) married Jane Hook, daughter of Thomas Hook, in 1826, in Hampshire County, Va. Jane remarried to Levi Scrivener on May 15, 1843; Henry Coe, Jr.; Elizabeth Coe married William Scrivener on April 27, 1816; Mary Coe married John Brunner on Nov. 1, 1818.

Coe, James, son of William and Elizabeth (Gore) Coe, was born in 1798 and died in 1858, in Frederick County, Va. His wife was Sophia Mary Groves, born in 1803 and died in 1874. They were married on Dec. 10, 1823, in Frederick County, Va. Henry Grove, who was buried at the Primitive Baptist Church on Timber Ridge, was Sophia's brother.

Coe, Samuel, died on Sept. 7, l872, in Frederick County, Va., aged 80 years. He married Catherine Bageant, daughter of John and Catherine (Whitnak) Bageant, on Feb. 28, 1822. She was born on Sept. 20, 1786 in Frederick County, Maryland, and died on Dec. 9, 1855. They were buried in the Timber Ridge Baptist Church cemetery in the northernmost section of Frederick County, Va.

Coe, Sarah (1830-1873) married J. Luther Green (1823-1880). Source: Tombstone inscriptions in Greenton Cemetery, Lafayette County, Missouri.

Coe, William Jr. was born on Dec. 1, 1808 and died on April 15, 1861, aged 52 years, 3 months, 15 days. Source: Tombstone inscription in Primitive Baptist Cemetery on Timber Ridge, Frederick County, Virginia.

Coe, William, was born circa 1755 in Maryland and died ca. 1834 on Timber Ridge, Frederick County, Va. After serving in the Revolutionary War, William Coe married Elizabeth Gore, daughter of Samuel Gore of Loudoun County, Va. They settled on Timber Ridge in Frederick County, about 1790.

Cole, Daniel, was born on Aug. 20, 1796 and died Jan. 15, 1879. He served in a Maryland militia during the War of 1812, and received a pension. He first married a person named Hannah; the remarried to Ruth Bumgardner, April 17, 1831, in Hampshire County. She was born on Aug. 11, 1795 and died Nov. 23, 1886. They were buried at Intermont, W.Va., on State Route 259, near Capon Springs.

Combs, David, died at Elizabeth, Harrison County, Indiana, on Oct. 29, 1871. He married Jane Rogers in Hampshire County, Va. on Feb. 22, 1808. Source: War of 1812 Pension Application, National Archives, Washington, D.C.

Combs, Peyton, died May 4, 1899, aged 79 years, 3 months, 17 days. Rebecca J. Combs, his wife, died July 24, 1896, aged 72 years, 8 months, 9 days. Source: Tombstone inscriptions in Mountain Dale cemetery, Hampshire County, W.Va.

Combs, Philip S., was born in 1850 and died in 1929. His wife, Malinda C., was born in 1857 and died in 1935. Source: Tombstone inscriptions in Mountain Dale cemetery, Hampshire County, W.Va.

Cookus, John T., died in Morgan County, W.Va. on Dec. 3, 1865, aged 79 years, 3 months, 14 days. He was born in

Shepherdstown, Va. and came to Morgan County to become a merchant. His wife was named Sophia. Source: Courthouse record in Berkeley Springs, W.Va.

Cookus, William, born on Feb. 14, 1822 and died on July 2, 1882. Wife, Mary C., was born in June 1823 and died in Dec. 1915. Source: Tombstone inscriptions in the Indian Mound Cemetery, Romney, W.Va.

Cool, Herbert, married Sarah Gulick, daughter of Ferdinand Gulick. Ferdinand was deceased before April 13, 1847, according to *Order Book II*, page 202, in the Circuit Court of Hampshire County, W.Va.

Coole, John, died Feb. 8, 1818, aged 69 years. Nancy M.Coole died May 4, 1823. Source: Tombstone inscriptions in Back Creek Quaker cemetery, Gainsboro, Va.

Cool, William, son of Herbert McCool, was born In Hampshire County, Va. in 1791 and died on May 15, 1869. His death record in the Hampshire County Courthouse states that he was a widower.

Cooper, Benjamin, died in October 1859, aged 53 years. He was born in Virginia, and worked as a farmer. Cause of death was "intemperance," of alcohol abuse. Source: 1860 Mortality Schedule for Frederick County, Va.

Cooper, Elizabeth, wife of G.W. Cooper, died on Feb. 2, 1855, aged 59 years, 1 month and 7 days. Source: Tombstone inscription in Ebenezer United Methodist Church cemetery near Romney, W.Va.

Cooper, Jacob, son of John and Mary Cooper, died in Hampshire County on March 7, 1875 at 75 years, 3 months, and 29 days. His wife was Anna Parks. Source: Hampshire County Death Records; the March 12, 1875 issue of the *South Branch Intelligencer*; and Mr. Norman C. Emerick, Baltimore, Md.

Cooper, John, son of George Cooper, was born in 1768, and died on Sept. 6, 1848. Note: Mr. Norman C. Emerick, 1323 Glendale Road, Baltimore, MD. 21239 is writing a comprehensive history of the Cooper and allied families of old Frederick.

Cooper, John, son of Leonard and Christina Cooper, died in January 1853, "at the head of the Potomac." He was 42 years old. Source: Death record in Virginia State Archives.

Cooper, Martha Jane, was born at Cold Stream on Feb. 11, 1846 and died in Kansas on Feb. 28, 1930. She was the second wife of John Cram Edwards, son of Anthony and Elizabeth (Cram) Edwards.

Copenhaver, Jacob, died in December 1859, aged 65 years. Born in Virginia. Occupation was farming. Suffered with cancer for 125 days prior to his death. Survived by his spouse. Source: 1860 Mortality Schedule for Frederick County, Va.

Copp, Susannah, "a widow," died in July 1859, aged 89 years. She had been ill for two months with "paralysis." Born in Virginia. Source: 1860 Mortality Schedule for Shenandoah County, Va.

Copsey, John, was born in 1757; died at Forks of Capon, Hampshire County, Va., on June 6, 1847. Allegedly he was a soldier of the Revolutionary War, and a wealthy landowner and innkeeper in the Bloomery District, near Forks of Capon. The old Copsey graveyard has been deteriorating for years, with fallen trees, theft and vandalism, no maintenance, and weathering age. Most of the old stones are unmarked, but the legible ones are reported in this volume. The graveyard is on a high knoll, on the east side of the Great Cacapon, on a side road (dirt) leading off the main road from Bloomery to Slanesville. Source: Tombstone inscription in Copsey Graveyard.

Corbin, Cornelius, was born in 1796 and died in Oct. 1859, "of consumption." He was listed as a "pauper." Source: 1860 Mortality Schedule for Hampshire County, Va.

Corbin, Elizabeth, daughter of James N. and Sarah Corbin, was born April 13, 1826. She married Andrew C. Groves. Source: *Winchester Reformed Church Records*, page 80.

Corbin, Humphrey, was born in Virginia in 1768 and died on July 5, 1837, in Franklin Township, Coshocton County, Ohio. His wife, Alice Powelson, daughter of Powel and Magdalena (Smock) Powelson, was born circa 1769, and was still alive at age 100 when the 1860 U.S. census was taken in Dolman Township, Clark County, Illinois. Alice was baptized in Millstone Reformed Dutch Church, Somerset County, New Jersey, June 16, 1775, in her fifth year. They had at least ten children, and emigrated from Hampshire County, Va. to Coshocton County, Ohio in 1830. Sources: *The American Family Powelson*, by Gladys Powelson Jones, Cheyenne, Wyoming, 1988; and *David Corbin of*

Hampshire County, by Elaine Corbin Artlip, 1988, Villisca, Iowa 50864.

Corder, The Rev. John Alexander, son of Alexander and Sadie (Arnold) Corder, was born Sept. 28, 1822, in Fauquier County, Va. and died Friday, March 2, 1882, in Hampshire County, W.Va. He was pastor of the Primitive Baptist Church at the Little Cacapon, Hampshire County. He married Sarah Lucretia Jones, daughter of James and Anna Jones, on Jan. 13, 1853, in Fayette County, PA. They had ten children. For further information contact: Mrs. Estelle Corder, P.O. Box 71, LaRue, TX 75770.

Cornet, Sarah, "Depart'b This Life FEBRUARY 7, 1795, AGE 34 Years 7 Months 7 Days." She married Richard Taylor, son of Harrison Taylor, June 11, 1782, in Frederick County, Va. After her death, Richard remarried to a woman named Dorcas, and they lived in Kentucky. Source: Tombstone inscription in Jeremiah Smith pioneer graveyard at Gore, Frederick County.

Cornwell, Elizabeth, died in June 1870, aged 70 years, "of dropsy." Source: 1870 Mortality Schedule for Hampshire County, Va.

Cornwell, Nancy, consort of Benjamin Cornwell, died at Pleasant Township, Madison County, Ohio on Tuesday, April 25, 1854, aged 44 years, 2 months, 23 days. Source: *Zion's Advocate*: Vol. I, No. 10, Sat. May 6, 1854, John Clark, editor. This semi-monthly periodical, published in Front Royal, Va., represented "Old School" or "Primitive Baptist" churches in Northern Virginia.

Cosner, Barbara, died in Grant County, W.Va. in September 1869, aged 82 years. Source: 1870 Mortality Schedule for Hampshire County, W.Va.

Cosner, Christian, aged 77, died on Aug. 2, 1874 in Grant County, W.Va. Source: Aug. 21, 1874 issue of the *South Branch Intelligencer*.

Cowgill, Ewing, son of Elisha and Martha (Ewing) Cowgill, was born on July 22, 1769, and died circa 1842, in Hampshire County, Va. His wife was named Susannah Buzzard, who was a daughter of Frederick and Susannah (Buckwalter) Buzzard. They lived in the Bloomery District of Hampshire County, Va. Susannah died prior to 1819, proven by the fact that she was deceased when her father's estate was settled. The estate papers listed only six heirs (children). Each one received a one-sixth share of their mother's part of the estate. The proven children were: (1) Martha Cowgill, born in 1796, married Michael Brown, born in 1776, in Ireland. They were both alive when the 1860 census was taken in Bloomery District, Hampshire County, Va. (2) Mary Cowgill married William Griffith (3) Henry Cowgill married Catherine Kerns, daughter of John and Elizabeth (Light) Kerns (4) Elizabeth Cowgill married John Murphy on July 3, 1819 (5) Frederick Cowgill, born in 1803, immigrated to Wyandot County, Ohio and (6) John Cowgill. Ewing Cowgill had other children. Were they too young to be mentioned in the court settlement? Were they Ewing's children by a second marriage or were their shares distributed through other means (than the settlement instrument)? Other known children of Ewing Cowgill were: (7) Milton Cowgill married Margaret Youngblood, on March 10, 1830, in Morgan County, Va. On Sept. 10, 1833, Milton remarried to Arianne McCauley (see reference to settlement of George McCauley's estate in Hampshire County, in 1836). Beatrice E. Cowgill reported in her book, *Cowgill History*, that Milton was born on Dec. 13, 1811 and died in Livingston, Iowa on June 19, 1889. (8) Elisha Cowgill immigrated to Crawford County, Ohio; (9) Valentine Cowgill, born in 1813, married Rebecca _____, and they settled in Pennsylvania; (10) Elias Cowgill, born in 1816, married Rebecca _____. They went to Wyandot County, Ohio in 1847; (11) Daniel Cowgill was mentioned in Maud Pugh's book on Capon Valley; and (12) the Rev. James Alexander Cowgill, born on April 22, 1818 and died on Nov. 18, 1882. James married Frances Hiett, daughter of Jeremiah and Lucinda (Kidwell) Hiett. The Bible of The Rev. Cowgill is in the hands of Mrs. Hannah Overholt, Romney, W.Va.

Cowgill, James W., son of John and Harriet (Alderton) Cowgill, was born on June 13, 1856 and died on Feb. 15, 1919. His wife, Electia V. Raigner, daughter of George Washington and Mary Elizabeth (McIntyre) Raigner, was born on Oct. 10, 1862 and died on Dec. 27, 1937. Source: Tombstone inscriptions in the Jacob Alderton graveyard, located near Bower's Run, below the Forks of Capon.

Cowgill, Nancy J., daughter of John and Elizabeth Grant, died on July 11, 1874, in Hampshire County, W.Va. Her husband was Frederick Cowgill, probably a son of Henry and Catherine (Kerns)

Cowgill. According to the courthouse death record, Ewing Cowgill, brother-in-law, made the report to the Courthouse.

Cox, John Ashby, was born in Delaware in 1771 and died in Hampshire County in 1850. His wife was Hannah Stoker, daughter of John and Elizabeth (Critton) Stoker. She was born on Oct. 4, 1776 and was still alive when the 1850 census was taken for Hampshire County, Va. See: "18th Century Grave of Early Hampshire County Settler Found," *The West Virginia Advocate*, published at Capon Bridge, W.Va., Aug. 17, 1987.

Critton, Elizabeth, daughter of William and Ann (Haggerty) Critton, I, was born in Hampshire County, Va. on Jan. 27, 1791 and died on Aug. 3, 1874. She married John Butcher and they had nine children.

Critton, Gabriel, son of John Critton, was born in Hampshire County, Va. on May 25, 1775 and died on Nov. 25, 1835. He was a veteran of the War of 1812. His wife was Catherine Johnson, born in "Va." on Jan. 8, 1782 and died in Ohio in Sept. 1867. They had ten children. Catherine's father was Griffin Johnson, veteran of the Revolutionary War.

Critton, John, was deceased before Sept. 1848, when his case (settlement of estate) came before the chancery court of law, Circuit Court of Hampshire County. Those involved in the court case were: (1) Sarah Critton Easter [could it be the Sarah who was born on Oct. 1, 1781 in Hampshire County and died on Oct. 29, 1861; buried in Newberry cemetery, near Addison, Pennsylvania? Sarah married Donald McDonald. After his death, she remarried to John Easter, son of John and Margaret (Thomas) Easter Sr., on Oct. 22, 1811.] (2) William Critton (3) Cresa or Cresida Critton married James Johnson, (4) Rebecca Critton married William Boxwell, (5) Isaac Critton married Elizabeth Athey (6) Jacob Critton (7) Elizabeth Critton (8) Mary Critton married _____ Hardy, and (9) John Critton, plaintiff. It is believed that this John Critton, dec'd, was a son of William Critton. Source: Hampshire County Circuit Court, Romney, W.Va., *Order Book II*, pages 308-309.

Critton, John, was deceased by Sept. 1849, in Hampshire County, Virginia. This is not the same John Critton as the one listed above. This John Critton was born circa 1792 and married Hannah _____. His heirs were: (1) Daniel Critton married

Eleanora Nellie Largent. Daniel was born in 1820 and died on April 27, 1893. She died in 1850 and Daniel remarried to Lucinda _____. At least one child was born to the second marriage, viz, Frances E. Largent (1856-1892), who married Emanuel King. (2) Harriett Critton married Moses Largent, (3) John Critton II, born in 1823, married Phebe Largent. They had three children: daughter Hannah Critton married Cicero Kerns; daughter Harriett Critton was born in 1849; and John Critton, III (1852-1873), (3) Sarah Jane Critton married _____ Largent, and (5) Martha Ann Critton married Thomas Largent, in 1850. Source: ***Order Book II***, page 336, Circuit Court of Hampshire County, Virginia (now West Virginia).

Critton, William, I, was born circa 1760 and died circa 1843 in Hampshire County, Va. His wife was Ann Haggerty. Possibly this was Letitia (Ann) Haggerty, daughter of John Haggerty (see entry), but not proven.   William had a son named John Critton who died in Hampshire County in 1846, who left no Will. This John would have been born during the late 1780's or early 1790's. But, this is only an estimate, as no birth year was given. The two above death dates came from a chancery case Box in the Hampshire County Circuit Court, Romney, West Virginia.

Critton, William, II, son of William and Ann (Haggerty) Critton, was born in Hampshire County on April 2, 1786 and died in Ohio on April 8, 1864. He married Mary Dever/ Deaver, daughter of Lloyd and Rebecca (Blue) Deaver, on Nov. 21, 1816. She was born on March 23, 1797, in Baltimore, Maryland, and died on Sept. 19, 1864. They raised a family of ten children. In 1837, they immigrated to Franklin Township of Shelby County, Ohio. Source: Family Bible records.

Crump, Catherine, died on March 8, 1842 on the main road leading from Winchester to Frankfort (now in Mineral County, W.Va.), near Isaac's Creek in Frederick County. A jury was appointed to make an inquisition re the cause of her death, and they decided that she died of natural causes. Members of the jury were: Casper Rogers, John Strickling, Richard Flowers, Thomas Adams, John Shutts, Joseph Clark, John Braithwaite, George Baker, Cornelius H. Heironimus, Hilery Baker, William Brown, Jr., and William Strickling.

Cundiff, John, was born in Northumberland County, Va. in 1759, according to a deposition given in 1832 at Romney, Hampshire County, Va. He served in the Revolutionary War, and settled in Hampshire County in 1788. His wife was named Sally.

Curlett, Frances "Fannie," died on May 2, 1813 in a cave behind her house in upper Back Creek Valley. Her husband was George Smith, son of Capt. Jeremiah Smith. The coroner's report, found in the State Archives in Richmond, stated that her throat had been cut with a razor and the death was ruled a suicide. The cave was located "twenty or more steps from the dwelling house." The coroner was a Dr. Wilson. A jury was appointed to make an inquisition on the "dead body": Joseph McKee, Thomas Marpole, Enoch Marple, David Cather, William Gore, Ezekiel Marker, Joseph Wilson, George Whitacre, Ezekiel Marple (another one!), James Lockhart and Sampson Smith, and Christian Shruk.

Curlett, Frances, died in October 1869, aged 62 years, "of consumption." She was born in Virginia. Source: 1870 Mortality Schedule for Frederick County, Va.

Curtis, Mary, died in Hampshire County, Va. in Feb. 1850, aged 72 years, "of dropsy." Source: 1850 Mortality Schedule for Hampshire County, Va.

Daily, Jacob, was born Jan. 17, 1798 and died Feb. 17, 1860. Source: Tombstone inscription, Springfield, W.Va.

Daily, James P., died on May 23, 1862, aged 24 years, 4 months and 4 days. Source: Tombstone inscription, on hill overlooking the town of Springfield, Hampshire County, W.Va.

Daily, John, died "of dropsy" in Feb. 1860, aged 62 years. He was born in Virginia. Source: 1860 Mortality Schedule for Hampshire County, Va.

Daily, Jane (nee Patterson), was born on Jan. 15, 1808 and died on Oct. 5, 1885. Her husband was Jacob Daily. Source: Tombstone inscription, Springfield, W.Va.

Daily, Rebecca (wife of John), was born on March 22, 1831 and died Sept. 28, 1862. Source: Tombstone inscription, Springfield, Hampshire County, W.Va.

Dalby, Elizabeth, daughter of Joseph and Hannah (Stonebridge) Dalby of Frederick County, Va., was born on Dec.

11, 1808 and died on Feb. 17, 1862. She married John McGinnis Johnston, son of Joseph and Harriett Ann (McGinnis) Johnston, on Feb. 18, 1830. He was born on April 1, 1807 in Frederick County, Va. and died on Oct. 23, 1892 and was buried at Oppy, KY. Source: Mrs. A.H. Lindsey, 26 Mt. Pleasant, Amherst, MA 01002.

Dalby, Rev. Joel, son of Richard and Susannah (Harris) Dalby, was born in Frederick County, Va. on July 24, 1777 and died on March 10, 1859 at, Frankfort, Clinton County, IN. He married: (1) Elizabeth Smith, (2) Nancy Curry, and (3) Miss Parrill. Source: Betty Lou Jones, 6162 South Popular Street, Englewood, CO 80111.

Dalby, William, died in January 1850, aged 75 years. Cause of death was "dropsy," and the duration of his illness was 100 days. Occupation was "shoemaker." Source: 1850 Mortality Schedule for Frederick County, Va.

Daniels, Alpheus, was born on Feb. 20, 1830 and died on July 29, 1881. Who was he and from where did he originate? Source: Tombstone inscription in the Baker Graveyard at Delray, Hampshire County, W.Va. Next to this grave was buried Florence V.L. H. Shull, a daughter of Alpheus Daniels. She was born on Aug. 20, 1857 and died on March 18th.

Daugherty, John was born on May 16, 1819 and died on May 8, 1894. He was a son of Valentine and Mary (Kelley) Daugherty. He married: (a) Elizabeth Beery and (b) Eliza (Haines) Offutt. Eight children were born to the first union and one to the second marriage. They lived at Pleasant Dale, Hampshire County, W.Va. Sources: Cemetery inscription at Augusta Methodist Church; Mrs. Celeste Arnold, Sedona, Arizona.

Daugherty, Valentine, was born in Ireland on Feb. 14, 1789 and died at Beaver Run, Hampshire County, on May 23, 1869. His parents were John and Elizabeth Daugherty, emigrants from Ireland to Rockingham County, Va. Valentine Daugherty married Mary Ann Kelley on May 1, 1812. Source: Mrs. Celeste Arnold, Sedona, Arizona.

Davidson, William, died in December 1849, aged 52 years. He was ill for eight days with typhoid fever. William was a carpenter, born in Virginia. Source: 1850 Mortality Schedule for Frederick County, Va.

Davis, James, was born circa 1710, probably in New Jersey, and died in old Frederick County, Va. (now Berkeley County, W.Va.), circa 1755 (see Frederick County Will, probated in 1756). He married Sarah Vanmetre, daughter of John Vanmetre. They were early settlers in old Frederick County, possibly as early as 1733.

Davis, John, died on May 19, 1865. His wife, Polly Brewer, died on July 10, 1876, aged 92 years. He was a veteran of the War of 1812. Source: Tombstone inscriptions in the Indian Mound Cemetery, Romney, W.Va.

Davis, John R., was born circa 1783 and died in 1859, according to a native tombstone inscription in the Dunlap Graveyard, LeHew, Hampshire County, W.Va. His wife, Margaret, died at age 82 years. See *William Davis Family*, by Lillian Virginia (Ludwig) Davis, Commercial Press, Stephens City, Virginia, 1972. Note: William Davis was a son of John R. Davis.

Davis, Margaret, was born in Ireland in 1775 and died in Hampshire County on June 8, 1871, aged 96 years. A tombstone in the Dunlap graveyard says that she died in her 82nd year. Further research is needed on this family. Her husband was J.R. Davis. Source: Hampshire County *Register of Deaths, 1866-1922*, Romney, W.Va.

Dawson, Nancy, died in August, 1869, aged 64 years. Cause of death was "epilepsy." Source: 1870 Mortality Schedule for Morgan County, W.Va.

Day, Ann, daughter of Jacob and Elizabeth Pugh, died on Oct. 7, 1874, age 70 years and 17 days. Her son, Alexander Day, reported the death to the Hampshire County Court Clerk. He stated that Ann's husband was named William Day.

Day, Mary was born in Culpeper County, Va. on April 5, 1768 and died in Romney, Va. on Aug. 10, 1855. Her husband was William Busby. Source: Death record in Virginia State Archives, and tombstone inscription in Indian Mound Cemetery, Romney, W.Va.

Deaver, Amy, died in Hampshire County, Va. in September 1859, aged 38 years. Source: 1860 Mortality Schedule for Hampshire County, Va.

Deaver, George S., son of William and Elizabeth Deaver, "drowned himself" on Oct. 1, 1875. He was born on Feb. 2, 1790, and never married. George was a veteran of the War of 1812, and received a bounty land grant. He jumped into the river at Croston's Ford, while in a despondent state of mind. Source: Hampshire County courthouse death record.

Deaver, Lucinda, died on March 10, 1898 at age 71, near North River Mills, Hampshire County. See Lucinda Hiett. Source: Courthouse death record.

Decker, Samuel, son of Garret Decker, died along the South Branch of the Potomac River, Frederick County, Virginia. Peter Scholl, coroner, stated that death was accidental, by a pen knife. A report on the inquisition of his death was made to the Circuit Court in Augusta County, Virginia, on April 15, 1749. Members of the inquisition team were: Abrah Vanderpool, Able Westfall (1696-1755), Henry Scarbrough, James Simpson, Johannes Cartright, Conrad Hoerner, Daniel Hornbeck, Anthony Logan, George Osburn, John Westfall (1728-1789), Cornelius and Curtwright. These were early settlers along the South Branch River, emigrating from New York, circa 1740.

DeHaven, John, died in November 1859, aged 75 years. He was a farmer, born in Virginia. Cause of death was "inflammation of the bowels," which was possibly an intestinal obstruction, considering the short duration of illness. His wife preceded him in death. Source: 1860 Mortality Schedule for Frederick County, Va.

DeHaven, Julia A., died in May 1869, aged 39 years, of childbirth. Source: 1870 Mortality Schedule for Frederick County, Va.

Delaplane, Isaac, was born in 1763 and died in April 1850, in Hampshire County, of "old age." Source: 1850 Mortality Schedule for Hampshire County, Va.

DeMoss, Louis, II, son of Louis and Catherine DeMoss, I, was baptized on Nov. 1, 1715, at Kingsville, Baltimore County, Maryland. On Jan. 1, 1743, he married Margaret Ramsey, in Baltimore County. Louis II filed a Will in Frederick County in 1743 and he died before 1749, when his widow received her dower. One unproven source stated that she remarried to John Largent, and that she was his first wife (of three). John Largent's children have been called "set one," "set two" and "set three." [Note: see

entry on John Largent, whose wife was named Elizabeth.]
Source: From a DeMoss History submitted by Roger Stubbs,
3020 Waterton Road, Long Lake, MN 55356.

DeMoss, William, son of Louis and Catherine DeMoss, I, was
baptized on Sept. 22, 1716, in Baltimore Maryland. He settled
along the Cacapon River, Hampshire County, Va., prior to 1761,
when he received a Fairfax grant. His wife was named Rachel
DeMoss. He sold lands in 1777, 1782, 1783, 1790, 1794, and
1795. Most of these lands were located near the Forks of Capon.
Source: Roger Stubbs, Long Lake, Minnesota.

Dew, Samuel Sr., son of William Dew of Richmond County, Va.,
was born Nov. 14, 1733, and died circa 1810, in Monroe County,
Va. He was twice-married. They settled along Kuykendall's Saw
Mill Run, a tributary of the South Branch River, Hampshire County,
Va., during the late 1750s. Then, he purchased Lot 12 (granted to
Garret and Catherine Decker in 1748), where he established a
permanent residence in South Branch Valley. In 1761, he was
deputy clerk of Hampshire County, working under Gabriel Jones.
Samuel became a large landowner and slave holder. He served
as a justice of the peace during the 1780s. In 1789, Samuel
moved to Botetourt County, Va., where he became clerk of district
court. His residence was in vicinity of Potts' Creek, a tributary of
the James River, (now in Monroe County, W.Va.), where he died
circa 1810. Betty Dew, widow of Samuel Sr., died circa 1817, in
Monroe County, Va. Their children were: (1) Sarah Dew was born
circa 1765. She married Thomas Conaway, Jan. 9, 1783. They
immigrated to Harrison County, Va. and raised a large family. (2)
Charles Dew was born June 17, 1767 and died Feb. 11, 1841. (3)
Mary Dew married Jacob Vanmeter (died in 1803). Their children
were: Henry Vanmeter, Sarah Vanmeter married Joel Hinkle, and
Rebecca Vanmeter married Nathaniel Cartmell. (4) William Dew
married Mary Flora and they settled in Allegheny County, Va. (5)
Samuel Dew Jr., born Sept. 20, 1771 and died in 1827. He
married Joanna Parks. (6) Elizabeth Dew was born April 17, 1774.
She married David Kean, and they lived in Monroe County, Va. (7)
Lucy Dew was born Dec. 18, 1775 and died Jan. 15, 1835,
unmarried. (8) Peter Dew immigrated to Kentucky. (9) John Dew
was born July 17, 1789. He was a Methodist preacher, church
administrator and president of McKendree College for two years.

Dew, Samuel Jr. was born in Hampshire County, Va., Sept. 20, 1771 and died in same county, February 1827. He married Joanna Parks, daughter of John and Susannah (Elrod) Parks III. Joanna died at West Milford, Harrison County, W.Va. Samuel served as Hampshire County surveyor. He patented a "universal compass." Their children: (1) Samuel Dew III died before 1840. He married Susan Largent. (2) Betsy Ann Dew died, single, in August 1828, Hampshire County. (3) John Lewis Dew was born circa 1813, and married Anna Duling, daughter of William and Elizabeth (Dean) Duling. They immigrated to Brown County, Indiana prior to 1855.[40]　(4) Susan Dew remained in Hampshire County, unmarried. (5) Sarah Dew married John R. Dyer and they moved to Lewis County, Va..[41] (6) Dr. William Henry Harrison Dew was born in Hampshire County, circa 1819, and died in Harrison County, W.Va., May 30, 1881. He married Jane Davis.

Dick, Elizabeth, died in September 1869, aged 66 years. Cause of death was "syphillis." Source: 1870 Mortality Schedule for Morgan County, W.Va.

Dickinson, Elder James, died on Oct. 31, 1827, aged 30 years. He was a companion preacher of the Rev. Christy Sine. Source: Tombstone inscription in Old Christian Church cemetery at Highview.

Dillon, William, was born Aug. 25, 1774 and died Dec. 29, 1832. Source: Tombstone inscription in White Hall Methodist Church cemetery, Frederick County, Va.

Doman, Henry, was deceased before April 15, 1840, according to a chancery suit in the Circuit Court, Hampshire County, Va. It mentions, Rachel Dorman, "widow and relicit of Henry Doman." Also mentioned: Sarah Inskeep, and Isaiah Burkett who was the administrator of Henry Doman's estate. Source: *Order Book I*, page 35, Circuit Court, Romney, W.Va. 26757.

Doman, George Nelson, was born on May 26, 1826 in Hampshire County and died in 1906 in Cameron, West Virginia. He married Mary Shanholtz, daughter of Samuel and Phoebe (Iden) Shanholtz. They lived in numerous counties in "West Va.." and in

---

40. See Hardy County (Va.) *Deed Book 26*, pp. 133-134.

41 . See Hardy County (Va.) *Deed Book 26*, pp. 133-134.

Greene County, Penn.; then divorced after a long and stormy marriage. Records in the Mormon Temple show that he remarried to Malinda Ault.

Doman, Jacob   Sr., was born circa 1755, probably in Lancaster County, Pennsylvania.   He died circa 1815 in Hampshire County, Va., near Romney. His wife was named Margaret. In 1794 he bought land from George Rogers. See Deed Book 17, page 553, Hampshire County, W.Va. court records. According to Mormon records in the Library in Salt Lake City, the children of Jacob and Margaret Doman were: Sarah Doman, ca 1775; John Doman, ca 1777; William Doman, 1779-1856, married Susannah _____; Anna, ca. 1781; Jacob Doman Jr., 1783-1865, married Rachel McGillian; Margaret Doman, ca. 1785; Mary Doman, ca. 1787, married Gabriel Cane; Catherine Doman, born ca. 1789; Rachel Doman, born ca. 1791;   and Joseph Doman, 1795-1881, was twice married (see below).

Doman Jacob, Jr., son of Jacob and Margaret Doman, Sr., was born on July 5, 1783 and died on May 5, 1865. His wife, Rachel McGillian, was born in 1785 and died in 1868. Both were buried on a wooded hillside in Fox Hollow, Hampshire County, Va., on Route 50/4. Fox Run flows into the South Branch just below Wapocomo. The Domans ran a mill, near the intersection of Long's Run and Fox Run. Mill Creek Mountain is to the east and Patterson Creek Mountain to the west. The graveyard is fenced, and these inscriptions are on the same large monument: William H. Doman (1818-1898) and Rebecca Doman (1820-1896); Lucy Doman (1873-1885); Tobias S. Doman (1828-1883) and Margaret C. Doman (1840-1895), wife.

Doman, Joseph, was born on Aug. 25, 1795 in Hampshire County and died in 1881 at Cameron, West Virginia. His parents were Jacob and Margaret Doman, pioneers to Hampshire County from Lancaster County, Penn. [Jacob Doman Sr. died in Hampshire County in 1815.] Joseph Doman was married to: (a) Mary or Margaret Nelson, who died in 1852 and (b) Betty Parks of Greene County, Penn, who died in 1880. Source: Private records kept by a descendant.

Donaldson, Anthony, was born in 1761 and died on June 3, 1847 at Springfield, W.Va. Source: Tombstone inscription in graveyard on Springfield Hill, Hampshire County.

Donaldson, James, born in 1736 and died on March 20, 1801. Elizabeth Donaldson, his wife, died on Oct. 1, 1816. Source: Tombstone inscription, Springfield, Hampshire County, W.Va.

Donaldson, John, was born in 1763 and died July 12, 1850. Mary Donaldson (wife of John), was born in 1761 and died March 14, 1848. Source: Tombstone inscription, Springfield, W.Va., in graveyard on top of hill overlooking the town.

Doran, William, died in Hampshire County, Va. in Feb. 1850, aged 54 years. He married Hannah Susan Gard, daughter of Samuel and Sarah (Caudy) Gard. [Note: Hannah S. was first married to William Carmichael]. Source: 1850 Mortality Schedule for Hampshire County, Va.

Douthit, Silas, was born Dec. 29, 1763, in Hampshire County, Va. He served in the Revolutionary War; moved to Fayette County, KY in 1786. A brother was named Caleb Douthit. Source: Pension application filed in Franklin County, KY courthouse, in 1833.

Doyle, John, died of "hydrothorax" in July 1869, age 53, in Hampshire County. Source: 1870 Mortality Schedule for Hampshire County, W.Va.

Doyle, Matthew, was born Feb. 14, 1803 and died April 4, 1879, in Hampshire County, W.Va. He first married Winney Corbin, daughter of Daniel and Jane Corbin, June 16, 1828. After her death, Matthew remarried to Harriett Swisher, who died on Jan. 28, 1909, aged 83 years, 4 months, 9 days. Sources: Hampshire County **Deed Dook 30**, page 358, dated May 25, 1835; Hampshire County marriage records; and tombstone inscriptions in Mountain Dale cemetery, located several miles southeast of Romney, W.Va.

Duling, William, was born on April 27, 1748 in Devonshire, England and died at Keyser, Hampshire County, Virginia on Dec. 24, 1839. He married: (1) Sarah Ann Campbell, and (2) Mary Marsh. Source: Contact Mr. O.E. Duling, 786 Los Palos Manor, Lafayette, CA. 94549, who possesses an excellent data base on this surname.

Duling, William, Jr., son of William and Sarah Ann (Campbell) Duling, was born in Hampshire County, Va. on April 5, 1779 and died on Oct. 10, 1856. He married Elizabeth Dean on April 14, 1807. She was born on May 22, 1788 and died on March 15,

1837. He remarried to Harriett ____. Children of William Duling Jr. were: (1) Sarah Jane Duling was born Nov. 29, 1829. She married John Welsh. (2) Ann Duling was born Oct. 3, 1812, and married John Dew. (3) Elizabeth Duling was born Sept. 25, 1814 and died March 15, 1840, unmarried. (4) William Duling III was born June 29, 1816. He married Elizabeth Poston. (5) Catherine Duling was born May 4, 1818 and died March 12, 1850. She married John Wineour of Cumberland, Md. (6) Mary Duling was born June 10, 1820 and died March 21, 1864. She married Joseph Davis, her cousin, Nov. 11, 1839. (7) Thomas Duling was born Aug. 17, 1824 and died June 2, 1842. (8) James Sanson Duling was born Aug. 17, 1824 and died in 1854. He married Emily Kitzmiller. (9) Caroline Eleanor Duling was born Aug. 24 and died July 4, 1842, unmarried. (10) David Gibson Duling was born Nov. 4, 1830 and died Jan. 6, 1865. He married Susan Rebecca Davis on Nov. 2, 1853. She was born in Nov. 1825. They lived at New Creek, Mineral County, W.Va. Source: Mr. O.E. Duling, 786 Los Palos Manor, Lafayette, CA 94549.

Dunbar, William, son of James and Grace Dunbar, died Jan. 18, 1764, aged 14 years. Source: Morgan's Chapel Records, Norborne Parish, old Frederick County, Va. (now Bunker Hill, W.Va.).

Duncan Sr., Matthew, son of James Duncan, was born circa 1700 and died in Frederick County, Va., in 1766. His son, Matthew Duncan II, was born circa 1725, married Sarah Johns (1723-1806), and he died in Berkeley County, Va., in 1793. They were early settlers in old Frederick County, emigrating from Lancaster County, PA., originally from Ireland. Most of their seven children immigrated to Kentucky prior to 1800. Source: Wilma Hill, 3040 Euclid, Wichita, KS 67217.

Dunkon, Patrick, and wife Catherine, were parents of: (1) Samuel Dunkon, born Dec. 12, 1749. (2) Patrick Dunkon Jr., born Dec. 15, 1751. (3) Elizabeth Dunkon, born Aug. 11, 1754. Source: Morgan's Chapel Records, Bunker Hill, Berkeley County (originally part of old Frederick County, Va.).

Dunlap, Abner, son of William and Flora (McMullen) Dunlap, was born in Frederick County, Va. in 1808 and died in Preble County, Ohio on Sept. 30, 1897. He married Elizabeth Sample, daughter of Samuel and Nancy Sample, May 30, 1830, in

Hampshire County, Va. Elizabeth was born in Frederick County, Va. on Nov. 20, 1811 in Frederick County and died April 27, 1890. Samuel Sample was born in 1780 and died in Preble County, Ohio in 1854. His wife was Nancy Ridenhour. These families immigrated to Preble County, Ohio in November 1830. Abner and Elizabeth Dunlap had eight children.

Dunlap, Archibald, son of William and Flora (McMullen) Dunlap, was born in Hampshire County, Va. on May 1, 1804 and died March 14, 1891. He married Mary C. Griffith, and they lived in Frederick County, Va. They were buried in the Dunlap graveyard on Timber Ridge.

Dunlap, John, son of William and Flora (McMullin) Dunlap, was born in Frederick County, Va., on August 9, 1799 and died Feb. 19, 1881. His wife, Eliza McKee, daughter of Bartholomew and Nancy (Reid) McKee, was born Dec. 24, 1807, and died Aug. 17, 1893. Their children were: (1) Rebecca Dunlap, born in 1830 and died in Iowa, on July 8, 1900. She married Azariah Slonaker, son of George and Nancy (Merchant) Slonaker, Sept. 5, 1854, in Frederick County. In 1882, when her father's estate was settled, her married name was Plotner or Platner, apparently the result of a subsequent marriage. (2) Lemuel James Dunlap, born April 18, 1831, in Frederick County and died April 3, 1899, at Winthrop, Buchanan County, Iowa. He married Mary Catherine Potterf (1832-1900) (3) Ellen Dunlap was born on Oct. 23, 1832 and died in Ohio on Aug. 9, 1859, unmarried. (4) Mercy Dunlap was born on Dec. 24, 1833, and died on Sept. 13, 1909. She married William B. Mason, 1830-1909. They lived in Hampshire Cunty, W.Va., near Yellow Springs. (5) William P. Dunlap was born on April 12, 1835, and died on Aug. 24, 1879, in Buchanan County, Iowa, aged 41 years, 4 months, 12 days. He first married Emily _____; then married Ellen Grove (1840-1919). (6) Aaron J. Dunlap was born Jan. 19, 1837, and died in 1913. He married Hannah E. Shane (1837-1919), daughter of John and Catherine (Mason) Shane, April 4, 1859. (7) Flora Ann Dunlap was born June 16, 1838 and died April 28, 1925. She married John F. Shane, son of John and Catherine (Mason) Shane, Oct. 10, 1861. John F. was born June 20, 1840 and died Oct. 8, 1915. They were buried in the Quaker graveyard at Gainsboro, Frederick County. (8) Bartholomew "Barton" Dunlap was born Feb. 6, 1840 and died Jan. 24, 1925. He received $100 from his father's estate in 1882. He married Nancy Gutherie on Jan. 30, 1868, and they lived in Winthrop, Buchanan County Iowa. (9) John Wesley Dunlap was born on Jan. 8, 1841 and died June 27, 1918, in Kansas City, MO. He married Sarah Ann Garrard, daughter of Harvey and Hannah (Gustin) Garrard, on Feb. 5, 1870, in Muncie, IN. Sarah was born June 12, 1850 and died June 9, 1932. They were buried in Mt. Hope cemetery, Kansas City. (10) George M. Dunlap was born on Aug. 27, 1844, and died in 1910. He married Margaret Ellen Elliott, daughter of Reuben and Mildred (Triplett) Elliott, Oct. 1, 1868, in Frederick County. She was born in December 1847 and died in 1911. (11) Eliza Catherine Dunlap was born on April 6, 1846 and died Dec. 16, 1927. She married John W. Marple, son of George and Livinia Marple, March 22, 1877. (12) Jeremiah J. Dunlap was born on April 2, 1848, and and died May 28, 1923. He first married Alwilda A. Reid, daughter of John and Mary A. Reid, May 12, 1870, in Frederick County. They were buried in the Shiloh Church Cemetery in eastern Hampshire County, W.Va. His second marriage was to Canzara Updike. (13) Joel P. Dunlap was born on June 25, 1853 and died on December 10, 1936. He first married Emily Belle Kerns, daughter of Benjamin F. and Julia Ann (Triplett) Kerns, July 30, 1874. She was born April 9, 1855 and died in 1911, in Frederick County. He remarried to Mary E. McCalham. Sources: Census and Bible records, court records (Frederick County *Will Book 34*, pp. 103-104), graveyard inscriptions, and information provided by Mrs. Patricia E. Brooks, 755 N.W. Kimo Lane, Seal Rock, OR 97376.

Dunlap, William (1775-1858) married Flora McMullen (1769-1851). They allegedly came from Belfast, Ireland, and arrived in Philadelphia with McVicker families during the late 1790s and settled on Timber Ridge in Frederick County, Va. See "History of the Dunlap Family," by Wilmer L. Kerns, in the February 1992 issue of *The West Virginia Advocate*.

Dunlap, William Jr., was born in Hampshire County, Va. on Dec. 28, 1807, and died Dec. 13, 1888. He married:(1) Margaret Ann Pugh, daughter of Mishall and Margaret (Rees) Pugh of Hampshire County. Margaret was born on June 30, 1810 and died Feb. 11, 1861. (2) Mary Jane Larrick, daughter of Jacob and Harriet (Good) Larrick. She was born in 1842 and died Dec. 24, 1909, in Philadelphia, Pa.

Edwards, Anthony, son of Thomas and Martha (Keener/Kisner) Edwards, was born on Nov. 18, 1786 at Edwards Run, Hampshire County, Va., and died on Sept. 19, 1860. His wife, Elizabeth Cram, daughter of John Cram, who came to Hampshire County, Va. from Philadelphia, PA, was born on Jan. 4, 1788 and died on Nov. 10, 1858. They were married on April 6, 1809. Source: Bible record in possession of William E. Edwards of Winchester, Va. (see more records below), and tombstone inscriptions in the Episcopal Cemetery, Cold Stream, Hampshire County, Va.

Edwards, Elizabeth Ann, daughter of Anthony and Elizabeth (Cram) Edwards, was born on Dec. 20, 1812, at Cold Stream, Hampshire County, Va., and died on Sept. 13, 1887 in Sherman County, Nebraska. She married: (1) William Largent, son of Lewis and Kezziah (Parrish) Largent, on Dec. 10, 1846 in Hampshire County. William was born circa 1796 and died circa 1848 at Cold Stream. They had one child. Then she remarried to (2) Mr. James Kidwell, son of John and Ellen (Hayes) Kidwell. Source: Bible record of Judge William E. Edwards, census records, courthouse records in Hampshire County.

Edwards, Elvirah Harrison, daughter of Anthony and Elizabeth (Cram) Edwards, was born on Aug. 11, 1810 at Cold Stream, Hampshire County, and died on March 1, 1844. She married a Mr. Harrison on March 11, 1830. It is believed that her husband was Nathan Harrison, son of Robert Harrison. Source: Bible record of Judge William E. Edwards.

Edwards, Hester Isabella Grubbs, daughter of Anthony and Elizabeth (Cram) Edwards, was born on June 3, 1815 and died on Nov. 15, 1866. She married James W. Grubbs of Cold Stream, Hampshire County, Va., on April 14, 1836. See the 1850 census for Hampshire County. Source: Bible record provided by Judge W.E. Edwards of Winchester, Va.

Edwards, James Anthony, son of Anthony and Elizabeth (Cram) Edwards, was born at Cold Stream on Oct. 20, 1820 and died on July 10, 1822. Source: Family Bible.

Edwards, John Cram, son of Anthony and Elizabeth (Cram) Edwards, was born at Cold Stream, Hampshire County, on March 26, 1819 and died on Jan. 26, 1903 in Kansas. His first wife, Harriett Baker, was born on Jan. 17, 1819 and died on Sept. 14, 1866. They were married on Dec. 6, 1843. She was buried in the

Episcopal cemetery at Cold Stream. He then remarried to Martha Jane Cooper? on Sept. 23, 1867. She was born on Feb. 11, 1846, at Cold Stream, and died on Feb. 28, 1930, in Kansas. She told her children that her maiden name was Cooper, but the marriage record in Romney says Caudy (signed by Evan Caudy). A third story says that her mother was nee Canon, the birth name of Martha J. Probably she was raised by a Cooper family, and adopted that name.

Edwards, Joseph, was born circa 1695 and died on his Capon Bridge farm in 1782. His wife was named Sarah. The first road leading west from Winchester, Va., in 1750, crossed his farm, known later as a wagon road. An old graveyard was located on the west bank of the Cacapon River, near the road, but has been lost in time, or destroyed. I and others have done extensive on-site research of the Edwards real estate. The northern half of the town of Capon Bridge, W.Va. lays on one section of his former 400-acre Fairfax grant. It is believed that Edwards emigrated from Chester County, PA to the Cacapon Valley circa 1734-35. One researcher contends that Joseph Edwards was a son of Joseph and Mary (Hickman) Edwards of Chester County, PA. A very compelling argument has been made in a research paper by: Mrs. Marie Quisenberry, 6852 Alderwood Drive, Carlsbad, CA. 92008.

Edwards, Louisa, daughter of Anthony and Elizabeth (Cram) Edwards, was born on Nov. 18, 1811 at Cold Stream, and died on April 10, 1881, unmarried.

Edwards, Robert, aged 72 years, married Ellen C. Brill, Aug. 19, 1879, in Hampshire County, W.Va. Source: Courthouse marriage record.

Edwards, Thomas, son of Joseph and Sarah Edwards, was born circa 1722 and died in 1791 in the Cacapon Valley, Hampshire County, Va. His Will was probated on July 14, 1791, per Hampshire County Will Book I, page 274. The Executors were his wife, Mary (Hiett) Edwards and her brother, Evan Hiett. Bondsmen were: John Slane, David Foreman and Evan Jenkins. He received valuable Fairfax grants, and Edwards' Run was named after this man. It is believed that he and his wife were buried on top of Edwards Mtn., on his own land. Their children were: (1) David Edwards was deceased by 1786. A book has been written on this branch, titled, **Edwards: Progenitors, Siblings, Descendants of Andrew Edwards**. Contact: Miss Lela Lillian Lones, 3400 Willis, Perry, Iowa 50220. (2) Margaret Edwards married William Alderton. (3) Sarah Edwards married James McBride. (4) Ann Edwards married Samuel Parke. (4) Naomi Edwards married: (a) John Owens (b) Bernard Brelsford. (5) Hannah Edwards married Samuel Parke and (7) Thomas Edwards, II, married Martha Keener. See Hampshire County **Will Book I**, pp. 369-370, for a list of legatees found in the administration papers, dated May 3, 1794, Hampshire County Court, Romney, W.Va. 26757.

Edwards, Thomas, II, son of Thomas and Sarah (Hiett) Edwards, was born in 1763 and died on Jan. 12, 1814. He married Martha Kesner (Kisner or Keener) on Dec. 13, 1785. Nearby in the same graveyard is a very old stone which says only, "E.E(dwards), Jan. 20, 1795." My guess is that this is the death date for one of the children of Thomas and Martha Edwards, possibly named Elizabeth. Source: Tombstone inscription in the Thomas Edwards, II, graveyard, behind the Cold Stream Assembly of God Church, Capon Bridge, W.Va.

Edwards, Thomas Austin, son of Anthony and Elizabeth (Cram) Edwards, was born at Cold Stream, Hampshire County, Va. on Oct. 13, 1816 and died on Feb. 20, 1853. The family Bible stated that he was married on Jan. 14, 1840, but didn't name the spouse, nor where they lived.

Edwards, William Meade, son of Anthony and Elizabeth (Cram) Edwards, was born at Cold Stream, Hampshire County, Va. on Nov. 26, 1829, and died at Martinsburg, W.Va. on Sept. 19, 1902. He married: (1) Mary Ann Kelly, daughter of James and Ellen (Frisellman) Kelly, on March 28, 1854. She was born on March 13, 1833 and died at Bowling Green, KY on May 12, 1864. (2) Elizabeth Catherine Peacemaker, on Oct. 23, 1866. She died on April 3, 1876 in Frederick County, Va. (3) Minnie Boxwell, on Nov. 16, 1880, in Frederick County, Va. He was an undertaker at Cold Stream, Hampshire County, during the 1850s and early 1860s; later moved to Frederick County where he served as postmaster in one of the postoffices. Source: Records of Judge William E. Edwards of Winchester, Va.

Effland, George, was born June 30, 1811. His wife, Mary Ann, was born Aug. 21, 1827. They had 11 children: (1) George W. Effland was born June 21, 1849, (2) John Effland was born Feb. 18, 1851, (3) Charles C. Effland was born Jan. 30, 1853, (4) Catherine Effland was born Dec. 27, 1855, (5) Jerry M. Effland was born Jan. 7, 1857, (6) David H. Effland was born June 22, 1859, (7) Mary E. Effland was born July 28, 1860, (8) Delilah Effland was born April 19, 1863, (9) William H. Effland was born Nov. 1, 1865, (10) Annie L. Effland was born Oct. 8, 1867 and died in Feb. 1968, aged 100 years, (11) Virginia Ellen Effland was born Jan. 12, 1871 and died Aug. 22, 1957. She was twice married, to John Gaver and John Thomas. They lived at Davis, W.Va. Source: Mrs. Peggy Frankenfeld, 1348 Green Road, Roslyn, PA 19001-2817.

Elliott, Reuben, died in January 1860, aged 49 years, from a spinal injury received in a fight with his son-in-law, Simeon Marple. Reuben was ill for two days before he passed away. He was survived by his wife, nee Mildred Triplett. Primary source of death record: 1860 Mortality Schedule for Frederick County, Va.

Ellis, David, son of Morris and Susannah Ellis Jr., was born March 1, 1782 and died Oct. 2, 1852, in Mahaska County, Iowa. He first married Nancy Hedrick, daughter of Nicholas and Jane Hedrick, Feb. 25, 1811. Nancy was born on Aug. 12, 1794 and died Feb. 27, 1823. David re-married to Sarah Jane Farmer, daughter of John and Frances (Seaton) Farmer, Oct. 2, 1828. Sarah J. was born Feb. 10, 1805 and died April 23, 1873, at Walla Walla, Washington. Source: Family Bible of John and Frances Farmer of Hampshire County, Va., and LDS records on the Ellis family.

Ellis, Eliza, daughter of David and Nancy (Hedrick) Ellis, was born in Hampshire County, Va. on Dec. 22, 1811 and died in Wabash County, Indiana on Sept. 9, 1874. She married Franklin Weaver, son of Abraham and Magdalene (Senseny) Weaver, on April 7, 1828, in Hampshire County, Va. He was born on Oct. 10, 1801 and died on May 15, 1877 in Wabash County, Indiana. Source: Hampshire County court records and tombstone inscriptions at LaGro, Indiana. Source: Mrs. Joann Ellsworth, Wampum, Wisconsin.

Ellis, Harriet, daughter of David and Nancy (Hedrick) Ellis, was born in Hampshire County, Va., Nov. 15, 1817 and died Sept. 19, 1845. She married David Ginevan, son of Mathias and Catherine Ginevan. Source: Bible record of David Ellis.

Ellis, Joel, son of Abraham Ellis, died on Dec. 17, 1865, aged 76 years, 8 days. Elizabeth his wife died on Feb. 10, 1871, aged 80 years, 5 months. It is believed that this family had a connection with Ellis families in Hampshire County, Va.; then went to western Pennsylvania before removing to Ohio. See Samuel Weaver below. Source: Tombstone inscriptions in the New Burlington Cemetery, near the Clinton/Greene, Ohio county line.

Ellis, Joel of Hampshire County, Va. was deceased prior to March 5, 1846, when an inventory was made on his estate. Samuel Baumgarner was the executor. Joel left no direct descendants, so the case was referred to chancery court to settle his Will. There were two sets of legatees; white heirs and black heirs. First, the whites: John Ellis, Nelson W. Ellis, Ira Ellis, sons of my deceased brother, Dudley Brown Ellis, of Kentucky; David Ellis, Jr.; Lucinda Dunlap, neice in Kentucky. Presumably Joel's sister married a William Dunlap; Mahala Clift (possibly a deceased sister) whose daughter Mary E. Clift ("niece") was to receive the silver. The black heirs: Judith was a slave of Joel Ellis, and she had Caroline, Abram, and Virginia Clay. Their father was a servant of Joel Ellis, but was freed and he went to Alexandria, Va. Judith (the female slave) died before Joel Ellis died. Celia was a servant of Joel and she became free and married Thomas Duncan. This case was kept open for many years, possibly because of the reluctance to turn over an estate to former slaves or servants. In 1868, Thomas Duncan gave a deposition that he was 70 years old. The name of the Ellis estate was called "Pleasant Retreat." The court finally agreed to give the white and black legatees equal shares. Source: Papers in Box 165, Circuit Court of Hampshire County, W.Va., dated June 27, 1848. In Box 232, dated March 1872, it shows that Samuel Baumgarner, Executor, had died and his widow, Ellen, was called Mrs. Racey. A tombstone inscription at Intermont, W.Va. shows that Samuel Bumgardner was born on Oct. 24, 1800, and died in 1864. It lists two different wives: Rachel F. (1816-1851) and Ellen Racey, born on Jan. 27, 1823, and died on Aug. 3, 1905.

Ellis, Jonathan Morris, son of David and Sarah (Farmer) Ellis, was born Sept. 27, 1829, and died Sept. 8, 1838. Source: Farmer family Bible record.

Ellis, Morris Jr., son of Morris and Sarah (Coleston) Ellis Sr., was born April 9, 1750. His second wife was Mary Smith, widow of Jeremiah Smith Jr. They were married in 1801 in Frederick County, Va. Children of Morris Ellis Jr. and his first wife were: (1) David Ellis was born March 1, 1782 and died Oct. 2, 1852. He married Nancy Hedrick and Sarah Jane Farmer. (2) Sarah Ellis was born May 3, 1783. (3) William Ellis was born Nov. 1, 1785. (4) Ann Ellis was born June 23, 1788 and died May 28, 1871, in Frederick County, Va. She married James Albin, Jan. 8, 1809, and George Smith, in 1819. (5) Jonathan Ellis was born Oct. 7, 1792 and died in Pickaway County, OH, on Aug. 10, 1842. His first wife, Catherine, was born in 1800 and died Aug. 11, 1824, in Pickaway County. His second wife, named Mary, was born in 1800 and died in Oct. 10, 1847. (6) Susannah Ellis was born Oct. 3, 1794. She married Casper Rogers. (7) Morris Ellis III was born Sept. 23, 1796. The date and place of Morris Ellis Jr.'s death is not known, but is being researched by descendants. Source: Contact Ms. Ann Aftanas, P.O. Box 77, Follansbee, W.Va. 26037.

Ellis, Samuel George, son of David and Sarah J. (Farmer) Ellis, was born Sept. 29, 1832 and died Feb. 8, 1904. He married Rhoda Ann Kennedy, May 8, 1856. Source: Family Bible record.

Ellis, Susan Frances, daughter of David and Sarah (Farmer, Sarah Ellis) Ellis, was born Jan. 1, 1831, and died May 12, 1916. She married Eli Zaring, in 1855. Source: Bible record of John and Frances (Seaton) Farmer, and LDS family group sheets.

Ely, William, died in 1844, aged 71 years. His wife, Sarah Ely, died in 1848, aged 76 years. Source: Tombstone inscriptions at Primitive Baptist Church Graveyard, Three Churches, Hampshire County, W.Va.

Emmart, Abraham, was born in 1809 and died on July 3, 1864, in Hampshire County, W.Va. His wife, Eliza Jane (Vance), widow of Abraham Emmart, died on April 25, 1881, aged 68 years, 15 days, according to the May 6, 1881 issue of the *South Branch Intelligencer*. Her parents were Andrew B. and Margaret (Batchelor) Vance, according to the research of Mr. Emil M. Sunley, 5421 Duvall Drive, Bethesda, MD 20816. A copy of the "widow's dower," including the survey plat for the division of Abraham Emmart's land, shows: Eliza Jane Emmart, widow's dower, 126 acres; George A. Emmart, 43 acres; Wilmot A.C. Emmart, 40 acres; Elmira V.C. Emmart, 40 acres; Martha A. McKee, 62 and one-half acres; Matilda A. Dellinger, 64 acres; Margaret E. Millslagle, 55 acres; Jonathan Emmart, 112 acres; and William S. Hook, assignee of Lewis Emmart, 51 and one-half acres.

Emmart, Andrew, son of Henry and Rebecca (Cheshire) Emmart, died on June 13, 1886, aged 79 years. The courthouse death record stated that Andrew was unmarried.

Emmart, Benjamin F., died on Feb. 15, 1895, aged 64 years, 2 months, 26 days. Source: Tombstone inscription on Dunmore Ridge, Hampshire County, on Ervin Poland's place.

Emmart, Eve, daughter of John and Nancy Emmart II, died on April 9, 1874, "of dropsey," aged 58 years, 2 months, 21 days. Nancy Emmart, sister reported the death. Source: Hampshire County courthouse death record.

Emmart, George W., died on June 7, 1878, aged 55 years. Source: July 14, 1878 issue of the *South Branch Intelligencer*. His tombstone inscription, at Three Churches Primitive Baptist Graveyard, shows that he was born on Aug. 23, 1822 and died on June 7, 1878. His death was reported, also, to the county courthouse. Maud Pugh stated on page 343, Volume II, *Capon Valley: Its Pioneers and Descendants...*, that George's parents were Henry and Rebecca Emmart. His wife, Barbara Adkins, was born on July 18, 1840 and died on May 6, 1899, according to her tombstone inscription at Three Churches, W.Va. A loose paper, found in an old family book, listed his children as: R.S. Emmart, H.M. Emmart, C.W. Emmart, M.E. Emmart, and G.E. Emmart.

Emmart, Hannah, daughter of Andrew and Elizabeth Emmart, died July 15, 1884, aged 58 years, unmarried. Death was reported to courthouse by her brother Jacob Emmart. In the same death register is listed Anna Emmart, who died Oct. 11, 1884, aged 54 years, "of consumption." The record stated that she was a daughter of Andrew and Elizabeth Emmart. Possibly this was the same person, whose death was reported by two persons. Courthouse death recrds are not considered to be a reliable source of information.

Emmart, Henry, son of Jacob and Barbara Emmart, was deceased by Feb. 2, 1858. His wife was Rebecca Cheshire. Their children were: Susan Jane Emmart married William Loy; George W. Emmart; Lemuel Emmart, born April 11, 1824, and died Oct. 3, 1900; Priscilla Emmart, died March 12, 1890, aged 71 years, unmarried; Samuel Emmart; and Andrew Emmart, died June 13, 1886, aged 79 years, unmarried.. The land, situated on the Tearcoat, was sold to James and Margaret Creswell. The witness was Adam Wolford.[42]

Emmart, Jacob F., was born on Sept. 22, 1818 and died on Sept. 3, 1895. His wife, Margaret Ann Cather, was born Sept. 23, 1822, and died on Aug. 24, 1891. My grandfather, Robert R. Kerns (1872-1961) was well-acquainted with this Jake Emmart. I have a letter written to my grandfather, from a friend in Frederick County, announcing the death of Jake Emmart. Grandfather was a college student at Shenandoah Institute in Dayton, Virginia, when the letter was received in 1895. Source: Tombstone inscription in Quaker Graveyard, Gainsboro, Virginia.

Emmart, John, II son of John and Nancy Emmart, died on Jan. 25, 1872, aged 55 years, 2 months, 5 days. His wife was named Barbara. Note: John Emmart I was born in 1783 and wife Nancy in 1777, according to the Hampshire County, Va. census for 1850. Source: Hampshire County Courthouse death record.

Emmart, Nancy (nee Cheshire), was born in 1777 and died in July 1859, in Hampshire County, of "old age." She was born in Virginia. Source: 1860 Mortality Schedule for Hampshire County, Va.

Emmart, Samuel, died Fe. 14, 1889 in Sherman Dist., Hampshire County, aged 68 years, 4 months, 16 days. Cause of death: "fatty heart." Undertaker was Welby McKee of Augusta, W.Va.

Engle, John, died on July 12, 1889, aged 83 years. His wife, Sarah Cooper, died on May 28, 1889, aged 79 years, 3 months. Source: Death record in Hampshire County courthouse. The *Undertaker Book* of John W. Mellon showed that John Engle was buried on July 13, 1889 and Sarah was buried on May 28, 1889.

42. Names of children proven by information in Hampshire County *Deed Book 50*, page 105, Romney, W.Va.

Evans, John, was born in Virginia in 1776 and died of "consumption" on March 28, 1850. He was a farmer. John's wife was Frances Hardesty, born ca. 1787 and died on Sept. 12, 1864. John was buried in Bethel cemetery near Gore, Va. and Frances was buried near Princeville, Illinois. Source: Mortality Schedule of 1850 U.S. Census, and records provided by Ms. Sue Mayer, Peoria, IL.

Evans, Peter, died on Feb. 20, 1874 in Frederick County, Va. He was aged 86 years, 6 months, 20 days. Source: March 6, 1874 issue of the *South Branch Intelligencer*.

Everett, Enos, died on April 4, 1867, aged 72 years. Source: *South Branch Intelligencer*, April 12, 1867 issue.

Everett, Jacob W., died on Feb. 8, 1873, aged 61 years, in Hampshire County, W.Va. Source: Feb. 14, 1873 issue of the *South Branch Intelligencer*.

Fahs, Joseph, was born on Aug. 12, 1805 and died on Nov. 26, 1892. His wife was Maria Slane, daughter of Thomas and Margaret (Nielson) Slane, was born on Jan. 22, 1805 and died on May 7, 1891. Source: Tombstone inscriptions in Slane graveyard, located behind the Slanesville, W.Va. Elementary School.

Fahs, Philip, was born on Oct. 1, 1760 and died on June 20, 1848. He was buried near Hoy, W.Va. (between Slanesville and Augusta, W.Va.) in the Fahs Graveyard. Philip was a member of the Old School Baptist Church. Source: Tombstone inscription.

Farmer, John, son of Gregory and Jane Farmer, was born April 2, 1775 and died in 1808, in Hampshire County, Va. His wife, Frances Seaton, daughter of John and Alice (Murrey) Seaton, was born Nov. 2, 1769 and died March 10, 1835. Alice Murrey, daughter of James and Lydia Murrey, was born Oct. 13, 1744 and died Nov. 11, 1830. She was buried on Leith Mountain in Hampshire County. John and Frances (Seaton) Farmer were married on Jan. 26, 1804. Their children were: Sarah Jane Farmer was born Feb. 10, 1805, and died April 23, 1873. She married David Ellis on Oct. 2, 1828; Alice A. Farmer was born Nov. 22, 1806, and married Jonathan Fletcher on March 25, 1830. Alice died Feb. 26, 1834; Samuel Farmer, born March 31, 1808 and died in 1847. He married Anna McDonald, daughter of Benjamin and Margaret (Hiett) McDonald.

Farmer, Samuel, son of John and Frances (Seaton) Farmer, was born on March 31, 1808 and died on May 8, 1848. They emigrated from Hampshire County after their marriage in 1838, to New Hope, Lincoln County, Missouri. It is believed that Samuel died there (or somewhere out west) and Anna returned with her small children to North River. Samuel married Anna McDonald, daughter of Benjamin and Margaret (Hiett) McDonald, on Jan. 4, 1838. Anna was born on March 25, 1811 and died on June 6, 1896, according to her tombstone inscription in the Benjamin McDonald Graveyard on North River, below Ice Mountain, Hampshire County. Old Benjamin Sr., was appointed guardian of the Farmer grandchildren. When "old Ben" died in 1856, James McDonald was appointed guardian. In 1872, a suit was filed in Hampshire County chancery court against James McDonald. See Box 238 in the Hampshire County Circuit Court. In this material I found the names of Samuel Farmer's children: (1) Margaret Frances Farmer was born Jan. 5, 1840, and married Zebulon B. McDonald, on Feb. 2, 1863; (2) Sarah Ann Farmer, born on Dec. 20, 1841, married Francis Marion "Frank" Kidwell on Feb. 16, 1869. Sarah A. died on Dec. 3, 1869; (3) Samuel James Farmer was born Feb. 8, 1846. He married Margaret E. Furr (See below); and (4) John Benjamin Farmer was born on Oct. 10, 1843 and died on Sept. 26, 1845. Source: Farmer family Bible, old letters from Benjamin and Margaret (Hiett) McDonald to the Samuel Farmer family in Lincoln County, Missouri, and Hampshire County Court records.

Farmer, Samuel James, son of Samuel and Ann (McDonald) Farmer, was born on Feb. 6, 1846 and died on May 6, 1936. He married Margaret E. Furr, daughter of Minor and Mary (McDonald) Furr. They were first cousins. She was born on May 31, 1846 and died on Sept. 3, 1916, aged 70 years, 3 months, 3 days. Buried nearby was Minnie B. Farmer, Born Oct. 23, 1874 and died on July 11, 1926. Source: Tombstone inscriptions in old Benjamin McDonald Sr., Graveyard, on North River, Hampshire County, W.Va., and the Farmer Family Bible (in possession of Mrs. Ellis Shanholtz, Capon Bridge, W.Va.)

Fawcett, Mary, died in February 1860, aged 72 years. She died of "dropsy," after a 114-day illness. Born in Virginia. Housewife. Source: 1860 Mortality Schedule for Frederick County, Va.

Fisher, Frances, daughter of William A. Kuykendall, was born in Hampshire County, Va. in 1777 and died in same county on Nov. 27, 1869. Source: Death record in Hampshire County courthouse.

Fisher, Thomas, son of Barak S. and Mary (Butler) Fisher, was born Nov. 18, 1763, in Frederick County, Va. and died on Aug. 28, 1802, in Frederick County. He married Margaret McKee, daughter of Robert and Elizabeth McKee Sr., Dec. 4, 1789. She was born May 8, 1764. Contact: Mrs. Martha Indermuhle, Box 504, Kittas, WA 98934.

Fletcher, Elizabeth Frances, daughter of Jonathan and Alice A. (Farmer) Fletcher, was born March 9, 1832. Source: Family Bible record.

Fletcher, George W., son of Jonathan and Alice A. (Farmer) Fletcher, was born Feb. 14, 1834. Source: Bible record.

Fletcher, Harriett, daughter of Jonathan and Alice A. (Farmer) Fletcher, was born on Jan. 2, 1831. Source: Family Bible record.

Fletcher, Jonathan, married Alice A. Farmer, daughter of John and Frances (Seaton) Farmer, March 25, 1830. Source: Family Bible record of John and Frances Farmer.

Fletcher, Joseph, was the first immigrant of that name to settle in the Timber Ridge section of Frederick County, Va. He died circa 1833 in Hampshire County, Va. His children were: (1) George Fletcher married Elizabeth _____ and they were living in "the Territory of Michigan, Kalamazoo, County," in 1834. (2) Benjamin Fletcher married Matilda _____ and they were also living in the Territory of Michigan, Kalamazoo County. (3) Thomas Fletcher married Barbara Oates. (4) James Fletcher was born on Aug. 8, 1796 and died on July 22, 1869. He married Catherine Ullery on July 26, 1818, in Frederick County, Va. According to the 1870 Mortality Schedule for Frederick County, James' father (Joseph) was not born in America. Also, the record stated that Catherine (spouse) survived James Fletcher. (5) Elijah Fletcher married Elizabeth Ann Queen on Jan. 20, 1826, in Hampshire County. (6) Ann Fletcher married John Milleson in Hampshire County. (7) Mary Fletcher married Jacob Ullery in Hampshire County. Sources: Hampshire County *Deed Book 29*, pages 153-156, dated June 9, 1833; *Deed Book 29*, pages 294-295, dated Feb. 7, 1834.

Fletcher, William (of Elijah Fletcher), married Elizabeth J. Ridgeway (of John Ridgeway), on Dec. 28, 1853, ???? at "B. White's," by "Rev. Russmisel." A tombstone in the Fairview Lutheran Church graveyard shows that William died on Dec. 3, 1861, age 50 years, and his wife, Elizabeth J. Ridgeway, died on April 8, 1910, age 88 years. Her birthdate was March 15, 1822, according to a court deposition in Hampshire County, W.Va. (See Box 236 in The Circuit Court). She and her brother, William G. Ridgeway, and her sister, Sarah M. Ridgeway, testified that the birthdate was taken from the Family Register of John Ridgeway, their father. Source: Note copied in margin of family Bible, and tombstone inscriptions, and court deposition.

Foley, Isaac, aged 69 years, died on June 25, 1877, in Grant County, West Virginia. Source: July 15, 1877 issue of the *South Branch Intelligencer*.

Foltz, John, born in Virginia in 1793, and died in Shenandoah County, Va. in December 1869, "of dropsy." Blacksmith. Survived by spouse. Source: 1870 Mortality Schedule for Shenandoah County, Va.

Foote, the Rev. William Henry, D.D., was born on Dec. 20, 1794 and died on Nov. 22, 1869. He was pastor of the Presbyterian Churches in Romney and Springfield. His wife, Arabella Gilliam, was born on Jan. 12, 1807 and died on March 18, 1892. Source: Tombstone inscriptions, Indian Mound Cemetery, Romney, W.Va. See, also, the Nov. 26, 1869 issue of The *South Branch Intelligencer*.

Foreman, Abbylonia, daughter of David and Catherine Foreman, Sr., was born in 1786 at Cold Stream and died on May 20, 1872 in Taylor County, West Virginia. She married John Shanholtzer, son of Peter and Magdalena (Hott) Shanholtzer, Jr., in 1818. Source: Mr. Howard L. Hunt, Coraopolis, Penn.

Foreman, Amos, was born circa 1778, and died in 1802 in Frederick County, Va. He married Hannah Goff on April 23, 1801. It is believed that he had a son named John A. Foreman, born in 1802, who married Mary Ann Clowser. After Amos' death, Moses Newbanks took out a marriage bond to marry Hannah (Goff or Gough) Foreman, widow, on July 29, 1803. Who were the parents of this Amos Foreman? One hypothesis is that he was the youngest son of Capt. William Foreman who was killed by

Indians in 1779.   Possibly he was a son of David Foreman. Source: Hon. Michael M. Foreman, Clerk of the Circuit Court, City of Winchester, Va.

Foreman, Catherine (Voglesong), died on July 17, 1825. Born circa 1752, she was married to David Foreman, son of William and Catherine (Dubois) Foreman. Source: Tombstone inscription, Foreman cemetery, Cold Stream, Hampshire County.

Foreman, Christina, unmarried daughter of David and Catherine Foreman, Sr., was born on Sept. 7, 1788 and died on April 28, 1869, at Cold stream. The Foreman graveyard at Cold Stream contains a slate with the inscription, "C.F." Source: Will and probate records.

Foreman, David, son of Capt. William and Anna (Dubois) Foreman, was born circa 1755 "on the South Branch" and died in 1795 near Cold Stream, Hampshire County. After his father was killed by Indians in 1777, David went to Berkeley County, Va. to live with relatives. He then married Catherine Voglesong and returned to Hampshire County, settling on the east side of Sandy Ridge. He was buried in an unmarked grave on the family farm, known locally as "Frog Hollow." There is some evidence that a church once stood on this land, referred to in an 1880 letter as no longer standing on the site. A manuscript on the Foreman family of Hampshire County, was published in the April 1989 issue of *The West Virginia Advocate*.

Foreman, Fannie, "wife of David Foreman (Jr.), died on June 23, 1824." She was a daughter of John and Ellen (Hayes) Kidwell. The David Foreman Jr. farm in Parks' Valley was sold to George Oates, Sr., whose Will was filed in 1844. Source: Foreman graveyard at Cold Stream and courthouse records.

Foreman, George, unmarried son of David and Catherine Foreman, was born ca. 1774; died Oct. 3, 1803 at Cold Stream. Source: Tombstone inscription in Foreman cemetery at Cold Stream.

Foreman, James William, son of Samuel and Anne (Richmond) Foreman, was born on Nov. 22, 1832 and died on Oct. 18, 1868. He married Harriett Hiett, daughter of John and Anna (Edwards) Hiett. Source: Letter written by Henry Haines in 1869 and tombstone inscription at Cold Stream.

Foreman, John, son of David and Catherine Foreman, was born in Hampshire County in 1777 and died in Aug. 1852 in Clinton County, Ohio. He married Catherine Rhinehart (born in 1783), daughter of Abraham and Margaret Rhinehart.

Foreman, Margaret, unmarried daughter of David and Catherine Foreman, Sr., was born ca. 1785 and died in Aug. 1856 at Cold Stream. Source: Census and courthouse records.

Foreman, Mary, was born in 1774 and died, unmarried, in Jan. 1850, of "palsy," at Cold Stream. Her parents were David and Catherine (Vogelsong) Foreman Sr. Source: 1850 Mortality Schedule for Hampshire County, Va.

Foreman, Samuel, was born on Jan. 10, 1784, and died on Oct. 26, 1851. His parents were David and Catherine Foreman Sr. Samuel married Anne Richmond, daughter of James and Jane (Allen) Richmond. She was born in 1812 and died on July 13, 1894, at Cold Stream, according to courthouse death records. John W. Mellon's *Undertaker Book* shows that she was buried on July 14, 1894, and the funeral cost was $18.00. Source: Buried in Foreman cemetery at Cold Stream, Hampshire County, W.Va.

Foreman, Samuel P., son of Samuel and Anne (Richmond) Foreman, was killed by runaway horses on June 17, 1864, aged 29 years, 7 months and 1 day. He was not married. Source: Letter written by Henry Haines in 1869 and tombstone inscription at Cold Stream.

Foster, Jonathan, was born in Chester County, Pa., March 9, 1766, and died in Frederick County, Sept. 20, 1824. His wife, Elizabeth Greenwood, was born May 15, 1768 in County of York, England, and died July 8, 1845. They immigrated to Winchester in 1807, to pursue commercial interests. They had a family of 12 children, only one of whom lived past the year 1850.

Fout, William, was born in 1797 and died in 1873. Margaret, his wife, was born in 1800 and died in 1872. Robert N. Fout, their son, was born in 1840 and died in 1922. Maria, wife of Robert Fout, was born in 1849 and died in 1917. Source: Tombstone inscriptions in family graveyard in field, near Purgitsville and Old Fields, W.Va. (Hardy County), along U.S. Route 220.

Fox, Gabriel, was born March 29, 1796 and died Dec. 18, 1877. His wife, Mary. M., was born Nov. 29, 1803 and died Oct.

27, 1869. Source: Tombstone inscriptions in Inskeep graveyard, located about one mile north of Fisher, Hardy County, W.Va.

Frank, Adam, died on Feb. 16, 1877, on Timber Ridge. He married Sarah Pugh on Nov. 28, 1815. Source: War of 1812 Pension application.

French, Susan Ann, daughter of John and Elizabeth Taylor, died on Feb. 17, 1866, aged 64 years, 8 months, and 3 days. Her husband was one William French. Source: Courthouse death record.

Fry, Elizabeth, died in Morgan County, Va., in February 1850, aged 80 years. She was born in Pennsylvania. Source: 1850 Mortality Schedule for Morgan County, Va.

Fry, Jacob, died on Nov. 23, 1838, aged 69 years, 9 months, 13 days. His wife, Elizabeth, died on March 16, 1838, aged 61 years. Source: Tombstone inscriptions at St John's Lutheran graveyard, near Hayfield, Frederick County, Virginia.

Fryback, Charity, was born in Hampshire County, Va. on Feb. 27, 1780 and died in Montgomery County, Ohio on Oct. 12, 1827. She married Jacob Stoker, son of John and Elizabeth (Critton) Stoker. Jacob was born in Hampshire County, Va. on March 22, 1780. Source: Tombstone inscriptions in Booher Graveyard, Butler Township, Montgomery County, Ohio.

Fryback, William, was born in Hampshire County, Va. on Aug. 3, 1793 and died on June 27, 1844, in Montgomery County, Ohio. His wife, Hannah, was born on Aug. 10, 1808 and died on June 20, 1844. Source: Tombstone inscriptions in Booher Graveyard, Butler Township, Montgomery County, Ohio.

Frye, Mrs. Fanny, wife of Cornelius Frye, died on Aug. 22, 1874, in Hardy County, W.Va. Source: Sept. 4, 1874 issue of the *South Branch Intelligencer*.

Furr, Newton, son of Enoch (1754-1845) and Sarah (Clawson) Furr, was born in 1797 and died in LaSalle County, Illinois, on Dec. 19, 1870. His wife was named Pleasant Matthews, daughter of Richard Matthews. She was born in Loudoun County, Va. and died in LaSalle County, Illinois, on Feb. 27, 1883. They lived a part of their lives on Timber Ridge, near High View, Frederick County, Va.

Furr, Nimrod, died on April 5, 1882, aged 69 years, in Mineral County, W.Va. Source: The April 14, 1882 issue of the *South Branch Intelligencer*. Note: There was one Nimrod Furr, son of Minor and Nancy (Murray) Furr, who was born on Dec. 2, 1809. This Nimrod married Betsy Inskeep.

Furr, Robert, died on Oct. 20, 1861. He was an adult, based on size of coffin (over six feet long) which was ordered by Joseph Furr. Source: *Coffin Book* of William Meade Edwards, undertaker at Cold Stream, Hampshire County, Va.

Gaddis, William, one of the early pioneers who settled in Mill Branch Valley, was buried on the eastern foothill of Bear Garden Mountain in Hampshire County, Va. The inscription on the solid rock erected as a monument simply says "W. Gad's." No date was given, but the inscription is at least 218 years old, (in 1991), because William Gaddis wrote his Will on Dec. 11, 1772 and it was probated on March 9, 1773. It is one of the oldest inscribed colonial tombstones in W.Va. Sometime after his death, his wife Priscilla, nee Bowen, moved to Fayette County, Pennsylvania. She was born circa 1718 and died in western Pennsylvania on Feb. 17, 1796. Gaddis was a Fairfax grantee, in both Frederick and Hampshire Counties. It is believed that he was connected with the Quaker church, at least during his earlier years. A 1792 deed in Romney shows that Frederick Buzzard Sr., of Hampshire County purchased Gaddis' 421 acre farm on Mill Branch, Hampshire County. See *The West Virginia Advocate*, issues of Sept., Oct. and Nov. of 1986 and Feb. of 1987, for a brief history of the Gaddis settlement in Hampshire County, W.Va. According to a leading researcher on the Gaddis family, Priscilla Bowen was a daughter of Henry and Jane (Carter) Bowen, early settlers along the Opequon Creek in old Frederick County, Va. Check with: Mr. James Gaddis, Jr., 511 Sandtree Drive, Palm Beach Gardens, FL 33403.

Gano, Stephen, Jr., son of Stephen and Abigail Gano, Sr., was born circa 1780 in Hampshire County, Va. and died in 1821. He was a veteran of the War of 1812. He married Jane Allen (Ca 1784-1854) who died in Hampshire County. Source: Data provided by Ralph L. Triplett, Gore, Va.

Gard, Samuel, son of John and Elizabeth (Dudley) Gard, was born on Oct. 27, 1770 and died on Sept. 14, 1840. His wife was

Sarah Caudy, daughter of David and Martha (Hiett) Caudy. Deed Book 42, pages 429-430, in Hampshire County shows that Sarah and her son John Gard had settled in Warren County, Ohio by 1846. Samuel owned and operated Merchant's Mill in "Capon Bridge," with James Caudy, his brother-in-law. Source: Grandfather Papers in DAR Library, and Hampshire County courthouse records.

Garrett, Alfred died in April 1880, aged 72 years, "of pneumonia." He and his parents were born in Virginia. Alfred was a farmer, and his wife survived him. Source: 1880 Mortality Schedule for Frederick County, Va.

Garrett, Andrew, served in a Pennsylvania militia during the War of 1812. He married Fanny Earles on Nov. 26, 1830. He died March 22, 1857, and she died Feb. 15, 1882, both at Wardensville, Hardy County, Va (W.Va.)

Garrett, Joseph, was born May 31, 1825, and died Dec. 10, 1884. He served in CSA Company "G," 10th Regiment, Virginia Cavalry. Buried in Asbury cemetery, Hardy County, W.Va. His children were: (1) Elizabeth C. Garrett was born April 25, 1846 (2) James F. Garrett was born April 25, 1846 (3) Salemma J. Garrett was born Feb. 22, 1851 (4) General W.S. Garrett was born Aug. 14, 1852 (5) George W. Garrett was born Aug. 19, 1854 (6) Ann Jemima Garrett was born Nov. 24, 1857. She married Benjamin Elias Shanholtz. (7) Millard Garrett was born Nov. 17, 1860 (8) Joseph Garrett Jr. was born March 18, 1864 and (9) Robert L. Garrett was born May 17, 1871. This Garrett family was from Hardy County, W.Va. Source: Bible record in possession of Mrs. Bertha (Shanholtz) Ritter, who was a granddaughter of Joseph Garrett. Bertha, a resident of White Post, Va., died in Dec. 1989. I visited her on her birthday every year in May. I played "Golden Slippers" on the mandolin and she danced to the music.

Garvan (Garvin), Catherine, died in February 1850, aged 61 years. She was born in Pennsylvania. She was ill for 400 days prior to her death caused by "pulminary disease." Source: 1850 Mortality Schedule for Frederick County, Va.

Gibbons, Elizabeth, died July 7, 1839, in her 66th year. She was buried in the Methodist Graveyard, Shepherdstown, Jefferson County, Va. (now W.Va.).

Gibbons, Jacob, son of James and Mary Gibbons, was born Sept. 10, 1745, probably in what is now Hampshire County, W.Va., and died during the early 1830s. After the Indian wars in Hampshire County, Jacob moved to Opequon Valley, about six miles southeast of Winchester, Va. Gibbon's Run, located in Hampshire County, W.Va., was named after this family. Sometimes the name was spelled Gibbens. See "History and Tragedy of the Gibbons Family," by Wilmer L. Kerns, *The West Virginia Advocate*, Capon Bridge W.Va., February 15, 1990. Source: Mrs. Mary T. Gibbens, R.R. # 2, Box 301, Center Point, Indiana 47840.

Gibbons, Sarah, probably a daughter of James and Mary Gibbons, was born in Frederick County, Va. on May 5, 1742 and died Sept. 16, 1832. It is believed that she was kidnapped by Indians in 1756 and held for several years before returning to her family. Sarah married Cornelius Lister, born in Frederick County in 1740 and died May 6, 1805. Information provided by: Mrs. Mary T. Gibbens (see above).

Gibbons, Sarah, was born Jan. 10, 1776 and died on Aug. 21, 1816. She was buried in a private graveyard near Kearneysville, Jefferson County, Va. ("Border Orchard").

Gibson, David, born on July 22, 1795 and died in Hampshire County on Nov. 10, 1871. His wife, Ann Markee Van Meter, daughter of Isaac Van Meter, was born on Dec. 5, 1805 and died on Aug. 24, 1859. Source: Tombstone inscriptions in the Indian Mound Cemetery, Romney, W.Va.

Gibson, Susan M., wife of O.W. Heiskell, died on Nov. 27, 1841. Source: Tombstone inscription in the Indian Mound Cemetery, Romney, W.Va.

Giffin, John was born in 1779 and died on May 16, 1850. Source: Tombstone inscription, Capon Chapel, Hampshire County, W.Va.

Gill ("black boy" of Charles Gill), died at Capon Bridge on Feb. 8, 1862. Source: Coffin-book of William Meade Edwards.

Gill, Dolly, daughter of Spencer and Nancy Walker, was born in Loudoun County, Va. in 1803 and died in Hampshire County, W.Va. on Oct. 19, 1880, "of paralysis." According to the death record in the Romney, W.Va. courthouse, her husband was named Charles Gill. They were married in Fauquier County,

Virginia on March 24, 1823. Their Bible record lists these children: (1) Nancy A. Gill was born on Jan. 30, 1824, and died May 6, 1880. She married a Benjamin P. McDonald, son of Gabriel and Catherine (Kackley) McDonald. They immigrated to Red Cloud, Nebraska. (2) Spencer Gill was born on Feb. 17, 1826, and died Jan. 9, 1900. See below. (3) Mariah Jane Gill was born on March 20, 1828 and died on Nov. 7, 1917. She was buried at Mt. Hebron E.U.B. Cemetery, Cross Junction, Va. Her first husband was William "Doc" Moreland, son of William and Sarah (Murphy) Moreland. He died in Peoria, Illinois and Mariah returned to Frederick County, Virginia, where she remarried to John Largent. (4) Alverna Gill was born on Sept. 17, 1829 and died on March 6, 1906. She married Wellington Herrell (1832-1899). Both were buried at Fairview Lutheran cemetery, Gore, Va. (5) Margaret Gill was born on May 11, 1831. She married Reuben DeHaven and they immigrated to Jefferson City, Missouri. (6) Catherine Gill was born on Jan. 14, 1833. She first married Benjamin F. Shane and then remarried to Gabriel McDonald, II. They died in Dawson County, Nebraska. (7) Franklin Gill was born on Dec. 11, 1834. He migrated to Nebraska. (8) Charles Washington Gill was born on Oct. 19, 1836. (9) Dolly Gill was born on Oct. 24, 1838. She married John Clark. (10) Lucinda Gill was born on Nov. 10, 1841 and died on Jan. 10, 1902. She married Joseph Allen Sprought (1844-1899). They were buried at Mt. Hebron E.U. B. graveyard, near Cross Junction, Frederick County, Virginia.

Gill, Elizabeth, was born in 1797 and died on Jan. 27, 1885. Her husband was Thomas Gill. Source: Hampshire County Courthouse death record.

Gill, Spencer, son of Charles and Dolly (Walker) Gill, was born Feb. 17, 1826 and died on Jan. 9, 1900, at Capon Bridge, W.Va. He married: (1) Mary Jane Hicks, who died on Jan. 13, 1866, aged 42 years, according to tombstone inscription at Fairview Lutheran Church, Gore, Virginia, and (2) Sarah Catherine Giffin, daughter of William and Sally (Pugh) Giffin, on April 29, 1868. Sarah Catherine was born on Oct. 21, 1838 and died July 2, 1913. Spencer and Sarah C. were buried in the Bethel (Trone) cemetery on Timber Ridge, near High View.

Gill, Thomas, died in Hampshire County, Va. on Nov. 30, 1861. He married Elizabeth Young in Jefferson County, Va., in Aug.

1817. Source: War of 1812 Pension Application, National Archives.

Ginevan, Catherine, died on May 11, 1900, aged 77 years, 3 months, 10 days. Source: Tombstone inscription in Ginevan Graveyard, Okonoko, W.Va.

Ginevan, Catherine, died on April 19, 1895. No other date given. This is hand-inscribed on an old slatestone. Source: Tombstone inscription in Ginevan graveyard, Okonoko, W.Va.

Ginevan, Elizabeth, daughter of Mathias and Catherine Ginevan, died May 29, 1883, aged 61 years, 3 months, 11 days. Source: Tombstone inscriptions, Ginevan Graveyard, Okonoko, Hampshire County W.Va., near Little Cacapon River.

Ginevan, Luther, son of Mathias and Catherine Ginevan, was born on April 22, 1808 and died on June 5, 1882. He was buried at Mt. Bethel, at Three Churches, W.Va.

Ginevan, Martin, son of Mathias and Catherine Ginevan, died on Sept. 19, 1845. This information was taken from a hand inscribed stone, Ginevan graveyard, Okonoko, W.Va.

Ginevan, Mary A., wife of David Ginevan, born in 1838 and died in 1914. She was nee Brelsford, because one Jesse Brelsford (born in 1829) testified in chancery court, Romney, W.Va., that his sister married David Ginevan. A marriage record in Hampshire County courthouse shows that David Ginevan, aged 56 years, married Mary Ann Brelsford, aged 38 years, on April 16, 1867, by the Rev. W.H. Foote. This was his second marriage, the first being to Harriett Ellis Source: Vital dates for Mary A. were secured from tombstone inscription in ."Shade graveyard," located a couple of miles west of the Neal's Run old Post Office, Hampshire County, W.Va.

Ginevan, Mathias, died on May 14, 1826, aged 45 years. His wife, Catherine, died on Feb. 26, 1869, aged 84 years, 11 months, 11 days. The name was sometimes spelled Genevan or Ginnovan. According to a suit in chancery court, in 1877, in Hampshire County Circuit Court, the children of Mathias and Catherine Ginevan were: Catherine, Elizabeth, Mathias, Jr., Luther Ginnevan, Harriett Burkett, Lueazr Mathews, Eveline Pratt, and David Ginevan, who married Harriet Ellis. Primary Source: Ginevan Graveyard, Okonoko, Hampshire County, W.Va.

Ginevan, Capt. Mathias, Jr., son of Mathias and Catherine Ginevan Sr., died on Aug. 23, 1875, aged 47 years, 2 months, 25 days. Source: Tombstone inscription under a 200-year-old, oak tree, in Ginevan graveyard, Okonoko, W.Va. The *South Branch Intelligencer*, Sept. 3, 1875 issue, stated that he died at Westernport, Maryland on Aug. 24, 1875 (a one-day discrepency between tombstone inscription and newspaper account of birth date).

Glaize, Henry, son of George and Catherine (Hetzel) Glaize, was born in Frederick County, Va. on Jan. 25, 1794, and died on Oct. 6, 1878. He married Ann Yeakley. Source: Records of Ralph L. Triplett, Esq.

Glaize, Sampson, son of George and Catherine (Hetzel) Glaize, was born in Frederick County, Va. on Oct. 3, 1791 and died on Feb. 6, 1850. He died of "dropsy" and was ill for 240 days. Sampson married Elizabeth Renner, who survived him. Sampson served in the War of 1812. Source: Records provided by Ralph L. Triplett Esq., Gore, Va.; 1850 Mortality Schedule for Frederick County, Va.

Glaize, Solomon, son of George and Catherine (Hetzel) Glaize, was born in Frederick County, Va. on Jan. 12, 1796 and died on March 11, 1878 in Frederick County. He married : (1) Elizabeth Streit, daughter of Charles and Catherine (Fries) Streit. She was born on Jan. 25 and died in 1837. (2) Elizabeth Fries. She died on July 6, 1875. Source: Records provided by Ralph L. Triplett, Esq.

Glaze, Andrew, died in Hampshire County on Feb. 12, 1872, aged 73 years. Source: *South Branch Intelligencer*.

Gochenour, Magdalene, died on May 16, 1885 near Augusta, W.Va. She married William Loy, son of Daniel and Christina (Millslagle) Loy, on April 25, 1838. William was born circa 1785 and died in 1861. William Loy's first wife was Mary Horn who died in 1827. (Note: This is to correct a mistake in my Shanholtzer history, re Magdalene's maiden name.) Source: Miss Mary Pugh, Romney, W.Va.; War of 1812 Pension folder.

Good, Elizabeth, died in March 1869, aged 79 years, "of bronchitus." She was born in Virginia. Source: 1870 Mortality Schedule for Frederick County, Va.

Good, Felix Sr., was born in Northampton County, Pennsylvania circa 1755 and died in Frederick County, Virginia circa

1816. Good served in the Revolutionary War and came to Frederick County, Va. prior to 1794, where he settled in upper Back Creek Valley. According to Ralph L. Triplett, Felix was buried in the Kale graveyard at the Burzie C. Baker farm near Capon Bridge, West Virginia. Felix married Anna Margaret DeLong, daughter of John and Maria Catherine (Dussinger) DeLong. She was born on Dec. 18, 1759. Her brother, John Nicholas DeLong, came to Frederick County, Va. He was born on July 19, 1756 and died on Feb. 21, 1823. The DeLong family came from Hudson Valley, New York prior to settling in Pennsylvania. Sources: Too many primary sources to list. Especially helpful was *The Lineage of Malcolm Metzger Parker From Johannes DeLANG*, by Dr. Irwin Hock DeLong, published in Lancaster, Pennsylvania in 1926. A copy of this book is in the DAR Library in Washington, D.C. See also, "Felix Good of Upper Back Creek Valley," *The West Virginia Advocate*, Capon Bridge, W.Va. 26711, June 19, 1991, for a discussion of these families.

Good, Felix, Jr., son of Felix and Anna Margaret (DeLong) Good Sr., was born on Aug. 30, 1794 and died in Frederick County, Virginia on Sept. 26, 1875. He married Rachel Orndorff, daughter of John and Margaret (Renner) Orndorff, on Dec. 14, 1820. Rachel was born Oct. 22, 1798 and died on June 3, 1857. Both were buried in the Good Cemetery, located on White Pine Ridge, on property now owned by Mr. Will Johnston of Winchester, Va. Felix, Jr. served in the War of 1812 and received bounty land. Source: Ralph L. Triplett was the major source. See *the West Virginia Advocate*, February 1991 issue, for an article on the Good family, and a photograph of Felix Jr..

Good, Jacob, son of Felix and Margaret (DeLong) Good Sr., was born April 6, 1799, and died March 12, 1881. He married Lucy Wigginton, Jan. 5, 1829, in Frederick County. Source: Hebron Lutheran Church Records, 1784-1850, Hampshire County, Virginia (birth); Tombstone inscription in Quaker graveyard, Gainsboro, Va. (death); and Frederick County marriage record.

Grapes, Mariah, daughter of Sylvanius Bennett, was born on July 25, 1807 and died on June 29, 1881. Her husband was John Grapes, according to Isaac Newton Grapes, who reported her death to the courthouse.

Grapes, Newton, died on April 4, 1878, aged 61 years, 10 months, and 27 days. He was a son of David and Harriett Grapes.

Greathouse, Harmon, Jr., son of Harmon and Mary (Stull) Greathouse, was born on June 30, 1762 (in either Frederick County, MD or Hampshire County, Va.) and died on July 5, 1849. He married Mercy Bukey, daughter of Captain John Bukey, born on March 19, 1768 and died on Feb. 25, 1841. They moved from Hampshire County, Va. to Nelson County, KY in 1790. He served in the Revolutionary War. Source: Mrs. Eleanor M. White received this from Barbara Maybury, 126 Inglewood Lane, Pittsburg, PA 15237.

Green, Dr. John, was born in Bolton, Lancashire, England, on Nov. 13, 1798 and died in Mineral County, W.Va., on Dec. 21, 1875. His parents were Richard and Ruth (Ridings) Greenhalgh. Green fought in the Battle of Waterloo, in the British forces, as a medic. He came to New York in May 1827 and then settled in Frederick County, Va., where he married Alice Ridings, on Aug. 19, 1835. He then resettled in Hampshire County, Va., where he remarried to Elizabeth Barnhouse, in 1841, and he was naturalized in 1844. He had eleven children. Green is considered to have been the first resident physician of Mineral County, W.Va., after it was formed from Hampshire County. See "Journey Through History," published in the April 17, 1989 issue of *The West Virginia Advocate*.

Gretzner, John C., was born in Mechiburg, Scheerin, Germany, on Feb. 17, 1807 and died on Jan. 13, 1876 in Romney, West Virginia. He married Henrietta D.E. Gelterine, born on April 20, 1814, in Bremen, Germany, and died on March 12, 1893. All of the above comes from the Family Bible, copied by Dan P. Oates of Romney, West Virginia. The Feb. 18, 1876 issue of the *South Branch Intelligencer*, stated, in John's obit, that he came to the U.S. (settling in New York) in 1837, and then to Romney, Va. in 1853. A copy of this Bible record is on file in the Genealogy Room of the Hampshire County Public Library.

Griffith, John, son of John and Mary Griffith, was born in Chester County, Pa., in 6th month, 13th day, 1737 and died in Frederick County, Va., on 1st month, 22nd day, 1833. He married Mary Faulkner, daughter of Jesse and Martha Faulkner, of York County, PA, on 10th month, 11th day, 1768. They immigrated to

Frederick County, Va. in 1776. Mary was born on 12th month, 18th day, 1746-47 and died in 1791. John remarried to Mary Ellis of Crooked Run, Va. Five children were born to the first union: (1) Martha Griffith, born 8th month, 22nd day, 1769, married Joseph Morgan, and they had issue. (2) Mary Griffith was born in 6th month, 21st day, 1771. She first married Asa Hoge Sr., and secondly to Joseph Sample. (3) Sibilla Griffith was born on 2nd month, 10th day 1774, and died unmarried. (4) Jesse Griffith was born in 8th month, 30th day, 1776 and died in 2nd month, 26th day, 1777. (5) John Griffith III was born on 9th month, 16th day, 1778, and died in Frederick County, Va., March 18, 1870. He married Rachel Hackney, daughter of Joseph and Martha Hackney, April 15, 1801. The 1870 Mortality Schedule for Frederick County, Va. stated that he died of pneumonia. Rachel was born in 9th month, 6th day, 1780 and died on March 20, 1863. Source: Handwritten genealogy by John Griffith III.

Griffith, John, died on March 8, 1851, near the residence of John F. Wall in Frederick County, Va. The coroner's report stated "the deceased came to his death from drunkeness and exposure, by laying out in a pool of water during the night and in a snowstorm." The document makes no further comments regarding age, marital status, residence, etc. Source: Frederick County, Va., "Inquisition of Dead Bodies," Virginia State Archives.

Griffith, John was born May 7, 1823. Mary Griffith was born March 7, 1826. Rebecca Griffith was born Dec. 1, 1828. These Griffith names were recorded in a Dunlap Bible. Mary Griffith married Archibald Dunlap. Nothing more is known about John and Rebecca Griffith.

Grove, Abraham, was born on Oct. 7, 1795, in Frederick County, and died on July 12, 1872. His wife, Sidney Ann (Wright) Mercer, was born on Oct. 18, 1791 and died on Dec. 13, 1861. Their marriage date was Sept. 26, 1819. Both were buried in the Heironimus cemetery at Whitacre, Frederick County, Va. Their proven children were: (1) William H. Grove was born on Aug. 3, 1820, and died July 22, 1828. (2) Mary Elizabeth Grove was born May 9, 1826 and died July 8, 1828. (3) Martha Jane Grove was born May 11, 1829 and died March 5, 1859. She married Aaron Kerns, son of Elisha and Rachel (Whitacre) Kerns, Jan. 20, 1850. After her death, Aaron remarried to Tamson Shanholtz. (4) Alcinda Grove was born Sept. 10, 1832, and died May 30, 1862.

She married Wilson Kerns, son of Elisha and Rachel (Whitacre) Kerns. (5) Francis Marion Grove was born on April 4, 1836 and died July 1, 1901. He married Sarah A. Bohrer, Jan. 9, 1858, in Morgan County, Va. All members of this family were buried in the Heironimus graveyard except for Francis M. Grove, who was buried in Salem Methodist cemetery in Morgan County, W.Va. Source: *Grove Fractur Book*, in possession of Joan Powell of Martinsburg, W.Va.[43]

Grove, George, son of Martin and Ann Maria Grove, was born on Aug. 11, 1794. On same page of scripture was written; Sarah Swigert was born in the year of Christ, 1803, 18th June. Quite possibly these two persons were married. Source: Letter written by Elmer M. Steele, Stephen's City, Va. on Aug. 8, 1934.

Grove, Henry, son of Henry and Mary (Lawyer) Grove, Sr., was born in 1806 in Frederick Co., Va. and died in 1882. Henry, Jr. married (1) Phoebe Mercer, daughter of William and Sidney (Wright) Mercer, May 9, 1833 and (2) Susan Duffy, daughter of Henry and Sarah (Fout) Duffy, March 20, 1856.

Grove, Henry, was born on Feb. 11, 1815 and died on Sept. 23, 1853 or 1858. Source: Tombstone inscription in the graveyard of the Primitive Baptist Church on Timber Ridge, Frederick County, Va.

Grove, James R., was born on Dec. 10, 1850 and died on May 25, 1904. Bettie, his wife, was born in 1847 and died in 1936. Source: Tombstone inscriptions at the Timber Ridge Primitive Baptist Church graveyard, Frederick County, Va.

Grove, John, was born on July 22, 1779 and died on June 16, 1849 in Frederick County, Va. The 1850 Mortality Schedule for Frederick County, Va. stated that he was a farmer, and that the cause of death was "gravel." Susan Grove was born on Jan. 1, 1777 and died on June 21, 1859. Source: Tombstone inscriptions near Stephen's City, Frederick County, Va.

Grove, the Rev. John, was born on May 23, 1787 and died on March 8, 1863. His wife Elenor Newberry/Newbraugh, was born in 1789 and died on Jan. 12, 1872. He was a Methodist preacher

---

43. An unproven daughter of Abraham and Sidney (Wright) Grove is Margaret Ann Grove, born in 1823. She married William R. Hart, a blacksmith in Frederick County, Va. Descendants have not been located.

and lived most of his life at Whitacre, Va., ministering in the Timber Ridge area of Frederick and Hampshire Counties. Source: Tombstone inscriptions in Heironimus cemetery, Whitacre, Va.

Grove, Samuel Jefferson, was born in 1788 and died in 1833/34, in Morgan County, Va. He married Elizabeth Newbraugh, daughter of John and Elizabeth (Grist) Newberry. Elizabeth was born on Oct. 4, 1789, in Chester County, PA. Their children were named: Susan, Elizabeth Ann, Rachel, John Wesley, William, Mary Ann, Martha Jane, Eli Maslin, and Sampson Grove. Source: Mrs. Kathern Allemong, Route 4, Box 27, Berkeley Springs, W.Va. 25411.

Groves, James V., died in July 1869, aged 49 years, "of consumption." Source: 1870 Mortality Schedule for Grant County, W.Va.

Guard, Henry, took his life on March 13, 1803 at New Town, Frederick County, Va. Source: Frederick County, Va., "Inquisition of Dead Bodies," Virginia State Archives.

Hackney, Joseph B., died in July 1859, aged 50 years. Cause of death was "intemperance," following a 200-day illness. Farmer. Born in Virginia. Survived by spouse. Source: 1860 Mortality Schedule for Frederick County, Va.

Hackney, Martha, was born at Greenspring, Frederick County, Va. on Dec. 25, 1786. She married Robert Daniel and they moved to Clinton County, Ohio in 1838.

Haggerty, John, died in Hampshire County, Va. in February 1787. His children were Catherine Barnes, Letitia Critton, Rebecca Haggerty, James Haggerty and John Haggerty. Source: Hampshire County *Deed Book 11*, page 111, Romney, W.Va.

Haines, Anna, was born in Hampshire County, Virginia on Sept. 22, 1833 and died on May 31, 1864 in Wilmington, Ohio. She married George McNemar on March 2, 1854. Source: *The Clinton Republican* newspaper, Wilmington, Ohio.

Haines, Barbara, was born in 1829; died on May 12, 1899. She was born in Hampshire County and was buried on Mouser's Ridge. She was married but the courthouse record did not name her spouse. NOW, let's look at the cemetery inscription for this same person: born Sept. 3, 1819 and died May 13, 1899. Her parents were Martin and Mary Magdalene (Emswiller) Fultz, and her husband was Jacob Haines. As a rule, tombstone inscriptions are much more reliable than courthouse death records.

Haines, Daniel, son of Henry and Ruth Haines, was born on July 30, 1792 in Maryland and died May 11, 1883 near Slanesville. He married Elizabeth, allegedly nee Haines. Source: Tombstone inscription.

Haines, Daniel B., son of H.B. and A.E. Haines, died on March 29, 1907, aged 20 years, 5 months, 7 days. Source: Tombstone inscription in Thomas Edwards, Jr. graveyard, later known as Brelsford graveyard, Cold Stream, Hampshire County, W.Va.

Haines, Eliza Jane, a daughter of Daniel and Elizabeth Haines, was born on Nov. 19, 1820 and died on Aug. 30, 1891. She married: (a) Zephaniah Offutt and (b) John W. Daugherty. She was buried in the Offutt cemetery near Slanesville.

Haines, Henry, died in Hampshire County on June 26, 1839, according to an entry in a family Bible. His wife was named Ruth. Deed Book 28, pp. 321-322, shows that Henry Haines purchased 150 acres of land in 1816. In 1832 this land was conveyed to Daniel and Elizabeth Haines. The U.S. Census shows that these Haines families lived in Maryland prior to coming to Hampshire County. The children of Henry and Ruth Haines were: Mary Haines married John Smoot; Daniel Haines married Elizabeth (Haines?); Henry Haines II, married Evaline Miller; Sarah Haines married John Timbrook; and Delilah Haines was unmarried.

Haines, Henry was born May 5, 1817 in Hampshire County and died on Aug. 5, 1894 near Wardensville, W.Va. He married Phebe Jane Snapp, daughter of John and Hannah (Milleson) Snapp. She was born on May 9, 1821 and died on June 4, 1886. Much of his life was spent farming at Cold Stream, Hampshire County, W.Va. Source: Tombstone inscriptions in Wardensville, Hardy County, W.Va. cemetery.

Haines, Isaac, died on Sept. 1, 1892, age 81 years, 2 months, 29 days. His wife, Nancy J., died on May 1, 1895, age 76 years, 4 months and 26 days, according to cemetery inscriptions at Ebenezer United Methodist Church, near Romney, W.Va. The above is probably more accurate than the death record in the courthouse, which says: Isaac Haines died on Sept. 4, 1892, aged 80 years, 2 months, 29 days. It stated that he was born on the Little Cacapon, Hampshire County.

Haines, Isaac, was born in 1785 and died in 1849. Source: 1850 Mortality Schedule for Hampshire County, Va.

Haines, Joseph, was born in 1763 in "Virginia." He died in Feb. 1850, of "pleurisy," in Hampshire County, Va. Source: 1850 Mortality Schedule for Hampshire County, Va.

Haines, Philip, was born on April 1, 1815 and died on Jan. 15, 1893. His wife, Catherine Fultz, was a daughter of Martin L. and Mary M. (Emswiller) Fultz. Catherine was born on March 13, 1817 and died on Dec. 23, 1901. Next to them is a gravestone which says: Lacy Haines, daughter of Philip and C. Haines, was born on Oct. 8, 1841 and died Sept. 1, 1863. Source: Tombstone inscriptions in Fultz Graveyard, in a field near Voit Road, Slanesville, W.Va.

Haines, Stephen Wheeler, "was accidentally shot to death by Samuel A. Rowzee," on Feb. 13, 1892, in Hampshire County, W.Va. Source: Inquest of Dead Body, Box 236, Circuit Court of Hampshire County, Romney, W.Va.

Haines, William, died on March 1, 1899, aged 78 years, 11 months, 26 days. Catherine (nee Mott), his wife, died on March 10, 1893, aged 73 years, 11 days. Source: Tombstone inscription in Ebenezer United Methodist Church, Romney, W.Va.

Hall, James, died on March 25, 1869, aged 98 years, in Grant County, W.Va. Source: The April 16, 1869 issue of the *South Branch Intelligencer*.

Hall, James L., son of Richard and Winifred Hall, was born in Loudoun County, Va. on June 10, 1794 and died on Dec. 22, 1880. The courthouse death record in Hampshire County stated that he was unmarried.

Hall, Richard, was born on April 18, 1770 and died on June 5, 1853. Source: Tombstone inscriptions at Branch Mountain United Methodist Church cemetery, Hampshire County, W.Va.

Hall, Rippen, black slave, born 1774, died August 1859 in Frederick County, Va. Farm laborer. Was ill for one year prior to death. Source: 1850 Mortality Schedule for Frederick County, Va.

Hamilton, Herbert was buried in the Powell cemetery near the Little Cacapon, along the Great Wagon Road. The stone appears to be old, but there is no inscription.

Hammack, Jacob, died on Nov. 18, 1845, aged 44 years, 5 months, 6 days. Buried nearby: Elizabeth D. Hammack, wife of Jacob, died on Jan. 29, 1869, aged 68 years, 2 months, and; John Hammack, son of Jacob and Elizabeth Hammack, died on Feb. 10, 1865, aged 39 years. Source: Tombstone inscriptions from a private graveyard near the old Poston Mill on North River south of U.S. Route 50 at Sedan, W.Va. These inscriptions were copied by Mrs. Eldora (Pepper) Park and given to me during a visit to her home on April 9, 1988.

Hannas, John was born in Hampshire County, Va. on Aug. 23, 1799 and died on Jersey Mountain on May 10, 1867. His widow, Debrah Hannas, reported his death to the county courthouse in Romney, W.Va.

Hardy, Martin, died on Feb. 22, 1861, aged 76 years, 10 months, 2 days. W.R. Hardy, born Dec. 9, 1807 and died May 28, 1859. Source: Tombstone inscriptions at Three Churches, W.Va.

Harris, Gabriel C., "widower," died in July 1869, aged 76 years. Born in Maryland. Farmer. Source: 1870 Mortality Schedule for Frederick County, Va.

Harris, Maria, died on March 1, 1904 at the age of 88 years, 7 months and 9 days. She was born in Hampshire County, Va. Source: Hampshire County, W.Va. death records.

Harrison, Charles, died on Sept. 10, 1857 at Capon Bridge. His father ordered a coffin, about five feet eight inches long. Source: **Coffin Book** of William Meade Edwards.

Harrison, Elvirah, of Cold Stream, Hampshire County, died on April 6, 1860. Her father handled the funeral arrangements. Elvirah was an adult, based on size of the coffin. It is believed that her parents were Robert and Mary (Straynton) Harrison, immigrants from England to Hampshire County, Va. during the 1820's. Corroborating evidence in the Mortality Schedule for 1860 shows that Elvira Harrison died in April 1860, aged 26 years, of "consumption." She was born in Virginia. Source: **Coffin Book** of William Meade Edwards and 1860 Mortality Schedule for Hampshire County, Va.

Hartley, John died at Patterson's Creek, Hampshire County, in 1784. His heirs were: (1) Mary Wilson (2) Margaret Hartley (3) Elizabeth Hardin (4) Ann Hardin and (5) Hannah Pearsall.

Source: Hampshire County Will, written in 1783 and probated on March 9, 1784.

Harrison, Robert, son of Hammon and Ann (Clarkson) Harrison, was born on Nov. 20, 1780 in Barmby Moor, York, England. His wife, Elizabeth Brigham, died in April 1815 at Barmby Moor. He died on April 21, 1864 in Hampshire County, Va. Source: Mrs. Mildred Ostfeld, 6851 N. Mendota Ave., Chicago, IL. 60646.

Harrison, William, formerly of Hampshire County, died on Nov. 22, 1881, in Cass County, MO. Source: Dec. 23, 1881 issue of The *South Branch Intelligencer*.

Hart, Adam, was born in 1727 and died on Dec. 19, 1816. Mary, his wife, died on Jan. 29, aged 70 years. Buried in Quaker graveyard at Gainsboro, Frederick County, Virginia.

Hart, Samuel was born in 1767 and died in 1838, aged 70 years, 8 months and 17 days. Source: Tombstone inscription in Quaker cemetery at Gainsboro, Frederick County, Virginia.

Harvey, Amos, born in 1808 and died in 1853. He was a "preaching companion" of the Rev. Christy Sine. Amos' wife, Esther Ann, was born in 1823 and died in 1868. Inscribed on the same monument are: Jonathan Wesley Pugh, born here in Park's Valley in 1845 and died in Phoenix, Arizona in 1926; Lydia Ross, 1861-1863; Margaret A. 1858-1864; Jerome and Angelo, born in May and died in Sept. 1856. The last names were not given for the four children, but assumed to be Pugh. Source: Tombstone inscriptions in the Park's Graveyard, Parke's Valley, Hampshire County, W.Va.

Hatton, Samuel, was born in England on June 6, 1758 and died in Wayne County, Virginia on Sept. 10, 1839. He was a soldier in the American Revolution. After his marriage to Rosannah Queen, daughter of John Queen, of Loudoun County, Virginia. They lived in Hampshire County, Va. during the early 1800's before moving to Cabell County, before 1820. Source: DAR records in the "Grandfather Papers."

Hawk, Henry, aged 91 years, died on Sept. 23, 1880, in Grant County, W.Va. Source: The Oct. 8, 1880 issue of the *South Branch Intelligencer*.

Hawkins, James, son of John and Catherine Hawkins, was born on Aug. 5, 1792 and died on Dec. 7, 1872. His wife was Elizabeth Orr, daughter of Anthony Orr of North River. Source: Courthouse death record; see also, settlement of Anthony Orr's estate, Hampshire County, found in *Order Book I*, page 147, dated Sept. 16, 1835, in Circuit Court, Hampshire County, Va.

Hawkins, Henry, son of James and Elizabeth (Orr) Hawkins, was born on Dec. 7, 1832 and died on July 8, 1894. He was killed by runaway horses, along with his daughter Annie L. Hawkins, who was born on Dec. 17, 1877 and died on July 8, 1894.; "In the bloom of life, she was called to her eternal rest." Henry married Louise J. Slonaker, who survived the accident, and died some years later. (Note: Maud Pugh is in error). Source: Tombstone inscriptions in the Slonaker family graveyard on the west side of Bear Garden Mountain, near the Cacapon River, and the *Undertaker Book* of John W. Mellon. The cost of the funeral was $20.00, which was an affluent funeral at that time.

Hawkins, William, son of John and Catherine Hawkins, was born in 1796 and died in Tazwell County, Illinois in 1881. He wife, Mary A. Orr, daughter of Anthony Orr, was born in Dec. 1796 and died on Feb. 5, 1864. See *Order Book I*, page 147, dated Sept. 16. 1835, Hampshire County, Va. Circuit Court, for proof of marriage.

Heare, Adam, was born on Nov. 12, 1760 and died on April 8, 1816. His wife, Margaret Todd, was born on Jan. 28, 1771 and died on July 17, 1844. Source: Tombstone inscriptions at Three Churches, W.Va. (behind the Mt. Bethel Church).

Heare, Eve, died of childbirth in Feb. 1850, aged 19 years. Source: 1850 Mortality Schedule for Hampshire County, Va.

Heare, James, son of Adam and Margaret (Todd) Heare, was born on Nov. 12, 1795 and died on May 10, 1875. James served in the War of 1812, according to the May 14, 1875 issue of the *South Branch Intelligencer*. He married Abigail Pownell, daughter of Elisha and Abigail Pownell. Source: Tombstone inscription and newspaper obit.

Heare, John Lyle, son of Adam and Margaret (Todd) Heare, was born in 1805 and died on June 4, 1855. He married Eliza Powelson, daughter of Rynear and Elizabeth Powelson on Oct.

20, 1828. Source: Robert Shanholtzer (deceased), Santa Barbara, CA.

Heare, J.W., born on Sept. 25, 1837, probably in Hampshire County, Va. and died on March 16, 1918. His wife, Mary M. was born on Aug. 16, 1846 and died on Dec. 19, 1912. These tombstone inscriptions were found in Collar cemetery, near Dawn, Livingston County, Missouri. It is believed that this family had roots in the Three Churches area of Hampshire County, Va.

Heare, Matthew, son of Adam and Margaret (Todd) Heare, was born on March 31, 1800 and died on Nov. 17, 1880. He married Mary Ann Powelson, daughter of Charles Powelson, on Nov. 25, 1825. After her death in 1843, he remarried to Martha Ruckman. Source: See article on "Family History: The Heare Family," *The West Virginia Advocate*, Dec. 5, 1983.

Heath, Jane, departed this life July 15, 1850, aged 20 years, 28 days. Source: Tombstone inscriptions in graveyard at Three Churches, W.Va.

Heatwole, John, died on Jan. 26, 1922 at the age of 93 years. He was born in Rockingham County, Va., according to George A. Lupton, who reported the death to the Courthouse.

Hedrick, Jane, departed this life on Aug. the 6th, 1836, aged 72 years and three months. This entry was found in the family Bible of David Ellis, who was born on March 1, 1782. David's wife, Nancy, was born on Aug. 12, 1794. In this same Bible are data on Joseph Weaver, who was a son of Abraham and Magdalene (Senseny) Weaver. Joseph was born on May 2, 1794 and his wife, Sarah Hedrick, was born on June 22, 1798. It is believed that the father was one Nicholas Hedrick, but not yet proven. He lived in the Mill Branch section of Bloomery District, in Hampshire County. Members of these families immigrated to Ohio. Source: Bible record in transmitted by Mrs. Joan G. Ellsworth, 5 Beverly Court, Waupun, WI 53963.

Hefflebower, David, was born in 1792; died on May 30, 1863. His first wife, Mary Ann Slifer, was buried next to him in the family cemetery at Capon Bridge, sometimes called "Carlyle's Cemetery." She was born on Aug. 28, 1803 in Washington County, MD. and died on Dec. 12, 1853. His second wife was Elizabeth Cookus. She died on April 22, 1872 at the home of J.H. Kanade in Jefferson County, W.Va., according to her obituary which was published in the **South Branch Intelligencer**. Source: Tombstone inscriptions.

Hefflebower, Samuel, son of David and Mary Hefflebower, died on July 2, 1844, aged 19 years, 5 months and 1 day. Source: Tombstone inscription in Carlyle cemetery near Capon Bridge, W.Va.

Heironimus, Andrew, son of Conrad and Christina Heironimus, died on March 1, 1840, aged 69 years, 2 months, 2 days. His wife, Catherine Allemong, died on Jan. 1, 1832, aged 48 years, 6 months, 2 days. Source: Tombstone inscriptions in Heironimus Graveyard at Redland community, Whitacre, Virginia.

Heironimus, Ann E., died in June 1860, aged 42 years. She had been ill for 1,195 days prior to her death, according to the attending physician. She was survived by her husband. Source: 1860 Mortality Schedule for Frederick County, Va.

Heironimus, Barbara, died in May 1850, aged 45 years, following a 400-day illness. She was born in Virginia. Source: 1850 Mortality Schedule for Frederick County, Va.

Heironimus, Conrad, was born on Dec. 1, 1842 and died on Sept. 14, 1921. M. Barbara, wife, was born on Sept. 12, 1844 and died on March 14, 1921. Source: Tombstone inscriptions at the Timber Ridge Baptist Church, Frederick County, Va.

Heironimus, Elizabeth, daughter of Conrad and Christina Heironimus, was born in Frederick County, Va. on June 6, 1766 and died on Oct. 24, 1853 on the Great Cacapon, in Morgan County, Va. She married: (1) William Cornelius Huff and (2) John Hardy. Source: Tombstone inscription.

Heironimus, Frederick,   son of John and Elizabeth (Null) Heironimus, died on May 23, 1863, aged 47 years, 8 months, 2 days. Maria Hutchinson, his wife died on Nov. 6, 1880, aged 65 years, 3 months, 2 days. Source: Tombstone inscriptions in private graveyard on their farm, between Silar and Shockeysville, Frederick County, Virginia.

Heironimus, Frederick, son of Henry and Mariah Catherine (Anderson) Hieronimus, died on April 28, 1877, aged 72 years, 11 months, 12 days. His wife, Maria Peacemaker, died on Sept. 7, 1894, aged 66 years, 9 months, 5 days. Source: Tombstone inscriptions in Heironimus Graveyard at Whitacre, Virginia.

Heironimus, Mary, wife of John W. Heironimus, died on Aug. 18, 1865, aged 28 years, 11 months, 13 days.   Source: Tombstone inscription in Timber Ridge Baptist graveyard, located near Reynold's Store in Frederick County, Va.

Heironimus, Nancy (nee Goram), died in August 1859, aged 63 years, after a 208-day illness. Cause of death was listed as "dyspepsia." Her husband, Conrad Heironimus, survived her. Source: 1860 Mortality Schedule for Frederick County, Va.

Heironimus, Overton Fink, son of Jacob and Elizabeth (Brown) Heironimus, died at Bloomery, Hampshire County, on Aug. 31, 1881, aged 71 years and 1 day, according to Hampshire County death record. His wife, Maria B. Taylor, died on June 25, 1880, aged 70 years, 11 months, 15 days, according to tombstone inscriptions in Heironimus Graveyard at Whitacre, Frederick County, Virginia.

Heiskell, Christopher, son of Adam and Margaret (Upp) Heiskell, was born on March 14, 1781 and died on Dec. 29, 1851 in the 71st year of his age (yes!!). Eleanor Abernathy, his wife, was born on Jan. 1, 1782 and died on Jan. 26, 1845. Buried nearby was Sarah Ann Heiskell, their unmarried daughter died on April 12, 1879, aged 67 years, 6 months, and 16 days. Source: Tombstone inscriptions in Indian Mound Cemetery in Romney, W.Va.

Heiskell, Emily, daughter of Adam and Margaret (Upp) Heiskell, was born in 1793, at Romney, Va., and died Aug. 31, 1814. She married Dr. John Snyder.

Heiskell, Francis William, son of Samuel and Sarah (Davis) Heiskell, was born on Feb. 19, 1822 and died on Oct. 2, 1881. His first wife was Harriett Elizabeth Heiskell, daughter of Christopher and Eleanor (Abernathy) Heiskell, born on March 28, 1822. They were married on Jan. 2, 1850. Francis W. remarried to Bettie V. Van Arsdale, daughter of Cornelius and Catherine (Huff) Vanarsdale. She was born on May 3, 1828 and died on Aug. 27, 1909. Other nearby graves of their children: Mary Florence Heiskell, born July 25, 1858 and died June 6, 1862; Charles Lee, born on Sept. 4, 1859 and died on June 4, 1862.

Heiskell, Isaac Noble, son of Adam and Margaret (Upp) Heiskell, was born on Jan. 21, 1778 and died on Oct. 28, 1855. His wife, Mary Sowers, was born on Nov. 3, 1777 and died on Jan.

17, 1829. They were married on May 2, 1802. Source: Typewritten copy of several pages of genealogy, without a source name.

Heiskell, Margaret Eleanor, daughter of Christoper and Eleanor (Abernathy) Heiskell, was born on March 3, 1817 and died July 4, 1902. She married James Caudy, who was a son of Evan Caudy of Capon Bridge. James Caudy was born Sept. 25, 1808. Source: Tombstone inscriptions in Indian Mound Graveyard, Romney, W.Va.

Heiskell, Martha, wife of I.N. Heiskell, died on Aug. 4, 1861 near the Capon Bridge area of Hampshire County, Va. She was nee Martha E. Muse, born in 1825, the first wife of Isaac Noble Heiskell. He was a son of Samuel and Sarah (Davis) Heiskell. I.N. Heiskell was born on Feb. 18, 1820 and died on Sept. 20, 1908. One Source: *Coffin Book* of William Meade Edwards, undertaker at Cold Stream, Hampshire County, Va.

Heiskell, Sarah (nee Davis), was born in 1800 and died on Feb. 24, 1876, according to her obit in the *South Branch Intelligencer*, Feb. 25 (yes), 1875 issue. Her husband was Samuel Heiskell, son of Adam and Margaret (Upp) Heiskell. Samuel was born in 1791 and died on Feb. 22, 1834.

Heiskell, Sarah (nee White), daughter of John and Elizabeth White, died on Aug. 25, 1842, aged 49 years. Her husband was John Heiskell. Source: Tombstone inscription in St. John's Lutheran Graveyard, near Hayfield, Frederick County, Virginia.

Heiskell, Senseny, born on Oct. 18, 1826 and died Sept. 16, 1896. Source: Tombstone inscription in graveyard at Three Churches, Hampshire County, W.Va.

Heiskell, General William Alexander, son of Christopher and Eleanor (Abernathy) Heiskell, was born in Hampshire County, Virginia on Nov. 16, 1807 and died at Paola, Kansas "on the Thursday before Aug. 20, 1870." He moved to Westport, Missouri in 1848, and then settled in Paola, Kansas, in 1849. His wife was nee Price. Source: Multiple, including an obit in the *South Branch Intelligencer*.

Henderson, Harriett, daughter of Larkin D. and Mary (Kees) Henderson, was born on Sept. 7, 1826 and died on Feb. 16, 1871. She died on Feb. 16, 1871, and was buried on the Henderson farm, now owned by Ronald Baker. She married Martin Tutwiler on Christmas Day, 1849. Source: Bible record and tombstone inscriptions.

Henderson, James, son of Larkin D. and Mary (Kees) Henderson, was born on Feb. 27, 1817 in Hampshire County, Va., and died on Feb. 17, 1892. He married Jane Patterson on Nov. 28, 1843. Source: Bible record. [Note: Jane Patterson was probably a daughter of John Patterson who lived nearby.]

Henderson, Larkin Day, was born on Sept. 28, 1790 and died on Dec. 30, 1872 at his home near Slanesville. According to the Henderson Bible record, his wife Mary Kees was born on Nov. 25, 1789 and died on Feb. 25, 1852. The Henderson cemetery is located at the end of Kedron Road, now the property of Ronald Baker. The graveyard has not been maintained during recent years. Note: Larkin D. Henderson was nee Day, [a son of William and Nancy Day] but was adopted by the Hendersons.

Henderson, Thomas F., died on Oct. 3, 1878, in Hampshire County, aged 61 years. Source: Oct. 25, 1878 issue of The *South Branch Intelligencer*. Apparently this was Thomas Frederick Henderson, son of Larkin Day and Mary (Kees) Henderson. If so, his Bible record shows a birthdate of March 14, 1817. His wife was Eliza Hiett, daughter of Jonathan and Hannah (Harrison) Hiett. Eliza was born on May 20, 1825 and died on July 21, 1913. They were married on Nov. 5, 1850. Both were buried in the Larkin D. Henderson Graveyard, on Kedron Road, near Slanesville, W.Va.

Henshaw, John, son of Nicholas and Rebecca (Smith) Henshaw, was born in 1734 and died in Frederick County, Va., May 6, 1793. His wife was Sarah Ann Caudy, daughter of James Caudy. Sarah died in 1807, in Frederick County. Source: Records in LDS Library, Salt Lake City, UT.

Henwood, William attended Frederick County Court for two days, as a witness in a court case "Hugh Fox vs Largent (the plaintiff)." Source: *Minute Book: 1761-63*, Frederick County records, Virginia State Archives.

Herriott, Ephraim, son of William and Elizabeth (Blue) Herriott, died on June 17, 1866, aged 68 years, 2 months and 24 days. Eliza Rees, his wife, died on Aug. 6, 1892, aged 86 years, 4 months, and 6 days. Other graves in this private cemetery are: Ephraim Herriott, "father," born on April 11, 1839 and died on April

22, 1916;   Isaac Herriott (1841-1908) and Sarah Blue, his wife, (1839-1931), "At Rest." Source: Family Graveyard on a hill overlooking the historic homeplace on Fox Run, Hampshire County, W.Va. This is located west of Mill Creek Mountain, on Route 50/4, in western Hampshire County, W.Va.

Hiatt, George, son of John and Mary (Smith) Hiett, Sr., was born circa 1698; died on Oct. 28, 1793 in Guilford Co., North Carolina. He married Martha Wakefield. It is believed that he was the first settler in what is now known as North River Mills, Hampshire County, W.Va. Source: The Descendants of Peter Simmons, by Gwen B. Bjorkman, 4425- 132nd Ave., S.E., Bellevue, WA. 98006.

Hickle, George, son of Devault and Eve Hickle, was born in Hampshire County, Va. on Oct. 1, 1769 and died in Guernsey County, Ohio in 1856. He married Mary Weaver in Shenandoah County, Va. on Nov. 12, 1811. They migrated to Ohio in 1816 and were parents of six children. Source: Mrs. Ernestine P. Moss, Memphis, TN.

Hickle, Henry, son of Devault and Eve Hickle, was born in 1779 in Hampshire County, Va. and died in 1842 in Ross County, Ohio. He married Rebecca Reed on Dec. 26, 1806, and she died in 1826. They moved to Ohio in 1814. After Rebecca's death, Henry married Eliza Smith. Henry had nine children by the first wife, and five by the second. Source: Mrs. Ernestine P. Moss, Memphis, TN.

Hickle, Samuel, was born in Hampshire County, Va. on April 5, 1760 and died in Preston County, Va. on May 13, 1832. He married Elizabeth Hoover on July 25, 1785 in Hampshire County, Va. They had eleven children. Source: Mrs. Ernestine P. Moss, 658 Stonewall, Memphis, Tennessee 38107.

Hickle, Stephen, son of Devault and Eve Hickle, was born in Hampshire County, Va. on Aug. 12, 1767 and died in Guernsey County, Ohio in 1854. His wife, Susannah Hoover, was born on Jan. 2, 1779. They had eleven children. Stephen, a "local preacher" in the Christian Church, took his family to Ohio during the late 1820's. His children married into many Hampshire County family names. Source: Mrs. Ernestine P. Moss, Memphis, TN.

Hickle, Tevault, son of Devault and Eve Hickle, was born in Hampshire County, Va. in 1775 and died in Ross County, Ohio on Nov. 15, 1830. He married Mary Groves, daughter of Philip (married an Arnold) Groves, in Frederick County, Virginia on March 7, 1801.

Hiett, Barbara, died in Hampshire County, Va. in July 1859, of "heart disease," aged 52 years. She was a housewife. It is believed that Barbara was the wife of Evan Hiett (nee Wise); that her actual date of death was Aug. 6, 1859. Source: 1860 Mortality Schedule for Hampshire County, Va.

Hiett, Benjamin, son of Evan and Jane L. (Easter) Hiett, died on Sept. 20, 1862. Source: Tombstone inscription in Hiett graveyard at the Forks of Capon, Hampshire County.

Hiett, Charlotte (nee Arnold), was born on Oct. 4, 1828 and died on Aug. 25, 1852. She married Asa Hiett, son of Jeremiah and Lucinda (Kidwell) Hiett. They had no children. Charlotte was buried in the Richard Sloan graveyard, near the "Stone House," on U.S. Route 50, west of Romney, W.Va. Source: Tombstone inscription.

Hiett, Eliza, daughter of Jonathan and Hannah (Harrison) Hiett, was born on May 20, 1825 and died on July 21, 1913. She married Thomas Frederick Henderson, son of Larkin Day and Mary (Kees) Henderson, on Nov. 5, 1850. He was born on March 14, 1817 and died on Oct. 3, 1878. Both were buried in the Henderson cemetery at the end of Kedron Road, Slanesville, W.Va. Source: Tombstone inscriptions, and Bible record in possession of Mrs. Irma Curtis, Weston, W.Va.

Hiett, Elizabeth, daughter of Evan and Sarah (Smith) Hiett, was born in Hampshire County on Jan. 6, 1779 and died on Aug. 17, 1873. Her husband was Thomas Gawthrop, born Jan. 22, 1772 and died in 1832 in Taylor County, W.Va.

Hiett, Elizabeth, daughter of John Hiett (of Evan) and Elizabeth (Tansy) Hiett, was born at North River, Hampshire County, Va., on July 16, 1819 and died on Nov. 15, 1872, at High View, Timber Ridge. Her husband, Jonathan Capper, was born on Dec. 28, 1813, on Timber Ridge, and died on Jan. 4, 1885. They were buried in the Timber Ridge Christian Church Graveyard, High View, W.Va.

Hiett, Esther, daughter of George and Martha (Wakefield) Hiett, was born on the 1st day, 4th month, 1731, in Lancaster County, PA and died in Frederick County, Va., March 6, 1778. She came with her parents as one of the first settlers along Opequon

Creek, in 1735. Esther married Thomas Wright, son of James and Mary Wright. See an article published in the May 1989 issue of *The West Virginia Advocate*, titled "The Opequon Settlement: Settler James Wright." Source: Quaker records, courthouse and Virginia State archives records.

Hiett, Evan, son of John Hiett, was born on Oct. 24, 1748 and died at Sandy Ridge, Hampshire County, Va. on Jan. 22, 1815. His wife was Sarah Smith, daughter of Captain Jeremiah Smith, Sr., of Frederick County, Va. It is believed that Evan and Sarah were buried in the Evan Hiett graveyard (called "Cowgill's" during recent years), in unmarked graves. The old house, next to graveyard and land are owned by Mr. John Whitacre. In 1991 the address is Capon Bridge, W.Va. 26711.

Hiett, Evan, son of Joseph and Alice (Sutton) Hiett, was born on Feb. 11, 1806 and died on April 4, 1886. His wife, Jane L. Easter, was born on March 8, 1814 and died on July 20, 1885. They were buried in the Hiett graveyard at the Forks of Capon. Source: Tombstone inscriptions in Hiett Graveyard.

Hiett, Frances Maria, daughter of Jeremiah and Lucinda (Kidwell) Hiett, was born on Jan. 30, 1813. and died on April 24, 1884. She married the Rev. James Alexander Cowgill, son of Ewing and Susannah (Buzzard) Cowgill, on Nov. 24, 1842, by the Rev. Christy Sine. He was born on April 22, 1818 and died on Nov. 18, 1882. Source: James A. Cowgill family Bible, and tombstone inscription in the Evan Hiett graveyard on Sandy Ridge, Hampshire County, W.Va.

Hiett, George W., son of Evan and Jane L. (Easter) Hiett, was born in 1856 and died in 1940. His wife, Elizabeth Ann McCool, was born in 1857 and died in 1933. Source: Tombstone inscriptions in Hiett graveyard near Forks of Capon, W.Va. He lived on the old homeplace, after his parents died.

Hiett, J.M., died on Oct. 13, 1925, aged 80 years. It is believed that he was a grandson of Joseph and Alice (Sutton) Hiett, because he was buried in that family graveyard near the Forks of Capon, Hampshire County. Source: Tombstone inscription.

Hiett, Jane, daughter of John and Mary (Locke) Hiett, was born Jan. 26, 1812, and died May 18, 1895. She married Martin Swimley, son of Jacob and Catherine (Snyder) Swimley. They were baptized in the Winchester Reformed Church on Aug. 25, 1840. Source: Church record.

Hiett, Jane E., wife of John Hiett, was born on April 23, 1843 and died on June 25, 1872. Next to her was buried an infant daughter, Louretta Hiett, born on June 13, 1872 and died on Oct. 15, 1872. Jane's parents were Deskin and Ann (Carmichael) Wills. She was buried in the Deskin Wills' private graveyard along North River, Hampshire County, W.Va.

Hiett, Jeremiah, Jr., son of Jeremiah and Lucinda (Kidwell) Hiett, was born in Hampshire County on July 9, 1825 and died at Tomahawk, Berkeley County, W.Va. on July 2, 1911. His wife Rachel Shanholtzer, daughter of Jacob and Hannah (Loy) Shanholtz, was born on June 1, 1834 and died on Aug. 1, 1903. Source: Bible record provided by Lee Rooney, Jones Spring, W.Va.

Hiett, John, son of John and Mary (Smith) Hiett, Sr., was born circa 1696 and died in 1764 in Frederick or Hampshire County, Va. His widow, Margaret, remarried to one James Largent, according to Frederick County, Va. court record. It is believed that this James Largent was a brother of John Largent II (ca 1720-1807) of Hampshire County, Va.

Hiett, John, son of Joseph and Alcinda (Sutton) Hiett, died in Hampshire County, W.Va. on July 30, 1883, at age 80 years. His wife was named Julia Ann Stump. Source: Courthouse death record, Hampshire County, W.Va.

Hiett, John, son of Jeremiah and Lucinda (Kidwell) Hiett, was born on Aug. 11, 1809 and died on Nov. 28, 1896. He married Anna Edwards, daughter of William and Ann (Albin) Edwards of Hampshire County, W.Va. Anna was born on July 15, 1812 and died on Jan. 8, 1895. They were married on March 27, 1834. Their children were: (1) James Walter Hiett was born Feb. 12, 1835 and died May 18, 1909. He married Margaret Largent, daughter of John Largent, Oct. 5, 1860. Margaret was born Feb. 24, 1837. It is through this line that family records were kept. The records were used as a basis for writing a Hiett History. (2) Samuel Patton Hiett was born April 3, 1836. (3) Lucinda A. Hiett was born Oct. 20, 1837. She married David Hawkins. (4) Harriett Hiett was born April 6, 1839. She first married James William Foreman (1832-1868). (5) Mary Ellen Hiett was born Sept. 27,

1841. She married John Kidwell, son of Hawkins and Nancy Kidwell. They had no children. (6) Martha Jane Hiett was born April 27, 1843. She was married to David Kidwell, son of John Spaulding and Mary (Hiett) Kidwell, and secondly to Isaac King. (7) Robert W. Hiett was born Nov. 18, 1844. He married Mary Elizabeth Largent. (8) Asa Hiett was born Feb. 11, 1847. He married Lydia McDonald. (9) Sarah F. Hiett was born Jan. 9, 1850. She married Harry Smith and they moved to Springfield, Illinois. (10) Jeremiah C. Hiett was born on March 7, 1852 and did not marry. Source: Copied from a copy of a copy of a Bible record.

Hiett, John S., son of John and Julia Ann (Stump) Hiett, was born in 1843 and died in 1906. His wife, Mary E. Noland, born in 1841 and died in 1905. Source: Hiett graveyard at Forks of Capon, W.Va.

Hiett, Joseph, son of Evan and Sarah (Smith) Hiett, was born on Jan. 11, 1774 and died on March 24, 1860. The 1860 mortality schedule of the U.S. census stated that he died of pneumonia. His wife, Alice Sutton, was born on Aug. 27, 1779 and died on May 31, 1866. They were buried in the Evan Hiett graveyard on Sandy Ridge, Hampshire County. Source: Clearly inscribed data on tombstones.

Hiett, Joseph W., probably a son of Evan Hiett, was born on Dec. 2, 1841 and died on March 8, 1900. His wife, Margaret, was born on Nov. 6, 1849 and died on March 10, 1918. Source: Tombstone inscriptions in Hiett graveyard mear Forks of Capon. This was the old homestead of Joseph and Elise (Sutton) Hiett.

Hiett, Joseph, son of John and Martha Elizabeth (Tansy) Hiett, was born on Nov. 11, 1815 and died on Aug. 3, 1897. His wife was Caroline Heiskell, daughter of Christopher and Eleanor (Abernathy) Heiskell. She was born on May 4, 1814. Joseph Hiett was elected to represent Hampshire County in the Virginia House of Delegates during 1863, with Alexander Monroe. He lived on a farm near North River Mills.

Hiett, Lemuel, son of John and Margaret Hiett, died in the Cacapon District of Morgan County, W.Va. on Dec. 3, 1884, aged 43 years, 7 months, 20 days. According to the death record in the courthouse at Berkeley Springs, W.Va., he was born in Morgan County, W.Va.

Hiett, Margaret, daughter of John and Margaret Hiett, was born circa 1728 and died after 1788, in Rockingham County, Virginia. She married: (1) William Dyer, the father of their two children, Roger Dyer and John Dyer, (2) John Cravens, son of Robert and Mary (Harrison) Cravens, circa 1760. He was born in 1722 and died on July 24, 1778. They had seven children born between 1760 and 1775, in Rockingham County, Va. (3) Dennis Lanahan, on March 20, 1782. They lived in Harrisonburg, Virginia.

Hiett, Margaret, age 58, died on Aug. 15, 1872. Her parents were Joseph and Elizabeth (Reid) McKee. Her husband was Jonathan Hiett, son of Jeremiah and Lucinda (Kidwell) Hiett. Source: Courthouse record in Hampshire County, W.Va.

Hiett, Margaret (nee Vanorsdale), died on Oct. 7, 1901 or 1907, aged 72 years, 0 months, 24 days. Her husband was Robert F. Hiett, son of Jeremiah and Lucinda (Kidwell) Hiett. Source: Tombstone inscription in Evan Hiett garveyard on Sandy Ridge, Hampshire County, W.Va.

Hiett, Mary, daughter of Evan and Sarah (Smith) Hiett, was born in Hampshire County on May 15, 1796 and died on July 17, 1882, according to the July 23 and 30, 1882 issues of the *South Branch Intelligencer*. She married John Spaulding Kidwell, son of John and Eleanor Kidwell. John and Mary (Hiett) Kidwell were buried in the Kidwell private graveyard, in a field behind the Mt. Union Christian Church, near Slanesville, West Virginia. Many of their descendants are buried in this well-kept graveyard.

Hiett, Sarah (nee Parks), wife of Samuel Sutton Hiett, who was a son of Joseph and Alicia (Sutton) Hiett, was born May 21, 1816 and died on Nov. 12, 1843. Source: Tombstone inscription in Park's Graveyard, Parke's Valley, Hampshire County, Va.

Hiett, Simeon, married a sister of Mrs. Eleanor Dunlap (deceased), wife of Robert Dunlap, per court document dated Nov. 4, 1777. Source: *Minute Book: 1773-1780*, Frederick County records, Virginia State Archives.

Hiett, Wesley, son of Evan and Jane L. (Easter) Hiett, died on Dec. 12, 1864, aged 21 years, 10 months, and 29 days. Source: Tombstone inscription, Hiett graveyard at Forks of Capon, W.Va.

Higby, Jonathan, was born in Connecticut in 1788 and died in Hampshire County, circa 1878. He was a school teacher. Jonathan married Prudence Marple, daughter of David and

Margaret (Purtlebaugh) Marple, in 1836, in Hampshire County. His first marriage was to Barbara Easter, a daughter of John and Margaret (Thomas) Easter. She was born on Dec. 17, 1793.

High, Catherine, daughter of Daniel High, died on Oct. 16, 1869, aged 84 years. She was born "in Virginia." Her husband was John Snider. Source: Courthouse death record, Morgan County, W.Va.

High, Frederick, died on Jan. 18, 1844, in his 83rd year, according to tombstone inscription. Another source gives his birthdate as March 22, 1761. Christina (Kale), his wife, "Gone to Rest" died on May 31, 1854, aged 83 years, 9 months, 20 days. Source: Tombstone inscriptions in cemetery on Davy Road, Hampshire County, W.Va.

High, John was born in 1726 (probably in Germany) and died on April 12, 1817. He was buried at Junction, W.Va., near the Hampshire/Mineral County line.

Hillman, Simeon, died in April 1860, after 1,500 days of illness with a kidney infection. He was born in New Jersey in 1789. Simeon was employed as a tollgate keeper in Frederick County. Source: 1860 Mortality Schedule for Frederick County, Va.

Hines, James, died on Aug. 6, 1872, age 54 years. Possibly he was related to the Haines families. which were buried nearby. Source: Tombstone inscription in Ebenezer United Methodist cemetery near Romney, W.Va.

Hines, James, died on July 27, 1867, aged 59 years. Source: Aug. 2, 1867 issue of the *South Branch Intelligencer*.

Hines, Thomas, was born on April 25, 1823 and died on Feb. 16, 1905. Harriett J., his wife, was born on Feb. 23, 1843 and died on April 13, 1913.

Hinkle, Ambrose, died in Shenandoah County, Va. in June 1870, aged 83 years, "of dropsy." Minister of the Gospel. Wife preceded him in death. Source: 1870 Mortality Schedule for Shenandoah County, Va.

Hite, Isaac, died Feb. 5, 1887, aged 85 years. Source: Tombstone inscription in Bloomery Presbyterian Church Graveyard, Bloomery, W.Va.

Hockman, Isaac, was born on Sept. 28, 1854 and died on Oct. 14, 1924. His wife, Annetta Murphy, was born on June 29, 1856 and died on June 3, 1931. In the same graveyard was: Philip Hockman, Dec. 29, 1822; Harvey Hockman (1858-1922) and Margaret (1862-1938). Source: Tombstone inscriptions in Hockman Graveyard, near Slanesville, W.Va.

Hockman, John Wesley, was a son of Mary Hockman (1826-1884). Mary married Henry Artz in 1851. Henry died in 1862. John Wesley was born on Feb. 8, 1846 and died on Feb. 5, 1901. He was a dentist. In 1870, he married Manerva Ann Copenhaver, who was born on Dec. 13, 1847 and died on April 8, 1884.

Hockman, Phillip, son of Jacob Funk and Elizabeth (Zimmerman) Hockman, was born on Dec. 29, 1822, according to his tombstone inscription in the Hockman Graveyard, located near Slanesville, W.Va., on Kedron Road. He married Diadem Daugherty. A researcher of the Hockman family is: Elsie H. Lambert, 219 Stonewall Jackson Drive, Conroe, TX 77302.

Hoge, Asa, was born in 1769, and died on Aug. 4, 1804. Buried in Quaker cemetery at Gainsboro, Va.

Hoge, Ruth, was born in 1760 and died in 1816. Buried in Quaker graveyard at Back Creek, Gainsboro (Pughtown), Va.

Hoge, Sarah, daughter of Solomon and Ann (Rollins) Hoge, was born on Nov. 11, 1752. She married Joshua Gore, who was a son of Thomas and Sarah Gore, in 1773. They lived in Loudoun County, Virginia. Joshua was born on Jan. 7, 1752 and died in 1830.

Hoge, Solomon, son of William Hoge, was born on May 21, 1729 and died on March 9, 1811. He married: (1) Ann Rollins, and they had eleven children. (2) Mary Nichols, on Nov. 11, 1773, by whom he had seven more children.

Hoge, William, died on Nov. 26, 1815, aged 88 years (born in 1727). He was buried in the old Quaker graveyard (Back Creek Meeting) at Gainsboro, Frederick County, Virginia.

Hoge, William (1660-1749) emigrated from Scotland to America in 1682, settling first in New Jersey. He married Barbara Hume (1670-1745), also from Scotland. They later moved to Delaware and, before 1735, to "the Opeckin settlement" in old Frederick County, Virginia. [Note: It was then called Orange County, Va., and before that, Spotsylvania County.] They located about 2-3 miles south of Winchester, on the Great Wagon Road, in or near what is known as Kernstown. Their land extended toward North Mountain and a creek was named after the Hoge family. When William Hoge Sr. was living in Nottingham, Chester County, PA, on April 18, 1729, he wrote a will which was later probated in Frederick County, Va., on Nov. 14, 1749. The Will provided for wife Barbara and eight children. The 1729 Will stated that he was weak in body. Children: (1) John Hoge was to possess tract of land given to him by Deed of Gift (2) William Hoge Jr. was given 120 acres that he lived on, secured by a bill of sale. (3) son-in-law Neal Thomson received 100 acres of land whereon he lived (4) son-in-law Robert White received 7 shillings (5) Alexander Hoge (6) James Hoge and George Hoge were to receive the remainder of the land, to be divided among the three of them. (8) Jorsebar Hoge, a daughter, was to received 50 pounds of money. Administrator for the estate was George Hoge (a justice of the peace), his son, and security was Matthew Rodgers. Source: Will Book I, Pages 338-339, Frederick County, Va.

Hogg, Peter, son of James Hogg of Edinborough, Scotland, filed a Will Oct. 5, 1773 and it was probated in Rockingham County, Va., April 22, 1782. It is believed this man lived near Winchester, in Old Frederick County, prior to going "west" to Greenbrier, where he received "Ohio land" for service in the French and Indian War. Peter was survived by his wife Elizabeth. Sons, named James Hogg and Peter Hogg Jr., were to be sent to Edinborough to receive an education under the care of their uncle, Walter Hogg. Peter Sr. left a son named Thomas Hogg, born in the early 1770s. Daughter Ann Hogg married William Hawkins, and Elizabeth Hogg married Jesse Bennett.

Holiday, William and Mary, were parents of twin children, James Holiday and Elizabeth Holiday, born Jan. 19, 1739. Source: Morgan's Chapel Records, Norborne Parish, old Frederick County, Va. (now Bunker Hill, Berkeley County, W.Va.).

Hollenback, Isaac, died on July 8, 1879, aged 85 years, in Mineral County, according to the July 11, 1879 issue of the *South Branch Intelligencer*. His wife was Susanna Johnson, born on July 6, 1787. Her parents were named Abraham and Catherine (Parker) Johnson, according to information in the DAR Library, Grandfather Papers.

Hollenbeck, Daniel, was deceased by 1840, according to **Order Book I**, page 316, Circuit Court, Hampshire County, Va. If I read the document correctly, his heirs were: 1) Margaret Hollenbeck married Abraham Rinehart 2) Marin Hollenbeck married Ellis Rinehart 3) Elizabeth Hollenbeck married Daniel Larimer (?) 4) Mary Ann Hollenbeck married Layton Raden 5) Caroline Hollenbeck 6) Warren Hudson 7) Daniel Smith. James Allen was mentioned.

Hollingsworth, David, died in September 1859, aged 69 years. He was a widower. Cause of death was "typhoid pneumonia," which he suffered for 60 days prior to his death, according to attending physician.   Source: 1860 Mortality Schedule for Frederick County, Va.

Hook, Archibald, son of Thomas and Eleanor (McVicker) Hook, was born in Hampshire County, Va. on Aug. 30, 1807 and died in Lafayette County, Missouri on Sept. 25, 1855. Source: Tombstone inscription in Greenton Cemetery, Missouri.

Hook, Addison, son of Thomas and Eleanor (McVicker) Hook, was born in Hampshire County, Va. on May 20, 1828 and died in Lafayette County, Missouri on Feb. 14, 1881. He married Mary C. Carlyle on Jan. 25, 1853, in Hampshire County. They migrated to Missouri in 1857. Mary Catherine Carlyle was born on July 8, 1837 in Hampshire County, Va. and died on Oct. 21, 1899. Her parents were Robert and Elizabeth (McCauley) Carlyle. Sources: DAR records submitted by applicants, and cemetery records in Lafayette County, Missouri.

Hook, David, was born May 20, 1810 and died April 16, 1894. He married Tacy Marple, daughter of Thomas and Abigail (Smith) Marple, Nov. 13, 1836. Source: Graveyard inscriptions in Bethel Church cemetery near Gore, Va.

Hook, Esther, daughter of William Hook, and wife of David Pugh, died on Aug. 2, 1871, age 68 years, 1 month. Source: Hampshire County, W.Va. courthouse record in Romney.

Hook, Joseph, son of Thomas and Eleanor (McVicker) Hook, was born in Hampshire County, Va. on Aug. 14, 1819 and died on March 1, 1897. His wife, Parthenia A. Carlyle, was born on April 22, 1822 and died on Sept. 11, 1884. Source: Tombstone inscriptions, Greenton Cemetery, Lafayette County, Missouri.

Hook, Mary, daughter of William and Mary (McKee) Hook, was born on Oct. 29, 1800. She received money from her father's estate, in 1835.

Hook, Nancy, daughter of Thomas and Eleanor (McVicker) Hook, was born on Jan. 28, 1806, in Hampshire County, Va. and died in Lafayette County, Missouri on July 17, 1879. Her husband was Jonathan Simmons. Source: Tombstone inscription in Greenton Cemetery in Lafayette County, Missouri.

Hook, Samuel, son of William and Mary (McKee) Hook, was born on March 23, 1795, and died on June 17, 1876 in Hampshire County, W. Va. Samuel and his first and third wife were buried at Capon Chapel. He married: (1) Anna McMorris, daughter of David and Nancy (McDonald) McMorris, on March 6, 1820. She was born on April 14, 1801 and died on Sept. 13, 1840. (2) Mary "Polly" Mauzy, daughter of Peter and Elizabeth (Buzzard) Mauzy Sr. She was born on Oct. 30, 1790 and died on Sept. 15, 1854. She was buried in the Mauzy graveyard on Timber Ridge, Hampshire County, Va., and (3) Elizabeth (McMorris) McKee, widow of Robert McKee and daughter of David and Nancy (McDonald) McMorris, on Feb. 15, 1855. She was born on April 23, 1797 and died on May 5, 1877. Elizabeth's obit was published in the *South Branch Intelligencer*, in the May 18, 1877 issue. Samuel Hook ran a tavern or inn, located a short distance east of Capon Bridge, W.Va., at the intersection of U.S. Route 50 and Smokey Hollow Road. Sources: Too numerous to mention, but primarily tombstone inscriptions. Samuel's vital dates were taken from a family Bible record (The dates given by Ralph L. Triplett are incorrect. The children of Samuel Hook were: (1) William Hook was twice married: (a) Sarah A. Mauzy, daughter of John and Elizabeth (Powell) Mauzy. This Sarah (Mauzy) Hook died on Aug. 21, 1858, aged 27 years, 10 months and 12 days, according to a tombstone inscription in the Peter Mauzy graveyard. (b) Elizabeth Leith, daughter of William and Mary (Powell) Leith. Elizabeth was born in 1829 and died on Feb. 4, 1880. (2) Robert Hook was born circa 1833, and was listed in his father's Will. (3) Elizabeth Hook was born Jan. 1, 1836 and died April 15, 1905. She married Howard Brooks, who died Sept. 1, 1893, aged 63 years, 6 months, 4 days. (4) Martha Hook was born on April 4, 1838 and died Sept. 28, 1861. She married James Richard Mauzy, son of Peter and Susannah (Powell) Mauzy. (5) Mary Ann Hook married first, Henry Mauzy and second, Andrew Jackson Bageant. (6) Davis S. Hook was listed as a son, in his father's Will. See "History of the Hook Family of Old Frederick County, Va.," *The West Virginia Advocate*, Jan. 16, 1989 issue.

Hook, Susannah, was born in Dec. 1824 and died on Jan. 28, 1897. She married Nathan Barrett on Sept. 29, 1842 in Hampshire County. He was born on Jan. 13, 1822 and died on Nov. 22, 1896. They were buried in the Christian Church cemetery at High View. Source: Submitted as a query by Ms. Sue MAYER, Peoria, IL.

Hook, Thomas, son of William and Mary (McKee) Hook, was born in Hampshire County on Oct. 8, 1783 and died on April 9, 1861 in Lafayette County, Missouri. His wife, Elenor McVicker, daughter of Dunkin and Jane McVicker, was born on March 22, 1785 in Hampshire County, Va. and died on Nov. 19, 1856 in Lafayette County, Missouri. They were married on March 14, 1805 in Hampshire County. Sources: Bible records submitted to DAR in application for membership, and tombstone inscriptions in Greenton Cemetery in Lafayette County, Missouri.

Hook, William, was born in 1759 in Gloucestershire, England and died in Hampshire County on Jan. 30, 1837. He served in the Revolutionary War. On Aug. 13, 1782, he married Mary McKee, daughter of Robert McKee Sr. She was born circa 1764 and died on Jan. 17, 1848. Source: DAR lineage records.

Horn, George, born in Hampshire County, Va. in 1807 and died in Shelby County, Missouri on July 6, 1882. Source: The July 23, 1882 issue of the *South Branch Intelligencer*.

Horn, John, was born on Aug. 1, 1792 and died on Feb. 3, 1873, aged 80 years, 6 months and 2 days, at Capon Bridge, W.Va., according to the *South Branch Intelligencer*, Feb. 14, 1873 issue of the newspaper. This corresponds with his tombstone inscription in the Capon Chapel cemetery. Catherine, his wife, was born on July 8, 1803 and died on Nov. 5, 1886 (also buried at Capon Chapel). Catherine was a daughter of Samuel and Sarah (Caudy) Gard.

Horner, William, born in 1811 and died on Jan. 3, 1872 in Hampshire County. He was buried in Capon Chapel. Source: The *South Branch Intelligencer* newspaper.

Hotsenpiller, Joseph, died in May 1850, aged 91 years. He was a farmer, born in Virginia. Source: 1850 Mortality Schedule for Frederick County, Va.

Hott: For extensive data on the Hott family, please refer to *Shanholtzer Family History and Allied Family Roots*, by Wilmer L. Kerns, Ph.D., Parsons, W.Va.: McClain Printing Co., 1980, 1054 pages.

Hott, Abraham, son of Samuel and Barbara (Shanholtzer) Hott, was born in Hampshire County on Dec. 12, 1812 and died on Aug. 8, 1883. His wife, Mary Ann Swier, was born in Frederick County, Va. on Sept. 14, 1814 and died in Indiana on Feb. 17, 1899. Source: Tombstone inscriptions copied by Mrs. Lorna Lou Collins, Kewanna, IN 46939.

Hott, Mrs. Conrad (nee Mary Ann Stipes), died on Dec. 3, 1861 at Cold Stream, Hampshire County. Source: *Undertaker Book* of William Meade Edwards, coffin-maker. The coffin was ordered by Levi Hott.

Hott, Ellanor, "widow," died in June 1870, aged 62 years, "of consumption." Born in Virginia. [Note: Could this have been Eleanor Barrett who married Martin Hott?] Source: 1870 Mortality Schedule for Frederick County, Va.

Hott, Elizabeth, daughter of Samuel and Barbara (Shanholtzer) Hott, was born in 1812/13 and died on Jan. 14, 1901, aged 88 years, in Indiana. Her husband was named Jesse Warfield (not George!) of Hampshire County, Va. Source: Mrs. Lorna Lou Collins, Kewanna, IN 46939.

Hott, George, was born in Germany in 1700 and died at White Hall, Frederick County, Va., in 1797. He married Magdalena Schantz in Germany, and she died in 1801 on the family farm at White Hall, Va. They moved from Lancaster County, Penn., in 1773, to Frederick County, Va. Sources: The immigration record gives George Hott's age when he arrived in Philadelphia, from which his birth year was calculated. The other information was obtained from courthouse records in Frederick County and tombstone inscriptions taken from the Hott farm. See *Shanholtzer History and Allied Family Roots*, McClain Printing Co., Parsons, W.Va., 1980, 1,054 pages, by Wilmer L. Kerns, Ph.D.

Hott, Mrs. John, died last Sunday, according to the Nov. 28, 1838 issue of The *South Branch Intelligencer*. She was in her

60th year, which suggests that she was born in 1779. It is believed that her husband was named John Hott Jr. (1780-ca1840), and that her first name was Sarah.

House, Nellie was buried in an old 18th century graveyard between Little Capon and the old Neal's Run Post Office. The old stone simply says "Nelle House, 1793." Nothing more was inscribed on the stone, and I believe the 1793 represents a death date. Next to Nelle was buried "Sara Johnson, 1778-1792. Quite possibly the graveyard was owned by a Johnson family at one time.

Huff, Catherine, died on July 1, 1865, aged 73 years, 3 months, 21 days. She was a widow at the time of her death, and her maiden name was Dinham, daughter of John and Mary Dinham. Her son-in-law- Hutchinson reported her death to the Clerk of the Court in Morgan County, W.Va.

Hull, Benjamin, wrote his Will on May 9, 1818 and it was probated in the Frederick County court on Oct. 5, 1818. He was from New Jersey. Benjamin mentioned his wife Elsa; daughters Margaret Hull who married Jacob Kerns, son of John and Elizabeth (Light) Kerns, on March 1, 1810. Margaret was first married to a Mr. Dawson; Elizabeth Hull married Lewis Largent; Hannah Eleanor Hull married Lewis Largent; and Naomi Hull. The two Lewis Largents were different persons. Source: Frederick County, Va.: *Superior Court Will Book 3*, page 62.

Hull, Benjamin, was born on May 22, 1738. He had immigrated to Hampshire County in 1792, where his Will was probated in 1809. His wife, Jemima, was born on Dec. 22, 1751. Their children: (1) Martin Hull was born April 2, 1775. (2) Elizabeth Hull was born July 25, 1776., and married a Mr. Barnes. (3) John Hull was born Feb. 2, 1778. (4) Anna Hull was born May 22, 1781. (5) Silas Hull was born Oct. 18, 1784. (6) Mary Hull was born Jan. 9, 1786, married Jacob Moon. (7) Stephen Hull was born Jan. 1, 1789. (8) Isaac Hull was born April 17, 1791. (9) William Hull was born April 10, 1795. His wife, Rebecca, was born July 1, 1794. (10) Jacob Hull was born Sept. 10, 1799. He married Elizabeth Cundiff, daughter of John Cundiff. Source: Bible record in hands of Mrs. Blanche Smith, Keyser, W.Va.

Hutchinson, Elizabeth, wife of John Hutchinson, was born on April 19, 1819 and died on May 28, 1868 in Frederick County, Va.

Source: Tombstone inscription at Timber Ridge Baptist Church, Reynolds Store, Frederick County, Va.

Iden, Jonathan, son of Jacob and Elizabeth Iden, was born in Loudoun County, Va. and died in Hampshire County, W.Va. on Dec. 4, 1875, aged 91 years, 3 months, 21 days. According to the **South Branch Intelligencer**, Jonathan died at the home of son-in-law Benjamin Loy. He moved to Frederick County during early life, and to Hampshire County in 1871. Jonathan was a Veteran of the War of 1812. Burial was in the Wesley Chapel Methodist Church Cemetery, on U.S. 522, south of the Frederick County, Va./Morgan County, W.Va. line. His wife, Catherine Jolley (1784-1872) was buried next to Jonathan.

Iden, Phebe, daughter of Jonathan and Catherine (Jolley) Iden, was born circa 1813 and died in Hampshire County, W.Va. According to the **Undertaker Book** of John W. Mellon, she was buried on Aug. 14, 1893. Her final grave was in the Foreman Graveyard, in Frog Hollow, on Cold Stream, Hampshire County. Phebe's husband was Samuel Shanholtz, son of Peter and Magdalena (Hott) Shanholtzer Jr. He was born in 1801, in Hampshire County, Va. and died on July 1, 1872. Samuel was buried on a knoll, near the Cacapon River. I have seen this site (escorted through the uninhabited "wilderness" by Mrs. Nellie Wilson, Charlie Harmison, Audrey Baker, et. al.) The slatestone was not inscribed, and it was in a prone position. See my book, **Shanholtzer History and Allied Family Roots**, for information on their descendants.

Iliff, Elizabeth, was born in 1778 and died on Nov. 30, 1881. Her daughter, Mary Siden (?), reported her death to the courthouse. Note: This record "doesn't add up," but that is what it says.

Inskeep, Susan, wife of Abraham Inskeep, was born in 1739 and died June 17, 1805. Source: Tombstone inscription in Inskeep graveyard located about one mile north of Fisher, Hardy County, W.Va.

Irick, Elizabeth, died in December 1859, aged 50 years. Cause of death was "neuralgia," after a 4-month illness. Her husband was living at the time of her death. Source: 1860 Mortality Schedule (U.S. Census) for Shenandoah County, Va.

Iser, Absolem, was shot to death on June 23, 1893, by Daniel R. Shawen. It happened two and one-half miles southwest of Romney, on a public road. Source: Record in Box 236, Circuit Court of Hampshire County, W.Va.

Iser, Elizabeth, died on May 27, 1888 at age 77 years. She was a daughter of David and Catherine (Shanholtzer) Hott. Her husband William Iser reported her death to the Hampshire County courthouse.

Iser, Silas, died on July 15, 1910, age 84 years. He was a widower. Source: Hampshire County courthouse death record.

Jackson, Benjamin, born circa 1783 and died about 1855, on Timber Ridge, near High View, Hampshire County, Va. He first came to the Frederick County side of the Ridge, from Loudoun County, Va. He was associated with the Bruner, Anderson, Furr, Scrivenor, and Muse families. Source: Mrs. Cheryl (Jackson) Malone, 140 Jackson Street, Morgantown, W.Va. 26505.

Jackson, Mary, widow of Benjamin Jackson, died in September 1890, aged 98 years. Daughter Emily Mason reported the death to the Hampshire County courthouse in Romney, W.Va.

Jackson, Aaron, son of Benjamin and Mary Jackson, married Jane Gray, daughter of Robert and Rosa Gray, Feb. 8, 1866, by the Rev. Simeon Ward. Source: Hampshire County marriage records. Aaron, listed as 26 years old, was born in Jefferson County, Va.

Jacob, the Rev. John J., was born in Ann Arundel County, Maryland on Jan. 17, 1757 and died on March 23, 1839, in Hampshire County. He served as a Captain in the Revolutionary War, and was ordained in the Methodist Episcopal Church in 1789. His wife, Susan, was born on April 26, 1795 and died on Nov. 30, 1880. Source: Tombstone inscriptions in Indian Mound Cemetery, Romney, W.Va.

Jenkins, Aaron, was born in 1750, and died in 1807. He married Charity Springer. Source: Cemetery inscription in New Burlington Cemetery, Clinton County, Ohio.

Jenkins, Jacob, was born circa 1725 and died in 1795 on Timber Ridge, probably on the Hampshire County side, in Bloomery District. His wife was named Elizabeth Rogers, and both were from Quaker families. Source: Hampshire and Frederick County courthouse records.

Jennings,Mary was born in Pennsylvania on July 2, 1799 and died in Hampshire County, on Jan. 11, 1882. She was married to Thomas Kesler. Source: Courthouse death record in Romney, W.Va.

Johnson, Daniel, was born in Virginia in 1789 and died in Hampshire County, Va. in Oct. 1859, "of asthma." Source: U.S. Census 1860 Mortality Schedule for Hampshire County, Va.

Johnson, David, was born on May 24, 1780 and died on Dec. 25, 1827, according to a tombstone inscription in the Old Johnson Graveyard, south of U.S. 50, on the road to Trone Methodist Church. Although it is located in Frederick County, Va., it is near the Hampshire County, W.Va. line. David served in the War of 1812. He married Catherine Bruner on Jan. 15, 1806, by the Rev. Christian Streit, in Frederick County, Virginia. According to an old letter provided by Nancy Cotton, 1704 Leawood Drive, Edmond, Oklahoma 73034, Catherine (Bruner) Johnson died at Timber Ridge in Virginia, on Jan. 27, 1863.

Johnson, Edward B., son of William S. and Carolyn (Garvin) Johnson, was accidentally killed in February 1887, in Capon District of Hampshire County. He was 22 years old, unmarried. Source: Courthouse death record.

Johnson, John W., died on March 15, 1875, in Hampshire County, aged 74 years. His parents were Thomas and Jane Johnson. He was survived by his wife, named Ellen. Source: Hampshire County, W.Va. death records, Romney, W.Va.

Johnson, Joseph H., was born on March 12, 1785 in Hampshire County, Va. and died on Sept. 25, 1834, in Montgomery County, Ohio. He married Mary Eve Stoker, daughter of John and Elizabeth (Critton) Stoker, on Oct. 5, 1805, in Hampshire County. She was born on Nov. 15, 1788 at Little Cacapon, Hampshire County, Va. and died on March 7, 1844. They had thirteen children. Source: Tombstone inscriptions in Old Johnson Graveyard, Wagner Ford Road, Wayne Township, Montgomery County, Ohio.

Johnson, Nancy, daughter of Thomas and Margaret Hollenback, was born in Hampshire County in 1789 and died at Patterson's Creek in Sept. 1854. Her husband was Okey

Johnson, born on Aug. 7, 1785, and died on Sept. 6, 1848, in Hampshire County. Okey was a son of William and Catherine (Parker) Johnson. Sources: Death record in Virginia State Archives, and DAR records in Washington, D.C.

Johnson, Okey, son of William and Catherine (Parker) Johnson, was born in Hampshire County, Va. on Aug. 7, 1785 and died on Sept. 6, 1848, in same county. He married Nancy Hollenback, in 1816. She was born on Sept. 23, 1789 in Hampshire County, and died on Sept. 28, 1854. Source: NSDAR records, DAR Library, Washington, D.C.

Johnson, Richard, buried "Mrs. Johnson" on May 22, 1887, according to the *Undertaker Book* of John W. Mellon, Timber Ridge.

Johnson, Robert, son of William and Jane Johnson, died in Morgan County, W.Va. in Aug. 1869, aged 80 years. He was a miller, born in Berkeley County, Va., and a "widower." Source: Morgan County, W.Va. courthouse death records.

Johnson, Sara, born in 1778 and died in 1792. This old stone was found in an 18th century graveyard, sometimes called the "Shade Graveyard," in the Little Cacapon area of Hampshire County, W.Va. The inscription is still very clear.

Johnson, Samuel, son of William and M. Johnson, was born in Berkeley County, Va. and died at Rock Gap, Morgan County, W.Va. on Sept. 2, 1876, aged 81 years. He was a farmer, and his wife was named Margaret. Source: Courthouse death record in Berkeley Springs, W.Va.

Johnson, William, son of Abraham and Rachel Johnson, was born in Hampshire County, in 1762, and died on May 2, 1801. His wife, Catherine Parker, was born on Nov. 21, 1764 and died on March 1, 1846. They were married on April 1, 1782, in Hampshire County, Va. Source: Genealogical Records Committee, N.S.D.A.R., Washington D.C. Library, at 1776 D. Street, N.W.

Johnson, William, "widower," died in June 1870, in Frederick County, Va. Blacksmith. Born in Virginia. Source: 1870 Mortality Schedule for Frederick County, Va.

Johnston, John was born in Morgan County, Va. (sic) on Jan. 6, 1780 and died on Sept. 26, 1854, "of diabetes" at Great

Cacapon. His parents were William and Elizabeth Johnston. Source: Death record in Virginia State Archives.

Johnston, Joseph, son of William and Elizabeth (Hancher) Johnston, was born on Dec. 4, 1785 in Va. and died on Jan. 6, 1854. He married Ann McGinnis on Feb. 28, 1805. She was born on May 18, 1782 and died on Aug. 20, 1864. They were residents of Frederick County, Va. Ralph L. Triplett believed that they were buried in the old Johnson Graveyard near the Trone Methodist Church, on Timber Ridge, Frederick County, Virginia. Source: Bible record provided by Mrs. A.H. Lindsey, Amherst, MA 01002.

Jones, Catherine, wife of Moses Jones, was born in Hampshire County in 1789 and died in Hardy County, Va. on Dec. 10, 1859. Cause of death was "consumption." Source: *West Virginia Vital Statistics: Hardy County Death Records*, Reel #3, Virginia State Library, Archives Division, Richmond, Va.

Jones, Jacob, died in Hampshire County on Jan. 25, 1867, aged 95 years. He was a Veteran of the War of 1812. Source: The *South Branch Intelligencer*.

Jones, John was born in 1795 and died Jan. 8, 1877. His wife, Martha Schinholtz, was born in 1798 and died April 26, 1884. It is believed that they emigrated from Hardy County, Va. to Ohio. One of their six children was named Mary Jones, born Feb. 17, 1827 and died Feb. 25, 1914. Mary married Robert Groves, Nov. 1, 1851, at Petersburg, Hardy County, Va. Robert was born Dec. 25, 1821 and died Dec. 4, 1899. Contact: Mr. Herman Gabriel, 7308

Judy, Elijah, died on Feb. 24, 1875, aged 65 years, on the South Fork. Source: March 5, 1875 issue of the *South Branch Intelligencer*.

Julian, Isaac, son of Rene Julian, was born on Dec. 30, 1716, in St. Ann's Parish, MD and died on July 8, 1788 in Randolph County, N.C. He was one of the early settlers on Hogue's Creek, Frederick County, Va. He was associated with Capt. Jeremiah Smith. Isaac married Barbara White, daughter of Dr. Robert and Margaret (Hoge) White, on Sept. 10, 1741, at North Mountain, Frederick County, Va.

Kackley, Abraham, son of Elias and Catherine Kackley, was born in Frederick County, Va. on Oct. 31, 1771 and died on June 15, 1849, in Smokey Hollow (on the Mill Branch of the Cacapon River), Hampshire County, Va. He was a Deacon in the Christian

Church. Abraham married Christina Wissent (Whisner?) on Nov. 26, 1793, in Frederick County, Va. The Kackley log house is still standing along Route 50, in deteriorated condition, one mile east of Capon Bridge, W.Va., and the family graveyard is on a knoll across the road. None of the field stones are inscribed.

Kackley, Benjamin, son of Jacob and Margaret (Secrist) Kackley, died in Frederick County, Va. in 1850. His wife was Mary Orndorff, daughter of John and Margaret (Renner) Orndorff.

Kackley, Jacob, was born in 1702, in Steinhelm, Wurenberg Germany and died in Frederick County, Va. on Feb. 16, 1788. He married Alice (1717-1805). They settled briefly in Lancaster County, PA; then moved to the east side of the Great North Mountain, near Mt. Williams, Va. They were buried nearby, in the St. John's Lutheran Church graveyard. The "plantation house," mentioned in his Will, in 1788, is now a part of the Shawnee Land Lodge. Allegedly the original house was built in 1750. They were among the early settlers of Frederick County. A book has been published on the Kackley family, titled, Jacob's House: *Cackley/Kackley/Keckley Family*. Contact Mrs. Elizabeth Qualls, Highway 56, Box 300, Evening Shade, AR 72532. Also, contact should be made with Mrs. Christine Garst, Route 1, Box 70, Webber, KS 66970, who is another serious researcher of the Kackley family. Mrs. Garst plans to publish the results of her research findings.

Kackley, John, son of Jacob and Alice Kackley, was born July 30, 1741 and died on April 23, 1823, at Pleasant City, Noble County, Ohio. His wife was Elizabeth Whiteman. Both were buried in the Lyons Cemetery, in Noble County.

Kackley, Magdeline, daughter of Jacob and Margaret (Secrist) Kackley, was born in Frederick County, circa 1790. She married John Clouser, son of Henry and Sarah (Fry) Clouser Jr. They were living in Lucas County, Iowa when the 1850 census was taken for that county.

Kackley, Margaret, daughter of Ellis Kackley of Capon Bridge, died on July 10, 1861, unmarried. Source: Coffin-book of William Meade Edwards, undertaker at Cold Stream, Hampshire County.

Kagey, Abraham, died in November 1859, aged 67 years. Occupation was "farmer." Born in Virginia. Cause of death was rheumatism.   Source: 1860 Mortality Schedule for Shenandoah County, Va.

Kale (Cale), John was born on April 19, 1726 and died on July 26, 1797, near Capon Bridge. His wife, Elizabeth Pugh, was born on Dec. 13, 1730 and died on Sept. 14, 1796.   Kale came to Hampshire County circa 1774 and settled on Fairfax grants originally issued to John Parks I, and Richard Arnold.   No indenture has yet been located which proves that John Kale purchased land in Hampshire County.   An 18th century mill, mentioned in a courthouse land record (1800), stood on Kale's land.   Much speculation has been made about the origin and roots of John and Elizabeth Kale. Source: Records submitted by descendants; cemetery inscriptions; land records.

Kaylor, Adam, son of Josiah and Mary (Shade) Kaylor, was born in Hampshire County, Va on March 6, 1832, and died on Sept. 24, 1910. He was twice-married: (1) Elizabeth Largent, died on April 5, 1889, aged 68 years, 4 months, 4 days, and (2) Mary Elizabeth Floyd, born on Feb. 9, 1847 and died on Nov. 24, 1914. A fence encloses these graves within a larger graveyard. Infant children are buried in the Kaylor plot.   Source: Tombstone inscriptions in the "Shade Graveyard" in the Little Capon area of Hampshire County, W.Va.

Kaylor, Josiah, son of Andrew and Alice Kaylor, died on Dec. 3, 1876, aged 72 years, 11 months, and 23 days. His wife, Mary Shade, daughter of Joseph and Sophia Shade, died in Hampshire County at age 74 years. Source: Courthouse death records in Romney, W.Va.

Kearns, Nancy, died in Berkeley County, W.Va., March 1870, aged 75 years. She was born in "West Virginia." Source: 1870 Mortality Schedule for Berkeley County, W.Va.

Kearns, Rosannah, was born in Virginia in 1810 and died in Oct. 1849, in Morgan County, Va., "of asthma."   [Comment: Possibly she was a daughter of Peter and Catherine Yost. If so, the 1855 Will of Peter Yost stated that his daughter Rosannah married Henry Kerns, and that four of her children were living.] Source: 1850 Mortality Schedule for Morgan County, Va.

Keesecker, Sarah, who was the wife of John Keesecker, died in Morgan County, W.Va. on March 11, 1873, aged 89 years, "of cancer." The courthouse death record in Berkeley Springs stated that Sarah's maiden name was Hickson. The death was reported by her son-in-law, H. Kerns.

Keiter, Elizabeth A., died in August 1849, aged 35 years. Born in Virginia. Suffered for 300 days from a pulminary disease. Survived by spouse. Source: 1850 Mortality Schedule for Frederick County, Va.

Keiter, Frederick, son of George and Esther (Buzzard) Keiter, was born on Dec. 10, 1797 and died on Sept. 19, 1871, in Greene County, Ohio. His death was announced in the *South Branch Intelligencer* newspaper (W.Va.). He married Mary Weaver, daughter of Abraham and Magdalene (Senseny) Weaver, in 1822. She (Mary) was born on Dec. 18, 1803 and died on Dec. 18, 1877. They migrated to Greene County, Ohio in 1833. Six children were born in Virginia and six more in Ohio. See the May 1987 issue of *The West Virginia Advocate*, for a history of the Keiter family.

Keiter, Frederick Theodore, son of John and Emily (Coe) Keiter, was born on July 12, 1857 in Hampshire County, Va. He married Lucinda Clark in April 1882. Source: Family Bible.

Keiter, George, was born on Dec. 25, 1756 and died on March 26, 1850. Next to him was buried wife Esther Buzzard, born in 1763 and died Sept. 12, 1828. Nearby was another broken stone which says, "died Oct. 28, 1848, ___ yrs, 8 mo., 28 days." The stone had been destroyed and it was impossible to read it entirely. Source: Tombstone inscriptions in Buckwalter cemetery. See the May 1987 issue of *The West Virginia Advocate*.

Keiter, George, Jr., born on June 16, 1790 and died on March 28, 1880. His first wife, Elizabeth Acre, was born in 1787 and died on March 11, 1862. His second wife was Margaret Peacemaker. Source: Tombstone inscriptions in the Buckwalter cemetery.

Keiter, George William, son of John and Emily (Coe) Keiter, was born on Oct. 8, 1838 and died on May 10, 1842. The tombstone inscription in Buckwalter's graveyard contains an error. Source: Keiter family Bible.

Keiter, Jacob, son of George and Esther (Buzzard) Keiter, Sr., was born on April 4, 1794 in Hampshire County, Va. and died on April 4, 1864. He married Mary Lewis, daughter of Jacob and Rachel (Hott) Lewis, on Dec. 31, 1816. She was born on Oct. 10, 1795 and died on Aug. 8, 1867. Source: DAR Grandfather papers, submitted by descendant.

Keiter, James C., "died July 1, 1900." Source: *Diary of George Edwards*, Cross Junction, Va.

Keiter, John, son of George and Esther (Buzzard) Keiter, Sr., was born on June 23, 1784 and died on May 24, 1870. Buried next to him was Sarah (Beall), born on Sept. 14, 1784 and died on Jan. 6, 1818, aged 34 years. They were married on Oct. 16, 1816 and had only one child. Buried on the other side was John Keiter's second wife, Emily Coe, daughter of William and Elizabeth (Gore) Coe, born on Feb. 13, 1812 and died on May 24, 1870. They were married on Jan. 4, 1838 and had eight children. Emily's death occurred only seven hours after John died. Sources: Tombstone inscriptions in Buckwalter cemetery in the Bloomery District and family Bible.

Keiter, John Coe, son of John and Emily (Coe) Keiter, was born Sept. 15, 1841. He married Mary E. Hammond on Oct. 13, 1870. Source: Keiter family Bible.

Keiter, Margaret, daughter of George and Esther (Buzzard) Keiter, Sr., was born in Hampshire County, Va. on Dec. 29, 1790 and died in Licking County, Ohio on July 10, 1873. She married, in 1811, John Weaver, son of Abraham and Magdalene (Senseny) Weaver. They migrated to Ohio in 1823.

Keiter Mariah "Marie," daughter of George and Esther (Buzzard) Keiter, Sr., was born at Bloomery, Virginia on May 22, 1806. She married John Smith (probably a son of Conrad Smith, the Hessian soldier born in 1754 in Germany) on Dec. 11, 1834 by the Rev. Herbert Cool. John Smith was born on June 6, 1806. They had seven children and later migrated to Greene County, Ohio in 1864.

Keiter, Mary Emily, daughter of John and Emily (Coe) Keiter, was born on March 2, 1853 and died on April 9, 1862. Source: Family Bible.

Keiter, Mary "Polly," daughter of George and Esther (Buzzard) Keiter, Sr., was born in 1788 and died unmarried on Jan. 31, 1861 in Hampshire County. Source: Hampshire County courthouse death record.

Keiter, Reese Babb, born in Hampshire County, Va., married Margaret Ellen Haines, Feb. 13, 1877, in Hardy County, W.Va. Both were residents of Greene County, Ohio at the time of their marriage,   according to a courthouse (marriage) record in Moorefield, W.Va.

Keiter, Robert George, son of John and Emily (Coe) Keiter, was born on Aug. 14, 1851. He married (Edmonia Hunnum ?) in Aug. 1875.

Keiter, Samuel Edward, son of John and Emily (Coe) Keiter, was born on Aug. 25, 1843 and died June 23, 1844. Source: Family Bible. The tombstone inscription contains an error.

Keiter, Sarah Elizabeth, born on Oct. 24, 1845 and died on June 22, 1851. (Note: Her sister Susan Maria died on Oct. 28, 1848, and was buried nearby. Her stone is almost disintegrated) Sources: Tombstone inscription, Buckwalter cemetery and family Bible.

Keiter, Susan Maria, daughter of John and Emily (Coe) Keiter, was born on Feb. 1, 1848 and died on Oct. 28, 1848. Source: Family Bible.

Keiter, Susannah, was born on Nov. 7, 1786 and died on Dec. 17, 1870. She married James Nelson, and they resided in Mill Branch Valley, near "U.S. 50." Her parents were George and Esther (Buzzard) Keiter. Source: Courthouse death record.

Keller, Jacob, a "widower," died in January 1850, aged 70 years. He was born in Virginia. Source: 1850 Mortality Schedule for Frederick County, Va.

Kelley, James died on Oct. 4, 1850. His wife, nee Ellen Frisellman, died on Oct. 5, 1850. They were married on Jan. 18, 1832.   They were immigrants from Ireland, and they died at Bloomery, Hampshire County, Va. Source: Record provided by retired Judge William E. Edwards of Winchester, Va.

Kelley, Patrick was buried on July 24, 1823. Source: *Journal* by the Rev. Christy Sine of Hampshire County, Va.

Kelley, Thomas, died on July 30, 1892, aged 82 years, according to J.P. Kelley, his son, who reported his death to the Hampshire County courthouse clerk. He was born in Ireland.

Kelso, James, son of William Kelso, was born in Ireland on July 8, 1774. He and his wife Anne (McVickers) resided on Timber Ridge, near LeHew, in Hampshire County, where he died on Sept. 5, 1854. Source: County death record in Virginia State Archives.

Kendall, Dorsey, was born in 1862 and died in 1941. Source: Tombstone inscription in Frederick County Poor House Graveyard.

Kenney, Mary E., born on July 9, 1869 and died on Sept. 27, 1927. It is believed that she was a daughter of William and Frances Sherwood. Source: Tombstone inscription in the Ginevan Graveyard, Okonoko, Hampshire County, W.Va.

Kercheval, Robert C., "brother of Samuel Kercheval, Jr.," died on Oct. 18, 1874, Ritchie County, W.Va. Source: *South Branch Intelligencer*, issue of Oct. 30, 1874.

Kern, Adam,Sr., was born circa 1735 and died in 1799 at Kernstown, Frederick County, Va. He married: (1) Marie Ester Moser on July 17, 1766 at York, Penn., (2) Mrs. Ruth Snyder on April 18, 1788, in Frederick County, Va., and (3) Mrs. Christina (Andrews) Enders, on Oct. 25, 1791 in Frederick County. Source: Courthouse records.

Kern, Adam, Jr., was born on Oct. 15, 1773 and died on Oct. 23, 1855 at Kernstown, Frederick County. He married: (1) Ella Bennett on April 2, 1796 and (2) Margaret Rittenour on May 10, 1807. Margaret was born in 1783, in Virginia, and died in June 1869, according to the 1870 Mortality Schedule for Frederick County, Va. Source: Tombstone inscriptions; Frederick County marriage records; and Kern family records in possession of compiler.

Kern, Elizabeth, daughter of Nicholas and Ann (Grove) Kern, was born in Frederick County, Va. on Dec. 29, 1796 and died on May 23, 1836. Her husband was John Beemer. Source: Family records.

Kern, Henry, son of Adam and Marie Ester (Moser) Kern, Sr., was born on Nov. 14, 1775 and died on Aug. 8, 1828 in Shenandoah County, Va. He was killed when a horse threw him to the ground. Henry married Rachel Kackley, daughter of Catherine (Rudolph) Kackley, widow of Benjamin Kackley, on Sept. 17, 1801.   By 1783, Catherine, had remarried to Henry Richards (1753-1847). Richards.   Rachel died in Shenandoah County on Sept. 2, 1874. Source: Family Bible of Henry Kern, now (1992) in the hands of Henry Kern, a Winchester businessman; Kern family papers in possession of compiler, including letters written during the early 20th century by descendants.

Kern, Jacob, son of Adam and Marie Ester (Moser) Kern, Sr., was born in Frederick County, Va. on July 4, 1779 and died in Indiana on Jan. 19, 1843. His wife was Sarah Ryan, daughter of Darby and Anna (Semmes) Ryan. Sarah was born on Oct. 5, 1780. Late in life, he remarried to Delphia Ann Stanley. Source: Mrs. Bessie (Kern) Regal (deceased), Iowa.

Kern, James M., son of John T. and Rebecca (Mason) Kern, died in New Orleans, LA on Oct. 12, 1876. He was born in 1838 in Romney, Va. Source: *South Branch Intelligencer*.

Kern, John Thompson, son of Adam and Ella (Bennett) Kern, Jr., was born on Jan. 26, 1797 in Frederick County, Va. and died in 1864 in Richmond, Va., where he, as a County Official, fled to the Confederate side as a member of the Administration of Jefferson Davis. He was the "John Kern Jr., Commissioner," whose name appears on thousands of documents in the Hampshire County courthouse, Romney, W.Va. His wife was Rebecca T. Mason. According to the *South Branch Intelligencer*, issue of May 1, 1874, she died several months earlier at the home of her son-in-law, John R. Dye, in Hancock County, Ohio. She was buried in the Indian Mound Cemetery in Romney, West Virginia. A death record in the Hampshire County courthouse states that Rebecca Kern died on Jan. 13, 1874, of "typhoid fever," reported by Miss Lou M. Kern.

Kern, Margaret, daughter of Nicholas and Ann (Grove) Kern, was born in Frederick County, Va. on April 9, 1790 and died on March 17, 1828. She married William Strother and they left descendants. Source: Bible record.

Kern, Mary, daughter of Nicholas and Ann (Grove) Kern, was born in Frederick County, Va. on Oct. 17, 1789 and died on Sept. 3, 1839. She married Elisha Smallwood. Source: Kern Bible record.

Kern, Nicholas, son of Adam and Marie Ester (Moser) Kern, was born in Frederick County, Va. on May 8, 1768 and died at Kernstown on Oct. 16, 1843. He married: (1) Ann Grove on Sept. 23, 1788 and (2) Mary Carroll in April 1802. Sources: Tombstone inscriptions; Bible record; and courthouse records in Winchester, Va.

Kern, Mrs. Eliza, wife of Nimrod Kern, died on Oct. 6, 1871, aged 72 years, in Winchester, Va.

Kern, Samuel, son of Adam and Marie Esther Moser Kern Sr., was born in Frederick County, Va. on Nov. 14, 1775 and died on July 6, 1857 in Shenandoah County, Va. He married Susannah Grabill, daughter of Christian Grabill, on April 9, 1801. She was born on Dec. 6, 1782 and died on Nov. 21, 1856. Source: Tombstone inscriptions on their farm in Shenandoah County, Va.

Kerns families: I am compiling a comprehensive data base on the Kerns surname, all spellings. This book is not the appropriate forum to publish voluminous Kerns files. For exchange of information, contact: Dr. Wilmer L. Kerns, 4715 North 38th Place, Arlington, Va. 22207.

Kerns, Albert L., son of Robert Algernon and Barbara (Keesecker) Kerns, was born on June 7, 1888, in Hancock, MD, and died on June 8, 1965, at Gore, Va. His wife, Sadie Giffin, was born on Aug. 12, 1905 and died on May 8, 1971. They raised a large family. See obituary in *The Winchester Star*, Winchester, Va.

Kerns, Barney, was born in March 1800 and died circa 1880 in Hampshire County, near Augusta. According to a court deposition, he was unmarried and left no heirs. Isaac and Emily (Oates) Shanholtz moved onto Barney's farm and maintained it for about forty years. Isaac [who was the father of Sol Shanholtz] was willed this farm because he took care of Barney Kerns. Mentioned in the court papers were Ann Davey and Elizabeth Kerns, but no relationship was stated. "Said Barney never having been married and his father and mother and brothers and sisters being long since dead..." It is believed that Barney was a grandson of Peter Kerns (1730-1799). The Will stated that Barney was to be buried in the Philip Malick cemetery, but I have found no marker. At least a tombstone could have been erected from the estate money, but it wasn't. Source: Records in Circuit Court, Box 221, Hampshire County, W.Va.

Kerns, Benjamin Franklin, son of Nathan and Elizabeth (Parrish) Kerns, was born in Frederick County, Va., June 15, 1827 and died July 3, 1901, in Frederick County. His name was not written in the Kerns family records. It is believed that Benjamin F. Kerns had a twin brother named Asa Kerns, same birthdate. If Asa was not his twin brother, then possibly Benjamin Franklin was named Asa at birth and changed his name (which is doubtful).

Benjamin's wife, Julia Ann Triplett, was born June 12, 1833, and died Feb. 13, 1885. Sources: Tombstone inscriptions in Rock Enon Cemetery, Frederick County, Va., and family record of Nathan Kerns.

Kerns, Catherine, daughter of John and Elizabeth (Light) Kerns, died on Aug. 20, 1886 at the age of 82 years, 5 months and 1 day. Her husband, Henry Cowgill, son of Ewing and Susannah (Buzzard) Cowgill, reported her death to the Hampshire County, W.Va. courthouse. [Note: Record erroneously reported John Cowgill.] According to *Cowgill History*, by Beatrice E. Cowgill, published by Gateway Press in 1986, Catherine Kerns was born March 19, 1804. Her husband, Henry Cowgill, was born April 19, 1798 and died Aug. 15, 1868. They raised a large family in Hampshire County, W.Va., leaving many descendants.

Kerns, David F., son of Robert Algernon and Barbara (Keesecker) Kerns, was born in 1876 and died on Oct. 6, 1954. His wife, Louisa Slonaker, was born in 1881 and died on April 19, 1971. Source: Tombstone inscriptions in Fairview Lutheran cemetery, Gore, Virginia.

Kerns, Earl J., son of Robert Algernon and Barbara (Keesecker) Kerns, was born in 1890 and died in 1960. His wife, Clara B. Hause, was born in 1911. Source: Cemetery inscriptions in Fairview Lutheran cemetery, Gore, Va.

Kerns, Elisha, son of Jacob and Rachel (Cowgill) Kerns, Jr., was born in Hampshire County, Va. on July 20, 1798 and died at Whitacre, Frederick County, Va. on Oct. 28, 1875. His wife, Rachel Whitacre, daughter of Joshua and Rachel (Wilson) Whitacre, was born in Frederick County, Va. on Nov. 14, 1804 and died on Oct. 23, 1875. Sources: Tombstone inscriptions in Heironimus cemetery, and Bible record in my possession.

Kerns, Elisha, son of John and Elizabeth (Light) Kerns, was born in Hampshire County, Va. on Aug. 27, 1793 and was alive in Aug. 1872, where he was living in Harrison County, W.Va. He married Margaret Gano on Oct. 18, 1827. My Shanholtzer history book, page 814, is in error, re his death. Source: Deposition given by Elisha Kerns, on Aug. 10, 1872, in Clarksburg, Harrison County, W.Va., re the will of John Critton of Hampshire County.

See Box 229, Hampshire County Circuit Court, "John Critton heirs vs William Critton."

Kerns, Elisha, son of Abner and Sarah (Davis) Kerns, was born in Frederick County, Va., on Sept. 10, 1830 and died on Aug. 16, 1872 in Vernon County, Missouri. Elisha was buried in the Lawrence cemetery near Hume, Missouri. He first married Margaret Noel, on Sept. 22, 1852, in Morgan County, Va. They moved to Leesburg, Kosciusko County, Indiana, where their two children were born. While there, Margaret (Noel) Kerns died on Dec. 25, 1859, after giving birth to two children. Elisha went into the military service and was discharged in Corinth, Mississippi in May 1862, for a service-connected disability. He returned to Leesburg, where he married Mary Jane McQuaid, daughter of Lewis and Susannah (Oates) McQuaid, on March 5, 1867. She was born in Frederick County, Va. on Feb. 25, 1833. Elisha's brother, Joseph H. Kerns, came to visit him after the war and was murdered by a former resident of Frederick County, Va. Elisha later moved to Rich Hill, Bates County, Missouri. Source: Ken Broadbeck, whose last known address was 4844 Eastwood, Wichita, KS 67218.

Kerns, Eliza, was buried on March 28, 1890. The cost of funeral was $14.00, which was paid from her estate. Source: *Undertaker Book* of John W. Mellon, Hampshire County, W.Va.

Kerns, Elizabeth died in March 1860, aged 70 years. She was born in Virginia, and her husband preceded her in death. Source: 1850 Mortality Schedule for Frederick County, Va.

Kerns, Ephrium, son of George and Elizabeth (Reid) Kerns Sr., was born in Frederick County, Virginia and died in the Bloomery District of Hampshire County, W.Va. on Jan. 14, 1897. He died at the home of his son, Aljourn Kerns, believed to have been Robert A. Kerns. Aljourn lived on an east bank of the Cacapon River, opposite the mouth of Edwards Mill Run, at the underwater bridge. Ephrium married Sarah Hoover on Oct. 4, 1836. She was born on May 10, 1814 and died on Aug. 21, 1890 at Warfordsburg, PA. Ephrium and Sarah Kerns lived briefly in Ellsworth County, Kansas during the 1880s, but returned to West Virginia and Maryland. Sarah was buried in Section B of the Warfordsburg Presbyterian Church cemetery. We have not located the burial site for Ephrium, but believe it to be somewhere in the Bloomery District of Hampshire County, W.Va., or possibly in a private graveyard on Timber Ridge. Source: Research findings of Mrs. Virginia L. Bachofer, 228 South 10th Street, Salina, KS 67401.

Kerns, Flora P., daughter of Robert Algernon and Barbara (Keesecker) Kerns, was born on March 15, 1897 and died on Aug. 14, 1970. She married: (1) Irvin Benar Kerns, son of Jacob and Alice (Dailey) Kerns, and (2) a Mr. Eshleman. Source: Tombstone inscription in Fairview Lutheran Cemetery, Gore, Va.

Kerns, Francis Marion, son of Ephrium and Sarah (Hoover) Kerns, was born in Frederick County, Va. on March 3, 1839 and died at Barnsdall, Oklahoma on Aug. 22, 1918. He married Eliza Jane Kerns, daughter of Washington and Elizabeth (Everett) Kerns. Eliza J. was born in Frederick County, Va. on Oct. 6, 1841 and died in Osage, OK on Feb. 28, 1926. They moved to Illinois; to Bates County, Missouri; to Greenwood County, Kansas; to Osage County, Oklahoma where they died and were buried in the Ethel Reece Cemetery. Source: Mrs. Jody Long, Rt. 2, Box 235, Beggs, OK 74421.

Kerns, Frederick, son of John and Elizabeth (Light) Kerns, was born in 1789 and died in 1848 in Hampshire County. He married Margaret Kesler, daughter of John S. and Rachel (Flora) Kesler. Sources: U.S. Census and courthouse records.

Kerns, Frederick, son of Henry and Catherine (HOTZENPILER) Kerns, was born at Stephensburg, Frederick County, Va. on Jan. 1, 1776 and died April 6, 1867, in Gallia County, Ohio. He married Susannah Syler, daughter of Christian and Margaret (Groover) Syler, on March 22, 1807. Susannah was born on Oct. 13, 1787 and died Nov. 6, 1874.

Kerns, Frederick, son of Jacob and Margaret (Hull) Dawson Kerns, was born in Hampshire County in 1812 and died in Frederick County, Va. in 1865, killed in a dispute with a Mr. Light (over stolen horses), at Cross Junction, Va. His common-law wife was Amelia Reid, according to his Will. One source says that her maiden name was Schuler. A court document stated that she was a granddaughter of Azariah Pugh.

Kerns, Harrison Ephrium, son of Robert Algernon and Barbara (Keesecker) Kerns, was born on Dec. 23, 1871 and died in 1956. His first wife, Mary F., was born on Aug. 4, 1873 and died on June

18, 1906. Both are buried in the Fairview Lutheran cemetery at Gore, Virginia. Buried nearby is their daughter, Ellen E. Kerns, born on Nov. 14, 1898 and died on Nov. 14, 1898. Source: Tombstone inscriptions and information from Harrison's son (personal interview by compiler).

Kerns, Henry, was born circa 1740 and died in 1781. He lived in Frederick Counties, Maryland and Virginia, and his Will was probated in Shenandoah County, Va. It is believed that he died as a soldier in the Revolutionary War. His wife was Catherine Hotsenpiller. Sources: Courthouse records and the Brumback family history.

Kerns, Henry's estate was settled in Morgan County, W.Va. on Sept. 16, 1875, John H. Buzzard, administrator. His widow, Mary C. Kerns to get one-third. Children: John W. Kerns, George E.B. Kerns, F.H.H. Kerns, Charles A. Kerns, Delila Kiner Kerns, James M. Kerns, Lawson A.H. Kerns, and Clarabell Cross, deceased, wife of George W. Cross. Source: Inventory and Estate Settlement Book # 1, page 332, Morgan County courthouse in Berkeley Springs, W.Va.

Kerns, Isaac, son of John and Elizabeth (Light) Kerns, was born in 1800 and died in Hampshire County, W.Va. on July 16, 1872. He married Elizabeth Kesler, daughter of John S. and Rachel (Flora) Kesler. Isaac and Elizabeth lived on Diamond Ridge, near Sandy Hollow, Hampshire County. They left many descendants. Source: Courthouse records in Romney, W.Va.

Kerns, Isaac Jefferson, son of Isaac and Elizabeth (Kesler) Kerns, was born in Bloomery District, Hampshire County, in July 1861 and died in 1948, at Winchester, Va. He married Emma Elizabeth Alabaugh, daughter of Mary Frances Alabaugh (who later married John Sanford Kerns). Emma was born in 1871 and died in 1956. Both were buried in Bloomery Presbyterian Church graveyard. They were married May 5, 1892, and had seven children. Source: Clarence Kerns, Bunker Hill, W.Va., only surviving child of Isaac J. Kerns.

Kerns, James, died Nov. 21, 1820, aged 33 years. Source: Tombstone inscriptions in Riner Graveyard in Berkeley County, W.Va.

Kerns, James, son of Robert Algernon and Barbara (Keesecker) Kerns, was born in 1883 and died in 1958. Source: Tombstone inscription in Fairview Lutheran cemetery, Gore, Va.

Kerns, Jacob Sr., was born circa 1738 and died in October 1811, in Frederick County, Va., on Timber Ridge. He married Sarah ____ who survived him. This was a German family. Sources: Courthouse records in both Hampshire and Frederick Counties, Va. See *Shanholtzer History and Allied Family Roots of Frederick and Hampshire Counties, Va.,* by Wilmer L. Kerns, published in 1980, 1,050 pages, $50.00 postpaid.

Kerns, Jacob, Jr., son of Jacob and Sarah Kerns, was born circa 1762 and died in 1826 in Hampshire County, Va. He married Rachel Cowgill, daughter of Elisha and Martha (Ewing) Cowgill, on Feb. 15, 1791. Rachel was born on Nov. 2, 1767. Source: Hampshire County courthouse records, and Quaker church record.

Kerns, Jacob, Jr., son of Jacob and Susan Kerns Sr., of Berkeley County, Va.; born in Berkeley County, Va.; died in Morgan County, W.Va., on May 22, 1869, aged 69 years, "of pneumonia." Occupation- farmer. He was buried at the Snyder's Church graveyard in the eastern part of Morgan County, near Cherry Run. His tombstone is inscribed. There is no proven relationship between this Kerns family and other Kerns' in Frederick and Hampshire Counties. Source: Morgan County, W.Va. courthouse death record.

Kerns, Jacob, was born June 12, 1829 in Hampshire County, Va. It is believed that his parents were John and Catherine Kerns, although not proven. Jacob worked for the railroad in Mineral, Morgan, and Berkeley Counties, W.Va. He died Aug. 23, 1884. Jacob married Emily Worth Souders, Oct. 12, 1858. Emily was born Aug. 7, 1840 at Orleans Crossroads, Morgan County, Va. and died Dec. 24, 1912, in Baltimore, MD. She was buried in Martinsburg, W.Va. They were Methodists. Children of Jacob and Emily Kerns were: (1) Anora Kerns was born in Piedmont, "Mineral County, W.Va." (sic), Feb. 22, 1860 and died May 13, 1864. (2) Sarah Catherine Kerns was born July 8, 1862 at Piedmont. She married Charles H. Shipley, son of Perry and Sarah Shipley, Feb. 22, 1881. (3) Margaret "Maggie" Kerns was born Nov. 24, 1864, at Piedmont, W.Va. She married Charles

Pennell, son of Andrew and Elizabeth Pennell, Oct. 28, 1886. (4) Virginia K. Kerns was born June 4, 1867 at Piedmont, and died Nov. 1, 1869. (5) Laura B. Kerns was born Dec. 14, 1869 at Piedmont, and died March 2, 1944, in Washington, D.C. June 24, 1891, she married Andrew F. Lambert, son of George T. and Maggie Lambert. (6) Emma Jane Kerns was born Sept 3, 1872 in Martinsburg, W.Va. and died Dec. 13, 1863, in McLean, Va. She married Joseph F. Barnett, son of Thomas and Sarah Jane Barnett, on March 31, 1897, in Martinsburg. (7) Mason Kerns was born July 19, 1876 at Orleans Crossroads, Morgan County, W.Va., and died Dec. 1, 1908. (8) Manirva Kerns was born April 22, 1875 and died May 23, 1875. (9) Jacob Humphrey Franklin Kerns was born Oct. 9, 1877 and died Jan. 4, 1951. He married: (a) Catherine Curtis and (b) Emma Rae Bell. Jacob worked for the U.S. Bureau of Fisheries and lived at 1653 Harvard Street, N.W., Wash., D.C. (10) Ida Kerns was born April 7, 1881. She married George Siebert on Nov. 27, 1899. Ida lived to reach the age of 100 or more years. We engaged in several phone conversations during her 90s, when she lived in Cumberland, MD. Source: Bible record maintained by Emma Jane (Kerns) Barnett of McLean, Va., plus courthouse research and information contributed by descendants.

Kerns, J.R., died Sept. 13, 1881, at the age of 35 years, 7 months and 26 days. His parents were Jonah and Eliza (Oates) Kerns. Source: Hampshire County courthouse death record.

Kerns, John Edward, was born "in Frederick County, Virginia" (although it could have been in Hampshire County, Va..), on Sept. 6, 1832 and died in 1916, in Ohio. He married Emily Sophia Coe (1836-1896), daughter of James and Sophia (Grove) Coe, of Timber Ridge, Frederick County, Va. Emily's birthdate was Oct. 10, 1836. When the 1860 census was taken, they were living on the Isaac Shanholtz farm near Cross Junction, Va. In 1870 and 1880 they were in Fayette County, Ohio. Then they settled in Mercer County, Ohio with one of their children, where both parents died. The death certificate of John E. Kerns stated that his mother's maiden name was Mary Grant. However, old letters hint that Mary was nee Kerns. John E. Kerns allegedly had a brother named Pierce Kerns and half-brothers surnamed Peacemaker. If anyone has information on this family, contact Clyde W. Kerns, 7643 South Race Street, Littleton, CO 80122.

Kerns, John William, son of Annie Kerns (of Isaac of John Kerns), was born Jan. 12, 1874 and died Jan. 7, 1960. He married Letha Mason, daughter of James Mason. She was born May 16, 1884 and died April 29, 1963. They lived in Sandy Hollow, Bloomery District, Hampshire County, and were buried in Bloomery Presbyterian Church graveyard.

Kerns, Jonas, son of Nathan and Sarah (Whitacre) Kerns, was born in 1819 and died March 24, 1899. His wife was Eliza Ann Whitacre, daughter of George and Rachel (Tumbleston) Whitacre II. Eliza was born in 1820 and died Nov. 11, 1899, near Paw Paw, W.Va. The 1860 census for Hampshire County, Va. listed these children: Sarah E. Kerns, age 20 years; Amanda E. Kerns, age 18; George W. Kerns, age 17; Mary J. Kerns, age 16; John R. Kerns, age 14; Nathaniel Kerns, age 11 years. Source: *Little Cacapon Primitive Baptist Church Records*, Hampshire County, W.Va.

Kerns, Joseph H., was a son of Abner and Sarah (Davis) Kerns. He was raised by Heironimus Hardy of Morgan County, W.Va. Joe Kerns served on both sides of the Civil War, being in a border state. He was born in 1836 in Frederick County, Va. and was murdered in Hendricks County, Indiana in 1867. There was conflict ("bad blood") with a Sherrard family. A grand jury convened, but no one was convicted of the murder. He married Lucy Maggie Shuler, daughter of Cornelius and Harriett (Kerns) Shuler. She was born on July 2, 1837 and died on Feb. 20, 1918. They were parents of a boy and a girl. She was buried in the Mt. Hebron E.U.B. Cemetery at Cross Junction, Va. Sources: Military records in National Archives; tombstone inscriptions and Kerns family records.

Kerns, Joshua, was buried on Dec. 22, 1886, according to the *Undertaker Book* of John W. Mellon, of Timber Ridge, Hampshire County.

Kerns, Kesiah, daughter of John and Sarah (Hickson) Keesecker, died in the Sleepy Creek District of Morgan County, W.Va. on Feb. 5, 1895, aged 75 years. She was born in the Sleepy Creek District. Samuel Thompson, a friend, reported the death to the courthouse in Berkeley Springs, W.Va. Although not stated, her husband was possibly named Henry Kerns.

Kerns, Lee Doil, son of Robert R. and Sophia Ann (Ritchie) Kerns, was born at Cherry Run, Morgan County, W.Va. and died in Richmond, Va., on Dec. 23, 1986. He married Madeline Grim, who was born on Aug. 7, 1912, in Harrisonburg, Va.   Source: Records of my parents.

Kerns, Lizzie, "died this evening at 2 o'clock, Nov. 12, 1900 and was buried the 13th." Source: *Diary of George Edwards*, Cross Junction, Va.

Kerns, Louvania, daughter of Nathan and Sarah (Whitacre) Kerns, Sr., was born in 1823, and died in 1853 at Cold Stream, Hampshire County. She married Enoch Whitaker, son of George and Rachel (Tumbleston) Whitaker. Source: Death record in Virginia State Archives.

Kerns, Lydia, wife of Robert Kerns, died on Christmas Day, 1897, of "consumption," at Bloomery, W.Va. She was buried on Dec. 26th, by Charles Shane of Cold Stream. Her attending physician was Dr. J.F. Gardner. Source: Hampshire County *Register of Deaths, 1894-1903*, page 16, # 193.

Kerns, Mahlon, son of Stewart and Mary Jane (Whitacre) Kerns, died on Dec. 11, 1880, aged 16 years and 25 days. Source: Hampshire County courthouse death record.

Kerns, Mary Margaret, daughter of George and Elizabeth (Reid) Kerns, Sr., was born on July 27, 1811 and died in Hampshire County in 1902. She married: (1) John Mellon and (2) Thomas Butler Riley, Jr. Source: Bible record and Hampshire County courthouse death record.

Kerns, Michael, died March 5, 1865, aged 74 years, 2 months, 22 days. His wife was named Nancy.   Source: Tombstone inscriptions in Riner Cemetery, Berkeley County, W.Va.

Kerns, Nancy, daughter of Abner and Priscilla Chilcott of Hardy County, died on May 23, 1881, aged 66 years and 8 months. Her husband was Edward Kerns. Further research located her grave in the Copsy Graveyard, near the Forks of Capon, Bloomery District. The tombstone gave her name as Nancy Kern, with the identical information that was given above. This graveyard has many unmarked stones, and it has not been maintained for many years. Next to Nancy are two stones. One has large initials inscribed, with the last being a C. (possibly the grave of Abner Chilcott) Sources: Courthouse death record, Hampshire County, W.Va., and tombstone inscriptions.

Kerns, Nathan Sr., son of Jacob and Sarah Kerns Sr., was born in Frederick County, Va., circa 1776, and died on Timber Ridge, Frederick County, Aug. 6, 1851. A daughter, Rebecca Kerns, died on Sept. 11, 1851, aged 26 years. Another daughter, Amy Kerns, died Aug. 18, 1851, in her 21st year. Obituary stated that the father and two daughters were members of The Christian Church. Source: **Winchester Republican**, issue of Sept. 26, 1851.

Kerns, Nathan, son of George and Elizabeth (Reid) Kerns Sr., was born in Frederick County, Va. on Feb. 3, 1801 and died on July 14, 1872, in Ritchie County, W.Va. His wife, Elizabeth Parrish, was born on Dec. 4, 1803 and died on May 4, 1865. They immigrated from Frederick to Ritchie County, Va. Their Bible record: (1) Mahala Kerns was born on Dec. 5, 1823 and died on July 3, 1865. (2) Delilah Kerns was born on April 11, 1825, and married Hiram Oates [see entry]. (3) Asa Kerns was born on June 15, 1827. [Note: It is believed that Asa had a twin brother named Benjamin Franklin Kerns, born on same day and died on July 3, 1901. If so, he married Julia Ann Triplett. [comment: see photo and biography in Ralph Triplett's book, **A History of Upper Back Creek Valley**, published in 1983.] (4) Barbara "Barbary" Kerns was born on Aug. 26, 1829 and died on July 4, 1883. (5) Henry Kerns was born on Sept. 17, 1831. (6) Sarah E. Kerns was born on March 2, 1834. (7) Jeremiah Kerns was born on Oct. 11, 1836. (8) Josiah Kerns was born on Dec..10, 1838 and died on June 13, 1865. (9) Mary E. Kerns was born on Sept. 24, 1840. (10) Alexander Kerns was born on Sept. 19, 1844 and died on Aug. 8, 1865. Sources: Family records maintained by Mrs. Norma Cook, Kenton, Ohio, and U.S. Census records.

Kerns, Perry Jefferson, son of Isaac J. and Emma Elizabeth (Alabaugh) Kerns, was born in Sandy Hollow, Bloomery District, Hampshire County, W.Va., Dec. 7, 1908 and died June 1, 1990. He first married Genevieve Amy Light, who was born Dec. 30, 1906 and died May 3, 1968; then married Mildred Peck. Buried in Chestnut Grove Methodist cemetery, Frederick County, Va. Their children: Frances, Hilda, Harold and Evelyn Kerns, of Bunker Hill, W.Va.

Kerns, Peter, born circa 1730 and died in 1799, in Hardy County, Va. He owned numerous properties in old Hampshire County, including two lots in Petersburg (now W.Va.), where he operated a retail store. His estate settlement record is located in the Hardy County courthouse. Peter's widow Elizabeth Kerans (spelled also Kerns) released her dower to Bryan Keran, Dec. 11, 1799. It appears that Peter owned 122 acres on the drains of Tearcoat Run, adjoining Joseph Saville, Martin Shaffer, Michael Brady and Henry Haines. See Hardy County **Deed Book A**, pp. 325-326 and **Deed Book 4**, pp. 179-185, and **Hardy County Record Book 1786-1791**, all of which are housed in the courthouse in Moorefield, W.Va.

Kerns, Robert R., son of Aaron and Tamson (Shanholtz) Kerns, was born on Dec. 23, 1872, at Cross Junction, Frederick County, Va. and died on Sept. 29, 1961, at Dayton, Va. He married: (1) Annie G. Files, daughter of Jacob and Mary C. (Parkinson) Files, on Oct. 19, 1898, at Shockeysville, Va. She was born on Aug. 11, 1874 and died on Dec. 14, 1900, at Cherry Run, Morgan County, W.Va. (2) Sophia Ann Ritchie, daughter of Isaac and Elizabeth (Showalter) Ritchie, on Nov. 13, 1901. She was born on Nov. 12, 1869 at Rushville, Rockingham County, Va. and died near her home, on July 17, 1953. They were buried in the Dayton (Va.) Cemetery. They had two children, Alvan Ritchie Kerns and Lee Doil Kerns (1906-1986). Source: Records of my grandparents.

Kerns, Rebecca, was born on May 1, 1821 and died on June 15, 1871, "of paralysis," aged 50 years, 1 month, 15 days. Her husband was Henry Kerns, and her parents were Thomas J. and Mary Hammond. Source: Death record in Morgan County, W.Va. courthouse.

Kerns, Rebecca, wife of Isaiah Kerns, died on Nov. 6, 1891, at Magnolia, W.Va., aged 53 years. Source: Courthouse death record, Morgan County, W.Va.

Kerns, Ruth M, "mother" was born on Feb. 17, 1875 and died on March 20, 1946. Source: Tombstone inscription at the Timber Ridge Baptist Church, Frederick County, Va.

Kerns, Sanford Aljourn, buried his mother on Aug. 7, 1886, according to the **Undertaker Book** of John W. Mellon, Timber Ridge, Hampshire County.

Kerns, Thomas (sometimes spelled Kearns, Keern, Keeran) was born in 1742, and died on March 3, 1799 in Shenandoah County, Va. Records of this family are found in both Frederick and Shenandoah Counties, Va. Source: Mrs. Edith Keeran, San Diego, CA.

Kerns, Thurman, son of Staton and Lydia (Keplinger) Kerns, was born on April 11, 1909 and died on April 31, 1973. He married Elsie Kelchner. Source: Tombstone inscription at Fairview Lutheran cemetery, Gore, Va.

Kerran, Sarah, "widow," died in April 1870, aged 90 years. Source: 1870 Mortality Schedule for Shenandoah County, Va.

Kesler, John Sanbach was born in Germany circa 1765 and died in Morgan County, Va. circa 1832. He married Rachel Flora, daughter of Thomas and Prudence (McDonald) Flora. Source: Mrs. Allene Lee Holmes, 513 East 820 South, Pleasant Grove, Utah 84062.

Kidner, Elizabeth, was born in 1806 and died in Oct. 1859, "of pleurisy." Source: 1860 Mortality Schedule for Hampshire County, Va.

Kidwell: See page 54 for an account of the first three generations of this surname.

Kidwell, Francis M., son of James and Rebecca (Slane) Kidwell, was born on Aug. 9, 1846 and died on Aug. 31, 1893. His wife, Isabella McDonald, died on Aug. 1, 1910. Source: Tombstone inscriptions in Kidwell graveyard.

Kidwell, James, died on June 13, 1895, aged 75 years. The identity of this man has not been established. Possibly this record contains an error. Source: Hampshire County courthouse death records.

Kidwell, William, died in Hampshire County, Va., March 1850, aged 20 years. Source: 1850 Mortality Schedule for Hampshire County, Va.

King, Athena, daughter of William and Susan King, married William Braithwaite, Jr., on April 22, 1814 in Frederick County, Va. He was born on Dec. 25, 1787.

King, Isabella, daughter of William and Susan King, died in Morgan County, W.Va. on Dec. 5, 1874, aged 75 years, 7 months, 3 days. She married Jesse Crouse. Isabell was "born in Va.," according to the death record in the Morgan County, W.Va. courthouse.

King, Reasin, son of William and Susan King, was born on Dec. 6, 1793 and died on June 12, 1871, according to the courthouse death record. His tombstone inscription appears to read: Reason King died on June 1, 1871, aged 77 years, 6 months, 16 days. His wife Elizabeth (Brelsford?) died on April 6, 1866, aged 71 years, 9 months, 13 days. In the same graveyard I found: Mary, wife of William King, died on April 8, 1892, aged 58 years, 5 months, 17 days. William King was apparently buried next to Mary in a marked grave, but the stone not inscribed. This graveyard is located in the mountains along an old wagon road which crosses North River at the Benjamin McDonald ("Kennedy") place and proceeds to Critton Owl Hollow. Researchers should look at the same primary sources that I have, before deciding on the correct vital dates for Reazin King above.

Kline, Adam, was deceased before April 12, 1849. His Executor was Jacob Kline. In *Order Book I*, page 305, Circuit Court, Hampshire County, Va., a chancery court suit was heard between Jacob Kline and the other heirs, viz: (1) David Pugh, executor of John Kline's estate (2) Elizabeth Swisher (3) Mary M. Kline (4) Eve Kline (5) Christina Kline (6) Henry Kline (7) Elizabeth Kline married Solomon Peters (8) Rebecca Kline married Elias Wickham (9) Christina Kline married Alpheus Wickham (10) Catherine Kline married Wilson Smith (11) Philip Kline (12) John Spaid. Jacob and Isaac Devore, "infants" were mentioned.

Kline, Benjamin, was born on Dec. 24, 1848 and died on Oct. 29, 1909, aged 60 years, 10 months, 5 days. Source: Tombstone inscription at Union Chapel Church, Delray, W.Va.

Kline, Catherine, wife of Jacob Kline, was born in 1794; died in Feb. 1887 in Hampshire County. Source: Courthouse records.

Kline, Henry, son of Jacob and Catherine (Brill) Kline, was born in Hampshire County on Dec. 4, 1801 and died on Aug. 30, 1870 in Wilmington, Ohio. He married: (1) Catherine Eaton and (2) Sarah Chipman. Henry migrated from Hampshire County in 1820. One of his parents died in Jan. 1802. Source: History of Clinton County, Ohio, Albert J. Brown, 1915, page 650.

Kline, Philip, was born on Jan. 1, 1760 and died on June 21, 1842; buried in Hebron Lutheran cemetery, Intermont, W.Va.

Kump, Henry, was born in 1757 in Berks County, Penn. and died in Hampshire County in July 1849. He served in the Revolutionary War. Buried in private cemetery on farm near Yellow Springs, W.Va.

Kump, Frederick, son of Henry and Julia Kump II, was born in 1798 and died circa 1889, on his farm at North River Mills, Hampshire County. He married: (1) Elizabeth Furr and they had: Elizabeth I. Kump; Mary K. Kump married E. Harvey Pennington; Julia Ann Kump married Mr. Foreman (living in Weston, W.Va. in 1891); Enoch F. Pennington and James F. Pennington, heirs from first marriage. (2) His second wife was named Juliann Earles, who was born in 1810 and died on June 26, 1890, according to death record in the Hampshire County Courthouse. John W. Mellon, in his **Undertaker Book**, stated that she was buried on June 29, 1890. According to courthouse record, in Romney, Juliann Kump was born in 1810 in Shenandoah County, Va., to John and Mary Earles (Carles?). Two children were born to the second union: Richard P. Kump and Harriett F. Kump [who died in 1931]. The Frederick Kump family settled on Moreland lands in 1847, where he set up a blacksmith shop on the Northwestern Grade (Slanesville to Capon Bridge), across the road from the John B. Miller house at North River Mills. First owner of this land was Rees Pritchard. Sources: Deed Books in Hampshire County, W.Va. courthouse, but especially **Deed Book 68**, p. 182; plus the 1850 U.S. Census for Hampshire County, Va., county death records and numerous other miscellaneous sources, such as Chancery Court Box 37, Hampshire County Circuit Court, Romney, W.Va.

Kump, Henry, was born in 1756 in Pennsylvania, and died suddenly in Hampshire County, Va. in December 1849, aged 93 years. Source: 1850 Mortality Schedule for Hampshire County, Va.

Kurtz, Abraham, died in February 1860, aged 69 years. He had suffered with rheumatism for 30 years. Occupation was "wheelwright." Born in Virginia. His wife preceded him in death. Source: 1860 Mortality Schedule for Frederick County, Va.

Kurtz, Christopher, died suddenly in Hampshire County, in November 1849, aged 61 years. He was born in Pennsylvania. Source: 1850 Mortality Schedule for Hampshire County, Va.

Kuykendall, Nathaniel, son of Jacob and Sarah (Westfall) Kuykendall, was baptized in the German Reformed Church, Oct. 6, 1728 (in New York). He immigrated to South Branch Valley (present-day Hardy County, W.Va.), where he became one of the first Justices of the Peace in old Hampshire County, Va.

LaFollette, William, son of George and Jemima (Minthorn) LaFollette, was born in 1774 (probably in New Jersey) and died in Hampshire County, Va. in 1857. On Jan. 6, 1795, he married Jane McKee, daughter of Robert and Elizabeth McKee Sr. Jane was born in 1778. They were buried in the Racey graveyard in southeastern Hampshire County. See "Family History: The LaFollette Family," *The West Virginia Advocate*, Capon Bridge, W.Va. 26711, newspaper issue of Monday, Aug. 1, 1983.

Largent: See page 62 for an early historical and genealogical account of the Largent family in this area.

Largent, Benjamin Offord, son of Samuel and Mary (Offord) Largent, was born in Hampshire County circa 1828 and died on Oct. 19, 1868 (according to a letter from his son B.O. Largent, Jr.). He married Elizabeth Beery on Dec. 11, 1866, according to the *South Branch Intelligencer*, issue of Jan. 4, 1867. Her son reported a marriage date of Dec. 13th, 1866. Elizabeth was born at Edom, Rockingham County, Va. on April 10, 1841, according to her son. Benjamin O. had a daughter named Etta C. Largent, born at Forks of Capon, W.Va. on Oct. 1, 1867. She lived in Long Beach, CA and did not marry.

Largent, Benjamin O., II, son of Benjamin Offord and Elizabeth (Beery) Largent, Sr., was born at the Forks of Capon, on May 7, 1869 and died in Springfield, Ohio, in 1950. He married Mary Hamilton in Grafton, W.Va., on April 9, 1896. They moved to Springfield, Ohio in 1899. Three children were born to this marriage. B.O. Largent, II, was a building contractor whose address was 224 South Clairmont Avenue, Springfield, Ohio, according to stationery used to write a letter to Roger A. Stubbs, dated March 2, 1942.

Largent, James (born circa 1716), was probably a son of John Largent I. James was first mentioned in the settlement of his father's estate in old Orange County, Va. during the late 1730s. This James married Margaret Hiett, second wife and widow of John Hiett (ca. 1696-1764). Proof of the relationship is found in several county deeds [e.g., Frederick County, Va. **Deed Book 12**, pp. 646-647 and in Fairfax land records]. James Largent was first mentioned in Fairfax records in 1762, when he served as a chainman for Evan Hiett's 24-acre survey in Hampshire County. [See page 32, **Northern Neck Warrants and Surveys** (Abstracts of), compiled by Peggy Shomo Joyner, 1987.] This James Largent has often been confused with his nephew, James Largent (1753-1813) of John Largent II.

Largent, James, son of Joseph and Mary (Largent) Largent, was born on Sept. 26, 1824 at Forks of Capon and died on March 30, 1899, at Benton, Kansas. He was buried in the Powell cemetery at Forks of Capon, Bloomery, W.Va. (Note: The courthouse death record in Romney is in error.) He married Mary Loy, daughter of Adam and Sarah (Hiett) Loy, born near Sandy Ridge, Hampshire County, Va. on June 30, 1825 and died in Towanda, Kansas on April 18, 1895.

Largent, James T., son of Major John and Sarah (Critton) Largent, was born on July 18, 1800, at Forks of Capon, Hampshire County, Va. and died on Aug. 31, 1888, at Paw Paw, W.Va. He lived in Peoria, Illinois, but returned home during later life and was buried at Forks of Capon. He married Elizabeth Boxwell on Oct. 6, 1825, in Cumberland, MD. Elizabeth died on April 7, 1887, at Peoria, Illinois. Source: Provided by Mr. Roger A. Stubbs, Long Lake, Minnesota.

Largent, Jeremiah, son of John and Rachel Largent (not John Largent II), was living in Frederick County, Va., in 1819, aged 77 years. This implies a birthyear in vicinity of 1741-42. Jeremiah was a veteran of the Revolutionary War. Source: Records in DAR Library, Washington, D.C.

Largent, Jeremiah, died on Aug. 3, 1916, aged 48 years. Effrona, his wife, died on June 12, 1910, aged 26 years. Source: Tombstone inscription in Little Cacapon Primitive Baptist cemetery, Hampshire County.

Largent, J. W., born Oct. 8, 1858 and died on Dec. 12, 1903. Source: Tombstone inscription in "Shade graveyard" in Little Capon area, Hampshire County, W.Va.

Largent, John W., son of William and Elizabeth Morgan (Frazier) Largent, was born on March 4, 1828, at Forks of Capon, Hampshire County, and died of typhoid fever on Oct. 7, 1874 in

Yamhill County, Oregon. He married Annie W. Matheny, daughter of Michael and Mahala (Pennington) Matheny, on July 16, 1857, in Oregon. She was born Oct. 1, 1842 in Pope, Illinois and died March 20, 1917. After John's death, Annie remarried to Davis Wooten (1832-1908). Source: Steven J. Largent, 1401 Jackson Street, Boise, Idaho 83705.

Largent, Jefferson, son of Thomas "Mad River" Largent (of Nelson), was born in 1820 and died on Aug. 30, 1891 (probably in Frederick County, Va..). He married Sarah Noel.

Largent, John A., born April 9, 1846 and died on Sept. 12, 1921. Sarah, wife, was born on April 14, 1849. Source: Tombstone inscription, Bethel Methodist Graveyard, Okonoko, Hampshire County, W.Va.

Largent, John W.C., born on April 2, 1826 and died on July 17, 1886. He married a daughter of Josiah and Mary (Shade) Kaylor. After John's death in 1886, she remarried to William Shade (born in 1833), her cousin, in 1895. William Shade was a son of Adam and Elizabeth (Hinckle) Shade of Frederick County, Va. John W.C. Largent was buried next to Adam and Elizabeth (Largent) Kaylor, in the "Shade graveyard" in the Little Capon area. He was a grandson of "Big Neck John" Largent. John W.C. willed his estate to "the poor," having no descendants. However, the Commisioner could not define "poor," and could not determine who should receive what part of the estate. Consequently, a thorough search was conducted to identify and locate all "heirs" determined by the Hampshire County Court of "Big Neck" John Largent. This discovery produced a major breakthrough on this branch of the family. Sources: Tombstone inscription on granite stone, and records in the Circuit Court of Hampshire County, W.Va.

Largent, Joseph, son of Lewis and Kesiah (Parrish) Largent, died on June 18, 1872, age 79. His wife was named Mary. Source: His son, John Largent, reported the death to the Hampshire County court, where the record is kept in Romney, W.Va. Also, his obituary was published in the *South Branch Intelligencer*. It stated that Joseph was a veteran of the War of 1812 (he was called Captain); that he was born on May 2, 1794 and died on June 18, 1872, in Hampshire County, W.Va. His wife was his cousin Mary Largent, daughter of Major John and Sarah (Critton)

Largent. Mary was born in 1798 and died on July 8, 1846. They had eleven children, according to their Family Bible. Source: Tombstone inscriptions in the Powell graveyard at Forks of Capon, W.Va. and Family Bible record.

Largent, Lewis, son of Thomas and Eleanor (Shivers) Largent, was born on Sept. 17, 1784 in Hampshire County, Va. He married Hannah Eleanor Hull, daughter of Benjamin and Elsa Hull, on Feb. 14, 1804. Source: Bible record, Frederick County, Va. marriage records, and Will of Benjamin Hull, Frederick County, Va., *Superior Court Will Book III*, page 62, dated May 9, 1818.

Largent, Louisa, daughter of Cornelius and Harriett (Kerns) Schuler, died on Aug. 8, 1921, aged 78 years, 7 months, 17 days. She was born in Frederick County, Va. and died in Hampshire County. Mary Jane Schuler reported the death. Source: Courthouse death record.

Largent, Lucy A., daughter of Deskin and Ann (Carmichael) Wills, was born on Oct. 22, 1847 and died on Oct. 14, 1920. She married Samuel H. Largent, daughter of Thomas and Sallie (Loy) Largent. Source: Tombstone inscription in Wills graveyard, near North River, Hampshire County, W.Va.

Largent, Malinda "Millie," was born July 5, 1814 and died on July 12, 1850, in Morgan County, Virginia. She married Absalom Kesler, born on Oct. 11, 1813 and died on Sept. 22, 1899. One source stated that she was a daughter of John and Sarah (Critton) Largent, but research is inconclusive at this time. Source: Tombstone inscriptions at Kesler's Curve, Morgan County, West Virginia, and Mrs. Allene L. Holmes.

Largent, Mary, daughter of William and Mary Alderton, was born in Hampshire County in 1797 and died on Dec. 6, 1875. Her husband was named Thomas Largent, according to her death record in the Hampshire County Courthouse in Romney, W.Va.

Largent, Samuel, son of Thomas and Eleanor (Shivers) Largent, was born on Nov. 4, 1786 and died in July 1865. His wife was Mary Offord, daughter of John and Ann Offord. She was born on July 31, 1790 and died Oct. 19, 1879, according to Bible record. [Note: Courthouse death record and tombstone inscriptions contain errors.] Sources: Bible record; courthouse death record in Romney; and tombstone inscriptions in Powell cemetery at Forks of Capon, where they were buried in Hampshire County, West Virginia.

Largent, Samuel, son of "Big Neck John" and Mary Largent, was born in Hampshire County circa 1798 and died on Nov. 17, 1879. His son Lemuel H. Largent reported the death to the Hampshire County Court. Samuel married: (1) Kezziah _____ and (2) Mahala Jane Pownell (a sister of Robert S. Pownell). Four children were born to Samuel, by the first union and five by second marriage. Source: Letters written by Samuel's children; courthouse death record; chancery court suit "John W.C. Largent" (Box 237) in Hampshire County Circuit Court, Romney, W.Va.

Largent, Sarah, daughter of Joseph and Mary (Largent, Mary) Largent, was born on July 11, 1832 and died on April 16, 1911, unmarried. Source: Tombstone inscription at Powell's cemetery, Forks of Capon, W.Va.

Largent, Silas F., son of Samuel and Mary (Offord) Largent, was born on Sept. 1, 1829 and died on June 20, 1901. His wife was Sarah Elizabeth Powell, daughter of Robert and Mary (Moreland) Powell. She was born on April 16, 1840, in Hampshire County, Va. and died on June 25, 1864. They were buried in the Powell graveyard at the Forks of Capon. Source: Tombstone inscriptions, Powell Bible record, et. al.

Largent, Susan A., daughter of John Largent, was born on June 11, 1791 at Little Capon and died on July 8, 1854 at Spring Gap. She was the biological, unmarried, mother of John C. Largent. Source: Hampshire County death record in the Virginia State Archives.

Largent, Thomas, son of John Largent II, was born on May 5, 1760 and died in 1830, in Hampshire County, Va. He married Eleanor Shivers. She was born on March 10, 1760. Their children: (1) Lewis Largent was born Sept. 17, 1784. (2) Samuel Largent was born Nov. 4, 1786. (3) Randall Largent was born Feb. 8, 1793. (4) Jane Largent was born July 2, 1795. (5) Thomas Largent Jr. was born Feb. 18, 1798. (6) Susannah Largent was born Aug. 25, 1800. (7) Fanny Largent was born July 22, 1803. (8) Davy Largent was born Nov. 6, 1807. (9) Elander Largent was born April 22, 1811, and (10) Deborah Largent was born Nov. 10, 1817. Source: Bible record in possession of Benjamin Offord Largent, Springfield, Ohio (in 1943, per Roger Stubbs of Long Lake, Minnesota).

Largent, Thomas, son of Nelson Largent, was born circa 1798 in Fleming County, KY. and died in Frederick County, Va. in 1850. His wife was Mary Alderton, daughter of William Alderton. Source: Courthouse and miscellaneous records.

Largent, Thomas, Jr., son of Thomas and Eleanor (Shivers) Largent, was born in Hampshire County, Va. on Sept. 7, 1798 and died on March 21, 1859. His wife was Margaret Easter, daughter of John and Margaret (Thomas) Easter. She was born on March 2, 1796 and died on Aug. 31, 1870. Source: Bible record.

Largent, Thomas F., son of Samuel and Mary (Offord) Largent, was born Jan. 27, 1813 and died on Nov. 20, 1874. He married Sarah Loy, daughter of Adam and Sarah (Hiett) Loy. She was born in 1819 and died in 1892. Source: Thomas' death was reported to the Clerk of Court, Hampshire County, W.Va. Death dates were taken from tombstone in Powell's graveyard, Forks of Capon, where both were buried.

Largent, William, died in Hampshire County, W.Va., on March 25, 1889, aged 70 years, according to son George Largent, who reported the death to the County Clerk. Although not proven, William was probably a son of John and Margaret (Slane) Largent. William's wife, Catherine, died on Feb. 24, 1899, aged 75 years. They lived in the Cold Stream section of Hampshire County. Source: Courthouse death records, Romney, W.Va.

Largent, William, son of Maj. John and Sarah (Critton) Largent, was born in Hampshire County, Va. on Sept. 16, 1798 and died on Jan. 24, 1862, in Peoria County, Illinois. His wife was Elizabeth Frazier, born in Virginia, Jan. 1, 1803 and died Aug. 22, 1879. They inherited one of the Hampshire County farms, of his grandfather James and Margaret Largent, via the Will of Maj. John Largent, in 1816 (See **Deed Book 31**, page 266, Hampshire County, W.Va.). The land was located near the Forks of Capon, Hampshire County. William sold it to Robert M. and Sarah (Moreland) Powell, on Oct. 2, 1835. At that time, William Largent reserved one-eighth acre of land for a graveyard. There were several burials already in the plot, including two 18th century members of the Nelson family. Known as Powell's graveyard, it is one of the historic cemeteries in the area, now owned by Jack Powell of Cumberland, Maryland.

L(arimore), J., "Deces'd Ju^y 31, 1817," eroded tombstone. Source: Inscriptions on tombstone in graveyard at Three Churches, Hampshire County, W.Va.

Larimore, Samuel, died in Licking County, Ohio, at the home of Richard Blue, on Jan. 13, 1873, aged 84 years. He was born in Hampshire County in Dec. 1788, and went to Ohio in 1848. Samuel was the 6th of 11 children, and was the last survivor. He served in the War of 1812. Source: Jan. 21, 1873 issue of the *South Branch Intelligencer*, Romney, W.Va.

Larrick, Elizabeth, died in April 1860, aged 81 years, of "dropsy." The duration of her illness was 123 days, according to the attending physician. She was born in Virginia. Source: 1860 Mortality Schedule for Frederick County, Va.

Larrick, Elizabeth, "widow," died in March 1870, aged 95 years, of "old age." Born in Virginia. Source: 1870 Mortality Schedule for Frederick County, Va.

Larrick, Henry, son of Casper and Elizabeth (Sundown) Larrick, was born in Va. in 1777; died in Va. in 1864. He married Ann Caudy. Source: W. Donald Larrick, 90 El Camino Drive, Yuma, AZ 85365.

Larrick, Frederick, son of Casper and Elizabeth (Sundown) Larrick, was born in 1783 and died in 1861. He married Elizabeth Secrist (1780-1870), daughter of Henry and Anna Maria Secrist. They lived near Highview, Frederick County, Va. Their children were: (1) Elizabeth Larrick, born circa 1807, married Jesse J. Pugh, son of Azariah Pugh, on June 28, 1835. (2) Henry Larrick was born in 1808 and died before 1867. (3) Caspar Larrick was born Feb. 13, 1809 and died Dec. 24, 1893, in Guernsey County, Ohio. His wife was Margaret Hellyer, born on Feb. 5, 1815 and died Sept. 14, 1876. (4) John Larrick was born Nov. 4, 1816 and died in 1892. He married Margaret Murphy, born circa 1821. (5) Robert Larrick was born in 1819 and died April 9, 1890. (6) Jacob Larrick was born April 1, 1820 and died Jan. 1, 1894. Jacob married Harriet Good, daughter of Felix and Rachel (Orndorff) Good Jr., on Nov. 18, 1841. (7) Anna Larrick was born in 1829 and died Nov. 27, 1898, unmarried. (8) Rebecca Larrick was born in 1831 and died Nov. 27, 1898, in a house fire. Sources: W. Donald

Larrick (See entry above);   Mr. Layne Secrist, 4020 Hallman Street, Fairfax, Va. 22030 (compiler for Secrist family history).

Lauch, Comfort W., was born on June 17, 1795 and died on July 18, 1862.   Source: Tombstone inscriptions at the Primitive Baptist Church Cemetery, Frederick County, Virginia.

Lawyer, Jacob, died in May 1850, aged 50 years. Farmer. Ill for six days with "arasypalis." Survived by spouse. Source: 1850 Mortality Schedule for Frederick County, Va.

Leith, Edmund S., son of James and Sarah (Rust) Leith, was born on June 12, 1811 and died on Jan. 27, 1877. He married Emeline Kyles. He was buried in the Powell-Leith graveyard at Bloomery, W.Va., where the tombstone inscriptions were copied by the compiler of this book.

Leith, Elizabeth, daughter of William and Mary (Powell) Leith, was born in 1829 and died on Feb. 4, 1880. Her husband was William S. Hook.   Possibly she was his second wife. Source: Death record in the Hampshire County courthouse.

Leith, James, Jr.,son of James and Mary (Goram) Leith, Sr., was born in Loudoun County, Va. on Nov. 17, 1760 and died in Bloomery, Hampshire County, Va., on June 29, 1848. He married Sarah Rust. Leith's Mountain in Hampshire County was named after him. Source: Tombstone inscription in Powell-Leith cemetery on Leith Mountain.

Leith, James F., son of James and Sarah (Rust) Leith, Jr., was born on April 1, 1819 and died on April 17, 1889, unmarried. He lived on the old homeplace and was buried in the family graveyard. Source: Tombstone inscription on Leith Mountain, Bloomery District, Hampshire, W.Va.

Leith, Mary (nee Goram), was born in 1738 and died on May 31, 18?9 (appears to be 1819). Her husband was James Leith Sr., of Loudoun County, Va., who died in 1800. Source: Tombstone inscription in Powell cemetery on Leith Mountain, Hampshire County, W.Va. Complete dates were chiseled on a native stone, but part of the dates have eroded.

Leith, Robert, was born on Dec. 30, 1853 and died on Dec. 3, 1863. He was buried next to Edmund S. Leith in the Powell-Leith cemetery at Bloomery, W.Va.

Leith, Sarah, died in Hampshire County, Va. in Feb. 1850, of consumption (TB), aged 18 years. Source: 1850 Mortality schedule of U. S. Census.

Leith, William P., son James and Sarah (Rust) Leith, Jr., was born on Aug. 22, 1795 and died on Dec. 9, 1833. Buried next to him in the Powell-Leith graveyard was his wife Mary Powell, daughter of Robert M. Powell. She was born on Nov. 13, 1790 and died on June 26, 1870. Source: Tombstone inscription in Powell/Leith graveyard at Bloomery, W.Va.

Leith, William Thomas, son of Joseph C. and Mary (McKee) Leith, was born in Hampshire County on Dec. 30, 1835 and died in Cass County, Missouri on Dec. 23, 1918. He married Rozella Pownell, daughter of John and Sarah Pownell. Source: Mrs. Margaret Norton (deceased), Brownwood, Texas.

Leps, Capt. (possibly George), died on Nov. 15, 1861 at Cold Stream, Hampshire County. His coffin was ordered by a Captain Sheets. Source: Coffin-book of William Meade Edwards.

Light, John W., was murdered on Nov. 5, 1844, by Robert W. Baker who knifed him in front of the residence of David Davis, in Frederick County, Va. Jacob Heironimus, a Justice of the Peace, asked constable John Giffin to summon a jury to make an inquisition. Members of the jury were: D.L. Brown (jury foreman), James Robinson, Hiram Murphy, David Davis, Casper Rogers, George W. Snider, Joshua Johnson, John F. Davis, William Hart, John B. Smith, Meredith Darlington, and Samuel Hart. Source: Frederick County, Va., "Inquisitions of Dead Bodies," Virginia State Archives.

Little/Littler, John, was born in Chester County, Penn. on March 28, 1708 and died on Dec. 6, 1748 in Frederick County, Va. He was one of the signers of a petition to set off Frederick County from Orange County, Va. His wife was Mary Ross, daughter of Alexander and Catherine (Chambers) Ross. She was born on Dec. 13, 1706 in Chester County, PA, and died in 1771 in Frederick County, Va.

Lockhart, John O., was born in Frederick County, Va. on Feb. 13, 1822 and died on Jan. 4, 1883. His wife, Mary F., was born on July 27, 1825 and died on April 13, 1903. Source: Tombstone inscriptions in Dover Cemetery, Lafayette County, Missouri.

Lockhart, Robert, was born in 1744 and died on May 13, 1817 at Gore, Virginia. Source: Tombstone inscriptions in the Lockhart family graveyard at Gore, Va.

Lochinger, John, was born in 1799 and died in 1881. His wife, Elizabeth Hott, died in 1873. Source: Tombstone inscriptions in Ruckman graveyard, located west of Grassy Lick Road, Hampshire County, W.Va.

Long, Conrad, was born on June 1, 1801 and died on Feb. 1, 1888. His wife Elizabeth Long was born on Feb. 7, 1811 and died on May 17, 1348. Source: Tombstone inscriptions at Three Churches, Hampshire County, W.Va.

Loy, Asa H., was born Oct. 21, 1814 and died March 29, 1886. His wife, Phoebe Loy, was born Aug. 16, 1816 and died Jan 17, 1899. Source: Tombstone inscriptions in Chestnut Grove cemetery, Frederick County, Va.

Loy, Benjamin, son of Adam and Sarah (Hiett) Loy, died on Feb. 22, 1898, aged 76 years, 3 months, 28 days. His wife, Martha Ann Iden, daughter of Jonathan and Catherine (Jolly) Iden, died on April 21, 1895, aged 73 years, 1 month, 2 days. In the same private graveyard: A.C. Loy, born Dec. 31, 1845 and died Dec. 24, 1911; Benjamin F. Loy, born Aug. 23, 1855 and died Aug. 22, 1863; Samuel W. Loy, died on Aug. 27, 1862; Jonathan H. Loy, born on Aug. 19, 1849; Bakie Loy, born on Feb. 13, 1863 and died on March 19, 1863; Emma Loy, born on Feb. 14, 1863 and died on March 18, 1863, twin; William L. Loy, son of Benjamin Loy, born Dec. 22, 1867 and died Dec. 27, 1867. Four graves are outside the family graveyard, probably slaves were buried there. Source: The Benjamin Loy private graveyard, along North River Road (north of U.S. Route 50), on what is known as "The River Bend Farm."

Loy, Julius, son of Peter Loy, died on Jan. 31, 1860, at Cold Stream, Hampshire County. Apparently he was a youngster because the coffin measured only three feet, eleven inches in length. Source: Coffin-book of William Meade Edwards.

Loy, Nancy, daughter of Adam and Sarah (Hiett) Loy, was born on June 10, 1810 at Sandy Ridge, Hampshire County, and died on Dec. 18, 1881 in Peoria County, IL. She married George Wolford. Source: Russel W. Wolford, Rt.2, Box 73-B, Brimfield, IL. 61517.

Loy, Peter, son of Adam and Sarah (Hiett) Loy, was born on Feb. 21, 1812 and died on March 18, 1867. His wife was Anna Foltz, daughter of Martin L. and Mary M. (Emswiller) Foltz. Anna was born on Nov. 20, 1820 and died on April 7, 1905. They were buried in the old Martin Fultz graveyard, on Voit Road, near Slanesville, W.Va. Several small children were buried nearby. One inscription says: John Hiett Loy, born June 13, 1850 and died on Sept. 2, 1853. Next to that is the oldest appearing gravestone (but uninscribed) in the graveyard. Cattle have knocked down most of the old graves, and nobody has organized to restore this very important historical graveyard. Members of the Haines, Fultz, and Loy families are buried here.

Ludwick, Joseph, died on Aug. 8, 1877, 76 years, 3 months, 12 days. His wife Ann died on Aug. 5, 1869, aged 61 years, 10 months, 22 days. Source: Tombstone inscription along the highway south of Junction, W.Va.

Ludwig, Leonard (1750-1804), served as a Private in Capt. Bayer's Maryland Company of the Revolutionary War. His wife, Catherine Rotruck (1751-1834) is buried beside him, in the Sloan Family Graveyard, On U.S. Route 50, west of Romney, West Virginia. Across the road is the "Old Stone House" built by Richard Sloan in 1790. In the same graveyard are: Andrew Ludwick, died on Aug. 20, 1872, aged 77 years, 6 months; James C. Ludwick (1840-1906) and his wife Sarah J., (1842-1915); Elijah H. Ludwick, born on Oct. 16, 1844 and died on Feb. 20, 1929; Annie Ludwick, July 6, 1836 to Feb. 13, 1915 "Romans 5:1"; and Sallie Ludwick, Jan. 24, 1887 to May 30, 1929. I think she "belonged to" James C. and Sarah J. Ludwick.

Luttrell, Richard, son of Robert and Barbara (Buzzard) Luttrell, was born on Aug. 14, 1797, on Timber Ridge, Frederick County, Virginia and died in Clinton County, Ohio on March 22, 1848. He married Mary "Polly" Groves, who was born on March 6, 1804 and died on Nov. 18, 1841. They migrated to Clinton County, Ohio in 1830, from Frederick County, Virginia. A son, Harrison Luttrell, was born on Feb. 3, 1835 in Clinton County, Ohio. He married Margaret Smith on Oct. 26, 1865, according to *History of Lafayette County (Missouri),* St Louis, Missouri: Missouri Historical Company, 1881, page 515.

Luttrell, William, son of James and Nancy Luttrell, was born in Frederick County, Va. and died in Morgan County, W.Va. on Aug. 9, 1879, aged 67 years. His wife was named "Christian" according to the death register in the Morgan County courthouse in Berkeley Springs, W.Va.

Lyle, the Rev. John, son of Daniel Lyle, was born in Rockbridge, Va. circa 1756. He came to Hampshire County as a Presbyterian pastor at Frankfort and Springfield. He died on July 5, 1807 and was buried at the back of the old church at Springfield. John married Sarah Glass, daughter of John and Elizabeth (Wilson) Glass. She was born in 1770 and died in 1850 in Madison, Indiana. Source: Presbyterian Church records in Richmond, Va., and a book, *Lyle Family*, Lecouver Press Co.: New York City, by Oscar Lyle, Brooklyn, N.Y. 1912.

Lyon, Archibald, son of Elijah and Margaret (Linthicum) Lyon, was born in Hampshire County, Va. on Jan. 1, 1810 and died in Kinderhook Township, Pike County, Illinois, on June 2, 1870. His burial was in the Aker's Chapel cemetery. He married Mary A. McKee, daughter of Joseph and Elizabeth (Reid) McKee, on May 28, 1835. Source: Kenneth W. Lyon, through Dale F. Bryant (see below).

Lyon, Elijah, son of Elisha Lyon, was born in 1776 and died in Hampshire County, Va. in May 1848. His wife Margaret Linthicum, daughter of Archibald and Mary Linthicum, was born in 1786 and died in Pike County, Illinois. She was buried in the Aker's Chapel Cemetery, in Kinderhook Township. Source: Kenneth W. Lyon of Ft. Scott, Kansas, via Dale F. Bryant, Box 987, Project City, CA 96079.

Lyon, Elisha, died in Hampshire County, Va. prior to 1832. In a chancery court suit, found in *Order Book I*, page 14, these persons were named: John W. Lyon; William Lyon; Naomi Lyon; Ann Lyon married George Baker; Daniel Lyon; Elijah Lyon married Margaret Linthicum; Massie Lyon; and David Lyon. James Gibson was the executor for the estate of Elisha Lyon. See also *Order Book II*, page 35, dated Sept. 1840, Circuit Court, (Romney) Hampshire County, Virginia.

Lyon, John, son of Elijah and Margaret (Linthicum) Lyon, was born in Hampshire County, Va. on Dec. 7, 1805 and died on Jan. 2, 1880, in Pike County, Illinois. He was twice-married: (1) Mary

Smith, on March 21, 1827, in Hampshire County, and (2) Elizabeth Harriett Poston, born in "Virginia." She was the widow of Branscom Poston of Hampshire County, and had two children by her first husband: James Higgins Poston and William Branscom Poston. Source: Kenneth W. Lyon, via Dale F. Bryant of Project City, CA.

Lyons, Samuel was born in 1813 and died at Paw, Paw, W.Va. in Dec. 1898. His death was reported to the Morgan County, courthouse by John H. Lyons.

McAtee, Samuel, died in January 1870, aged 52 years, 'of asthma." He was born in Maryland, and pursued the occupation of farming. Source: 1870 Mortality Schedule for Morgan County, W.Va.

McBride, Capt. Alexander, was born on Feb. 15, 1759 in Ireland and died on May 15, 1835 in Richland County, Ohio. His Hampshire County estate was settled on March 16, 1832. His wife, Jean Reiney, was born on May 1, 1761 and died on Feb. 3, 1815 in Hampshire County, Va. They were married on Jan. 1, 1783 in Ireland. Source: Collected by and submitted to me by Mrs. Delores Mustaine, Phoenix, AZ 85024.

McBride, the Rev. Isaac, moved from Virginia (now West Virginia) to Georgia on Aug. 17, 1824. He moved to a warmer climate, hoping to cure a chronic case of TB, but he died shortly thereafter. Source: Journal of the Rev. Christy Sine, of Hampshire County, Va.

McBride, John, immigrant to Hampshire County, Va., was born in Ireland. He married Elizabeth Stodoman on Nov. 18, 1777. They had eleven children as follows: (1) Sarah McBride was born Aug. 3, 1778. (2) Margaret McBride was born Nov. 2, 1779 and died on Oct. 9, 1783. (3) Alexander McBride was born Oct. 10, 1781. (4) Mary McBride was born Sept. 23, 1783. (5) Thomas McBride was born on Nov. 2, 1785. (6) Elizabeth McBride was born Oct. 27, 1789. (7) John McBride was born Nov. 26, 1790. He married Elizabeth Arnold. (8) Welton McBride was born on Jan. 17, 1793. (9) Peter McBride was born on Dec. 23, 1794 and died May 7, 1884. He was buried in the Salem Methodist Church cemetery at Slanesville, W.Va. (10) Robert McBride was born on June 12, 1798. (11) Anna McBride was born May 12, 1799. She married John Smith, who was born in December 1796. [They had

12 children, including Margaret Smith, born Feb. 23, 1828 and died Feb. 18, 1907. Margaret married Isaac Haines, who died March 20, 1900.] Source: Bible records.

McBride, Joseph, was born on Feb. 14, 1814. He married Elizabeth Ann Henderson, daughter of Larkin Day and Elizabeth (Kees) Henderson, on Nov. 16, 1837. Source: Bible record submitted by Mrs. Irma Curtis, Rt. 3, Weston, W.Va. 26452.

McBride, Mary, was born in 1812 at Cold Stream and died on July 16, 1899 at Slanesville. Her husband was John Moreland.

McBride, Robert, was born in 1762, and died in Jan. 1850 in Hampshire County. It is believed that he married Nancy, widow of Thomas McBride, in Jan. 1825. Source: Mortality Record from 1850 U.S. Census.

McBride, Stephen, was born on Feb. 10, 1759 and died on Aug. 8, 1837 in Columbiana County, Ohio. He lived in Frederick County, Va., where he met and married Hannah Smith, daughter of Capt. Jeremiah Smith, in 1781. She was born in Frederick County, Va. on March 31, 1761 and died on Dec. 24, 1823. The names of Stephen's parents have not been proven. Source: Mrs. Delores Mustaine, 2550 E. Beardsley Road, # 28, Phoenix, AZ, 85024.

McBride, Thomas, was born in 1771 in Callabackey, Ireland and died on April 27, 1824 in Richland County, Ohio. He married Mary McVicker, daughter of Duncan and Jane (McConnell) McVicker, on March 9, 1797. They were residents of Hampshire County after the Revolutionary War.

McBride, William, died on March 28, 1899, aged 76 years, in Hampshire County, W.Va. He was unmarried. Courthouse death record stated that he died of congestion after going into ice water. Buried in Mt. Zion Church cemetery.

McCauley, Addison, died "in bed" at Tearcoat Creek, Hampshire County, W.Va. on March 20, 1867, aged 82 years. He was born in Maryland. Occupation: carpenter. Source: Death record in Hampshire County courthouse, Romney, W.Va.

McCauley, George Sr., was deceased prior to Sept. 15, 1836, in Hampshire County. A chancery suit in the Circuit Court lists these heirs: George McCauley, Jr.; Addison McCauley; Alfred McCauley married Elizabeth Edwards, daughter of Thomas and

Martha (Keener) Edwards of Cold Stream; Jehosephat McCauley; John McCauley; Elizabeth McCauley married Robert Carlyle, son of Charles Carlyle; Arianna McCauley married Milton Cowgill, son of Ewing and Susannah (Buzzard) Cowgill. Alfred Simpson was listed as an heir, but no relation was stated. George's wife, named Parthenia, was remarried to John Baker. Source: *Order Book I*, page 186, Circuit Court of Hampshire County, Va.

McCauley, George, Jr., son of George and Parthenia McCauley, died on Feb. 4, 1881, aged 87 years, 3 months. He was a farmer, born in Maryland; his wife was Julia Ann Pepper, daughter of John and Catherine (Emmart) Pepper Sr. Source: Hampshire County, W.Va.Courthouse death record.

McCauley, George, died in Hampshire County on Jan. 12, 1875, aged 61 years. Source: *South Branch Intelligencer*.

McClune, William and his wife Maria, were found dead on March 23, 1888 in Frederick County, Va. Their deaths were ruled as murder-suicide. Jacob Hinckle, Justice of the Peace, appointed a jury to make an inquisition of their deaths. Members of the jury were: Jesse Boyd, Joshua Place, Jacob Catlett, Benjamin F. Omps, Nun Place, and Thomas Hinckle, M.D. Source: Frederick County, Va., "Inquisitions of Dead Bodies," Virginia State Archives, Richmond, Va.

McCool, A. Gertrude, wife of P.C. McCool, was born on Oct. 26, 1869 and died on Dec. 28, 1900. Nearby, are buried Hattie McCool, daughter of P.C. and G.A. McCool, died on Sept. 23, 1890, aged 1 year and 10 months; and James McCool, son, died on Feb. 19, 1896, aged 1 year, 8 months, 15 days. Source: Tombstone inscriptions in the Deskin Wills graveyard on North River, below Ice Mountain, in Hampshire County, W.Va.

McCool, Lewis, was born on Aug. 16, 1780 and died on Nov. 14, 1828. A marriage record in Frederick County, Va. shows that a Lewis McCool married Nancy Weaver on Sept. 22, 1808. Source: Tombstone inscription in Gaddis cemetery in Union Township, Clinton County, Ohio.

McCormack, James, was born in Virginia in 1776 and died of "asthma" in June 1849/1850, in Hampshire County. Source: Mortality records of 1850 Census.

McCullough, John, was born in 1752 in Hampshire County (in section which later became Hardy County), Virginia and died on April 6, 1821 in Wheeling County. In 1776, he married Mary Bukey. Source: Grandfather Papers, DAR Library, Washington, D.C.

McDonald, Abraham Kackley, son of Gabriel and Catherine (Kackley) McDonald I, was born May 2, 1822 in Frederick County, Va. He first married Rebecca V. Elliott, daughter of William and Nancy (Wright) Elliott. Rebecca was born circa 1829, and died Nov. 1, 1858. She was buried in an Elliott family graveyard at Hayfield, Va. After her death, Abraham remarried to Isabella Catherine Triplett, daughter of Edwin S. and Elizabeth (Poole) Triplett. Isabella was born on July 12, 1842 and died Oct. 18, 1932. Sources: Family Bible of Benjamin McDonald I; Records of Ralph L. Triplett Esq.; and information provided by Ms. Lois C Marbert, 10110 Farmington Drive, Fairfax, Va. 22030-2049.

McDonald, Benjamin, II, son of Benjamin and Margaret McDonald, was born on Jan. 12, 1774 and died in 1856, at his North River farm, several miles above the Forks of Capon, Hampshire County, Va. His wife, Margaret Hiett, was a daughter of Evan and Sarah (Smith) Hiett. According to a tombstone inscription in the Benjamin McDonald graveyard, on the homeplace, Margaret was born on Jan. 9, 1778 and died on Sept. 9, 1846. They were buried side-by-side, but his fieldstone was not inscribed. Source: Will of Benjamin McDonald was filed and probated in 1856, in Hampshire County Court; Benjamin McDonald I family Bible and; 1850 U.S. Census: and tombstone inscriptions in McDonald Graveyard, and Bible record of Benjamin McDonald I.

McDonald, Benjamin, III, was born on Dec. 30, 1807 and died May 20, 1874, of "heart disease." His wife was Amy Park (according to court record) and his parents were Benjamin and Margaret (Hiett) McDonald. The March 28 issue of the *South Branch Intelligencer* reported that Amy died on Jan. 14, 1873, aged 60 years. The same newspaper later reported the death of Benjamin McDonald, giving a July 20 death date rather than May 20th. Source: Courthouse death record and local newspapers.

McDonald, David, was born in 1809 at Bloomery, Va..(?) and died on May 14, 1887 at Darkesville, Berkeley County, W.Va. He married Hannah Kerns, daughter of John and Elizabeth (Light) Kerns. She was born in 1814 in Hampshire County and died on June 28, 1889 at Darkesville. (Note: In this record was a notation, "Andrew McDonald was born Feb. 22, 1791"). Source: Mrs. Madeline Miller, Martinsburg, W.Va.

McDonald, Evan, son of Benjamin and Margaret (Hiett) McDonald, was born in Hampshire County, Va. in 1805. He died on Jan. 6, 1882, in Hampshire County. His obit appeared in the Feb. 3, 1883 issue of *The South Branch Intelligencer*, Romney, West Virginia. His first wife was named Mary White, daughter of Francis White. Proof of this marriage may be found in *Order Book II*, page 133, Circuit Court, Hampshire County, W. Va. His second marriage was to Margaret Ann Stump, daughter of Benjamin Stump, circa 1840. This is proven by a letter from Benjamin McDonald, II, to Samuel Farmer, dated Dec. 20, 1840. His third marriage was to Arah Ann Millslagle, daughter of Jacob and Elizabeth (Cooper) Millslagle.

McDonald, Gabriel I, son of Benjamin and Mercy (Wilkinson) McDonald I, was born in Frederick County, Va. on Oct. 14, 1789, and died in Feb. 1874. He married Catherine Kackley, daughter of Abraham and Christina (Whissen) Kackley. Catherine was born in 1794 and died in Frederick County, Va. on May 4, 1872. Their children were: (1) Elizabeth A. McDonald was born on Nov. 13, 1816 and died Jan. 26, 1894, at Paw Paw, W.Va. She married Isaac Van Horn, who was born Jan. 1, 1815, and died Sept. 23, 1887. They had ten children. (2) John W. McDonald was born on June 18, 1818. (3) Benjamin P. McDonald was born Feb. 13, 1820. His first wife was Ruth Whitacre, daughter of Wilson and Rachel (Kerns) Whitacre. After her death he remarried to Nancy A. Gill, daughter of Charles and Dolly (Walker) Gill. Nancy died on May 20, 1880. (4) Abraham Kackley McDonald was born May 2, 1822. See separate entry above. (5) Gabriel Russell McDonald II, was born Jan. 31, 1827 and died Jan. 2, 1901, at Lexington, Dawson County, Nebraska. He first married Elizabeth Whitacre, daughter of Wilson and Rachel (Kerns) Whitacre (1838-1862) and, after her death, remarried to Catherine V. (Gill) Shane, widow of Benjamin F. Shane. Source: Bible record of Gabriel McDonald I provided by Ms. Illyce MacDonald.

McDonald, George, of the Sandy Ridge/North River section of Hampshire County, died on Dec. 22, 1889, of "dropsy," aged 80 years, 5 months, 9 days. His wife was Mary Miller, who died on Jan. 3, 1884, aged 75 years, of "rheumatism." The death was reported to the courthouse in Romney by her son John McDonald. Another courthouse record shows that after George McDonald died, an Executor's bond, value $200.00 was taken on William Miller, for the estate of George McDonald, Circuit Court, Hampshire County, W.Va., dated Jan. 10, 1890.

McDonald, George W., (1843-1927) and wife, Mary S. _____ (1846-1892), were buried in the old Benjamin McDonald Graveyard, North River, below Ice Mountain, Hampshire County, W.Va.

McDonald, James, son of Benjamin and Margaret (Hiett) McDonald II, was born on July 22, 1800 and died on May 26, 1876. He married: (1) Margaret Stump, who died before 1850, and (2) Priscena (Spaid) Moreland, widow of David Moreland, who was killed by lightening. Priscena was born on Nov. 24, 1823 and died on Aug. 27, 1861. He lived in various places in Hampshire and Frederick Counties.

McDonald, Lemaryan, wife of James H. McDonald, died in Winchester, Va. on Jan. 2, 1866, aged 34 years, 10 months, and 12 days (according to the Winchester paper). She left seven small children.

McDonald, Margaret, daughter of Benjamin and Margaret McDonald, was born Jan. 14, 1772 and died in 1817, in Back Creek Valley. She was the second wife of George Smith, son of Capt. Jeremiah Smith.

McDonald, Mary, daughter of Benjamin and Margaret (Hiett) McDonald II, was born on Sept. 12, 1814 and died on Jan. 11, 1909. Her husband, Minor Furr, was born on June 19, 1814 and died on July 5, 1880, according to his obit in the July 23, 1880 issue of the *South Branch Intelligencer*. (Note: His tombstone inscription appears to say June 25, 1880). They were married in Sept. 1840, according to an 1840 letter from Benjamin McDonald to Samuel Farmer, in Lincoln County, Missouri. Source: Tombstone inscriptions in the Benjamin McDonald Graveyard, on North River, below Ice Mountain, Hampshire County, and newspaper obit and old letter.

McDonald, Sarah, daughter of Benjamin and Margaret (Hiett) McDonald, was first married to Thomas McClure [see "Family

Histories of Two Benjamin McDonalds of Old Frederick County, Virginia," *The West Virginia Advocate*, Sept. 14, 1987] However, when Benjamin's estate was being settled in Hampshire County, Va. in 1856, it mentioned daughter Sarah McClure who had three children, viz, Benjamin Lockhart, Aaron Lockhart, and Mary Ann Lockhart. Can anyone explain this? The same document mentioned that Benjamin's daughter Rebecca (McDonald) Foreman was deceased in 1850, and monies were allocated- $100 each- to Benjamin F. Foreman and David Foreman, presumably Rebecca's two sons. Maud Pugh stated that Rebecca married to a David Foreman. Primary source: Court Box 233, Circuit Court of Hampshire County, W.Va.

McDonald/McDaniel, Valentine, was born on Jan. 11, 1760 on the South Branch of the Potomac, Hampshire County, Va. and died in Brown County, Ohio on Jan. 13, 1845. He served in the Revolutionary War (Pennsylvania records). He married Sarah Jones, on Oct. 15, 1798 in Mason County, KY., according to her own testimony on March 4, 1853 in Brown County, Ohio. Source: Military pension record. Contact Mr. R. Neil McDonald, 522 Pine, Arthur, IL 61911, who is researching this McDonald lineage.

McDonald, Zebulon Benjamin, son of Benjamin and Amy (Park) McDonald, III, was born in Hampshire County, Va. in 1834 and died in 1919. He married Margaret Francis Farmer, daughter of Samuel and Annie (McDonald) Farmer, on Feb. 2, 1863. They were first cousins. Margaret was born on Jan. 5, 1840 and died on Sept. 13, 1912. They were buried in the Benjamin and Margaret (Hiett) McDonald Graveyard, on North River, Hampshire County, W.Va. Buried in same plot was: Calvin E. McDonald, 1867-1894, "A Good Son." Source: Tombstone inscriptions, and Box 238 in Hampshire County Circuit Court, chancery suit against guardian James McDonald, their uncle.

McDowell, Joseph, was born in Ireland in 1801, and died Feb. 12, 1890, in Mineral County, W.Va. His wife, Marion B. Walker, was born in 1808, in Ireland, and died in Mineral County, Va., in 1861. They arrived in New York on May 16, 1826, and settled, in 1845, in a log cabin along the headwaters of Wild Meadow Run, a tributary of Patterson's Creek, Mineral County, about five miles south of Burlington. Joseph earlier worked on construction of C&O Canal, and later worked for the B&O Railroad. Source: George T. McDowell Sr., P.O. Box 44 Grantsville, MD 21536.

McGraw, Lutitia, died in September 1859, aged 95 years, after an ilness of 400 days. Source: 1860 Mortality Schedule for Frederick County, Va.

McIntire, Charles, was born on Oct. 7, 1783 and died May 3, 1858. Catherine, his wife, was born on May 21, 1783 and died May 19, 1857, aged 73 years, 11 months, 23 days. Source: McIntire Graveyard inscriptions, Frederick County, Va. (on Morgan County, W.Va. line).

McIntire, Thomas, died Dec. 9, 1774 in Berkeley County, Va. Thomas McIntire Jr. died on Sept. 28, 1847, aged 80 years. Mary McIntire, wife of Thomas Jr., died Dec. 5, 1838, aged 55 years. Source: Tombstone inscriptions in Hedgesville Cemetery, Berkeley County, W.Va.

McIntire, William, was born Sept. 27, 1788 and died Jan. 15, 1863. Source: Tombstone inscriptions in McIntire Graveyard, located on the Morgan County, W.Va./Frederick County, Va. line.

McKee, Ann, daughter of Robert and Elizabeth McKee, Sr., was born in Frederick County, Va. in 1780 and died in Noble County, Ohio in 1858. She married Thomas Davis, son of Elijah and Ann Davis Sr., born in 1780, probably in Hampshire County, and died in 1853, in Noble County, Ohio. They were married in Frederick County, Va. on Nov. 1, 1801.

McKee, Bartholomew, son of Robert and Elizabeth McKee Sr., was born on Feb. 10, 1779 in Frederick County, Va. and died on June 3, 1864 in same county. He married Nancy Ann Reid, born on Sept. 12, 1786 and died on April 21, 1868. He served in the War of 1812. Their children: (1) Mercy McKee was born Jan. 22, 1803, and died in Sept. 1855. She married Abraham Cline. (2) James McKee was born Aug. 25, 1805, and died May 28, 1831, from falling timber while building a barn. (3) Eliza McKee was born Dec. 24, 1807. She married John Dunlap, son of William Dunlap. (4) Elenor McKee was born Oct. 6, 1810, and died Nov. 3, 1876. She married George Smith II on Feb 5, 1835. (5) Aaron McKee was born Oct. 10, 1812, and died Dec. 12, 1893. He had six children: Abraham, Isaac, Jacob, Bartholomew, Massa, and Sarah McKee. (6) Lavinia McKee was born Nov. 26, 1814, and died in February 4, 1874. She married George W. Marple. (7) Mary Ann McKee was born Feb. 9, 1817, and died April 1, 1882. She married William Parrish on April 14, 1873. (8) Miriam McKee was born Dec. 1, 1818, and died Dec. 20, 1843. (9) George Read McKee was born Jan. 22, 1821, and died May 26, 1859. (10) Rebecca McKee was born Dec. 19, 1824, and died Jan. 27, 1838. Source: Family Bible of Bartholomew McKee, in possession of Wilmer L. Kerns, 4715 North 38th Place, Arlington, Va. 22207.

McKee, Barthalomew, son of Robert and Jane (Cather) McKee, was born in Frederick County, Va. on April 10, 1799 and died in Nov. 1870. He married Elizabeth Ann Evans, daughter of John and Frances (Hardesty) Evans, on May 4, 1837, in Frederick County. She was born in Feb. 1806 and died in 1868. They immigrated to Princeville, Illinois. These two Barthalomew McKees have been confused by some researchers.

McKee, Elizabeth, died in November 1879, aged 67 years, "of dropsy." She was born in Virginia, and she was survived by her husband. Source: 1880 Mortality Schedule for Frederick County, Va.

McKee, Joel, son of Joseph and Elizabeth (Reed) McKee, was born in Frederick County, Va. on April 24, 1800 and died in 1835, of typhoid fever. He married Rebecca Kline, daughter of Philip and Elizabeth (Schweitzer) Kline, on Dec. 22, 1822. Rebecca was born on March 25, 1801, according to one family Bible record provided by Miss Mary Pugh of Romney, W.Va. Children of Joel and Rebecca McKee were: (1) Elizabeth Jane McKee was born Sept. 21, 1823, and died on Oct. 30, 1896. She married John J. Wolford, son of Martin and Mary (Crim) Wolford. John J. was born on May 30, 1816 and died on July 22, 1896. See the Oct. 12, 1987 issue of *West Virginia Advocate*, "Old Families of Hampshire County: Wolford Family Roots," by Wilmer L. Kerns. (2) Josiah McKee was born on March 22, 1825 and died on Oct. 13, 1825. (3) Rebecca Ann McKee was born on Aug. 29, 1826, and died on Dec. 24, 1826. (4) Margery D.L. McKee was born on Nov. 3, 1827, and died on Oct. 28, 1843. (5) Joshua M. McKee was born on Jan. 10, 1830. (6) Mary Margaret McKee was born on April 28, 1832, and died on Oct. 18, 1899. She married Daniel Pugh, son of Jesse and Charity (Gard) Pugh, Jr. He was born on June 27, 1826. (7) John Wesley McKee was born on March 17, 1834, and died on March 1, 1892, in Illinois. According to an obituary, he married Mrs. S.E. French, and he had no children. Primary source of information: Miss Mary Pugh, Box 111, Romney, W.Va. 26757.

McKee, John, son of William and Martha (Hammond) McKee, was born in Frederick County, Va. on Jan. 1, 1810, and died Jan. 3, 1865, in Long Creek Township, Decatur County, Iowa. He married Mary Ann Bain, Jan. 13, 1831, in Muskingham County, Ohio. She was born on April 14, 1814, in Virginia. They had ten children. Contact: Mrs. Vera L. Woodstock, 1564 Piikea Street, Honolulu, HI 96818.

McKee, John W. died on Dec. 11, 1911, aged 77 years, 9 months and 11 days. His wife, Maggie Baker, daughter of Aaron L. and Malinda Baker, was born in 1852 and died in 1937. Source: Tombstone inscriptions in the Baker Graveyard near Delray, Hampshire County, W.Va.

McKee, Joseph, son of Robert McKee, Sr., was born in 1777 and died in 1852 in Frederick County, Va. He married Elizabeth Reid, daughter of Jeremiah and Elizabeth (McMahon) Reid on Feb. 5, 1799. They were buried at Bethel Methodist Church, Trone, Frederick County, Va. According to one source (tradition), they had nine daughters and four sons. After studying the U.S. census, I'm inclined to think there were nine children; four boys and five girls. The sons were: (1) Joel McKee (1800-1835) married Rebecca Kline. (2) Joshua McKee drowned in Back Creek, at a young age. His grave is at Trone Church, with name engraved but no dates. (3) Jeremiah McKee settled in Camden, Arkansas, where he married, raised a family, and died. (4) Mary A. McKee was born June 19, 1810, on Timber Ridge, Frederick County, Va., and died at the home of her son, Joseph H. Lyon, April 25, 1899, at High Prairie, Missouri (possibly in Andrew County). She married Archibald Lyon, son of Elijah and Margaret (Linthicum) Lyon, on May 28, 1835. He was born on Jan. 1, 1810 and died on June 2, 1870. Archibald was buried in Akers' Chapel, Kinderhook Township, Pike County, Illinois, and Mary A. was buried in Missouri. (5) Rebecca McKee married John Cowgill. Joseph McKee was living with them on Timber Ridge, when the 1850 census was taken. Rebecca was listed as 45 years old (born circa 1805). (6) Margaret McKee was born in 1814 and died on Aug. 15, 1872, in Hampshire County. She married Jonathan L. Hiett, son of Jeremiah and Lucinda (Kidwell) Hiett, on Jan. 24, 1837. He survived her. (7) Robinson Joseph McKee was born at Back Creek, Frederick County, Va. on Dec. 5, 1819 and died on Jan. 9, 1906, in Lathrop, Missouri. He married Maria Sommerville, daughter of James and Elizabeth (Mauzy) Sommerville, on March 20, 1844. (8) name of a daughter not identified, and (9) name of another daughter not identified.

McKee, Margaret A., died in May 1869, aged 27 years. She was born in Virginia. Source: 1870 Mortality Schedule for Frederick County, Va.

McKee, Mary, daughter of Robert and Elizabeth McKee, Sr., was born in 1762; died on Jan. 30, 1847 in Hampshire County, Va. She married William Hook on Aug. 13, 1782 in Frederick County, Va. He was a Revolutionary soldier. Source: Family records deposited in DAR Library.

McKee, Mary daughter of Robert and Jane (Cather) McKee, Jr. was born on Jan. 13, 1808 and died on June 20, 1876, Bloomery District of Hampshire County. Her husband was Joseph Leith, son of James and Sarah (Rust) Leith, Jr. Joseph was born in 1798 and died in 1873. Apparently he lived on the old Leith homeplace, or nearby, because this couple and some of their children were buried in the family graveyard. Source: Hampshire County courthouse death record and cemetery inscriptions.

McKee, Robert Jr., son of Robert and Elizabeth McKee, Sr., was born in 1767 and died in Frederick County, Va. on Oct. 30, 1830. He married Jane Cather, daughter of Jasper and Barbara (Lawrence) Cather, on Sept. 5, 1793 in Frederick County. His father, Robert McKee, Sr., has often been confused with two other Robert McKee's, one of whom was a surgeon in the Revolutionary War. Robert of Frederick County was not the same person as Robert of Rockbridge County, Va.!

McKee, Robert, son of William and Martha (Hammond) McKee, was born on April 26, 1792 and died in Frederick County, Va. on June 9, 1850. He married Elizabeth McMorris, daughter of David and Nancy (McDonald) McMorris, on March 3, 1816. She was born on April 23, 1797 and died on May 5, 1877. Her second husband was named Samuel Hook of Capon Bridge, W.Va.

McKee, Sarah, daughter of Robert and Elizabeth McKee, Sr., was born circa 1786 and died on June 25, 1865. She married John Giffin. They lived on Timber Ridge, near the boundary between Hampshire and Frederick Counties, Va. Source: Records from Ralph L. Triplett Esq.

McKee, Vincent Dorsey, died Aug. 31, 1899, aged 71 years, 10 months, 15 days, at Capon Bridge, W.Va. His third wife, Susan Johnson, daughter of Amos and Elizabeth Johnson. They were buried in the Fairview Lutheran Cemetery on Timber Ridge. Undertaker was "Oats and McKee."

McKee, William, son of Robert and Elizabeth McKee, Sr., was born in 1765 and died on July 9, 1837 in Frederick County, Va. He married Martha Hammond on May 4, 1791. The Hammond origin has not been determined at this time, but researchers are probing for clues. Source: Private family records.

McKeever, Hugh, was born March 14, 1804 and died Feb. 15, 1882. His wife, Lucinda O., was born Nov. 3, 1804 and died April 18, 1890.   Source: Tombstone inscriptions in town cemetery, Wardensville, Hardy County, W.Va.

McQuaid, John W., son of Lewis and Susannah (Oates) McQuade, was born in Frederick County, Va. on May 5, 1831 and died in Mapleton, Kansas on Feb. 3, 1906. His sister, Mary Jane McQuaid, was born on Feb. 25, 1833 in Frederick County.   Their mother [Susannah] went to Leesburg, Indiana by covered wagon in 1849. Mary Jane married Elisha Kerns, son of Abner and Sarah (Davis) Kerns Sr. Source: Mrs. Mary F. (Kerns) Brouchard, 12925 N.W. Westlawn Terrace, Portland, Oregon 97229.

McVicker, Duncan ("Dunkin") and wife Jane (nee McConnell) were residents of Hampshire County. Duncan died sometime prior to Dec. 15, 1815, the date that his real estate was settled among his heirs. Their children were: Eleanor McVicker married Thomas Hook; Catherine McVicker married Charles Capper; John McVicker married Jane _____; Nancy McVickers married James Kelso; Archibald McVicker married Elizabeth _____, and they resided in Ohio, in 1815; Mary McVicker married Thomas McBride; Margaret McVicker married Frederick Spaid; and James McVicker purchased the Hampshire County farm. Source: Deed Book 20, pages 258-260, Hampshire County, W.Va. courthouse. Note: McVicker descendants have submitted information for membership in the DAR, but the papers are confusing. It states that Duncan McVicker was born in Scotland in 1739 and died in Schellsburg, Bedford County, Pennsylvania, citing a tombstone inscription on Chestnut Ridge, in Napier Township. This account gives the names of eight children and states there are other daughters, not named in the report. It states that his wife was named Nancy (Annie Laurie) McCollum. The children were listed: Alexander McVicker, "Justice of the Peace," born on July 14, 1773 and died on Aug. 5, 1832. He married Jane Taylor (1774-1834); Daniel McVicker married Margaret ____; David McVicker died in 1833. He married Eve Wertz; Duncan McVicker Jr.; James McVicker was born on Jan. 16, 1768 and died on Oct. 31, 1852. He married Pernelia McNamar; John McVicker; Joseph McVicker (1776-1852) married Mary Prudence McMullen; Mary McVicker married Thomas McBride in 1797; William McVicker married Dianah Mercer in 1797, and they lived in Hampshire County during the early 1800s. My fellow researchers, as you can see, there is a great variance between these two accounts. Your comments are solicited. I am inclined to go with the Hampshire County list of his heirs, as stated above. If anyone has the answers, please get in touch with me.

McVickers, Margaret, daughter of Duncan McVickers, was born on May 18, 1789 and died on Aug. 24, 1831. She married Frederick Spaid, son of George Nicholas and Margaret Elizabeth (Kale) Spaid, on May 5, 1805. Frederick was born on Dec. 3, 1785 in Hampshire County, Va. and died on Jan. 28, 1872. He remarried to Priscilla Capper (1794-1863), on May 22, 1832.

M., J., is on an old tombstone in the Thomas Edwards cemetery at Cold Stream, Hampshire County, Va. It says, "J.M. (died in) 1796." Nearby is another member of the family, whose stone reads, "T.M. (died in) 1822."

Malick, Aaron, son of John and Mary (Todd) Malick, was born in Hampshire County, Va. on Sept. 30, 1801, at 7 o'clock in the morning (Bible record) and died on April 21, 1895. Aaron's first wife was Sarah Pownall, born on July 15, 1802. His second wife was Catherine Saville, daughter of Oliver and Mary (Shanholtzer) Saville. Aaron was clerk of the Primitive Baptist Church (Union) near Mouser's Ridge. Catherine was born on Nov. 8, 1810 and died on Aug. 20, 1889. Aaron and Catherine were married on Oct. 9, 1879, in Hampshire County, according to a wedding announcement in the Oct. 31, 1879 issue of the *South Branch Intelligencer*. They were buried in the Malick cemetery near Augusta, West Virginia. Sources: Aaron Malick's Bible record, newspaper article, graveyard inscriptions, and county court records.

Malick, James, died Oct. 30, 1890, aged 79 years, 4 days. Mariah, his wife, died March 10, 1891, aged 81 years, 1 day. Source: Tombstone inscriptions in Mountain Dale cemetery, Hampshire County, W.Va.

Malick, Emsey, daughter of Aaron and Sarah Malick, was born in Hampshire County, Va., on May 15, 1823 and died on Aug. 11, 1862, in Tazwell County, Illinois. The Bible record does not name her husband, but she married a Mr. Grapes of Hampshire County, Va. Many of their children died young, per old letter written from Illinois to Hampshire County in 1862. It gave these death dates of the Grapes children, who died with their mother: Alonzo Calvatta Grapes died on Aug. 17, 1862; Belzora Virginia Grapes died on Aug. 25, 1862; Lydia M. Ann Grapes died on Oct. 26, 1862; and Sarah E. Grapes died on Nov. 12, 1862. The letter was signed by R. Grapes.

Malick, Johannes (spelled Moelick), was born in Frankfurt, Germany on Feb. 25, 1702 and died at Bedminster, Somerset County, N.J., on Nov. 16, 1763. He married Maria Cathrina Kirberger on Nov. 1, 1723, at Bendorf, Germany. They immigrated to America on the ship *Mercury*, arriving at Philadelphia on May 29, 1735. They were the immigrant ancestors of Malicks who later settled in Berkeley and Hampshire Counties, Va. Source: From information provided by Mr. Tommy McDonald of Winchester, Va. [see below]

Malick, John, son of Philip and Mary Malick, was born in Somerset County, New Jersey on Jan. 11, 1762 and died in Hampshire County, Va. on March 11, 1844. His wife, Mary Todd, was born on July 19, 1762 and died on July 27, 1839. Both were buried in the Malick cemetery, located in the Hoy/Augusta area of Hampshire County. John was a Revolutionary War veteran. Source: Tombstone inscriptions In Malick cemetery, Maud Pugh, Joseph T. McDonald of Winchester, Va., and Malick Family Bible in possession of Afton Malick, Augusta, W.Va.

Malick, John, Jr., son of John and Mary (Todd) Malick, was born on Jan. 2, 1791. Source: Family Bible.

Malick, Mary, daughter of John and Mary (Todd) Malick, was born in Somerset County, New Jersey on March 8, 1785 and died in Hampshire County, Va. on Dec. 6, 1841. She married David

Shaffer, son of Martin Shaffer. They were both buried in the Malick cemetery in Hampshire County, but David's grave is not marked.

Malick, Margaret, daughter of John and Mary (Todd) Malick, was born on Dec. 6, 1796 and died on May 5, 1863. According to the Malick family Bible, Margaret drowned.

Malick, Nancy, was born on Sept. 4, 1836 and died May 31, 1902. Source: Tombstone inscription in Mountain Dale cemetery, Hampshire County, W.Va.

Malick, Philip, son of Johannes and Maria Katriṇa (Kirberger) Moelick, was born on Oct. 8, 1736 (in either Pennsylvania or in New Jersey) and possibly died in Hampshire County, Va., near Augusta, but not yet proven. His wife was named Mary or Mary Margaret. The Malick family came to America on May 29, 1735, on the ship "Mercury." A Bible record of Philip Malick's family is in the hands of Afton Malick of Augusta, W.Va. The best source of information on the Malick family is Joseph T. McDonald, who is writing a book on the family, and he would like to communicate with Malick descendants. I urge you to contact him, because he is a very effective researcher, as well as a knowledgeable person. His name and address: Mr. Joseph T. McDonald, 1312 Ambrose Drive, Winchester, Va. 22601.

Malick, Philip, son of John and Mary (Todd) Malick, was born on July 17, 1788 and died on March 1, 1885, at 11 o'clock in the morning. Source: Malick Family Bible.

Malick, Sarah, daughter of Martin Shaffer, died on Aug. 16, 1872, aged 74 years, 11 months, and 26 days, according to a courthouse record in Hampshire County. However, it appears that the recording date was mixed up with her death date. It appears that the correct dates are: born Aug. 20, 1797 and died Aug. 17, 1871. But further verification should be done before accepting any of these dates. Her husband was David Malick, born in "Berkeley County, Va." on Feb. 27, 1794 and died on July 8, 1882. Source: Hampshire County death records and tombstone inscription in Malick cemetery.

Malick, Uriah, son of John and Mary (Todd) Malick, was born in Hampshire County, Va. on Feb. 10, 1808 and died in DeWitt, Arkansas on Sept. 25, 1882. He married Chloe Powell, daughter of Henry and Precious Ann (Queen) Powell. She was born on July 17, 1811, in Hampshire County. They migrated to Mercer

County, Ohio. Source: Bible record of Powell family, and records provided by Joseph T. McDonald, 1312 Ambrose Drive, Winchester, Va. 22601. Mr. McDonald is researching the Malick family.

Malick, Uriah, son of Martha Malick [daughter of John and Mary (Todd) Malick], was born on May 24, 1802. Martha was born on April 16, 1782. Source: Malick family Bible.

Malick, William, son of Aaron and Sarah Malick, was born in Hampshire County, Va., on June 19, 1835 and died in Pottsville, PA, on Feb. 11, 1864. Source: Family Bible of Aaron Malick.

Malin, Rebecca, 1775-1793, was buried in the Quaker cemetery, Gainsboro, Frederick County, Virginia.

Maphis, George, died of "cancer" on Jan. 13, 1881, aged 79 years. He was born in Hampshire County. Wife was named Elizabeth. Source: Courthouse death record.

Maphis, Luther, was born on Oct. 22, 1881 and died on Sept. 28, 1910, aged 28 years, 11 months, 6 days. Buried in the same cluster of locust trees on a farm were: Effie J. Hurd, born on Sept. 11, 1868 and died on Nov. 11, 1910; Basil W. Maphis, born on July 29, 1909 and died on Sept. 29, 1906; Annie E., daughter of N. and L. Maphis, died on Sept. 2, 1901, aged 16 years, 10 months, 28 days, and; Catherine Shavill, wife of Samuel Shavill (Saville?), died on Sept. 19, 1888, aged 54 years, "Gone but not forgotten." This graveyard is in deplorable condition, with the stones knocked down. It is located at Delray, W.Va. on a farm owned by Helen Botts, formerly the Clint Haines place.

Maphis, William, was born in 1790 and died in May 1860. He was ill for nine days, and the cause of death was "erysipelis." Born in Virginia. Occupation was farmer. His wife survived him. Source: 1860 Mortality Schedule for Shenandoah County, Va.

Manker, William, was born on Jan. 7, 1765, in Maryland and died in Highland County, Ohio. He served in the Revolutionary War, and married Rachel Jenkins, daughter of Jacob Jenkins of Hampshire County, Va. Source: Raymond G. Manker, 4530 E. Pepper Tree Lane, Paradise Valley, AZ 85253.

Marple, Ezekiel, son of Enoch and Sarah Marple, was born on March 4, 1757 and died on March 18, 1815 in Frederick County,

Va. He married Prudence Kennedy, born on March 1, 1758. Source: Jennie McIntyre, via Joyce Liepins of Charlotte, MI.

Marple, Sarah, a daughter of Thomas and Abigail (Smith) Marple, died on July 29, 1880, age 79. Her husband was George Moreland. Source: Hampshire County courthouse death record, Romney, W.Va. 26757.

Marshall, John L., born in Oct. 1757; died in Nov. 1817. His wife, Prsicilla, died in her 80th year, on Nov. 1, 1844. Source: Tombstone inscription at Indian Mound Cemetery, Romney, W.Va.

Martin, Joseph, died "of paralysis" on Oct. 10, 1868, age 88 years, at North River, Hampshire County, W.Va., where he was born. He was a farmer was was survived by his widow. Source: Courthouse death record in Romney, W.Va. See, also, the *South Branch Intelligencer*, Sept. 18, 1868 issue, which reported that Joseph Martin died on Sept. 10, 1868, aged 91 years. These are conflicting reports, and the U.S. Census gives a third birthyear.

Mason, John, was born on Feb. 22, 1753 in Berkeley County, Va. and died on Aug. 16, 1805, in Fayette County, PA. His wife, Hannah Frost, was born on Dec. 25, 1751, and died in Fayette County, PA. after 1805. He was a soldier of the Revolutionary War. Source: DAR application records.

Mason, Jonathan, was born on Jan. 20, 1793 and died on Nov. 17, 1860. He lived in the Timber Ridge area, and was buried in the Heironimus Graveyard, at Whitacre, Virginia. Jonathan married Helen Braithwaite, March 20, 1822, by the Rev. Joseph Dalby, in Frederick County, Va.

Mason, Reason Jr. was born circa 1793 and died Sept. 12, 1837, in Frederick County, Va. He married Mary Dick, daughter of Peter Dick, Nov. 14, 1821, in Frederick County, Va. The exact composition of his family unit is not known at this time. He had at least one son, named William C. Mason, born Nov. 14, 1824 in Frederick County, and died Nov. 6, 1888, in Grant County, W.Va. His wife was Mary M. Lewis. Two of Reason Jr.'s children were bound out as indentured servants, on October 5, 1839. A daughter, Nancy Mason, was born Nov. 1, 1827. She was bound to Jacob Null of Cross Junction, Frederick County, Va., "to spin, sew and knit." A second daughter, Elizabeth Ann Mason, was born March 15, 1829. She was bound to Aaron Largent of Acorn Hill, Frederick County, Va., "to spin, sew and knit." These indentured servant records are located in the Virginia State Archives (restricted access). Contact: Mr. William D. Mason, 633 Bridger Drive, Colorado Springs, CO 80909.

Mason, William, a black slave, died in August 1859, aged 81 years. He was ill for four days prior to his death that was caused by "old age." Source: 1860 Mortality Schedule for Frederick County, Va.

Mason, William, was born on May 2, 1826 and died on April 4, 1878 in Frederick County, Va. His wife, Lavina, was born on Dec. 12, 1834 and died on July 16, 1912. Source: Tombstone inscriptions in Timber Ridge Primitive Baptist Church, located near Reynold's Store in northern Frederick County, Va.

Mathew, John, son of Levi and Rhoda (Hilburn) Mathew, was born in Hampshire County, Va. on Sept. 4, 1775 and died in Sept. 1854, in Clinton County, Ohio. He married Rachel Parke, probably a daughter of Samuel and Hannah (Edwards) Park. Rachel was born on June 13 (June 12 by another account), 1781, and died Dec. 18, 1820, in Clinton County, Ohio. They were buried in Centerville cemetery. Source: Mr. John K. Maddy, 4310 43rd Street, Des Moines, IA 50310.

Mauzy, Emily, daughter of William Henry and Massie (Whitacre) Mauzy, was born on Dec. 8, 1860 and died on July 11, 1888. She married George Oates on April 4, 1880. Source: Bible record, court record, and tombstone inscription in Ebenezer cemetery near Gore, Virginia.

Mauzy, George, died on Nov. 9, 1836, aged 40 "YER," according to a tombstone inscription in the Mauzy graveyard, Timber Ridge/Smokey Hollow, Hampshire County, W.Va. In *Order Book II*, page 286, Circuit Court of Hampshire County, dated Sept. 1848, it stated that George Mauzy, deceased, left these infant children: Jonathan Mauzy, David Mauzy, and Susan Mauzy. George's wife, Margaret (Fout) Mauzy, moved to Clinton County, Ohio, as did their daughter Mary Susan Mauzy. Jonathan T. Mauzy returned from Ohio to marry Mary Jane Smith, daughter of John and Susan Smith, on March 10, 1857. He then went to Charlton County, Missouri. David H. Mauzy settled in Missouri, too. The Mauzy heirs brought suit against the estate of William Fletcher (died in 1861). The family connection has not been determined.

Mauzy, Henry was deceased by Oct. 28, 1850 because on that date William S. Hook was appointed guardian for orphan children, named Samuel Alexander Mauzy and Mary Susan Mauzy. William S. Hook married Sarah A.Mauzy, daughter of John Mauzy. This Sarah (Mauzy) Hook died on Aug. 21, 1858, aged 27 years, 10 months and 12 days, according to a tombstone inscription in the Mauzy graveyard. A cemetery inscription in the Mauzy graveyard on Timber Ridge/Smokey Hollow shows that Henry Mauzy was born on March 1, 1803 and he died on Sept. 2, 1850. In the same graveyard is Ann E. Mauzy, daughter of Henry and Mary Mauzy, born on Aug. 5, 1845 and died on Sept. 2, 1850, and daughter Mary Susan Mauzy, born on Sept. 18, 1850 and died on Oct. 5, 1852. From another source I learned that Henry Mauzy was married to Mary Ann Hook, daughter of Samuel and Anna (McMorris) Hook. Source: Guardian Bond in Hampshire County courthouse, and cemetery inscriptions.

Mauzy, Henry, son of William and Sarah (Leith) Mauzy, was born in Hampshire County, Va. on Sept. 21, 1832 and died on Nov. 27, 1910. Source: Tombstone inscription in Greenton Cemetery, Lafayette County, Missouri.

Mauzy, James Richard, son of Peter and Susannah (Powell) Mauzy, Jr., was born in Hampshire County in 1830 and died in Salem, Missouri on May 8, 1886. Martha Hook, first wife of James R. Mauzy, was born on April 4, 1838 and died on Sept. 28, 1861. She was buried in the Mauzy graveyard in Smokey Hollow, Hampshire County, W.Va. They had three children: Peter Luther Mauzy immigrated to Little Rock Arkansas; Ann Elizabeth Mauzy married Asa Larrick; and George William Mauzy married Alverna Elizabeth Moreland. James R. Mauzy remarried to Amy Elizabeth Heironimus, daughter of Frederick and Maria (Hutchinson) Heironimus, and they had six sons: Edgar, Lemuel, Frederick, Offutt, Mack and Walter Mauzy. James R. Mauzy died only three weeks after moving to Missouri, and was buried there. Amy Elizabeth (Heironimus) Mauzy died on May 22, 1915 in Dent County, Missouri, aged 78 years. See the Dec. 14, 1987 issue of **The West Virginia Advocate**, for further detail on the Mauzy family, and photographs.

Mauzy, John, son of Peter and Elizabeth (Buzzard) Mauzy IV, was born in Hampshire County, Va., circa 1795, and died in 1866, in Chariton County, Missouri. John married Elizabeth Powell, daughter of Robert Massey and Elizabeth (Leith) Powell, on Jan. 11, 1825 in Hampshire County, Va. Contact: Gilbert F. Sacco, 11123 Canterbury Street, Westchester, IL 60154.

Mauzy, Mary "Polly," second wife of Samuel Hook, was born on Oct. 30, 1790 and died on Sept. 15, 1854. She was a daughter of Peter and Elizabeth (Buzzard) Mauzy, III, and buried next to them in the Mauzy graveyard in Smokey Hollow, Hampshire County, W.Va. Samuel Hook, son of William and Mary (McKee) Hook, was born on March 23, 1795. It doesn't appear that Mary had children, because she was married later in life, after age 45, when her father stated in his Will that she was unmarried. Samuel's first and third marriages were to Anna and Elizabeth McMorris, daughters of David and Nancy (McDonald) McMorris.

Mauzy, Mary, daughter of Peter and Susanna (Powell) Mauzy, Jr., was born in Hampshire County, Va. on July 14, 1832 and died on Aug. 31, 1916. She married Robert Whitacre, son of George and Elizabeth (McKee) Whitacre. He was born Nov. 20, 1827 and died on July 2, 1893.

Mauzy, Peter II, son of Peter and Elizabeth (Sumners) Mauzy I (1713-1750), was born May 19, 1738 in Stafford County, Va. and died in Oct. 1799 in Fairfax County, Va. He received a Fairfax grant on Mill Branch of the Cacapon River, Hampshire County, in 1753. He married Priscilla Waugh, born on Oct. 27, 1741. Their children were: George Mauzy; Sarah Mauzy married John Heriford; Mary Mauzy married Isaac Hutchinson; Thomas Mauzy; Margaret Mauzy married Tapley Frye; Peter Mauzy III, (1764-1835) married Elizabeth Buzzard; John Mauzy died unmarried ca. 1835; and Ann Mauzy married Lewis T. Waugh. The Hampshire County land was divided into eight shares, valued at $148.75 each. Sons Peter, III, and John bought all of the shares.[44] On March 4, 1802, 29 acres were conveyed from George Mauzy to his brother Peter Mauzy, III. John D. Hinkle, a Mauzy descendant and family researcher who lives in Fairfax, Va., has listed three more children of Peter Mauzy II: Michael Mauzy; Mildred Mauzy m. John Bladen; and Elizabeth Mauzy m. Nicholas Grimes.

---

44. Several deeds in Hampshire County **Deed Book 13** reveal the distribution of Peter Mauzy's land. See especially **Deed Book 13**, pages 112-113.

Mauzy, Peter, III, died on May 18, 1835 on Timber Ridge, Hampshire County, Va., aged 69 years. His wife, Elizabeth Buzzard, daughter of Frederick and Susannah (Buckwalter) Buzzard, died on April 8, 1840, aged 74 years. Both were born in 1765-66. They were buried on their Hampshire County farm. Their tombstones have broken into pieces, but are still legible. Their daughter Susan Mauzy married John Heironimus, according to Hampshire County Circuit Court, *Order Book II*, page 286. The marriage occurred after 1835 and before 1848.

Mauzy, Peter, IV., was born on Nov. 6, 1791 and died on Jan. 20, 1858. His wife, Susannah Powell, daughter of Robert Massey and Elizabeth (Leith) Powell, was born on April 26, 1797 and died on July 18, 1863. Buried on the Mauzy farm in Hampshire County. Source: Tombstone inscriptions.

Mauzy, Peter, was deceased by June 27, 1853 or 1858 (not a death date), because his orphan children were placed under guardianship of William P. Stump on that date. The children of this Peter Mauzy, under this guardian bond, were: Margaret, Sarah, James and John C. Mauzy. Source: Hampshire County, Va. Guardian Bond in basement of courthouse, Romney, W.Va.

Mauzy, Samuel A., born on Nov. 20, 1848 and died on June 4, 1897. His wife, Julia A. Paskel died on Feb. 22, 1910. Source: Tombstone Inscriptions in the Mauzy graveyard in Smokey Hollow, Hampshire County, W.Va.

Mauzy, William, son of Peter and Elizabeth (Buzzard) Mauzy, III, was born in Hampshire County, Va. on May 22, 1805 and died on May 3, 1887 in Lafayette County, Missouri. His wife, Sarah Leith, daughter of James and Sarah (Rust) Leith, Jr., was born on Dec. 12, 1804 and died on Oct. 31, 1878. During the l850's a slave ran away, and William advertized in a Winchester paper, offering a reward. They sold their Hampshire County land during the 1870's and migrated to Missouri with relatives. Source: Tombstone inscriptions in Greenton Cemetery, Lafayette County, Missouri, plus many records in the Hampshire County, Va. courthouse.

Mauzy, William Henry, son of Peter and Susanna (Powell) Mauzy, IV, was born in Smokey Hollow, Hampshire County, Va. Nov. 19, 1819 and died on Sept. 6, 1895 in Frederick County. His wife, Massy Whitacre, daughter of Wilson and Rachel (Kerns) Whitacre, was born June 21, 1825 and died in 1910. They were married on Feb. 8, 1844, by Rev. Christy Sine, at Wilson Whitacre'S house. FROM THE BIBLE RECORD: The children of William H. and Massie (Whitacre) Mauzy: (1) Alexander Mauzy, born on Oct. 25, 1844. He married Rachel Peacemaker on Sept. 29, 1881. (2) Emaline Mauzy born on July 2, 1846. (3) Isabella Mauzy, born on Aug. 16, 1847. She married John C. Oates on Oct. 12, 1865. (4) Ruth Mauzy, born on Oct. 1, 1849. She married John W. Hinkle on Oct. 15, 1874. (5) Henry Mauzy, born on Aug. 21, 1851. (6) Mary Mauzy, born on March 14, 1855. (7) Lydia Mauzy, born on March 10, 1857. She married T.M. Dolan on July 16, 1876. (8) Emily Mauzy, born on Dec. 8, 1860. She married George Oates on April 4, 1880. (9) John William Mauzy, born on Feb. 16, 1866. Both William and Massie were buried at Ebenezer Christian Church, Gore, Virginia. Source: Family papers copied from a family Bible.

Mellon, John W., was born Oct. 24, 1827 and died Dec. 18, 1899. It is believed that he was a son of Margaret (Kerns) Riley. John was an undertaker on Timber Ridge. His wife, Catherine, was born on June 5, 1830 and died May 3, 1907. Source: Tombstone inscriptions in Fairview Lutheran cemetery, Gore, Va.

Mendenhall, Eliza, died on April 5, 1875, aged 70 years. Source: Tombstone inscription on high bank of North River, inside a wooded area on property of Kenneth Baker, North River Mills. In this same small private graveyard was buried George S. Williams.

Merrifield, Samuel, was born Aug. 12, 1720, in Croat, England, and died in Monongalia County, Va., Feb. 26, 1781. His wife was named Mary Elizabeth. One of their children, Richard Merrifield, was born in 1747, in Frederick County, Va., and died in 1798, in Monongalia County, Va. Richard married Phoebe Tucker (1754-1801), daughter of Richard and Elizabeth Tucker. Samuel Merrifield was an early settler in old Frederick County, in the Opequon settlement. His neighbors in 1750 were: Joseph Lupton, Benjamin Smith, Andrew Vance, and Nathan Cartmell. Source: Sara H. Rice, 4020 Southwest 77th Street, Gainesville, FL 32608-3604.

Michael, Christopher, died in Morgan County, W.Va., in July 1849, aged 80 years. He was born in Maryland. Source: 1850 Mortality Schedule of U.S. Census.

Michael, John, died on June 29, 1876, aged 80 years, in Morgan County, W.Va. Source: The **South Branch Intelligencer**, issue of July 7, 1876.

Michael, Martha, died in Morgan County, W.Va., March 1870, aged 36 years. Cause of death was complications from childbirthing. Source: 1870 Mortality Schedule of U.S. Census.

Michael, Sarah, died on Nov. 18, 1882, aged 94 years, 1 month, 28 days. Her husband was named Philip Michael. Source: Death record in Hampshire County courthouse.

Miles, C. (a male) died on March 28, 1899, aged 88 years. He was a widower, born in Hampshire County and buried at Cold Stream. Source: Hampshire County death record.

Miles, Elizabeth J., daughter of James and Rosannah (Binegar) Powell, died in 1878, aged 43 years. She was married to Joseph Miles. According to the Hampshire County death record, she was born near the Forks of Capon, Hampshire County.

Miles, James, was born April 21, 1767 and died April 23, 1846. Buried next to James was Mary A. Miles, born Sept. 16, 1770 and died July 18, 1842. In same graveyard was buried Owen and Sophia Thomas (1764-1838). Source: Tombstone inscriptions in private graveyard on mountainside, on Turkey Mountain Road, near Fisher, Hardy County, W.Va. Tombstones have fallen and the graveyard has become "lost and forgotten."

Millar (Miller), Isaac, died in Hampshire County, Va. on Jan. 23, 1816, aged 64 years, 11 months, and 20 days, according to a tombstone inscription. His parents were William and Catherine (Dubois) Millar. Issac was a soldier in the Revolutionary War. He married Elizabeth See in 1777.

Millar, Michael, died on the South Branch, on Nov. 10, 1872, aged 87 years, 7 months, 9 days. He travelled in the South and West when young; then returned to Hampshire County where he married and died. Source: **South Branch Intelligencer** newspaper.

Miller, Abraham, died in June 1860, aged 62 years. Was ill for 28 days with consumption. Born in Virginia. Survived by spouse. Source: 1860 Mortality Schedule for Shenandoah County, Va.

Miller, Christena, widow of Abraham Miller, died on April 11, 1873 in Augusta County, Virginia, aged 80 years. Abraham died on April 11, 1847. Source: May 2, 1873 issue of the *South Branch Intelligencer* (which was copied from the *Rockingham Register*). The Rev. Frank L. Baker's manuscript on the Miller family showed that Christina was a daughter of Daniel and Elizabeth (Thomas) Arnold; that she was born on Nov. 2, 1793 and died on April 11, 1873. He gave the birthdate of Jan. 16, 1788 for Abraham Miller, son of Jacob Miller.

Miller, Christina, died in April 1860, aged 48 years, of "liver disorder." Listed as a housewife, she was born in Maryland. Source: Mortality Schedule for 1860 Census, Hampshire County, Va.

Miller, David, "died Saturday night and was buried at Ebenezer Christian Church (Frederick County, Va.) today." Source: Entry in *Diary of George Edwards*, dated Monday, June 19, 1899.

Miller, Jacob, of Shenandoah County, was found dead on Dec. 4, 1818, in Frederick County, Va., "about a mile at the end of Isaac Hite's lane." It is believed that he was thrown from a horse or wagon while traveling.   Source: Frederick County, Va., "Inquisitions of Dead Bodies," Virginia State Archives, Richmond, Va.

Miller, Mary, wife of Jeremiah Miller, died on Sept. 22, 1898, aged 72 years, 11 months, 25 days, according to a tombstone inscription in the Larkin D. Henderson graveyard, on Kedron Road, near Slanesville, W.Va. Her Bible record states that she was born on Sept. 28, 1820, and her marriage to Jeremiah Miller was on Jan. 16, 1850. Source: A person who has assisted me and who seems to be most knowledgeable on the Henderson family is: Mrs. Irma Curtis, Route 3, Box 106A, Weston, W.Va. 26452.

Miller, Moses, was deceased before Aug. 10, 1898, when the newspaper in Romney, W.Va. published a list of heirs. He married Elmira Gilmer, daughter of Henry Gilmer of Rockingham County, Va. (Note: Henry made his Will in 1855, which is included with the documentation.) The children of Moses and Elmira (Gilmer) Miller were: (1) Margaret Naomi Miller married R.H. Main. They were living in Sprague, Bates County, Missouri, in 1900. (2) Barbara A. Miller was single, living with her sister in Missouri, in 1900.   (3)

Mary Ellen Miller married Josiah McKee; (4) Rebecca Miller married John Alger, and they resided at Baker's Run, Hardy County, W.Va. (5) Levina Miller married Joseph Householder and they immigrated to Peoria, Illinois; (6) Robert H. Miller married Miami _____ and they moved to Okarche, Oklahoma; (7) Samuel A. Miller was a businessman at Rich Hill, Bates County, Missouri. This Miller family lived near North River. The 200-acre Miller homeplace was sold to H.B. Daugherty, on Feb. 11, 1899, for $1,100. Source: Chancery court suit, Box 232, Circuit Court, Hampshire County, W.Va.

Miller, Rebecca, widow of the late Jacob Miller, died April 16, 1854, at her residence near the Baptist Church at Lost River, Hardy County, Va. She was about 80 years old. Source: *Zion's Advocate*: Vol. I, No. 9, Saturday, May 6, 1854. This church periodical, published in Front Royal, represented the "Old School" or Primitive Baptist Church in Northern Virginia.

Miller, Sarah "Sallie" A., daughter of Benjamin and Charity (Furr) Wills, and the wife of John B. Miller, of North River Mills, Hampshire County, W.Va., died on Jan. 28, 1872, at the home of her son-in-law, Clark Loy. She was born on Dec. 14, 1819. Her husband, John B., was a son of William and Christina Miller. John B. Miller was born on May 20, 1808 and died on March 21, 1886, at North River Mills, W.Va. Apparently, John B. Miller remarried, because a death record in the Romney Courthouse shows that his second wife was Sallie Stump, daughter of Adam and Parthenia Stump. Sallie #2 died on March 7, 1886, aged 56 years, 6 months, 6 days. John B. Miller established the first post office at North River Mills, on March 25, 1843. Source: U.S. Census; The *South Branch Intelligencer* newspaper; postal records in the National Archives; and Miller Family Bible.

Miller, Silas, son of William and Christina Miller, died on Sept. 13, 1826, aged 21 years. Source: Miller Family Bible, in possession of Mrs. Charles L. Miller, North River Mills, Hampshire County, W.Va.

Miller, Stephen, allegedly a son of John Miller (not proven), was born on Dec. 19, 1819. He married Anna Krizer, on Oct. 21, 1840, in Frederick County, Va. Source: Mrs. Delores Glass, Farmington, N.M.

Miller, William, died on Aug. 16, 1826, aged 48 years, 10 months, 4 days (born on Oct. 12, 1777). His wife, Christina, was born on Jan. 23, 1778 and died on June 26, 1854. They were buried at Three Churches, Hampshire County, W.Va.

Milleson, Johnston (1813-1874) and his wife Phebe McDonald (1816-1891) were buried in the old Benjamin and Margaret (Hiett) McDonald graveyard, North River, Hampshire County, W.Va. Buried in the same graveyard were George W. Milleson (1855-1929) and his sister, Mary Ann Milleson (1862-1884). Also: Benjamin E. Milleson (1843-1845), Isaac Milleson (1846-1847), and Margaret Milleson (1851-1853). Maud Pugh stated, on page 331 of *Capon Valley..*, that Phebe (McDonald) Milleson was a granddaughter of old Benjamin McDonald, but I'm inclined to believe Phebe was a daughter, given the dates on the tombstones.

Milleson, Martha, daughter of Silas and Harriett Milleson, aged 21 years, married David Sylvester Powell, son of Robert M. and Mary Powell, aged 28 years, on Feb. 20, 1867. Source: Hampshire County courthouse marriage record.

Milleson, Silas, was born on March 31, 1807 and died on May 23, 1885. His wife Harriett Slane was a daughter of Thomas and Margaret (Nielson) Slane, and she was born on Oct. 4, 1808 and died on May 11, 1885. Several children died as infants: Benjamin A. Milleson, born on March 7, 1832 and died on May 18, 1837; Phebe Milleson, born on Feb. 21, 1834 and died on Dec. 18, 1839; Thomas W. Milleson, born April 18, 1836 and died on May 27, 1837; Samuel J. Milleson, born on June 8, 1838 and died on Dec. 15, 1839; Robert N. Milleson, born Aug. 18, 1848 and died on Aug. 27, 1848; and Philadelphia B. Milleson, born Nov. 6, 1851 and died on Nov. 29, 1859. Source: Tombstone inscriptions, all on a single monument in a field near Slanesville, W.Va. The farm was once known as the Robinson farm and is now owned by James Pyles. The grave monument has been knocked over, apparently by farm animals, and is in need of maintenance.

Mills, John Jr, son of John and Rachel (Bates) Mills, was born 10-12-1712 in Chester County, PA and died 4-18-1794, in Guilford County, N.C. He married Sarah Beals, daughter of John and Sarah (Bowater) Beals, on 7-14-1732. Sarah was born in PA, 5-20-1713, and died on 9-9-1800 in N.C. Sarah was a Quaker minister. John Mills Sr. was one of the first settlers in old Frederick County, a recipient of a Bryan-Ross grant in 1735. Also, it is believed that Mills Branch of the Cacapon River was named after him, although he left the area before Fairfax land grants were issued. These were pioneer Quaker families.

Mills, Thomas, son of John and Rachel (Bates) Mills, was born in Chester County, PA, in 1709, and died in Guilford, N.C., 9-10-1793. He married Elizabeth Harrold, daughter of Richard and Mary (Beale) Harrold, on 1-18-1730. Elizabeth was born 3-10-1711 and died 9-9-1771. Source: From information provided by Charity G. Monroe, 4315 West Lora Ann Lane, Peoria, IL 61615.

Millslagle, George, died on Oct. 9, 1866, aged 81 years and 2 months, unmarried. Source: Hampshire County death record.

Millslagle, Sarah, died June 2, 1904, aged 90 years, 9 months, 4 days. Possibly she was unmarried. On the 1850 census for Hardy County, Va. she was living with a Baker family. Her tombstone inscription was found in the cemetery of Baker United Methodist Church, near Baker, Hardy County, W.Va.

Mitchell, Robert, was born on Feb. 7, 1816 and died on Oct. 14, 1872. His wife, Ellen, was born on March 16, 1830 and died on March 8, 1870. Source: Tombstone inscriptions in Slonaker private graveyard on west side of Bear Garden Mountain, along the Cacapon River, Hampshire County, W.Va.

Monroe, Alexander II, son of Alexander and Margaret (Lang) Monroe I, was born in Fauquier County, Va. circa 1758 and died in Southport, Indiana on Nov. 20, 1842. His wife was Elizabeth "Betsy" Chenoweth (1764-1829), daughter of John and Eleanor Chenoweth (1735-1812). Alexander II was a Baptist minister, and a veteran of the Revolutionary War. Source: Mrs. James Monroe, 2933 Truwood, Trenton, MI 48183.

Monroe, Alexander, son of George Monroe, was born in 1794-probably in Fauquier County, Va.- died in 1875 in Pendleton County, KY. He married Anna Monroe, his cousin, daughter of the Rev. Dr. John and Eleanor (Asberry) Monroe. They were married on Oct. 2, 1817. She was born on July 28, 1794. Source: Family Bible of the Rev. Dr. John Monroe.

Monroe, Alexander, was born in Hampshire County, Va. in 1816 and died in same county on March 16, 1904. Source: Courthouse death record in Romney, West Virginia.

Monroe,   Alexander, was born April 2, 1814, in Hampshire County, Va., and died Jan. 17, 1877, in Wirt County, W.Va. He married Lydia Ann Hiett, daughter of John and Martha E. (Tansy) Hiett. Lydia Ann was born in Hampshire County on Sept. 24, 1812, and died in Wirt County, W.Va., on April 29, 1868. It is believed that Alexander was a son of William and Hannah (Edwards) Monroe, based on the fact that all these persons were buried together in a farm plot (now almost destroyed). Source: Tombstone inscriptions in Monroe family graveyard [William Monroe (1793-1876) buried here], Wirt County, W.Va.

Monroe, Alexander, M.D. and surveyor, son of John and Eleanor (Asbury) Monroe, was born circa 1774 and died in Pendleton County, KY on Sept. 18, 1814. He married Sallie C. Mountjoy, daughter of Alvin and Mary (Edwards) Mountjoy, on April 24, 1806. Alexander was named in his father's Will, but not named in the family Bible, which remains a mystery for Monroe researchers.   Source: Mrs. Sue Schneider (deceased), 210 Adams Street, Benson, IL. 61516.

Monroe, Alexander, son of Robert and Elizabeth Monroe, married Margaret E. Pugh, daughter of Benjamin and Sarah Pugh, on Nov. 21, 1866. He was listed as a widower, aged 47 years, and she as 26 years old, her first marriage. Another marriage record, in same Hampshire County court book, stated that one Alexander Monroe, aged 45 years, resident of Wirt County, W.Va., married Ephinia Pugh, aged 40 years, Jan. 23, 1869

Monroe, Dr. James, son of John and Eleanor (Asbury) Monroe, was born in Hampshire County, Va. on Feb. 16, 1786 and died on Feb. 11, 1855. His wife, Margaret Pugh, was a daughter of Robert and Margaret (McDonald) Pugh, II. She was born on Jan. 17, 1797 and died on Jan. 10, 1858. Both are buried on the historic Robert Pugh farm, not far from Capon Chapel. A cast-iron fence was placed around these two well-marked graves, located on the side of an old abandoned roadbed. James was a physician and a Baptist preacher. Source: Tombstone inscriptions on the old Monroe farm at Capon Bridge, originally belonging to pioneer Robert Pugh.

Monroe, Jeremiah, M.D., son of John and Eleanor (Asbury) Monroe, was born on Oct. 19, 1787, in Hampshire County, Va., and died in 1831 in Pendleton County, KY. He married Anna Maria Clarkson in May 1817. Source: Mrs. Sue Schneider.

Monroe, Lt. Jeremiah, CSA, about 41 years old, died on April 14, 1875, on the Capon, in Hampshire County, W.Va. Source: The *South Branch Intelligencer*, issue of April 23, 1875.

Monroe, Jesse, son of John and Eleanor (Asbury) Monroe, was born on Jan. 9, 1785 and died in Hampshire County on May 11, 1857. Jesse was an attorney and a minister. His wife was Eleanor Blue, daughter of Garrett Blue. His gravestone appears to say that Rev. Jesse Monroe, died on May 12, 1857, aged 81 years, 3 months, _?_ days. He and Eleanor were buried at Three Churches, W.Va., on Branch Mountain. An obit in the March 8, 1878 issue of The *South Branch Intelligencer* stated that Eleanor Monroe, wife of Jesse, died on Feb. 1, 1878, aged 89 years, in Hampshire County. Their tombstones were broken off and then repaired and set into a concrete base. The lower part of the inscriptions are not visible. Further research is needed.[45]

Monroe, The Rev. Dr. John, son of Alexander and Margaret (Lang) Monroe, was born on April 10, 1750 in Fauquier County, Va. and died in Hampshire County, Va. on Aug. 19, 1824. He married Eleanor Asbury, daughter of George and Hannah (Hardwick) Asbury, on Oct. 10, 1770. Eleanor was born on June 13, 1754 in Stafford County, Va. After her death, John Monroe married Mrs. Lucy Louther, widow, on April 12, 1812. She died in Aug. 1824 and was buried next to her husband at the Capon Chapel. John Monroe was a Baptist preacher and a physician. Source: Mrs. Sue Schneider (now deceased), 210 Adams, Box 343, Benson, IL 61516; Family Bible of the Rev. Dr. John Monroe. See, also, Robert Semple's history of the Baptists in Virginia, which gives a biography of John Monroe.

Monroe, John Jr., son of John and Eleanor (Asbury) Monroe, was born on Nov. 26, 1780 and died on Dec. 3, 1820, at Glasgow, Barren County, KY. He married Lucy Rogers, born in Albermarle County, Va., Dec. 27, 1787 and died on Sept. 18, 1834, in Coles County, Illinois. [Research question: Who was the John Monroe who married Sarah Craig in Frederick County,

---

45. A letter in my possession, dated March 3, 1855, stated that "Old Dr. Jesse Monroe is dead."

Va. on Jan. 6, 1805?]   Source: Mrs. James Monroe,   2933 Truwood, Trenton, MI 48183.

Monroe, Marquis, son of John and Eleanor (Asbury) Monroe, was born on March 28, 1792, per family Bible. Allegedly he was a preacher in the Methodist church. What was his relationship to Alexander Ambler? On Sept. 12, 1853, one Marquis Monroe was ordered to pay interest to Alexander Ambler, from March 28, 1824 (on his 32nd birthday), to "the present time." Source: *Order Book III*, page 270, Hampshire County, Va. Circuit Court record.

Monroe, William, son of James Monroe, was born June 24, 1793, probably in Hampshire County, and died Jan. 9, 1876, in Wirt County, W.Va. He married Hannah Edwards (born in 1794), daughter of Thomas Edwards, II. Source: Courthouse record in Hampshire County, dated in 1823, Deed Book 23, page 472, and tombstone inscriptions in Monroe Family Graveyard, Wirt County.

Montgomery, Alice, (wife of Hugh H. Montgomery), born on Sept. 13, 1803 and died July 15, 1876. Source: Tombstone inscription, Springfield, W.Va.

Montgomery, Edward, died on May 27, 1867, aged 35 years, 8 months, 27 days. Source: Tombstone inscription, Springfield, W.Va. cemetery on top of hill.

Montgomery, Hugh H., was born on March 7, 1793 and died on May 12, 1854. Source: Tombstone inscription.

Montgomery, James W., was born Feb. 11, 1812 and died Feb. 15, 1900. His wife, Priscilla, died July 6, 1895, aged 60 years, 9 months, 22 days. Source: Tombstone inscriptions in Salem Methodist Church graveyard, Slanesville, Hampshire County, W.Va.

Montgomery, Louisa, died on Oct. 28, 1860, aged 31 years, 5 months, 4 days. Source: Tombstone inscription at Springfield, W.Va.

Moore, Abraham, son of Henry and E. Moore, died in Hampshire County on Oct. 10, 1881, aged 80 years, 8 months and 2 days. According to a tombstone inscription, he was born on Feb. 8, 1801. Born in Loudoun County, Va. He married Sarah Stump, daughter of Joseph Stump, on Oct. 1, 1828. Sarah was born on Aug. 5, 1802 and died on Oct. 10, 1881. Both were buried in the Stump/Noland graveyard at Little Capon, Hampshire

County, W.Va. Source: Courthouse death record and tombstone inscriptions in Noland cemetery.

Moore, Abraham, son of Henry and Elizabeth (Stump) Moore, was born on Feb. 8, 1801. His wife was Sarah Stump, daughter of Joseph and Elizabeth (Boggess) Stump. Sarah was born on Aug. 5, 1802. Their children were: Malinda Catherine Moore was born on July 17, 1829; Elizabeth Jane Moore was born Oct. 14, 1831. She married Robert Dade Noland; Joseph Stump Moore was born on Nov. 4, 1833; Ann Rebecca Moore was born Oct. 21, 1840. She married John W. Noland. Source: Family Bible in hands of Mrs. Marvin Keesecker, Route Box 52, Great Cacapon, W.Va. 25422.

Moore, Jemima (wife of Dr. John W. Moore), was born in 1811 and died on Aug. 11, 1868. [Sorry, but source misplaced]

Moore, John W. (M.D.) was born on Dec. 12, 1805 and died on Oct. 7, 1881. Source: Tombstone inscription, Springfield, W.Va.

Moore, Joseph S., 1833-1919, and Mary E. Moore, 1845-1931. Source: Tombstone inscriptions, "Noland Graveyard" at Little Capon, Hampshire County, W.Va. A Bible record states that Joseph Moore was born on Nov. 4, 1833.

Moore, Peter, died on Oct. 27, 1874, age 60 years. "Here lies an honest man" is inscribed on his tombstone, in Noland graveyard at Little Capon, Hampshire County, W.Va. The *South Branch Intelligencer*, issue of Nov. 6, 1874, stated that he died at the home of his aunt, Mrs. Samuel J. Stump, near Slanesville, West Virginia.

Moore, Philip, Jr., son of Philip Moore, Sr., was born in 1747 and died in 1778 in Hampshire County. [Note: Philip Moore Sr. died in Hampshire County, Va. in 1762. It was a German name, Mohr.] The wife of Philip, Jr. was Mary Dosher/Tosher. The town of Moorefield, W.Va. was named after this surname, specifically after Conrad Moore (whose Will was probated in Hardy County on April 9, 1800). Conrad was a son of Philip Moore Sr. Source: Ms. Wilma Hill, 3040 Euclid, Wichita, KS 67217.

Moore, Rebecca (second wife of Dr. John W. Moore), was born in 1819 and died Feb. 10, 1876. Source: Tombstone inscription at Springfield, W.Va. cemetery, on top of hill, overlooking the town.

Moreland, Bazil was born in Charles County, MD on Feb. 25, 1782 and died on Sept. 19, 1857 in Knox County, Ohio. He married Margaret Fahs, born in Hampshire County on Nov. 6, 1785 and died in Knox County, Ohio on Sept. 11, 1864. Source: Archive Record, Mormon Library, Salt Lake City, Utah.

Moreland, Bazil, was born in Hampshire County on Sept. 27, 1812 and died on Aug. 15, 1846. His wife, Margery Stump, was born on April 23, 1812. They were married on Nov. 27, 1834. Source: Mrs. Pansy S. Bennett, Hagerstown, MD.

Moreland, David, son of William and Eleanor Moreland of Dillon's Run, was killed by lightning on July 8, 1854 at Spring Gap. He was aged 38 years, 8 months and 28 days. According to Maud Pugh's record, David Moreland married Priscena Spaid (1823-1861), daughter of Frederick and Margaret (McVickers) Spaid. Source: Death record in Virginia State Archives, Richmond, Va.

Moreland, Evan, son of George H. and Sarah Moreland, was born on Dec. 14, 1821 and died on Oct. 13, 1913. He was buried at the Little Cacapon Primitive Baptist Graveyard, Hampshire County. His wife, Eleanor Moreland, was born on March 24, 1824 and died on May 8, 1890. She was buried in the "Shade Graveyard," located in a field, about 1 mile east of the P.B. Church. In same graveyard, buried with her: G.W. Moreland, born June 19, 1853 and died Sept. 8, 1860; B.E. Moreland, born April 30, 1856 and died Feb. 18, 1857. Source: Tombstone inscriptions.

Moreland, George, died Nov. 30, 1897. His mother was Rachel Moreland. Source: Cemetery inscription in Poor House Graveyard, Frederick County, Va.

Moreland, George W., was deceased by Sept. 12, 1851. His widow was named Sarah, daughter of Thomas and Abigail (Smith) Marple. These were his heirs: Levin Moreland; Mary Moreland (later married John J. Largent); George H. Moreland; James Moreland; Evan Moreland (married Eleanor Stump); Harrison Ullery; and Sarah Moreland. Source: *Order Book III,* page 8, Circuit Court, Hampshire County, W.Va.

Moreland, Mrs. Mary, wife of Newton Moreland, died in Hampshire County, W.Va. on July 9, 1876, aged 24 years, 4 months. Survivors included a widowed mother, a husband and infant child. Source: *South Branch Intelligencer*, July 21, 1876 issue.

Moreland, Mary, daughter of George and Sarah (Marple) Moreland, died Oct. 25, 1881, aged 53 years, 6 months, 15 days. Death was reported to Hampshire County courthouse by her husband, John J. Largent.

Moreland, Sarah Ellen, daughter of James William and Margaret J. (Martin) Moreland, was born on Nov. 17, 1859 and died in Hampshire County, W.Va. on Oct. 4, 1921. She married Benjamin Alexander "Alex" Kidwell, son of Samuel and Nancy (Largent) Kidwell, on March 25, 1880. Source: Mrs. Frank Perdew, R-6, Box 172, Bedford, PA. 15522

Moreland, William H., born on June 17, 1777 and died on Dec. 30, 1863. His wife, Eleanor, was born Sept. 17, 1786 and died on March 10, 1862. Source: Tombstone inscriptions at Capon Chapel, Hampshire County, W.Va.

Morgan, Col. Morgan, was born Nov. 1, 1688 and died Nov. 17, 1766. His wife was Catherine Garretson, born on May 16, 1692 and died May 16, 1773. He was one of the founding fathers of Old Frederick County. He lived on Mill Creek in present day Berkeley County, W.Va. Source: Tombstone inscriptions in Morgan Chapel Cemetery at Bunker Hill, W.Va.

Morgan, Zackquill, son of Morgan and Mary Morgan Jr., married Rachel Marpel, daughter of Enoch and Mary Marple, May 29, 1798. Source: *Morgan's Chapel Register, 1741-1838* (Norborne Parish), Bunker Hill, Berkeley County, Va.

Morris, Margaret, daughter of David and Mary (Slifer) Hefflebower, died on Sept. 4, 1852, aged 26 years, 2 months. Her husband was Pythagoras Morris, son of Joseph Morris. Buried next to her were two children: Mary F. Morris, died on Jan. 13, 1851, aged 4 months and 13 days; Josephine Morris, born and died on ___ 8, 1848. Source: Tombstone inscriptions in Carlyle cemetery, Capon Bridge, W.Va.

Mouser, Jacob, son of John Mouser, was born Nov. 3, 1763 in old Frederick County, Va. and died in Marion County, Va. in 1835. His wife, Eve Benner, was a daughter of John and May (Livingston) Benner. Eve was born on June 4, 1768 and died Oct. 3, 1831. Jacob and Eve were married on Nov. 10, 1789, in Frederick County, Va. by the Rev. Christian Streit.

Murphy Bible record: Benjamin Fowler Murphy, born April 26, 1783; Susan Murphy, born April 6, 1786; John Murphy, born Dec. 23, 1789; Rebecca Murphy, born Jan. 6, 1792; Barrick Murphy, born Jan. 5, 1794; Elizabeth Murphy, born Jan. 27, 1796; Martha Murphy, born July 24, 1798; Robert Murphy, born _____ 25, 1802; and Priscilla Murphy, born Feb. 24, 1804. The above names, presumed to be siblings, were found on a Family Record loose page. Names of parents were not given on that page. Also, included in same Bible record was: Jeremiah Read died Aug. 14, 1827. Was this Jeremiah Reid a son of Jeremiah Reid Sr., of Timber Ridge, or from one of the other Reid families living in that vicinity of old Frederick County, Va.? Source: Family record page in private hands.

Murphy, James, was born on Nov. 13, 1750 and died on March 21, 1799. He was buried on a farm about 3 miles from Green Spring, Hampshire County. Source: Tombstone inscription.

Murphy, Thomas, was born on Nov. 8, 1776 and died on March 7, 1857, on Timber Ridge. He was buried in the Trone Methodist Church Graveyard, several miles south of U.S. Route 50, located just inside the Frederick County, Va. line.

Muse, Robert (pioneer), born on March 25, 1769 and died on Jan. 16, 1846. His wife, Elizabeth Browne, was born on April 12, 1788 and died on Nov. 27, 1846. Numerous other members of the Muse family were buried here. See *Cemeteries of Hampshire County, West Virginia and Vicinity*: Volume 3, by Ralph L. Triplett Esq. Source: Tombstone inscriptions, Trone Methodist Church, Timber Ridge, Frederick County, Va.

Naylor, the Rev. James, son of William and Susan (McGuire) Naylor, was born on July 4, 1821 in Romney, W.Va. and died near Waterford, Mississippi, on Jan. 30, 1874. He went to Mississippi in 1861. He was twice-married. Source: *South Branch Intelligencer*, issue of March 20, 1874.

Nelson, Harry, son of Evan Atwell and Mary (Pugh) Nelson, was born on June 20, 1870 and died on Oct. 17, 1893. The footstone on his grave says "Brother." Next to him was buried his sister, Mollie E. Nelson, born on Aug. 2, 1872 and died on Jan. 1, 1892. According to Maud Pugh, the authoress, Evan A. Nelson was born in 1834 and died in 1890. After his death, Harry Horn Nelson, assumed his father's role, but lived only three years longer than his father. Harry's mother, Mary Pugh, was born in 1832 and died in 1899. Mary Pugh's parents were Jesse and Charity (Gard) Pugh, II. Mollie E. Nelson was a student at Fairmont College. The graves of Harry H. and Mollie E. Nelson are located high on a foothill of Cooper's Mountain, overlooking Edward's Run, in Parks' Valley. The closest path is about one-half mile from the graves. Ruins of an old house are nearby. The tombstone is unprotected, and was knocked down by cattle in 1986 or 1987. The property is now owned by Mrs. Margaret Moreland.

Nelson, James, born on Aug. 24, 1830 and died on died on May 21, 1882, aged 51 years, 8 months, 27 days. His wife, Susan J. Nelson, was born on Aug. 23, 1837 and died on Feb. 9, 1912. Other inscriptions on the same monument are: Charles L. Nelson, born June 21, 1869 and died on July 21, 1902, age 33 years and 1 month; Ollie M. Nelson, born on Sept. 3, 1875 and died on Oct. 20, 1875, 3 months, 17 days. Source: Tombstone inscriptions in Park's Graveyard, Parke's Valley, Hampshire County, W.Va.

Nelson, John, was born in 1742; died on May 2, 1797 in the Bloomery District of Hampshire County. This is a very old river stone, and one of the first burials in an old graveyard on land first owned by the Enoch family, then James Largent. I wonder whether there was a connection between the Largent and Nelson families, in that old John Largent named one of his sons Nelson Largent. Another very old stone, possibly older than John Nelson's, appears to say Robert (Nelson?), illegible. Source: Tombstone inscription in Powell's Graveyard, Forks of Capon.

Nesmith, Hiram Newton, son of Thomas and Barbara Nesmith, was born in 1803; died on July 12, 1874. He married Nancy Hoyle on Feb. 11, 1836 in Morgan County, Va. Source: Courthouse death record in Hampshire County, W.Va.

Nesmith, Joseph, wrote his Will on March 27, 1837 in Morgan County, Va. He named his wife Elizabeth. "Big" Jacob Miller was named executor. Please contact me, Wilmer L. Kerns, if you have information to share on the Nesmith family!

Nesmith, Joseph T., was born on July 5, 1821 and died Nov. 23, 1904. His wife, Mary, was born Aug. 6, 1821 and died June 27, 1909. Source: Tombstone inscriptions in Shanghai Presbyterian Church Cemetery, Berkeley County, W.Va.

Neville, General Joseph, was born in 1733/1734 in Gloucester County, Va. and died in Hardy County, Va. on March 4, 1819. He served in the Virginia House of Burgesses for Hampshire County, 1773-1776, and served in the U.S. Congress, 1793-1795; was a Brigadier General in the Virginia Militia. He married Nancy Brown, of Scotland. Source: His obituary was published in the *Winchester Gazette*, Winchester, Va. Also, *The Neville Family of England and the United States*, privately published by Mrs. John Hart Wilson, Wichita Falls, TX, in 1964.

Newman, John was born circa 1753 and died July 26, 1826, in Hampshire County, Va. He was a veteran of the Revolutionary War, serving in several Maryland regiments. In 1781, his residence was Middletown, Frederick County, Maryland. His first wife was named Hannah. After her death, John remarried to Elizabeth (Stump) Moore, widow of Henry Moore. They had four children, born between 1812 and 1823. Source: Tombstone inscriptions in Stump–Noland graveyard, Little Cacapon, Hampshire County, W.Va., and Revolutionary War pension record. The relationship between John and the numerous Newman families of Hampshire County has not been established at this time. Contact: Don and Carol Newman, 5135 Kirby Road, Cincinnati, OH 45223.

Nixon, George Sr., son of James and Sarah (Edwards) Nixon, was born March 27, 1687, in Ireland. He married Mary Janney, daughter of Joel Janney, June 1, 1727. Three children were born to the union: (1) John Nixon was born March 23, 1728 (2) Jonathan Nixon, born May 4, 1729 and died in May 1791, in Virginia. Allegedly he came to America with his brothers George Nixon II and John Nixon. (3) George Nixon II was born Feb. 25, 1730. He married Mary Combs, daughter of Jonah Combs, of Clogh, County Antrim, March 8, 1750. Children of George and Mary (Combs) Nixon II were: (a) Jonah Nixon was born Dec. 28, 1750 (b) George Nixon III was born Sept. 30, 1751. (c) John Nixon. This Nixon family is possibly related to the Nixons in old Frederick County, Va., but I have not been able to identify or to establish a connection. Nixon researchers should consult Grace Kelso Garner, *Earliest Settlers Western Frederick-Eastern Hampshire*, privately printed in 1978. Source: Correspondent sent information, citing two articles which appeared in *The*

Baltimore Sun (Maryland), Nov. 24, 1907 issue, page 17. Compiler of the Nixon information was Emily Emerson Lantz.

Nixon ("child of George Nixon"), died on Feb. 1, 1862 at Capon Bridge, Hampshire County. Source: Coffin-book of William Meade Edwards (mortician).

Nixon, William, died on Feb. 19, 1869, at an advanced age. He served on the Hampshire County Court and the Virginia State Legislature, according to the **South Branch Intelligencer**, March 12, 1869 issue. His wife, Mary Ann Caudy, died on Jan. 9, 1867, aged 71 years, at Capon Bridge, W.Va., according to the Feb. 1, 1867 issue of the **South Branch Intelligencer**. They were buried at Capon Chapel.

Noel, Mary M., died on Feb. 12, 1890, aged 50 years and 10 days. She married J.G. Noel. "Dearest mother." Source: Tombstone inscription, Buckwalter cemetery, Bloomery, W.Va.

Noland, Elisha, son of Pierce and Mary (Powell) Noland, was born on Aug. 1, 1815 and died on Aug. 1, 1882. Jane (Stump) Noland, his wife, was born on March 23, 1814 and died on Jan. 30, 1875. A daughter named M.E. Noland was born on Jan. 9, 1845 and died on Sept. 13, 1864. All three of these inscriptions are on one monument in the Pierce Noland cemetery on top of Spring Gap Mountain.

Noland, Pierce, son of Charles and Elizabeth Noland, was born in Fairfax County, Va. on July 5, 1777 and died on Jan. 4, 1853, of "paralysis" at his home on Spring Gap Mountain, Hampshire County, Va. Buried in family graveyard on homeplace, but marked grave has not survived. Source: Death record in Virginia State Archives.

Oates, Christopher, son of Jacob and Catherine (Harmon) Oates, was born in Thurmont, MD. on April 21, 1783 and died in Hampshire County after 1850. The church record gives his name as Johan Christian, but he was commonly known as Christopher Oates. It is believed that his wife was named Mary; that he remarried to Nancy Simpson; and that some of his descendants live in Hardy County, W.Va.

Oates, Christopher, was born in 1818 and died in March 1888 in the Capon District, and was buried there. Source: Courthouse record.

Oates, Daniel, son of Jacob and Catherine (Harmon) Oates, was born at Thurmont, MD. on April 12, 1790 and probably died in Hampshire County, W.Va., circa 1861. His wife was named Mary _____, probably a native of Timber Ridge. Their children were: (1) Jonathan Oates was born on May 27, 1813 and married Eve Shanholtzer, daughter of Peter and Magdalena Shanholtzer, II. According to an 1837 letter, Jonathan and Eve were living in Jennings County, Indiana. (2) Peter Oates was born on June 9, 1814 and died on Feb. 9, 1863. (3) Lucinda Oates was born on Jan. 28, 1815 and died on Dec. 18, 1883 in Hampshire County, W.Va. She married Joseph Abrell, son of Joseph and Margaret (Reid) Abrell. (4) Jacob Oates was born on July 17, 1816 and married twice: Rebecca Myers and Elizabeth Messick. [see separate entry] (5) Elizabeth Oates was born on Feb. 8, 1817 and died on March 5, 1898. She married Washington Whitacre. (6) Lorenzo Oates was born on Nov. 18, 1818 and died on Aug. 3, 1901. He married: (a) Sarah Grove and (b) Mary C. Harper. (7) Barbara Oates was born in Aug. 1821. ((8) Hiram Oates was born on Jan. 10, 1823 and died on March 23, 1901. He married Delilah Kerns, daughter of Nathan Kerns. [see additional entry] (9) Mahala Oates was born on April 22, 1825 and died in 1877. She married James M. Lockhart. [see separate entry]   (10) Drusy "Druscilla" Jane Oates was born on Sept. 8, 1827 and died on Aug. 27, 1898, in Berkeley County, W.Va. She married William H. Abrell, son of John Abrell. (11) Mary Oates was born on Sept. 8, 1830 in Hampshire County. On April 9, 1855, she became the second wife of Enoch Whitacre, son of George and Rachel (Tumbleston) Whitacre. (12) Sylvester Oates was born on March 10, 1832. He married Levinia Whitacre, daughter of Wilson and Rachel (Kerns) Whitacre. (13) Sarah Ellen Oates was born on Feb. 28, 1834. On Oct. 17, 1854, she was married to Mahlon Kerns, son of Nathan and Sarah (Whitacre) Kerns. (14) George Oates was born in 1837 and immigrated to Peoria, Illinois at a relatively young age.

Oates, Elizabeth, daughter of Christopher and Ellen (Noel) Slonaker, was born on Aug. 16, 1788 in Frederick County, Va. and died on July 16, 1854 at her home on Timber Ridge, Hampshire County, Va. Her husband was Jacob Oates, Jr., son of Jacob and Catherine (Harmon) Oates Sr. Source: Death record in Virginia State Archives.

Oates, Elizabeth, daughter of John and Mary (Kerns) Oates, died on Dec. 5, 1883, aged 68 years, 8 months and 26 days. Her husband was Jacob Sirbaugh and they lived in the Cold Stream area of Hampshire County. Source: Courthouse and family records.

Oates, Elizabeth, daughter of Jacob and Catherine (Harmon) Oates, was born in 1790 at Thurmont, Maryland, according to a church record (Apple Church). She married John Carlyle, in Hampshire County, Va. See the deeds in the Hampshire County courthouse which settled the real estate of her father, Jacob Oates, such as Deed Book 30, pages 466-467, dated Feb. 1, 1835. [Comment: Something is wrong. Please see page 25, entry of John Carlyle. More research needed on this!]

Oates, Emily Jane, daughter of Christopher Oates, was born on April 17, 1829 and died on Sept. 29,1910, at Augusta, W.Va. She married Isaac Shanholtz, son of John and Eve (Hott) Shanholtz, on March 27, 1845 in Cumberland, MD. They resided near Augusta, W.Va. Source: Family records given to me.

Oates, George, Sr., was born at Thurmont, Frederick County, MD on March 25, 1786 and died in 1844 in the Parks Hollow section of Hampshire County. His wife was Catherine Slonaker, daughter of Christopher and Mary Ellen (Noel) Slonaker.

Oates, George, Jr., died on Feb. 11, 1889, aged 81 years. This courthouse death record was created by George A. Lupton, a nephew. However, family records show his birth as being on Dec. 22, 1809 and died on Jan. 12, 1890 in Hampshire County. He lived on the "old Foreman place" mentioned in father's will. His parents were George and Catherine (Slonaker) Oates Sr. George, Oates, Jr. married Mary Furr, born on Feb. 13, 1819 and died on Jan. 14, 1899. Sources: Too numerous to mention.

Oates, Harmon, son of John and Mary (Kerns) Oates was born on Oct. 7, 1816 and died on Feb. 11, 1874 in Hampshire County. He lived on the county line. Harmon married: (1) Ruth Kerns, daughter of Nathan and Sarah (Whitacre) Kerns Sr., on Jan. 31, 1837 and (2) Sarah E. Mauzy, daughter of Peter and Susannah (Powell) Mauzy. Source: Courthouse records.

Oates, Hiram, son of Daniel and Mary Oates of Hampshire County, Va. (now W.Va.), was born on Jan. 10, 1823 and died on March 23, 1901 in Hardin County, Ohio. He married Delilah Kerns, daughter of Nathan and Elizabeth (Parrish) Kerns, on Nov. 25, 1845. Delilah was born on April 11, 1825, in Frederick County, Va. According to an old handwritten record, Nathan Kerns was born in Frederick County, Va. on Feb. 3, 1801 and died on July 11, 1872. His wife, Elizabeth Parrish, was born on Dec. 4, 1803 and died on May 4, 1865, the place of death not stated. Source: Mrs. Norma Jean Cook, 15099 CR 155, Kenton, Ohio 43326.

Oates, Jacob, was born in 1757 and died in 1831 in Hampshire County, Va. His name was Hawver (German) prior to 1800. Jacob married Catherine Harmon in Frederick County, MD or possibly in Pennsylvania. Source: Extensive research by W.L. Kerns and Dan P. Oates, including the Apple Church records in Thurmont, MD. and an estate settlement in Hampshire County, Va. [Comment: A history of the Oates family is being compiled by Dan P. Oates, 206 East Main Street, Romney, W.Va. 26757. You are urged to contact him if you have any interest in this project. He is collecting information on all Oates descendants.]

Oates, Jacob Jr., son of Jacob and Catherine (Harmon) Oates Sr., died in Hampshire County on Feb. 21, 1876, aged 92 years, *South Branch Intelligencer*, March 17, 1876 issue of newspaper. He died at the home of his son Daniel Oates. He was born near Thurmont, Maryland, in 1784. Jacob married Elizabeth Slonaker, daughter of Christopher Slonaker. She was born on Aug. 16, 1788 and died in Hampshire County, on July 16, 1854, according to death record in the Virginia State Archives.

Oates, Jacob, son of Daniel and Mary Oates, was born on July 17, 1816 and died on Aug. 4, 1878. He married: (1) Rebecca Myers on Jan. 15, 1839. She was born on Aug. 5, 1822 and died on Sept. 14, 1842. (2) Elizabeth (Swartz) Messick on Sept. 5, 1844. She was born on Oct. 15, 1814 in Rockingham County, Va. and died on June 22, 1906. Source: Dan P. Oates of Romney, W.Va.

Oates, John, son of Jacob and Catherine (Harmon) Oates, Sr., was born in Frederick County, MD on Jan. 17, 1788 and died in Frederick County, Va. circa 1823-24. He married Mary Kerns, daughter of George and Elizabeth (Reid) Kerns, Sr., on April 2, 1814. Mary was born on March 14, 1794 and remarried to Asa Rosenberger, in 1828. Sources: Kerns Bible record; church record, and courthouse record.

Oates, Lanor, daughter of Capt. Sampson Oates of Mineral County, died on Feb. 22, 1874 in Mineral County. Source: March 6, 1874 issue of the *South Branch Intelligencer*, Romney, W.Va.

Oates, Lorenzo, son of Daniel and Mary Oates, was born on Nov. 18, 1818 and died on Aug. 3, 1901 in Frederick County, Va. He married: (1) Sarah Grove on Jan. 11, and (2) Mary C. Harper on April 9, 1863.

Oates, Lucinda, daughter of Daniel and Mary Oates, was born on Jan. 28, 1815 and died on Dec. 18, 1883 in Hampshire County. She married Joseph Abrell, Jr., son of Joseph and Margaret (Reid) Abrell. Sources: Bible record and courthouse death record.

Oates, Mahala, daughter of Daniel and Mary Oates, of Timber Ridge (Frederick and Hampshire Counties, Va..), was born on April 22, 1825, according to a copy of information taken from a Bible record. According to another descendant [Ann Gregath, publisher of the first printing of this book], Mahala Oates died in Webster County, Nebraska during the summer of 1877. Mahala married James Madison Lockhart, son of Josiah and Elizabeth (Triplett) Lockhart, on Feb. 8, 1848. He was born on Oct. 21, 1828 in Frederick County, Va. and died in 1920 at Wardensville, W.Va.

Oates, Mary, was born in Hampshire County, Va. on Feb. 25, 1813 and died on April 22, 1877, in Indianola, Vermillion County, Illinois. Her husband, Charles E. Rinehart, was born in Martinsburg, Va. (Berkeley County) on Feb. 15, 1813 and died on Nov. 21, 1886. Charles was a son of David and Barbara (Ohlinger) Rinehart. Both were buried in the Woodlawn Cemetery at Indianola. They were married On June 4, 1840, in Frederick County, Va., by the Rev. Christy Sine. In 1862, they emigrated from Hampshire County to Randolph County, Indiana. Source: Mr. Roy E. Sheppard, Mattoon, Illinois 61938.

Oates, Mary. died on Jan. 13, 1899, aged 83 years. She was buried in the "family burying ground" in the Capon District of Hampshire County, according to Courthouse death record. It is believed that Mary was nee Furr, and that her husband was George Oates, Jr.

Oates (daughter of Michael Oates), died on March 7, 1862, at Capon Bridge, Hampshire County. Source: Coffin-book of William Meade Edwards (mortician).

Oates, Michael, sixth child of George and Catherine (Slonaker) Oates, was born in Hampshire County, Va. in 1825 and died at Clarksdale, llinois, in 1910. His second wife, Harriet Shivers, was born in 1848 and died in 1912. Source: Wanda Lucas, Pana, IL 62557.

Oates, Mrs. Susan, wife of Sampson Oates, died in Mineral County, W.Va. on Feb. 8, 1875. Their daughter, Lanor Oates, died on Feb. 22, 1874, in Mineral County. Source: *South Branch Intelligencer* newspaper, Romney, W.Va.

Oates, Samuel, son of John and Mary (Kerns) Oates, was born on March 15, 1822 and died on June 1, 1891. He married Sarah Jane Noel, born on July 8, 1833 and died on Jan. 19, 1913. Source: Mrs. Kathleen Fletcher, 6332 West Morraine Place, Littleton, CO 80123.

Offutt, Mrs. Elizabeth (nee Roberts), widow of Solomon W. Offutt, died on Sept. 13, 1870, aged 84 years ("in her 85th year"), at Slanesville, W.Va. She was born in Montgomery County, Maryland. Her husband, Solomon Offutt, was a son of Nathaniel and Elizabeth (Owen) Offutt, was born in 1776 in Montgomery County, Maryland and died at Slanesville, Va. on Feb. 7, 1848. They were married on April 6, 1804. Source: Sept. 30, 1870 issue of the *South Branch Intelligencer*; Maud Pugh's *Capon Valley: It's Pioneers and Their Descendants,* Records in the DAR Library; and tombstone inscriptions in the Offutt graveyard, Slanesville, W.Va.   ·

Offutt, Dr. John James Thornton, son of Nathaniel and Margaret Ellen (Frazier) Offutt, was born in 1826 and died on July 21, 1886. His wife was Sarah C. Nixon, daughter of William C. and Mary Ann (Caudy) Nixon. Sarah was born on Nov. 16, 1827, in Hampshire County, and died on Aug. 5, 1882. She was buried in the Capon Chapel cemetery. Source: Records in DAR Grandfather Papers, 1776 D St., Wash. D.C.

Offutt, Nathaniel, son of Samuel Owen and Elizabeth (Hite) Offutt, was born on Nov. 18, 1792 and died in 1861. His wife was Margaret Ellen Frazier. They were ancestors of numerous Hampshire County families.

Offutt, Owen O., son of Solomon and Elizabeth (Roberts) Offutt, was born on April 5, 1807 and died on April 31, 1848.

Source: Tombstone inscription in Offutt family graveyard, near Slanesville, Hampshire County, W.Va.

Offutt, Samuel Owen, son of Nathaniel and Elizabeth (Owen) Offutt, was born in Frederick County, Maryland on Oct. 18, 1760 and died on Jan. 3, 1829, in Charles Town, Va.   His wife, Elizabeth Hite, was born on Jan. 13, 1765 and died on April 4, 1845.   Source: Maud Pugh's *Capon Valley: Its Pioneers and Their Descendants*, and DAR records (NSDAR).

Offutt, Sarah (nee Snapp), daughter of John and Hannah (Milleson) Snapp and wife of Thornton W. Offutt, was born May 31, 1832 and died on Dec. 4, 1871. Thornton Washington Offutt was born on April 25, 1830 and died on May 12, 1907. His tombstone inscription says, "For 35 years deprived of his earthly companion Lonely, but never alone I'll never forsake thee Nor leave thee alone." Source: The *South Branch Intelligencer* (Sarah's obituary), in the Dec. 15, 1871 paper, and tombstone inscriptions in the Offutt graveyard, near Slanesville, W.Va.

Offutt, Zephaniah, son of Solomon and Elizabeth (Roberts) Offutt, was born on Oct. 20, 1821 and died on April 9, 1848. His wife was Eliza Jane Haines, daughter of Daniel and Elizabeth Haines. She was born on Nov. 10, 1820 and died on Aug. 30, 1891. She remarried to John H. Daugherty. Source: Tombstone inscriptions in the Offutt graveyard, near Slanesville, West Virginia.

Omps: See page 71-72 for graveyard data on this surname.

Omps, Richard Lafayette (1864-1943) married Phena Catherine Dick and their children were: Myrta Izetta Omps, born on April 3, 1888; Luella Omps, born March 5, 1889; Calvin E. Omps, born on Jan. 14, 1892; Letha M. Omps, born on Sept. 7, 1893; Lena F.Omps, born on July 18, 1895; Ora Ethel Omps, born on Feb. 8, 1897; Clarence E. Omps, born on Feb. 18, 1900; Delma C. Omps, born on March 5, 1902; Richard A. Omps, born on March 10, 1904; Ervil J. Omps, born on March 5, 1905; Lewis R. Omps, born on Nov. 14, 1907; Harry K. Omps, born on Nov. 14, 1907; and Katye B. Omps, born on Jan. 19, 1910. Source: Bible record in possession of Mrs. Kila (Hottle) Merica, who lives on the Omps homeplace in Frederick County, Va.

Orndorf, David, died in Capon Valley on June 12, 1855. He was an adult. His funeral arrangements were made by Isaac

Lockmiller. Source: William Meade Edwards' *Undertaker Book* (called *Coffin Book*).

Orndorff, Ellen, was born circa 1791, and died in February 1860. Her maiden name was Young. She was paralyzed for 725 days prior to her death. Ellen married Levi Orndorff, who survived her. Born in Virginia. Source: 1860 Mortality Schedule for Frederick County, Va.

Orndorff, James, died in Hampshire County on Aug. 28, 1872, aged 66 years. Source: *South Branch Intelligencer.*

Orndorff, John Jr., son of John and Elizabeth (Mentz) Orndorff, was born in Pennsylvania, circa 1755, and died in 1830 in Frederick County, Va. He married Margaret Renner, daughter of George Renner, on June 5, 1792. Margaret was born in Pennsylvania in 1763 and died in Frederick County, in February 1850, aged 87 years. She was ill for six days prior to her death, according to the 1850 Mortality Schedule for Frederick County, Va. Their children were: (1) John Orndorff III was born Nov. 19, 1791. He married Elizabeth Margaret Pitcock, March 13, 1812. (2) Mary Orndorff was born Aug. 10, 1794 and died Sept. 13, 1867. She married Benjamin Kackley, July 3, 1818. They lived at North Mountain, Frederick County. (3) Isaac Orndorff was born Aug. 8, 1796, and he married Margaret Lee, April 19, 1842. They were buried at St. John's Lutheran Church. (4) Rachel Orndorff was born Sept. 17, 1798, and she married Felix Good II, Dec. 14, 1820. (5) William Orndorff was born Oct. 20, 1800 and died Jan. 15, 1885. He married Salome Wisecarver, who was born on June 16, 1808. (6) Sarah Orndorff was born on Dec. 25, 1806. She married Joseph Clouser. Source: Records of the late Ralph L. Triplett, Esq., Gore, Va.

Orndorff, Margaret, widow of Joseph Orndorff, aged 59 years "died last Sunday in Springfield." They were married on Jan. 13, 1823 in Frederick County, Va. Source: Jan. 26, 1872 issue of the *South Branch Intelligencer*, Romney, W.Va.

Orndorff, Mary, died in Shenandoah County, Va. in January 1870, aged 48 years, "of a tumor." Survived by spouse. Born in Virginia. Source: 1870 Mortality Schedule for Shenandoah County, Va.

Orr, Anthony, was deceased before April 1836. He lived in the North River Mills section of Hampshire County. According to

Order Book, page 273, in the Circuit Court of Hampshire County, his children were: (1) Catherine Orr married William Edwards, (2) Elizabeth Orr married James Hawkins, (3) Charlotte married Peter Shanholtzer, Jr., (4) Mary Orr married William Hawkins, (5) Daniel Orr, (6) Sarah Orr, and (7) Christopher Orr.

Orr, Charlotte, daughter of Anthony Orr, was born in 1797 and died in April 1851 near Cold Stream. She was the second wife of Peter Shanholtzer, Jr. Source: Letter written by Samuel Foreman, in 1851.

Osman, Jabez, son of Charles and Kezziah (Higgins) Osman, was born in Hampshire County, Va. in 1788 and died in Davies County, Indiana in Aug. 1849. He married Mary "Polly" Baker in Adams County, Ohio on Nov. 17, 1810. The purpose of this entry is to solicit information on the Osman family. Contact Mrs. Ethel F. Chambers, 150 Forest Avenue, Seaman, Ohio 45679. She is researching also the Chrisman, Martin, DeMoss, Larue, Morgan, Higgins, Marquis, Flora, and Biggerstaff families of this area.

Owens, William, son of William and Judah Owens, was born in Frederick County, Va. in 1750 and died in 1836 in Pulaski County, KY. He married Nancy Owens, daughter of Vincent and Winifred (LeHew) Owens, on Sept. 20, 1773. She was born on March 15, 1754 in Frederick County, Va. and died in 1840 at Somerset, KY. Source: Revolutionary War record. A Bible record of their 13 children is included in the pension folder.

Page, Emily, died in July 1859, aged 70 years. Cause of death: consumption. Ill for about 15 years. Survived by spouse. Born in Virginia. Source: 1860 Mortality Schedule for Frederick County, Va.

Painter, Barbara died in November 1869, in Shenandoah County, Va., aged 81 years. Born in Virginia. Source: 1870 Mortality Census for Shenandoah County, Va.

Painter, Philip, died in June 1860, aged 73 years. Farmer. Survived by spouse. "Sudden death" of unknown cause. Source: 1860 Mortality Schedule for Shenandoah County, Va.

Pangle, Jacob, died in Frederick County, Va. in March 1870, aged 84 years, "of old age." Born in Virginia. Farmer. Survived by spouse. Source: 1870 Mortality Schedule for Frederick County, Va.

Park, Allen was born before 1745 and died before Dec. 2, 1805, in Madison County, KY. He married Elizabeth Giles. This Allen Park was mentioned in the early records of Hampshire County, Va. (Fairfax records in Virginia State Archives) He later lived in Rowan Co., N.C. between 1767 and 1795. Source: Mrs. Warren R. Park, P.O. Box 525, Chandler, OK 74834.

Park(e), Amos, son of Andrew and Rachel Parke, was born on June 10, 1758 and died on July 27, 1827, in Licking County, Ohio. He married Susannah Miller, daughter of Isaac Miller, in Hampshire County, Va., in 1790. She was born in 1770 and died on March 20, 1839. Source: Letter from Mrs. Dorothy Becker, (formerly of) 4901 Bryce Ave., Fort Worth, TX 76107. [Note: see next entry]

Park, Amos, was born in 1770, and married Susannah _____. According to a Bible record, circa 1835, referenced as "the Earnheart version," the children of Amos and Susannah Parke were: (1) Elizabeth Parke was born Jan. 5, 1796. (2) Amos Parke II was born Aug. 28, 1797. (3) Rebecca Parke was born Sept. 19, 1798. (4) Phebe Parke was born May 7, 1800. (5) Freida Parke was born Dec. 31, 1801. (6) Mary Parke was born Dec. 17, 1803. (7) John Parke was born Nov. 13, 1805. (8) Amy Parke was born Jan. 28, 1808. (9) Isaac Parke was born Nov. 8, 1809. (10) Wesley Parke was born Nov. 11, 1811. Comment: See Dorothy Becker's book on the Parke family for a comparison of names. It is believed that this entry contains a reliable list of children in Amos Parke's family unit; that Becker's list was developed from miscellaneous records and circumstantial evidence. Contact: Bruce Earnheart, 1075 South Jefferson Street, #205, Arlington, Va. 22204.

Park, Amos, son of Samuel and Nancy A. (Edwards) Parks, was born in Hampshire County, Va., on June 4, 1794 and died on Dec. 23, 1825, in Ohio. He married Sarah Horn on June 12, 1815. They immigrated to Licking County, Ohio right after their marriage. She was born on Oct. 7, 1794 and died on April 8, 1869, in Illinois. Sarah remarried to Aaron Duckworth. Source: Bible record maintained by Mrs. James Parks, Ventura, CA.

Park(E), Andrew, was born on Nov. 11, 1709 and died on March 18, 1790, in Hampshire County, Va. Rachel, who was possibly nee Mosley, was born on Oct. 26, 1723. Source: Letter to compiler from Mrs. Dorothy Becker, Ft. Worth, Texas.

Park, Anna, daughter of Jacob Parks, was born on Feb. 4, 1817 and died on Jan. 22, 1899, according to death record in Hampshire County court house. She was the second wife of Samuel Sutton Hiett, son of Joseph and Alice (Sutton) Hiett.

Park, Catherine, wife of George Park, died on March 27, 1871, aged 26 years. Her parents were Amos and Catherine Poland. Source: Hampshire County courthouse record.

Park, Enoch, died in Aug. 1859, aged 65 years, "of bronchitis" He was a farmer. It is believed that he was a son of John and Mary (Millslagle) Park, and that his wife was named Margaret Ruckman. Source: 1860 Mortality Schedule of U.S. Census, Hampshire County, Va.

Park, Col. George, died on July 28, 1842, aged about 80 years. His wife, Hannah Millslagle, died on Dec. 19, 1859, aged 86 years, according to tombstone inscriptions in Park's Graveyard in Parke's Valley, Hampshire County, W.Va. (Note: The Mortality Schedule of the U.S. Census lists a Hannah Park, born in 1773 and died in Dec. 1859, "of dropsy." She was born in Virginia.) According to *Order Book II*, page 373, Circuit Court, Hampshire County, Va., the proven children of George and Hannah Park were: (1) George Park, Jr. (1806-1875), (2) John Park, (3) William Park married Susan Brill, (4) Elizabeth Park married James Thompson, (5) Mary "Polly" Park married a Mr. Price, (6) Philena Park, (7) Susan Park married Washington Stuart, and (8) Sarah "Sally" Park married Samuel Hiett.

Park, George, son of Col. George Park, died on Feb. 9, 1875 in Hampshire County, aged 69 years. according to the *South Branch Intelligencer*, March 12, 1875 issue. His handcarved tombstone, in the family graveyard in Parke's Valley, Hampshire County, shows a birthdate of Oct. 16, 1806 and deathdate of Feb. 9, 1875.

Park, John and Suzanna Elrod (no dates given), and the grave of Solomon Parke (no dates). Source: Park's Graveyard, Parke's Valley, Hampshire County, Virginia.

Park, John, son of Samuel and Nancy A. (Edwards) Park, was born in Hampshire County, Va. on Feb. 16, 1786. He married

Margaret McBride in 1809. It is believed that he moved to Ohio soon after his marriage.

Park, Philemia, died on April 3, 1870, aged 76 years, 2 months, ___ days (inscription is difficult to read). Source: Tombstone inscription in Park's Graveyard, Parke's Valley, Hampshire County.

Park, Rebecca, died in Hampshire County on Oct. 11, 1872, aged 47 years. Source: The Oct. 11, 1872 issue of the *South Branch Intelligencer*, Romney, W.Va.

Park, Rhoda Ann, wife of James M. Combs, was born Oct. 29, 1857 and died April 16, 1928. James M. Combs was born April 16, 1857 and died Oct. 24, 1934. Source: Tombstone inscriptions in Mountain Dale cemetery, Hampshire County, W.Va.

Park(es), Samuel, son of Andrew and Rachel Parks, was born in "Hampshire County," Va. on March 14, 1754 and died on Feb. 18, 1815. He married two daughters of Thomas and Mary (Hiett) Edwards: (1) Hannah Edwards on April 18, 1775. She died on Oct. 7, 1784. (2) Nancy A. Edwards, who died on Oct. 14, 1829 in Licking County, Ohio. Source: Mrs. Robert D. Hughes, 1970 Grape Avenue, Boulder, CO 80302.

Parke, William, son of George and Hannah (Millslagle) Parke, was born on Nov. 14, 1810 and died on Feb. 18, 1904. On the same stone; Susan A. Parke [nee Brill, daughter of John and Cinderella (Cooper) Brill], born Nov. 14, 1841 and died Oct. 18, 1921. Source: Tombstone inscription in Park's Graveyard, Parke's Valley, Hampshire County, W.Va.

Parker, Sarah, was born in 1782 and died in May 1859, "of dropsy." Source: 1860 Mortality Schedule for Hampshire County, Va.

Parrish, William, was born in 1797 and died on Jan. 21, 1883. His wife was Margaret Slonaker, daughter of Christopher Slonaker. She was born in 1797 and died on Nov. 15, 1872. They lived on Timber Ridge, Frederick County, Virginia, just north of U.S. Route 50. A post office called Parrishville was once located there.

Parsons, James, was born on July 8, 1773 in Hampshire County and died on Jan. 25, 1847. His wife, Catherine Casey, daughter of Nicholas and Grace (Foreman) Casey, was born on

Oct. 3, 1776 and died on June 2, 1846. They were married on March 6, 1795. Source: Records in DAR application.

Paskel, George B., aged 80 years, died "Monday of last week" at the home of his son-in-law, Dr. E.W. Canfield, at Paw Paw, West Virginia.   Source: Oct. 8, 1880 issue of the *South Branch Intelligencer*.

Paskel, Madison H., was born on March 21, 1816, and died in 1860. He was an illegitimate son of Ruth Mahew. His wife, Sarah, was born in 1815 and died in 1896. Buried in private graveyard near Cross Junction, Frederick County, Virginia.

Patterson, Mrs. Annie (nee Mullins), 81, wife of Alexander Patterson, died on June 4, 1871 on Little Cacapon in Hampshire County. Source: The *South Branch Intelligencer*.

Patterson, Elizabeth (nee Abernathy) was born on Nov. 1, 1780 and died on July 4, 1864. Buried in plot with Jacob and Jane (Patterson) Daily, and the inscription says "our grandmother." Source: Tombstone inscription, Springfield, W.Va.

Patterson, John, Sr., died on July 14, 1828, in his 49th year. Mary, his wife, was born on May 11, 1783 and died on July 7, 1828. Alexander Patterson, son of John and Mary Patterson, was born and died in 1818. Source: Tombstone inscriptions in private graveyard on farm owned by Earl Combs, Hickory Corner Road, Augusta, W.Va.

Patterson, John, Jr., son of John and Mary Patterson, died on July 3, 1899, aged 87 years, 6 months, and 28 days. His wife, Margaret Smith, died on Oct. 2, 1920, aged 92 years, 1 month, and 28 days. William Patterson was buried nearby, no inscription nor stated relationship.   Source: Tombstone inscriptions in Patterson private graveyard, now on property owned by Earl Combs, Hickory Corner Road, Augusta, W.Va.

Patterson, Mrs. John (nee Nancy Offutt), daughter of Solomon Offutt, died on Jan. 2, 1872, aged 68 years. She was twice-married: (1) Jonathan Pugh III and (2) John Patterson. She was stricken by paralysis in 1870. Source: The *South Branch Intelligencer*.

Patterson, Robert, son of James and Jane Patterson, was born in Hampshire County on March 5, 1790 and died in same county on Dec. 21, 1876. Source: Courthouse death record, Romney, W.Va.

Patterson, Thomas, died on April 30, 1851, aged 50 years, 11 months, 8 days. Source: Tombstone inscriptions in graveyard at Three Churches, Hampshire County, W.Va.

Payne, Sarah, died in February 1870, aged 88 years. Born in Pennsylvania.   Source: 1870 Mortality Schedule for Frederick County, Va.

Peacemaker, Barbary, born on Feb. 9, 1824 and died July 22, 1893. Source: Tombstone inscription in Buckwalter cemetery.

Peacemaker, David, was born on Aug. 10, 1789 and died on April 6, 1850. Source: Tombstone inscription in Buckwalter cemetery.

Peacemaker, Delilah, wife of Adam Peacemaker, died on May 28, 1882, in Frederick County, Va., according to a death record in the county courthouse in Winchester. The old Adam Peacemaker graveyard was destroyed by a road being widened at the corner of Sleepy Creek Road and Virginia State Route 127 (near Timber Ridge).   Delilah was a daughter of Jacob and Rachel (Cowgill) Kerns Jr.

Peacemaker, Elizabeth, born on May 15, 1815 and died on Feb. 5, 1892. Source: Tombstone inscription in Buckwalter cemetery.

Peacemaker, Elizabeth, daughter of Richard and Hannah Johnson, was born on Oct. 31, 1838 in Licking County, Ohio. She died in Hampshire County on Nov. 29, 1922.   It is believed that she married Adam Peacemaker.   Offutt Peacemaker (a son?) reported her death to the county courthouse.

Peacemaker, George, died on April 30, 1889, aged 68 years, 6 months, and 23 days. Source: Tombstone inscription in Buckwalter cemetery.

Peacemaker, Jacob, was born on July 3, 1794 and died on July 9, 1871. His parents were John and Catherine Peacemaker. Source: Tombstone inscription in Buckwalter cemetery.

Peacemaker, Jacob, born on Jan. 10, 1822 and died on Oct. 19, 1896. Source: Tombstone inscription, Buckwalter cemetery.

Peacemaker, Margaret (nee Smith), wife of Jacob Peacemaker, was born on Dec. 9, 1797 and died on March 30, 1875. Source: Tombstone inscription in Buckwalter cemetery.

Peacemaker, Mary E., daughter of Conrad Smith, died on Nov. 22, 1881 at the age of 88 years, 10 months, 3 days. She was born in Pennsylvania. She married David Peacemaker. Source: Tombstone inscription, Buckwalter cemetery, Bloomery District, and courthouse death record.

Peacemaker, Philip, son of John and Mary Ann Peacemaker, was born in 1800 and died on Jan. 8, 1860 at Cold Stream, Hampshire County. The coffin was ordered by Jacob Cooper. Source: Coffin-book of William Meade Edwards.

Peacemaker, Simeon, died on Feb. 3, 1900, aged 67 years, 8 months and 6 days. Next to him was buried Catherine Peacemaker, born on Nov. 24, 1818 and died March 4, 1899. The *Diary of George Edwards* said, "Simon Peacemaker was found dead in his bed on Feb. 3, 1900 and was buried Feb. 5." Source: Tombstone inscription, Buckwalter cemetery, Hampshire County, W.Va. and diary.

Pearsall, Job, son of John Pearsall was born circa 1705, in Chester County, PA., and died at Patterson's Creek, Hampshire County, Va., in 1770. He first settled at the site of what later became Romney, W.Va.; built a fort during French and Indian War; then moved to Patterson's Creek during later years. Job married Bithia Bull, daughter of Thomas Bull, of Chester County. Their children were: (1) John Pearsall married Hannah Lyons. (2) Benjamin Pearsall married Rebecca Ann Babb, daughter of Peter Babb. (3) Eleanor Pearsall married Daniel Hall (or HALE). (4) Rachel Pearsall married a Mr. Berkeley of Stafford County, Va. (according to one biographer of the Pearsall family). (5) Margaret Pearsall married Richard Jackson. (6) James Pearsall was killed in the Revolutionary War, serving in 4th Virginia Regiment. (7) Richard Pearsall was born circa 1741. He moved to Washington County, PA, and then to Green County, KY.

Peasmaker, Michael, died on "The Branch" on April 14, 1876, in Hampshire County. Source: The April 21, 1876 issue of the *South Branch Intelligencer*.

Peasmaker, William, was born on Sept. 7, 1823 and died on Dec. 23, 1902. Rebecca, his wife, was born on June 24, 1827 and died on Sept. 8, 1899. It is believed that they came from Hampshire County, W.Va. Source: Tombstone inscription in Miller Cemetery in Clinton County, Ohio, and obituary in The Clinton Republican.

Peacemaker, William W., died in Hampshire County, W.Va. in 1878. William Meade Edwards made his coffin for $15.00. W.W. married Mary E. Bageant, widow of James Bageant, on Aug. 16, 1872. She had at least two children by her first marriage: John W. Bageant was born on July 21, 1860 and James Bageant was born on Nov. 30, 1861. These were listed as step-children of William W. Peacemaker, when his estate was settled. The children of William W. and Mary E. Peacemaker were: Mary Florence Peacemaker was born on Jan. 6, 1871. She married George William Largent; David Sampson Peacemaker was born on July 31, 1873; Edward Francis Peacemaker; and George C. Peacemaker was born on Jan. 28, 1879. Source: Chancery Court papers in Box 232, Circuit Court, Hampshire County, W.Va.

Peck, Philip W., "teacher," died Oct. 25, 1845, aged 71 years. Source: Vanmeter graveyard inscription at Old Fields, Hardy County, W.Va.

Pepper, Benjamin Franklin, son of John and Catherine (Fahs) Pepper, was born near Hanging Rock, North River of the Great Cacapon, on April 24, 1821 and died on Oct. 7, 1916 at San Diego, CA. He married: (1) Rebecca Baker on June 2, 1842. She was born in Hampshire County, Va. on March 29, 1820 and died at Walker, Vernon County, Missouri on Dec. 7, 1866. (2) Sally Ann Coyle, on May 16, 1867.

Pepper, Catherine, was born in 1790 and died in Hampshire County, Va. in March 1850, of cholera, according to the Mortality Schedule of 1850 U.S. Census for Hampshire County, Va. To clarify this record, Maud Pugh, in *Capon Valley ...* stated that Catherine was nee Fahs, born on Oct. 18, 1789 and died on March 12, 1849. Her husband, John Pepper, Jr., was born Sept. 1, 1790 and died on Jan. 19, 1861. One Pepper researcher resides on the Delray Road at Sedan, W.Va., not far from the original settlement of the Pepper family. She is willing to help with local research of the family: Mrs. Eldora (Pepper) Park, Star Route 2, Box 97, Augusta, W.Va. 26704.

Pepper, Jacob, son of John and Catherine (Fahs) Pepper, II, was born on April 5, 1815 and died on Aug. 1, 1877. His wife, Frances Alverson, was born on May 29, 1824 and died on June 20, 1902. Source: Tombstone inscriptions at the Pepper graveyard on property owned by Ivan Park, on west side of North River, north of U.S. 50.

Pepper, Jacob B., son of John and Catherine (Emmart) Pepper, was born on Sept. 6, 1792 and died on Oct. 3, 1866. His wife, Martha Heare, daughter of Adam Heare, died on Oct. 24, 1886, aged 84 years, 3 months, 20 days. Source: Tombstone inscriptions in old Jacob Pepper graveyard, Dunmore Ridge Road, near Pleasant Dale, on Ervin Poland's farm.

Pepper, John was deceased by May 6, 1835, the date of a court case, in *Order Book II*, in the Circuit Court of Hampshire County, Va. Maud Pugh, in *Capon Valley: Its Pioneers and Their Descendants*, stated that John Pepper died on Aug. 28, 1826, but I have not yet been able to locate his tombstone in any of the Pepper graveyards in the North River area. His wife Catherine, nee Emmart, was still living in 1835, when the case came to court. The children (heirs) were listed: (1) John Pepper, Jr. married Catherine Fahs, (2) Jacob Pepper married Martha Heare, daughter of Adam Heare, (3) Henry Pepper married Rachel Tate, according to Maud Pugh's account, (4) Frederick Pepper married Deborah Slocum, (5) Sophia Pepper married Robert Carter, (6) Juliana Pepper married George McCauley Jr. (7) Mary Pepper married _____ Cheshire, and (8) Elizabeth Pepper married Andrew Emmart. Note: Maud Pugh listed two daughters Hannah and Arabella Pepper, who are doubtful, and she failed to mention Mary (Pepper) Cheshire. I'm inclined to use the court document as the legal and authoritative source of information on this family unit.

Pepper, Martha, daughter of Adam and Margaret (Todd) Heare, was born on July 14, 1802 in Hampshire County, Va. and died on Oct. 24, 1886. She married Jacob Pepper in 1827. She was buried on Dunmore Ridge, Hampshire County, on Ervin Poland's property. Source: Tombstone inscriptions, and a Bible record furnished to me by the late Robert Shanholtzer of Santa Barbara, California. He had much genealogical data on families in this area, and I made an airplane trip to Santa Barbara to spend a couple of days with him, in 1978.

Peters, John, died June 17, 1859, aged 64 years, of pneumonia, in Hardy County. His wife was named Ann. Death was reported by Jacob Johnson, son-in-law. Source: *West Virginia Vital Statistics: Hardy County*, Reel #3, Virginia State Archives, Richmond, Va.

Peters, Tunis, was born on Oct. 26, 1749 and died in Fairfield County, Ohio on Sept. 24, 1826. He married Francina Adams, born on Aug. 18, 1758 and died on May 3, 1839. He served in the Revolutionary War, and as a sheriff of Hampshire County, Va. They were buried in the Turkey Run Primitive Baptist cemetery at Ashville, Fairfield County, Ohio. According to Bible record, they had 13 children; 4 married into the Ashbrook family. Source: Mrs. Eleanor Walkey, a correspondent in Convent Station, New Jersey. 07961.

Pettit, Moses, was born in 1768, died in March 1837. He resided in the Three Churches area of Hampshire County, Va. Source: Cemetery inscription in Three Churches cemetery.

Pettit, Sidona, "wife of M(oses) Pettit," died on Dec. 13, 1857 in the 94th year of her age. It has been suggested that her maiden name was Ruckman, but not proven. Source: Tombstone inscription in Ebenezer United Methodist cemetery, near Romney, W.Va.

Philips, Mary, died in May 1850, aged 90 years (born circa 1759-60). Cause of death was paralysis. Born in Virginia. Source: 1850 Mortality Census for Frederick County, Va.

Piper, John, died in November 1869, aged 76 years, "of gangreen." He was a farmer, born in Virginia. Survived by spouse. Source: 1870 Mortality Schedule for Frederick County, Va.

Piper, Martha, died in March 1870, aged 76 years, "of typhoid fever." She was born in Virginia. Source: 1870 Mortality Schedule for Frederick County, Va.

Place, John, died in April 1850, aged 45 years. He was born in Virginia. Farmer. Ill for 180 days with pulmonary disease. Source: 1850 Mortality Schedule for Frederick County, Va.

Poland, Achsah, wife of W. J. Poland, was born on March 20, 1825 and died on May 12, 1892, aged 67 years, 1 month, 22 days. Buried near her was Susan P. Poland, born in 1861 and died ??. Source: Tombstone inscription in Poland Graveyard, located near Long's Run which flows into Fox's Run (tributaries of the South Branch of the Potomac River), in western Hampshire County. The deteriorated graveyard is located several hundred yards from the nearest dirt-road, high on a ridge, believed to be Middle Ridge.

Poland, Comfort (nee Hopkins), wife of Amos Poland was born in 1778 on the Eastern Shore of Maryland and died of "paralysis" in 1855 at South Branch, Hampshire County, Va. Source: Hampshire County death record in Virginia State Archives.

Pool, Nancy, died on Sept. 9, 1895, aged 77 years. Her husband preceded her in death. Source: Reported to the Hampshire courthouse by Mr. Davis Farmer.

Poston, Alexander, son of Col. Elias and Rebecca (Cheshire) Poston, was born in 1783 in Hampshire County, Va. and died on Feb. 18, 1851, in Wapello County, Iowa. He married thrice: (1) Martha Green, sister of Thomas Green of North River, Hampshire County, (2) Mrs. Nancy (Greene) Stephenson, but no record of this marriage, and (3) Malinda Poston, daughter of Samuel and Jane (Slane) Poston, Alexander's neice. See the Nov. 4, 1985 issue of *The West Virginia Advocate*.

Poston, Ashford, son of Col. Elias and Rebecca (Cheshire) Poston, Sr., was born in Hampshire County, Va. circa 1792 and died in Adrian County, Missouri on May 18, 1879. He married Mary McVickers on Nov. 19, 1827, in Hampshire County, Va.

Poston, Catherine, daughter of Col. Elias and Rebecca (Cheshire) Poston, was born in Hampshire County, Va. on Jan. 14, 1777 and died on May 16, 1847. She married George Nixon on Jan. 17, 1793. They immigrated to Illinois.

Poston, Col. Elias, son of William and Priscilla Poston, was born in Charles County, Maryland on Nov. 14, 1747 and died on July 4, 1802 at Capon Bridge, West Va. He came to Virginia circa 1775 as a surveyor for Lord Fairfax. When the Revolutionary War broke out, he served under General Morgan. Elias married Rebecca Cheshire, daughter of Samuel and Ann (Robbins) Cheshire. Rebecca remarried to John Johnson, and she died in 1832, in Athens County, Ohio. For an extensive history of this family, see the Oct. 7 and Nov. 4, 1985 issues of *The West Virginia Advocate*, Capon Bridge, West Virginia.

Poston, Capt. Elias, Jr., son of Col. Elias and Rebecca (Cheshire) Poston, Sr., was born in Hampshire County, Va. on May 7, 1787 and died in Moline, Illinois on Sept. 30, 1866. His wife was named Harriett.

Poston, Elias C., son of Samuel and Jane (Slane) Poston, was born in Hampshire County, Va. on Dec. 21, 1804 and died on Jan. 22, 1876. His wife, Amanda, was born on July 11, 1813 and died on June 2, 1898. They were buried at Netawaka, Kansas. Source: Photo and tombstone inscriptions supplied by: Merna M. Hansen, 16803 SE Webster Road, Gladstone, OR 97027.

Poston, Nancy, daughter of Col. Elias and Rebecca (Cheshire) Poston, was born in Hampshire County, Va. in 1786 and died in Delaware County, Ohio on June 30, 1840. She married Elias Slane, oldest son of John and Phoebe (Hiett) Slane. Source: Tombstone inscription in Delaware County, Ohio.

Poston, Nancy, daughter of Samuel and Jane (Slane) Poston, was born in Hampshire County, Va. on Aug. 7, 1800 and died on May 7, 1866 in Johnson County, Kansas. She married William Stephenson, son of Thomas and Nancy (Greene) Stephenson, who died in Johnson County, Kansas on July 28, 1865. In 1825 they emigrated from Hampshire County, Va. to Athens, Ohio, and, in 1841, to Lee County, IOWA. They had twelve children. Source: Mrs. H. Tolivaisa.

Poston, Richard, son of Col. Elias and Rebecca (Cheshire) Poston, was born in 1790 in Hampshire County and died in Athens County, Ohio in 1863. He married: (1) Elizabeth Thompson, allegedly killed by runaway horses in Hampshire County, Va., (2) Malinda (Murphy) Brammel, and (3) Mary Cool, daughter of Herbert and Ann (Sebring) Cool.

Poston, Samuel, son of Col Elias and Rebecca (Cheshire) Poston, was born June 5, 1777 in Hampshire County, and died on Aug. 13, 1823. He married Jane Slane, daughter of Daniel and Nancy Ann (McDonald) Slane, of Hampshire County, Va. She was born in Ireland in 1778 and died in Sept. 1852 near Fort Madison, Iowa, at the home of her daughter, Nancy (Poston) Stephenson.

Poston, William, son of Col. Elias and Rebecca (Cheshire) Poston, was born in Hampshire County, Va. during the mid-1770s according to the 1850 census for Hampshire County. He immigrated to Ohio during the 1830s, but returned to Hampshire

County during the 1840s, where he presumably died sometime after 1850. He lived on the North River Road, now called the Delray Road, and he operated the Poston's Mill on North River, several miles south of U.S. Route 50. This discovery was recent (1988) and is being researched further. Mrs. Audrey S. Baker, of Capon Bridge, W.Va., and I have found the site of the mill, but local residents know nothing about the mill being owned by the Poston family.

Powell, Abraham, son of Joseph and Christina Powell, was born on Oct. 20, 1754 and died on Jan. 3, 1817 in Champaign County, Ohio. He married Ann Smith, daughter of James and Mary (Capon) Smith, early settlers in Hampshire County. Both of these families emigrated from New Jersey to Hampshire County during the 1750's.

Powell, Albert Patterson, was born on May 29, 1854 and died on Dec. 4, 1937. His wife, Mary Virginia, was born on March 1, 1858 and died on Aug. 16, 1900. On this very unusual stone were recorded the births of their children, all Powell: James Edward Powell, born Dec. 23, 1878 and died Sept. 28, 1909; Harvey Reece Powell, born March 26, 1881; William Burr Powell, born Feb. 18, 1883; Albert Thomas Powell, born Jan. 30, 1885 and died Sept. 10, 1885; Clarence John Powell, born Oct. 14, 1886; Ira Benjamin Powell, born March 8, 1889; Sensony Eugene Powell, born Dec. 17, 1891; Henry Alexander Powell, born March 27, 1895; and George Dennis Powell, born July 4, 1898. Source: Tombstone inscriptions in family cemetery, located east of the Little Cacapon River and north of U.S. Route 50.

Powell, Alexander, died on March 9, 1875, in Hampshire County, W.Va. Source: March 19, 1875 issue of the *South Branch Intelligencer*, Romney, W.Va.

Powell, Dade, son of Robert and Elizabeth (Leith) Powell, was born in 1786 and died before the 1850 census was taken for Hampshire County, Va. He married Mary Leith, on Feb. 10, 1808. The 1850 census shows Mary as head of the household, aged 61 years, and: Winifred Powell, age 33; Robert D. Powell, age 29; Susan A. Powell, age 26; John W. Powell, age 24; Mary E. Powell, age 22; and Edward A. Powell, age 20. He lived west of Bear Garden Mountain, in the Bloomery District. Dade inherited the

Powell family Bible, according to courthouse records. The Bible is still being sought for its genealogical records.

Powell, Elizabeth was born on Jan. 6, 1763 and died on Sept. 8, 1828. My source for these dates is an inscription on her tombstone in the "Powell-Leith graveyard" on Leith Mountain, Bloomery District, Hampshire County, W.Va. Elizabeth was nee Leith, daughter of James and Mary (Gorham) Leith Sr. She married Robert Massey Powell, son of Elisha and Winifred (Massey) Powell Sr. I found no grave for him, but have learned that this Robert M. Powell was born on Oct. 5, 1762 and died on May 18, 1851.

Powell-Leith graveyard: This historic graveyard is located on Leith's Mountain in eastern Hampshire County. It is not accessible to an automobile, and one must walk more than a mile to reach the site [with permission of the owner]. The crypts were handcarved from native stone on Leith Mountain, and pulled downhill by oxen between 1815 and 1831, the period of crypt-burials. Numerous of the inscriptions go back to the 1700s [birth], with one or two being in the 1730s or 1740s. There are other inscribed stones in this graveyard, but many, many stones have no markings. All inscriptions have been recorded in this volume, and identified with this graveyard. I call it the "Powell-Leith graveyard," after those buried here.

Powell, James, was born circa 1759, possibly in New Jersey, and died in 1823 in Wayne County, Indiana. He married Mary Reeder, daughter of Joseph and Elizabeth Reeder, on Oct. 7, 1780, in Hunterdon County, N.J. She was born ca 1760 and died on March 15, 1821, in Wayne County, Indiana. They lived briefly in Loudoun County, Va.; then moved to Hampshire County, Va.; to Montgomery County, Ohio in 1815-16; to Wayne County, Indiana in 1820. They lived on the Little Capon River, in Hampshire County. Their children were: (1) Henry Powell was born on Nov. 12, 1781 in Loudoun County, Va. and died in the War of 1812, at Norfolk, Va. He married Precious Ann Queen in 1803. (2) Reeder Powell died circa 1832 in Wayne County, Indiana. (3) William Powell was born on Dec. 19, 1784 and died in 1849, in Wayne County, IN. (4) James Robert Powell, born circa 1790, married second, Precious Ann Queen, widow of his brother Henry Powell. (5) Jemima Powell allegedly married William

Spicer. (6) Sarah J. Powell and (7) Elizabeth Powell. Source: Mr. Robert A. Fetters, 215 Dun Road, Chillocothe, Ohio 45601.

Powell, James H., was born on July 13, 1871 and died on Nov. 27, 1943. His wife was named Virginia, but no inscriptions for her. There are numerous members of the Arnold family buried nearby, and this was the family graveyard established by the Rev. John Arnold, a Primitive Baptist preacher. There are many unmarked slates in this cemetery, sometimes known as Powell's graveyard at Little Cacapon.

Powell, James Leith, married Mary Jenkins, widow of Jacob Jenkins, Jr., on May, 13, 1824, in Hampshire County, Va. I believe that she was nee Buzzard, one of the daughters of Frederick Buzzard. This is based on a statement made in the Will of Jacob Jenkins. Mary's children by Frederick Jenkins were: (1) Frederick B. Jenkins (2) John Z. Jenkins (3) George S. Jenkins (4) Elizabeth Ann Jenkins (5) Susan Marie Jenkins (6) Mary Eveline Jenkins. Mary's children by James L. Powell were: (7) Elisha Powell (8) Alfred H. Powell (9) Susan Ann Powell and (10) Amanda Powell.[46]

Powell, John B. (1846-1930) and Mary Elizabeth (1845-1930), his wife, "Saved by grace." Source: Cemetery inscriptions in Powell graveyard near Little Cacapon, on land owned by Paul Roomsburg. Originally, this graveyard was established by the Rev. John Arnold, as the family burial ground.

Powell, John V., born in 1857 and died in 1922, according to tombstone inscriptions in the Slonaker graveyard, on west side of Bear Garden Mountain, near the Cacapon River. His wife was Mary Jane Slonaker, daughter of Christopher and Sarah Jane (Leith) Slonaker, III. A footmarker shows that she was buried next to her husband.

Powell, Mary, daughter of Elisha and Winifred (Massey) Powell, was buried in the Powell-Leith graveyard on Leith's Mountain in Hampshire County. Her tombstone inscription says, "Sacred to the Memory of Mary Rust, born on Oct. 6 A.D. 1766, died on Aug. 2,A.D. 1821." The inscription was hand-hewn on a native stone which measures about 4'x 8'x 6," an amazing piece

---

46. Names of children were obtained from **Order Book I**, page 299, Circuit Court, Hampshire County, Va., circa 1838.

of work. The grave is located about 50 feet behind the old Powell house on Leith Mountain. The chimney is still standing but the stones in the house have fallen to the ground because of cement erosion. This Mary Powell was first married to John Middleton. After his death she remarried to Peter Rust, the family name inscribed on her tombstone.

Powell, Mary, daughter of Robert Massey and Elizabeth (Leith) Powell, was born on Nov. 13, 1790 and died on June 26, 1870. Her husband was William Powell Leith, son of James and Sarah (Rust) Leith, Jr. His tombstone inscription reveals that he was born on Aug. 22, 1795 and died on Dec. 9, 1833. Source: Tombstone inscriptions in Powell-Leith private cemetery on Leith Mountain.

Powell, Mary Eleanor, daughter of Robert M. and Mary (Moreland) Powell, was born in Hampshire County, Va. on April 22, 1828 and died in Henry, Illinois on Aug. 16, 1870. She married George F. Paskell in 1854. Source: Bible record.

Powell, Robert Dade, son of Robert M. and Mary (Moreland) Powell, was born on Dec. 5, 1835 and died in 1918. He married Elizabeth Gore. Both were buried in the Powell's Forks of Capon Cemetery in Hampshire County.

Powell, Robert Massey, Sr., son of Elisha and Winifred (Massey) Powell, was born on Oct. 5, 1762 and died on May 18, 1851. His wife was Elizabeth Leith, born on Jan. 6, 1763 and died on Sept. 8, 1828, according to tombstone inscription in Powell-Leith graveyard near Bloomery. (Note: See Leith family records.)

Powell, Robert Massey, Jr., son of Robert Massey and Elizabeth (Leith) Powell Sr., was born on Sept. 12, 1795 and died on April 10, 1857. His wife Susannah Leith, daughter of James and Sarah (Rust) Leith, Jr., was born on July 28, 1801 and died on Sept. 8, 1878. Source: Tombstone inscriptions in the Leith-Powell graveyard on Leith Mountain in Hampshire County. The old Leith stone-house has crumbled to the ground but the chimney is still standing. The old graveyard, now in a deteriorated condition, is located behind the house.

Powell, Robert Massey, son of Elisha and Mary Ann (Leith) Powell, was born on Feb. 4, 1800 and died on Oct. 17, 1858. He married Mary Moreland, daughter of William and Eleanor Moreland, on June 18, 1821, in Hampshire County, Va. She was born on Oct. 10, 1806 and died on Jan. 17, 1895. Source: Tombstone inscriptions in Powell's Forks of Capon Cemetery.

Powell, Samuel, son of Joseph and Christina (Fry?) Powell, was born on Sept. 9, 1760 in Hampshire County and died on Oct. 5, 1823 in Champaign County, Ohio. He married: (1) Sarah Randall on July 3, 1783 in "Va.," and (2) Phoebe Yasle. It is believed that this Powell family was of German origin, and came to Hampshire County via New Jersey.

Powell, Samuel D., was born on April 17, 1810 and died on Aug. 1, 1901. His wife, Martha E., was born on July 19, 1840 and died on July 30, 1894. In same graveyard: Charles B. Powell, born Feb. 18, 1866 and died on Jan. 12, 1930; and Flora Powell. Source: Cemetery inscriptions, on farm owned by Irvin Poland, Dunmore Ridge Road, Hampshire County, W.Va.

Powell, Sarah Elizabeth, daughter of Robert M. and Mary (Moreland) Powell, was born on April 16, 1840. She married Silas Largent.

Powell, Walter J., (1861-1935) and wife, Mary E., (1863-1934), were buried in the Ginevan Graveyard, Okonoko, Hampshire County, W.Va. Source: Tombstone inscriptions.

Powell, William M., was deceased prior to April 13, 1838. According to a chancery court suit in the Circuit Court, Hampshire County, Va., found in *Order Book I*, page 255, dated April 13, 1838. The heirs (presumably children) of William M. Powell were: 1) Horatio Powell 2) Sarah Powell 3) Elizabeth Powell 4) Sarah M. Powell 5) Mary Powell 6) Elisha F. Powell 7) Peter R. Powell 8) Bartella Powell married Joseph Walker 9) Johanne Powell was deceased and had two children, Sarah and Elizabeth Powell.

Powell, Winifred Massey, daughter of Elisha and Mary Ann (Leith) Powell, Jr., was born on June 4, 1797 and died on July 6, 1847. She married John William Kyle on Feb. 20, 1818. He was born on Nov. 11, 1789. They had seven children. Source: Margaret Norton, Brownwood, Texas.

Powelson, Elizabeth G., "wife of Rev. J. L. Luttrell," was born on April 5, 1872 and died on July 13, 1950. Hampshire County courthouse records state that John Lee Luttrell, son of John Luttrell, died July 3, 1920, aged 82 years, 10 months, 10 days. His occupation was listed as a carpenter. His marriage record shows that he married Elizabeth Gertrude Powelson, Jan. 28,

1914. Source: Tombstone inscription in Powell private graveyard at Little Cacapon, on property owned by Paul Roomsburg.

Powelson, James R., died in Hampshire County, aged 62 years, on Dec. 8, 1871. Source: The *South Branch Intelligencer*.

Powelson, John, died on Dec. 3, 1872, aged 64 in Hampshire County. His wife, Katherine, died on Dec. 6, 1872, three days after her husband. They lived near the Ebenezer Church. Source: Dec. 13, 1872 issue of the *South Branch Intelligencer*.

Powelson, John W., was born on Aug. 25, 1844 and died on Aug. 30, 1875. His wife, Nancy Jane, was born on Feb. 21, 1844. Source: Cemetery inscription in Powell graveyard at Little Cacapon, now owned by Paul Roomsburg.

Power, Elder B.W., was born in 1836 and died in 1929. His wife, Mary F., was born in 1841 and died in 1916. He was a minister in the Primitive Church. Source: Tombstone inscriptions in the Little Cacapon Primitive Baptist Church Graveyard, near Levels, Hampshire County, W.Va.

Pownall, Elisha, was born in New Jersey on Aug. 6, 1759 and died on July 17, 1837. His wife, Abigail, was born in 1764 and died on Feb. 18, 1854. Source: Cemetery inscriptions at Three Churches, Hampshire County, W.Va.

Pownell, Isaac J., died on March 11, 1898, aged 75 years, 28 days. It appears that someone named Rebecca is buried nearby. Source: Tombstone inscriptions at Three Churches, Hampshire County, W.Va.

Pownall, Isaiah, was born on April 25, 1799 and died on March 6, 1887. His wife, Mary (Heare) Pownall, daughter of Adam Heare, died on July 6, 1896, aged 91 years, 3 months. *The Hampshire Review* stated that he was an elder in the Mt. Bethel Church, and one of the most respected citizens in the County. Rev. G.K. Finley preached the funeral. Source: Tombstone inscriptions at the Mt. Bethel Church, at Three Churches, Hampshire County, W.Va.

Pownall, Jonathan, aged 94 years, was born in Berks County PA on Sept. 4, 1784 and died in Hampshire County on June 3, 1878. He served in the War of 1812, and was the father of ten children. Source: July 7, 1878 issue of the *South Branch Intelligencer*.

Pownell, Jonathan, died on Feb. 1, 1851, aged 76 years. Source: Tombstone inscription in Old Bethel Cemetery, Hampshire County, W.Va.

Pownell, wife of Elisha Pownell, was born Nov. 10, 1814 and died Feb. 7, 1902. Source: Tombstone inscriptions in Mountain Dale cemetery, Hampshire County, W.Va.

Pritchard, Rees, son of Samuel and Margaret (Weaver) Pritchard, was born in Sept. 1744 and died on Sept. 30, 1830 in Morgan County, Va. During the late part of the 18th century, the Rees Pritchard family lived along North River, between Hanging Rock ond Pleasant Dale (along what is now U.S. Rt. 50) in Hampshire County, W.Va. Rees Pritchard also owned land along North River at North River Mills, and in other locations along the Great Cacapon River. According to a deed which I found in Hampshire Courthouse in Romney, W.Va., Rees' wife's maiden name was Barthama Davis. I have misplaced the citation, but it was related to the track of land at North River Mills, sold to the Moreland family, which was then sold to the Kump family during the 1840's, and the land is now owned by the Paul Gilson family.

Pritchard, Rees, II, son of Rees Pritchard I, of Samuel Pritchard, was born in Hampshire County circa 1783 and died in Morgan County, W.Va. on May 8, 1865, according to a death record in courthouse. His wife was named Arabella "Amy" Johnston. According to the physicians certificate of death, she died at Rock Gap on Aug. 2, 1893, aged 102 years. Their children were: (1) Rees Pritchard, III, born in 1813 and died on Feb. 14, 1899 in Morgan County; married Sarah Iden. (2) Nancy Pritchard, born on April 6, 1816 and died on Oct. 9, 1903; married Elijah Hovermale, born on Jan. 18, 1816 and died on April 8, 1869. (3) Amelia Pritchard was born in 1818 and died in 1899. She married Cyrus Dawson. (4) Sarah Pritchard was born in 1827 and married John Michael. (5) Isom S. Pritchard married Ellen Kidwell, born on Jan. 15, 1830 and died on Jan. 15, 1905, and (6) Parker Pritchard, 1830-1919, married Delilah Foutch and Sarah E. Widmyer. Source: The Hunter papers in the Morgan County, W.Va. Public Library.

Pritchard family: The Will of Joseph Pritchard, dated Feb. 4, 1768 in Hampshire County, Va., proves the relationships of three brothers, viz: (1) Joseph Pritchard (ca. 1718-1768) married Alice

_____ (2) Rees Pritchard of Frederick County, Va. (Will filed in 1758), married widow Eleanor Evans on Sept. 7, 1743 in Philadelphia, and (3) Samuel Pritchard married Margaret Weaver and they settled in Hampshire County as early as 1760, if not earlier. On Oct. 7, 1770, George Washington visited Samuel Pritchard on the Cacapehon River, and wrote in his Journal, "Pritchard's is a pretty good house, there being fine pasturage, good fences, and beds tolerably clean." It is believed that Robert Pritchard who settled in North Carolina was a brother, too. Eleanor Pritchard, a sister, married Jenkins James and they lived in Frederick County, Va. Pritchard is a Welsh name, and members of the family were associated with the Quakers. It is believed that the name came to old Frederick County, Va. during the mid-1740's.

Pugh, Jane, wife of Robert Pugh, died Dec. 18, 1886, aged 77 years. Source: Hampshire County Courthouse death record.

Pugh, Jesse, son of Thomas and Jane Ann (Rogers) Pugh, was born on Sept. 16, 1711, in Pennsylvania and died in 1797 in Frederick County, Virginia. He married Alice Malin, born on Sept. 29, 1711. They came to Frederick County, Virginia in 1741; took up a Fairfax grant in 1752 on Back Creek; and participated in the Quaker life of that community.

Pugh, Jesse, son of Robert and Mary (Edwards) Pugh, was born in Capon Valley, W.Va., on March 18, 1760 and died on Aug. 3, 1847 in Washington County, Ohio. His wife was Sarah McDonald, daughter of Benjamin and Margaret McDonald. She was born Feb. 8, 1766, and died on Sept. 29, 1849. Source: Tombstone inscriptions in Gard cemetery in Washington County, Ohio, and the McDonald family Bible.

Pugh, Jesse, was born in Frederick County, Va., Sept. 5, 1776. His wife, Elizabeth Hampson, was born June 4, 1778. They moved to Fairfield County, Ohio in 1803.

Pugh, Jesse J., died on July 9, 1882 at age 72, in the Capon District. He married Elizabeth Larrick. He was listed as a "farmer," born in Hampshire County, according to his son Thomas Pugh. Source: Hampshire County death records. Also, the private records of Ralph L. Triplett Esq. show his birthdate as being on Sept. 13, 1809, and his parents names being Azariah and Elizabeth (Reigle) Pugh of Highview.

Pugh, Job, son of Jesse and Alice (Malin) Pugh, was born on July 4, 1737 and died in Frederick County, Virginia in 1809. In 1769, he married Ruth John, of York County, Pennsylvania. They were members of the Quaker Church and buried in the Old Quaker Cemetery at Gainsboro, Virginia. Job founded this town, in 1797, which was first named Pughtown, but later changed to Gainsboro, Virginia. It is located north of Winchester, Virginia, on U.S. Route 522.

Pugh, John, son of Samuel and Sarah Pugh, was born in Hampshire County, Va. on Feb. 12, 1782 and died on Oct. 10, 1858. His wife, Nancy A. Keller, was born on March 5, 1787 and died on Feb. 19, 1862. They were buried in the Pugh Graveyard "located off of Homestead Drive, Williamstown, W.Va." Source: Mrs. Jeanie P. Wines, 1912 Cameron Ave., Parkersburg, W.Va. 26101.

Pugh, Jonathan, son of Evan and Mary Pugh, was born circa 1720 and died in 1794 in Hampshire County, Virginia. His wife was Margaret Wood. Their children were: Margaret Pugh married a Parsons; Daniel Pugh married Sarah Hiett; Lucy Pugh married Francis Taggart; Jonathan Pugh, II (1757-1834), married Mary Ellen Tansy; David Pugh settled in northeastern Ohio; Jesse Pugh settled in Lancaster, Ohio; Hananiah Pugh settled in Newark, Ohio in 1804; Sydney Pugh married Harvey Westfall; John Pugh married Florinda Murphy, and they lived in Ohio. Source: Miss Mary Pugh, Box 111, Romney, W.Va. 26757. [Note: Jonathan and Margaret (Wood) Pugh were buried on his farm along North River, on the east side about 2-3 miles downstream from U.S. Route 50. The farm is now owned by Chalmers R. Souders. The gravestones were not inscribed, but descendants knew where they were and to whom they belonged. However, these stones have been "farmed over" during the 20th century, and have disappeared.]

Pugh, Jonathan, son of Jonathan and Mary Ellen (Tansy) Pugh, was born on April 14, 1795 and died on Feb. 29, 1832, aged 36 years, 10 months, 1 day. He married Nancy Offutt, daughter of Solomon and Elizabeth (Roberts) Offutt, on June 14, 1827. She was born on Jan. 15, 1805 and died on Jan. 2, 1872. After Jonathan's death, she remarried to John Patterson, on May 3, 1836. Source: Tombstone inscriptions in the Offutt Family Graveyard, near Slanesville, W.Va.

Pugh, Mary M., died on Oct. 18, 1899 at age 68. She was a daughter of Joseph and Rebecca McKee. Source: Hampshire County death records.

Pugh, Maud (1862-1952) was buried in the Indian Mound Cemetery, Romney, West Virginia. She was author of *Capon Valley: Its Pioneers and Their Descendants, 1698-1940*, a monumental work on genealogy and local history.

Pugh, Samuel, son of Robert and Mary (Edwards) Pugh, was born in Hampshire County, Va. on April 1, 1758 and died on July 27, 1862. His wife, Sarah, was born circa 1763. They were buried in the Pugh Ridge Cemetery in Belmont County, Ohio. Source: Mrs. Jeanie P. Wines, 1912 Cameron Ave., Parkersburg, W.Va. 26101.

Pugh, Thomas, son of Jesse and Alice (Malin) Pugh, was born on Nov. 16, 1731 in Pennsylvania and died in Frederick County, Virginia in 1798. He married Anna (Wright) McCool, widow of James McCool and daughter of James and Mary Wright. Ann was born on the 29th day, 1st month, 1725, in Chester County, PA, and died at Back Creek, Frederick County, Va., on April 7, 1801. See "The Ellis Pugh Family History," *The West Virginia Advocate*, June 6, 1983. [Capon Bridge, West Virginia, 26711.

Pultz, Isaac, was born on Oct. 16, 1824 and died on Aug. 15, 1909, aged 80 years, 3 months, 28 days. His wife, Mary M. Pultz, was born on July 3, 1832 and died on Oct. 24, 1911, aged 79 years, 3 months, 25 days. Source: Tombstone inscriptions in the Green Lane cemetery, located near Delray, West Va.

Pultz, Rebecca, was born on July 4, 1825 and died on June 5, 1897. She was a daughter of Jacob and Mary (Fahs) Shanholtzer Sr., of the Gibbons Run section of Hampshire County. Rebecca married Jacob Pultz, son of Michael Pultz. An old Pultz graveyard (unmarked slates) is located on the southside road between Augusta and Slanesville, near the residence of Mrs. Ruth (Fultz) Beyer. However, Rebecca was not buried there, as previously believed. The source for Rebecca's death date was a tombstone inscription at the Mt. Bethel Primitive Baptist Church, at Three Churches, which corrects an error on page 64 of my *Shanholtzer History and Allied Family Roots*.

Pyles (Piles), Francis, died on March 16, 1872 in the Hampshire County Poor House, aged 89 years and 4 months. He was born in Nov. 1782. Source: The *South Branch Intelligencer*.

Queen, Absalom, died in June 1850, in Lincoln County, W.Va., aged 78 years. Cause of death was "lung hemorage." Source: 1870 Mortality Schedule of U.S. Census.

Queen, Elizabeth, daughter of Stephen and Mary (Moreland) Queen, was born on Nov. 12, 1827, and died on July 5, 1870, in Hampshire County, W.Va. She married Silas Haines, son of Isaac Haines, on Nov. 11, 1847. Source: Bible record, and *The South Branch Intelligencer*.

Queen, John Jr., son of John and Mary Queen, Sr., was born in Loudoun County, Va. in 1755; died in Hampshire County, Va. on May 12, 1842. He married Chloe Carrick. Source: DAR records.

Queen, Stephen, son of John and Chloe (Carrick) Queen, was born in Hampshire County on March 1, 1800 and died in 1870. He married Mary Moreland, daughter of Richard and Elizabeth Moreland, on Feb. 8, 1827. She was born on Nov. 28, 1803 and died on Dec. 31, 1861. Source: See *The West Virginia Advocate*, Capon Bridge, W.Va., June 1984.

Race, Augustus, migrated from Hampshire County to Greene County, Illinois, where he died on March 31, 1872. Source: *South Branch Intelligencer*.

Race, James William, was born in Hampshire County, Virginia on March 17, 1832 and died on April 1, 1906 in Decatur, Illinois. His father, James R. Race, died during the early 1830's and his mother brought the family to Ohio shortly thereafter. Source: Decatur, Illinois newspaper.

Race, John R., was born in Hampshire County on Dec. 6, 1828. His mother moved to Columbus, Ohio when he was but four years old. He later went to Decatur, Illinois where he became prosperous, and died in Jan. 1910. Source: *Decatur Daily Herald*, Decatur, Illinois, Jan. 10, 1910.

Racey Sr., John married Elizabeth Aiken, daughter of James and Elizabeth (Roland) Aiken. This family lived in the southeastern section of present-day Hampshire County, near Lehew, W.Va. Their children were: (1) Cynthia Racey was born in 1781 and died Nov. 16, 1860 in Montgomery County, Missouri. She married Thomas Hellyer, who was born in 1776 and died

Sept. 9, 1860. (2) John Racey Jr., born in 1782, and died in Hampshire County, Va. on March 15, 1831. He married Rebecca Orndorff on June 20, 1808William Racey was born on April 24, 1786 and died Nov. 29, 1870, in Hampshire County. His wife, Mary Myers, was born in 1790 and died on March 8, 1844. They were married in Frederick County, Va. on June 16, 1808. Her grave in the Shiloh Cemetery at LeHew, W.Va. does not have inscribed dates. Source: Letter from Simeon Ward to John Bruner, dated May 23, 1844. (4) Thomas Racey, born in 1787, and died in Hampshire County, Va. on July 1, 1822. He married Margaret Hinslip, born in 1786 and died on March 4, 1861. (5) Landon Racey was born June 13, 1796 and died Dec. 3, 1855, in Noble County, Ohio. He married Susannah Barnhouse on April 4, 1822, in Harrison County Ohio. Source: Information from LDS files in Salt Lake City, edited and transmitted to me by Arlene N. Lombard, 2022 Custer Avenue, Billings, MT 59102. We believe the above record is incomplete. Also, tombstone inscriptions were copied from cemeteries in Hampshire County, W.Va.

Rannels, Jane, daughter of John Rannels [of William Rannels] was born in 1781, probably in Hampshire County, Va., and died on Aug. 15, 1867 at Uniontown, Fayette County, PA. She married James Gaddis, son of Col. Thomas and Hannah (Royce) Gaddis. He was born on March 28, 1774 at Uniontown, PA. and died on Dec. 14, 1812, at Ft. Niagra, N.Y., during the War of 1812. Source: Mrs. Warren R. Park, P. O. Box 525, Chandler, OK 74834.

Rannells, John, "Ruling Elder of Bethel Church," died May 11, 1852, aged 57 years. Source: Tombstone inscription at Three Churches, Hampshire County, W.Va.

Rannells, Samuel, son of William and Jane Rannells, was born on Dec. 10, 1766 and died in Bourboun County, KY on March 24, 1817. He married Margaret Gilkeson on May 10, 1798. She was born on March 28, 1777 and died on Oct. 30, 1821. Before emigrating west, they were from Frederick and Hampshire Counties, Va. Source: Copied from a copy of a Bible record.

Rannells, William, son of John Rannells, was born in Hampshire County, Va. in 1782 and died on April 6, 1864 near Wilmington, Ohio. In 1800 he settled in Uniontown, PA, and married Leah Gaddis, daughter of Col. Thomas and Hannah

(Royce) Gaddis. His wife Leah was born on Sept. 28, 1784 and died on Dec. 24, 1855. They lived about two miles northeast of Wilmington, Ohio, and were buried in the Gaddis cemetery at that place. See *The Clinton Republican* newspaper (1864), local histories and cemetery inscriptions for additional information.

Rannells, William, died in Hampshire County, Va. in 1794. His wife Jane died in 1797. They were immigrants to Hampshire County. Their children were: (1) James Rannells died in 1807. (2) Samuel Rannells immigrated to Bourboun County, KY. (3) John Rannells went to Fayette County, PA around 1800. (4) Nancy Rannells married a Mr. Hume and lived in Washington County, PA. (5) William Rannells lived in Washington County, PA. (6) David Rannells married Ruth Beckett and they lived in Washington County, PA. (7) Margaret Rannells married a Mr. Earsom. (8) Robert Rannells married Mary Earsom, daughter of John and Christina Earsom. Robert allegedly died in Hampshire County, Va. in 1819. Major source: Will filed in Hampshire County, Va. courthouse, on Oct. 15, 1794.

Raymond, Rev, Moses, was "born Jan. 9, 1798 in Norwalk, Connecticut and died in Green Spring Valley, Hampshire County on May 19, 1875." The *South Branch Intelligencer* stated that he graduated from Yale University. Source: Tombstone inscription.

Reed, Elizabeth, died in December 1859, aged 67 years. Died a sudden death after being parlyzed. Born in Virginia. Source: 1860 Mortality Schedule for Frederick County, Va.

Reed, James, died on Dec. 4, 1816, aged 41 years; heighth 5 feet 4 inches tall; "from want, supposed the direct cause was from cold and hunger." He was found dead in a field near the dwelling house of William Wilson. (Note: Today we would call him a homeless person.) Source: Frederick County, Va., "Inquisitions of Dead Bodies," Virginia State Archives.

Reid, Jeremiah Sr., born about 1750 and died on April 12, 1822 in Hampshire County, Va. His wife, Elizabeth McMahon, died on June 25, 1828. I am currently researching this family. Source: Records collected by Ralph L. Triplett, Esq., Gore, Va.

Reid, Jeremiah, Jr., was born in 1785 and died in Frederick County, Va. in 1852. He married: (1) Elizabeth Hickle, daughter of Devalt and Eve Hickle, in 1807, and (2) Nancy (Ann) Cowgill, daughter of Elisha and Martha (Ewing) Cowgill, in 1815. She was born on Oct. 5, 1786. There is still a question about the veracity of this Nancy Cowgill being the second wife of Jeremiah Reid, Jr. Further proof is requires.

Reid, Jeremiah, died Aug. 14, 1827. Jane Reid died Oct. 5, 1868, aged 81 years, 11 months. Presumably, Jane was Jeremiah's wife. Anderson Reid/Read died May 28, 1899. On same Bible page was a list of Murphy siblings, born from 1783 to 1804, with notation at a later date "unkles and aunts of Anderson Read." One hypothesis is that this Jeremiah Reid belonged to the Timber Ridge Reid families. Source: Loose Bible page from Murphy Bible, with no notations of geography or location.

Reid, John, son of Jeremiah and Elizabeth (McMahon) Reid, was born in 1780 and died in 1854. He married: (1) Nancy Ann Orndorff, a daughter of John and Hannah (McIlwee) Orndorff, Jr. She died in 1822-23. (2) Mary or Elizabeth Ann Brunner, in 1824 and (3) Mary Pugh.

Reid, Rebecca, daughter of Jeremiah and Elizabeth (McMahon) Reid, was born in Hampshire County in 1781; died in Ross County, Ohio in 1824. She married Henry Hickle, son of Devalt and Eve Hickle, on Dec. 6, 1806. Source: Mrs. Ernestine P. Moss, Memphis, TN.

Reid, Tilberry, son of John Reid, was born in Hampshire County on Dec. 15, 1810 and died at Holly Springs, Mississippi on Jan. 1, 1863. His death was service-connected. Tilberry was Captain of Company C, 99th Regiment of Indiana Volunteers. He married Rebecca Caudy, daughter of James and Elizabeth (Lyons) Caudy, on Jan. 10, 1831, in Hampshire County. Rebecca was born in Hampshire County, Va. on Dec. 20, 1811. Source: Declaration For Widow's Pension, filed in Marion County, Indiana in 1863. See also the published works of Maud Pugh and Grace Kelso Garner, who researched certain Hampshire County families.

Renner, Peter, died in May 1860, aged 80 years. Survived by spouse. Farmer. Was ill for seven days prior to death. Source: 1860 Mortality Schedule for Frederick County, Va.

Reynolds, James, was born on June 2, 1771 and died in Mineral County on Feb. 24, 1872, aged 100 years, 8 months and 10 days. Source: The *South Branch Intelligencer*.

Rhinehart, Christina, died on Sept. 20, 1868 at North River, aged 75 years old according to a Hampshire County courthouse record (which I believe to be in error). A tombstone inscription at the Sedan Church on top of the ridge, to the left of the church, says: Christina Rhinehart was born on June 12, 1798 and died on Oct. 20, 1863, aged 75 years, 3 months, 28 days. The latter appears to be correct.

Rhinehart, David, died in Frederick County, Va. on Dec. 31, 1833, "under mysterious circumstances." Josiah Lockhart, Justice of the Peace, appointed a jury consisting of: Joseph McKee, John Piper, Isaac White, Jacob Junkins, William McKee, Thomas Anderson, William Smith, Samuel Smith, Jacob F. Sybert and William Howard. Jonas Whitacre was the Deputy Sheriff, and the hearing was held on New Years Day, 1834 at the home of Alfred T. Newbanks in Frederick County, Va. Source: Frederick County, Va. "Inquisition of Dead Bodies," Virginia State Archives.

Rhinehart, Margaret, daughter of Abraham and Margaret Rhinehart, was born on Feb. 26, 1787 and died on Aug. 26, 1854, of "diphtheria." Her husband was Henry Wolford, son of John and Catherine (Sydener) Wolford. Source: Death record in Virginia State Archives, and other sources.

Rhodifer, Edward, died on March 9, 1929, aged 84 years. Source: Tombstone inscription in the Timber Ridge Primitive Baptist Church, Frederick County, Va.

Richard, Henry, was born on June 5, 1789 and died on March 12, 1847, aged 57 years, 9 months, 7 days. His wife Leah was born on Feb. 9, 1789 and died on Aug. 26, 1853, aged 64 years, 6 months, 6 days. Buried in the same private graveyard were: John W. Richard, born Jan. 25, 1823 and died on Dec. 26, 1860, aged 37 years, 6 months. Sarah M. Richard, wife of John W. Richard, was born on March 27, 1829 and died on April 19, 1856; Mary E. Richard, daughter of John W. and Sarah M. Richard, died on June 10, 1856, aged 2 months, 3 days; _____ Richard, was born on Nov. 30, 1819 and died on Feb. 20, 1855, aged 35 years, 2 months, 20 days. Caroline Richard was born on Dec. 17, 1826 and died on Jan. 21, 1847, aged 20 years, 1 month, 4 days; Mary Richard died in 1843, aged 22 years, 22 days; Joseph Shanholtzer was born on May 29, 1808 and died on Nov. 27, 1892. His wife was Mary M. Saville, daughter of Isaac Saville. Mary's tombstone has been broken into small pieces; Erasmus Bean died on Feb. 21, 1896, aged 74 years, 10 months, 20 days.

His wife, Emily Bean, died on Oct. 30, 1883, aged 56 years, 7 months, 9 days. Source: Richard private graveyard located in a field near Delray, Hampshire County, W.Va.

Richards, John, died in March 1850, aged 87 years, of "old age." He was ill for 35 days prior to his death. Farmer. Born in Virginia. Source: 1860 Mortality Schedule for Frederick County, Va.

Richards, Lydia, died in May 1870, aged 88 years. Born in Virginia. Source: 1870 Mortality Schedule for Frederick County, Va.

Richman, Jane (probably Richmond), was born on Nov. 14, 1830 and died on July 8 (no year given). Source: Foreman cemetery at Cold Stream.

Richmond, James W., died on Nov. 9, 1890, aged 42 years. Source: Cemetery inscription, Foreman cemetery.

Richmond, Jane, daughter of John and Ann Allen, died on April 20, 1870, age 83 years (born circa 1787). Her husband was James Richmond. They lived in the Capon Valley basin, Hampshire County, Virginia.

Richmond, Kate E., died on Oct. 8, 1894, aged 48 years, 1 month and 14 days. Source: Tombstone inscription in Foreman cemetery.

Richmond, William, died on Sept. 23, 1894, aged 82 years. Buried next to him was his wife, Eliza (McDougan), died on May 21, 1878, aged 63 years. The tombstone inscription states that she was a daughter of William and Mary McDougan. In Hampshire County *Deed Book 70*, pages 58-61, the children of William Richmond are listed as: John A. Richmond; Joseph L. Richmond; Samuel P. Richmond; Margaret Hoffman, wife of Jacob Hoffman; Rebecca Light, wife of John W. Light; Mary Jane Richmond, dec'd, and; Catherine Richmond, dec'd. Apparently the latter two children died unmarried. Mary Jane Richmond had a daughter named Lucy B. Richmond who married William Shanholtz; and Catherine Richmond had a daughter named Laura B. Richmond. Source: Cemetery inscriptions, Foreman cemetery at Cold Stream, and courthouse records.

Ridgeway, Elizabeth Jane, daughter of John Ridgeway, was born on March 15, 1822. Her husband was William Fletcher, who died on Dec. 3, 1861, aged 50 years. Their children, according to chancery court document, Box 236, Hampshire County Circuit Court, were: Joseph Fletcher, Mary Catherine Fletcher, Margaret Frances Fletcher, and Rebecca Fletcher.

Ridgeway, John, was born in 1770; died on April 6, 1866 at Highview, according to a Hampshire County death record.

Riley, George L., son of Thomas Butler and Mary Margaret (Kerns) Riley, was born on July 4, 1841 and died on Oct. 26, 1863. He served in the War Between the States; contracted pneumonia; then came home to recuperate, where he died suddenly. George was not married. He was buried in the Riley graveyard, on the east bank of the Cacapon River, between Darby's nose and the underwater bridge. There are several other graves, but inscriptions have eroded. Source: Tombstone inscription.

Riley, James R., was born on March 16, 1844 and died Dec. 29, 1936. His wife, Mary E. Kidwell, was born on Nov. 10, 1849 and died on April 7, 1904. Source: Tombstone inscriptions in Kidwell graveyard, two miles east of Slanesville, Hampshire County, W.Va.

Riley, Sarah Mariah, daughter of Thomas Butler and Mary Margaret (Kerns) Riley, Jr., was born on June 14, 1838 and died on Nov. 27, 1898. She married Isaac Sylvester Sirbaugh, son of Jacob and Elizabeth (Oates) Sirbaugh, Jr. Source: Tombstone inscription in the Evan Hiett graveyard on Sandy Ridge, Hampshire County, W.Va.

Riley, Thomas, died on April 12, 1874, aged 59 years, 5 months and 12 days. The death record in the Hampshire County courthouse stated that he was a blacksmith; that he was born in Loudoun County, Va. Note: Records in the possession of the late Rev. Melvin Lee Steadman, Jr., Falls Church, Va., show that Thomas Riley, Jr. married Margaret Kerns (1811-1904), daughter of George and Elizabeth (Reid) Kerns, Sr., on Aug. 8, 1833. Also, his records showed that Thomas B. Riley Jr. was a son of Thomas and Sarah (Savage) Riley Sr. The April 17, 1874 issue of the *South Branch Intelligencer* stated that Thomas Riley died on April 9, 1874; that his widow and eight children survived him, three of whom were married.

Riley, Sarah (nee Savage), died at Cold Stream, Hampshire County, Va. on Dec. 30, 1860, at the home of her son, Thomas

Butler Riley II. Her husband was Thomas Riley Sr. Source: *Coffin Book* of William Meade Edwards. Another source states that she was nee Trowbridge and a third source states that she was a Strawbridge (the latter name I have not yet encountered in this geographic area).

Rinker, Casper, born in 1727 and died on Feb. 11, 1804, according to a tombstone inscription in the Quaker Graveyard (Back Creek Meeting) at Gainsboro, Va. Buried next to him in the Quaker cemetery (Back Creek Meeting at Gainsboro, Virginia) is wife Mary Rinker, born in 1729 and died on Jan. 26, 1820. In a Circuit Court record in Augusta County, Va., Mary testified in a deposition that she and her husband, Casper, moved to Frederick County, Va. in 1757. A correspondent sent this information to me: "Hans Jacob Rinker, was baptized on Christmas Day, 1727 in Zurich, Switzerland. He died on Feb. 17, 1804 in Frederick County, Va. On April 11, 1757, in Germantown, Penn., Rinker married Maria Schultz. He immigrated to Pennsylvania on Aug. 30, 1743." Please note the difference of death dates, Feb. 11th versus the 17th.

Rinker, Casper, was born Nov. 29, 1789, and died April 9, 1861. Wife, Isabelle, was born June 20, 1800 and died Aug. 7, 1853. Wife, Rebecca A. Light, died Aug. 21, 1873, aged 62 years. Source: Tombstone inscriptions in Back Creek Quaker graveyard at Gainsboro, Va.

Rinker, Joshua, son of John and Betsy (Biser) Rinker, was born on Sept. 9, 1831 and died on July 2, 1890. "Joshua Rinker and Susan C. Lear was married July 10, 1862"; "Joshua Rinker and Susan E. High was married on Oct. 24, 1867." Susan E. High was born on March 7, 1850. Source: Bible record submitted by Dan P. Oates, Romney, W.Va.

Ritter, Elizabeth, died in August 1859, aged 60 years. Born in Virginia. Cause of death was "dropsy," following an illness of 155 days. Classified as "an idiot." Source: 1860 Mortality Schedule of Frederick County, Va.

Roberson, John, a veteran of the War of 1812, died at 92 years in Hampshire County, on May 17, 1877. Source: May 25, 1877 issue of the *South Branch Intelligencer*.

Robinson, Benjamin was born on April 14, 1779. He emigrated from Hampshire County, Va. to LaSalle County, Illinois, where he died on May 26, 1877, aged 98 years, 1 month, 12 days. His obit appeared in the July 1, 1877 issue of the **South Branch Intelligencer**. It is believed that his wife was Catherine Peacemaker, daughter of John and Mary Ann Peacemaker, of Timber Ridge, Hampshire County, Va., although not proven. They were still residents of the Timber Ridge area in 1835, when John Peacemaker's estate was settled. See article in March 11, 1987 issue of **The West Virginia Advocate**, "Regional History: German Immigrants to Smokey Hollow, the Peacemaker Family."

Robinson, James, died "of cholic cramp" in Hampshire County, June 1850, aged 65 years. He was born in Virginia. Source: 1850 Mortality Schedule of U.S. Census.

Robinson, John, aged 75 years, died in Hampshire County, W.Va. on "Tuesday last" (who knows?). Source: March 22, 1878 issue of the **South Branch Intelligencer**.

Rogers, Casper, son of John and Mary (Rinker) Rogers, was born circa 1792, probably in Frederick County, Va. His death date is not known, but believed to have been between 1855 and 1860. His first marriage was to Susannah Ellis, April 24, 1815, probably a daughter of Morris Ellis. Susannah died on April 12, 1831, aged 31 years, and was buried in the Quaker graveyard at Gainsboro, Va. Casper remarried to Eliza Ann Brown, daughter of Adam and Christina (Zuber) Brown, Aug. 16, 1832. They had at least eight children according to source, Mr. Sid Rogers, 1006 Cameron Street, Alexandria, Va. 22314.

Rogers, Evan, was born on Dec. 26, 1793 and died on Dec. 12, 1876. His wife, Hannah Dalby, was born on Jan. 5, 1800 and died on June 12, 1845. In this same graveyard, near Gainsboro, Frederick County, Virginia, was buried John Dalby, but no readable inscriptions.

Rogers, James, was born in 1769 and died Nov. 17, 1804, in Frederick County, Virginia. It is believed that he was a son of Evan and Sarah (Ballenger) Rogers, whose birthdate was listed in Hopewell records as March 17, 1768. Source: Tombstone inscription in Quaker graveyard, Gainsboro, Virginia.

Rogers, Mary, was born in 1759 and died June 23, 1823 in Frederick County, Virginia. It's possible that she was the oldest daughter of Frederick and Susannah (Buckwalter) Buzzard, of Timber Ridge. If so, she married William Rogers. However, more than likely she was an unmarried daughter of Evan and Sarah (Ballenger) Rogers, whose birthdate is given as Feb. 20, 1759 in Hopewell Quaker records. More research needs to be done on this person. Source: Tombstone inscription at Back Creek Meeting (Quaker), Gainsboro, Virginia.

Rogers, Mary, died in May 1860, aged 72 years, of "consumption." Her husband survived her. Was ill for eight years prior to death. Source: 1860 Mortality Schedule for Frederick County, Va.

Roland, Samuel, "widower," died in May 1870, aged 87 years. Farmer. Born in Virginia. Source: 1870 Mortality Schedule for Frederick County, Va.

Rosenberger, Erasmus, was born in 1723 in Germany and died in the 1790's (probably in Shenandoah County, Virginia. He married Anna Catherine Baumgardner, and after her death, remarried to Regina _____. He was the father of twelve children. Source: Mr. Francis Coleman Rosenberger, family historian of Alexandria, Virginia. He died on Oct. 19, 1986 at Fairfax Hospital, in Virginia.

Rosenberger, Jacob, son of Erasmus and Regina Rosenberger, died in Frederick County, Virginia in 1815. He married Betsy Brubeck on Sept. 11, 1799. They left many descendants in the area. Source: Courthouse records.

Rosenberger, John, son of Erasmus and Anna Catherine (Baumgardner) Rosenberger, was born in Oct. 1761 and died on Timber Ridge, Hampshire County, in 1831. He served in the Revolutionary War. Wife was named Elizabeth, and their two children were named Asa and Elizabeth Rosenberger.

Rosenberger, Michael, son of Erasmus and Regina Rosenberger, died in Frederick County, Virginia in Nov. 1817. He married Betsy Jennings on Aug. 31, 1799. Source: Court records.

Ross, Alexander, was born circa 1682, probably in Ireland. He was orphaned in 1693 when his father, John Ross (1658-1693) died. On April 11, 1706, in Philadelphia, Penn., he married Catherine Chambers. They were among the first settlers in the Shenandoah Valley of Virginia, in 1730; were members of the Friends (Quakers); and were pioneer developers of "the Opeckin settlement," meaning the Opequon Creek in old Frederick County,

Virginia. He died in late 1748 and she in early 1749, near Winchester Va.

Ross, Philip, was born in 1732 in Dorchester County, Maryland and died in 1813, at Mansfield, Allegheny County, PA. He married Elizabeth Casey, daughter of Peter and Magdalena (Dupuy) Casey, in Hampshire County, Va. during the 1760s. There is no proven connection between this Philip Ross and pioneer Alexander Ross of the Quaker settlement. A knowledgeable person on the Ross surname: Mrs. Virginia Day Wright Stevens, 509 Franklin Drive, San Marcos, TX 78666.

Royce, Daniel, son of John and Hannah Royce, was born circa 1743 and died in 1804 in Hampshire County, Virginia. In 1823, when his real estate was divided among his children, only four children survived Daniel Royce, viz, Frederick Royce, John Royce, Hannah (Royce) Critton, wife of John Critton, and Sarah (Royce) Slane, wife of Daniel Slane. Source: Hampshire County, W.Va. courthouse, *Deed Book 23*, pages 58-59.

Ruble, Ulery and Peter (deceased), left these heirs: George Ruble and Elizabeth his wife; Morris Evans and Elizabeth his wife; Owen Ruble and Eleanor his wife; David Ruble and Sarah his wife; Samuel Ruble and Mary his wife; Isaac Mahlin and Susanna his wife; William McDowell and Susannah his wife; Peter Lester and Jane his wife; William Murdock and Mary his wife. Source: Frederick County *Superior Court Book II*, page 323, dated Oct. 6, 1796.

Ruckman, James T., was born July 10, 1835 and died March 18, 1913. Buried next to James was Caroline Ruckman, born January 26, 1838 and died May 26, 1904. Source: Tombstone inscriptions in the Rev. Joseph Ruckman family graveyard, Hampshire County, W.Va.

Ruckman, Joseph, was deceased by Sept. 10, 1855, in Hampshire County., according to **Order Book III**, page 376, located in the Circuit Court. A tombstone inscription in a private graveyard, located several miles southeast of Romney, W.Va., says that he was born on May 16, 1786, and died on July 22, 1855. Buried next to Joseph was Eliza Ruckman, born Oct. 25, 1814 and died Nov. 10, 1851. Rev. Joseph was ordained as an elder in the Primitive Baptist Church, and served as clerk of the Patterson's Creek Baptist Association. His heirs were: (1) Martha

Ruckman married Matthew Heare, (2) Rachel Ruckman married James Poland, (3) Juliet Ruckman married Thomas Hines, (4) Rebecca Ruckman married William Taylor, (5) Emily Ruckman married Caleb Evans, (6) John Ruckman, (7) Elijah Ruckman, (8) Joseph Ruckman, II, and (9) Harriett Ruckman.

Russell, Andrew, was born in 1764/65 and died Dec. 26, 1853, "in 89th year." Source: Tombstone inscription in Old Fields Methodist graveyard, Hardy County, W.Va.

Russell, Antony was born in 1759/60 and died in March 1831, in "82nd year." Molly Russell, buried next to him, died May 6, 1851, "in 86th year." Source: Tombstone inscriptions in Vanmeter graveyard, Old Fields, Hardy County, W.Va.

Russell, John, was born in Virginia in 1791 and died in Nov. 1859, "of heart disease." Source: Mortality Schedule for Hampshire County, 1860 U.S. Census.

Russell, Joseph, was born in Frederick County, Va. circa 1775 and died in Belmont County, Ohio in 1820. He married Elizabeth Kackley, who was born in Frederick County, Va. in 1777 and died in Morgan County, Ohio, in 1837. She was a daughter of Jacob and Margaret (Secrist) Kackley, Jr. One researcher for this branch of the family is: Mrs. Janet Russell, 3546 Zinnia Ave., N.E., Canton, Ohio 44705. She is researching other families who came from old Frederick County, Va., including Joseph Anderson, born on May 10, 1791 and immigrated to Noble County, Ohio, where he died on April 27, 1869. Joseph's wife was named Sarah. Also, Mrs. Russell is researching the Elijah Davis family of Hampshire County, W.Va., a surname of interest to this compiler.

Russell, James, had a daughter Lydia Russell who married Henry Richards in Frederick County.

Rust, Mary, was born on Oct. 6, 1766 and died on Aug. 2, 1821. It is believed that she was a daughter of Elisha and Winifred (Massey) Powell, Sr., and that her second husband was named Peter Rust. She was buried in the Powell-Leith graveyard, next to James Leith, Jr. Source: Tombstone inscription at Bloomery, W.Va.

Sample, Joseph, son of Samuel and Nancy (Ridenour) Sample, died on Jan. 12, 1828, aged 8 years, 3 months. Source: Graveyard inscription, Old Timber Ridge Church graveyard at Highview.

Saville, George, son of Oliver and Mary (Shanholtzer) Saville, was born in Hampshire County on April 14, 1814 and died on March 20, 1901. Sarah J. Robinson (wife), daughter of Moses and Elizabeth Robinson, was born on July 10, 1829 and died on Dec. 12, 1904. In same graveyard were their descendants: J.J. Saville, born June 14, 1861 and died Dec. 31, 1956. His wife was born on Jan. 18, 1862 and died on Jan. 5, 1911; William T.L. Saville, son, born Nov. 14, 1864 and died on Dec. 4, 1904; George Loy Saville, 1868-1947. Source: Tombstone inscriptions in the Ginevan Graveyard, Okonoko, W.Va.

Saville, John, was born in Hampshire County in 1806 and died in Berkeley County, W.Va. on Dec. 28, 1881. His wife was Rebecca Asbury. They were buried in the Tomahawk cemetery in Berkeley County.

Saville, Joseph, son of Oliver and Mary (Shanholtzer) Saville, was born on April 6, 1802 and died on June 10, 1886, aged 84 years, 2 months, 4 days. Source: Tombstone inscriptions in the Oliver Saville graveyard near Augusta, W.Va.

Saville, Martha, daughter of Joseph and Lydia (Pultz) Saville, died on July 10, 1869, aged 89 years. The 1870 Mortality Schedule of the U.S. Census stated that she died of "consumption." Source: July 23, 1869 issue of the *South Branch Intelligencer*.

Saville, Mary, daughter of Abraham and Eliza (Haines) Saville, was born in 1827. Her husband was Robert McBride.

Saville, Oliver, son of Joseph and Lydia (Pultz) Saville, was born in 1773 and died on Oct. 19, 1855. His wife was Mary Shanholtzer, daughter of Peter and Elizabeth Shanholtzer. Mary was born on June 2, 1783 and died on Oct. 12, 1870. Source: Tombstone inscriptions from gravestones on the former Oliver Saville farm, located almost two miles northeast of Augusta, W.Va., and War of 1812 Widow's Pension application records.

Saville, Oliver, Jr., son of Oliver and Mary Saville, was born on Sept. 12, 1822 and died on March 12, 1888. He was buried in the Saville Graveyard near Augusta, W.Va., with his father. His wife was Elizabeth Combs, born on April 27, 1842 and died in Oct. 1904. She was buried in the Malick Graveyard at Augusta, W.Va.

Schaffenaker, Charles William, son of William and Catherine Schaffenaker, was born in Trenton, New Jersey in Feb. 1856. He moved with his family to Capon Bridge, Hampshire County, several years later. One unofficial source says that he married Emma Horner. A marriage record in the courthouse in Winchester, Va. shows that he married Emma Clayson, born in Pennsylvania, in 1858, to Stephen Clayson. They were married on Dec. 17, 1879. His occupation was listed as blacksmith. Another marriage record, dated March 8, 1883, states that he was widowed and then remarried to Mattie F. Arnold, daughter of Elias and Harriet J.F. Arnold.

Schaffenaker, Clyde, son of William and Catherine Schaffenaker, was born on May 30, 1865 and died in 1944. He was buried at Capon Chapel. He married Rena Pugh, 1868-1938, daughter of Louise A. (Carpenter) Pugh, according to Ralph L. Triplett Esq. Source: *Journal of Ray Wolford*, Capon Bridge, W.Va.

Schaffenaker, Frank L., son of William and Catherine Schaffenaker, born in Aug. 1873, married Bessie L. Himmelright, daughter of John F. and Hattie Himmelright, of Frederick County, Va. Marriage took place Nov. 8, 1899.

Schaffenaker, Henry, was born on Sept. 25, 1863 and died on Sept. 15, 1890. He married Fannie Pugh, according to Mr. Ralph L. Triplett Esq. Source: Tombstone inscription at Capon Chapel, Hampshire County, W.Va.

Schaffenaker, William, was born in Hollenberg, Germany in 1823 and died at Capon Bridge, W:Va. on Jan. 21, 1892. His wife, Catherine, was born in Saxon, Germany in 1833 and died on June 4, 1917. They were buried at Capon Chapel. They emigrated together from Germany, and landed at Trenton, New Jersey during the 1850's. After several years in that State, they came to Winchester, Virginia where they lived briefly. Then they settled at Capon Bridge, West Va., where he worked as a wagonmaker, and then a well-known blacksmith. Source: Tombstone inscriptions, U.S. census, and *Journal of Ray Wolford*.

Scott, William, was deceased by 1779, in Hampshire County. His widow, Sarah, remarried to Isaac Ely. William and Sarah Scott had a daughter, Mary, who married Benjamin Ely. Source: *Northern Neck Warrants and Surveys*, in folio of Benjamin Ely, Virginia State Archives.

Scribner (Scrivner), Levi, was born in Hampshire County, Va. in 1804 and died on Aug. 5, 1885, in Lafayette County, MO. His wife, Jane Coe (a widow), died on Oct. 20, 1858, aged 47 years. A letter, dated May 23, 1844, from Simeon and Sarah Ward to Uncle John Bruner, stated that "...the widow Jane Coe is married to Mr. Levi Scrivner." This widow Jane Coe was nee Hook, and her first husband was named Wesley Coe. A copy of letter was provided by Nancy J. Cotton, Edmond, OK 73034. Sources: Cemetery inscriptions in Greenton Cemetery, Lafayette County, Missouri.

Scrivner, Benjamin, was born in 1796 and died on Sept. 12, 1878. Source: Tombstone inscription in Trone Methodist Church Graveyard, Timber Ridge, Frederick County, Va.

Scrivner, Eliza, died in August 1879, aged 59 years, "of consumption." Her husband survived her. Eliza was born in Virginia. Source: 1880 Mortality Schedule for Frederick County, Virginia.

Scrivner, Emily C., died in December 1869, aged 35 years, 'of fever." Born in Virginia. Survived by spouse. Source: 1870 Mortality Schedule for Frederick County, Va.

Scrivner (Scrivenor), William, was born in 1793 and died on March 2, 1879. His wife, Elizabeth Coe, was born in 1790 and died in Oct. 1852, at High View. They were buried in the Trone Methodist Church Graveyard, on Timber Ridge. Possibly, William, Benjamin, Elijah and Levi Scrivner were brothers. Quoting from an letter dated May 22, 1848, written by Pleasant (Matthews) Furr of High View, Va., to Henry and Mary Ann (Matthews) Bruner, of Ottawa, LaSalle County, Illinois, "Katherine Johnson lives at Simion Ward's. Mary is single and Susan is single. Elizabeth is dead. Elijah Scrivner have brought a young wife from the Ohio, a very fine girl. Edward Muse [(1807-1855), husband of Eliza A. Scrivenor (1803-1876)] lives where Mrs. Scrivner lived. She is dead six years ago (approximate death year for their mother would be 1842). James and John Scrivner is in Indiana. Nancy Scrivner is married to Jefferson Murphy. Eliza Scrivner is single, and her and Benjamin Scrivner lives at E.R. Muse." Information from the letter was provided by Mrs. Nancy J. Cotton, 1704 Leawood Drive, Edmond, OK 73034. Mrs. Cotton is a researcher of the Bruner family.

Seaman, Jonah, and wife Jean, had these children: (1) Jonathan Seaman, born Dec. 5, 1744. (2) Elizabeth Seaman, born March 10, 1745. (3) John Seaman, born Aug. 16, 1747. (4) Jeremiah Seaman, born Nov. 3, 1749. (5) Jonah Seaman Jr., born Feb. 21, 1750. (6) Hannah Seaman, born Sept. 20, 1752. (7) Peter Seaman, born Dec. 2, 1753. (8) Charles Seaman, born April 5, 1754. (9) William Seaman, born July 1757. (10) Catherine Seaman, born March 10, 1758. (11) Phebe Seaman, born Jan. 16, 1760. Source: Morgan's Chapel Records, old Frederick County, Va. (in Virginia State Archives, Richmond).

Seaton, Alice, was born on Oct. 13, 1744 and died on Nov. 11, 1830. She was one of the oldest persons buried in the Powell-Leith graveyard in the Bloomery District of Hampshire County, West Virginia. Alice was nee Murrey or Murray, daughter of James and Lydia Murrey. She married John Seaton, Dec. 21, 1768, in Fauquier County, Va. Source: Cemetery inscription, Bible record of John and Frances (Seaton) Farmer, and courthouse marriage record.

Secrist, Henry, Swiss immigrant to Frederick County, Va., was born circa 1725 and died in Sept. 1799 in Frederick County. He married: (a) Maria "Mary" Elisabetha Printzler, daughter of Nicholas and Anna Margaretha (Ort) Printzler, in 1754. She died Nov. 21, 1767, of childbirth. (b) Anna Maria _____, 1n 1768. For more information on the Secrist family, contact family researcher Mr. Layne Secrist, 4020 Hallman Street, Fairfax, Va. 22030.

Secrist, Henry Jr., died on July 30, 1835, aged 76 years, according to tombstone inscription in St. John's Lutheran graveyard, located several miles south of Hayfield, Frederick County, Virginia. A Secrist history, provided by Mr. Layne Secrist, Stated that Henry Jr. was born Feb. 16, 1759 and he died unmarried.

Seevers, Henry, son of Casper Seevers, was born July 25, 1768 in Penn., and died Feb. 1, 1857. He married Hannah Grapes, born Oct. 22, 1772 in Frederick County, Va. and died Jan. 8, 1843. They were married Dec. 14, 1790 in Frederick County, Va. and were both buried in the Mt. Hebron cemetery in Winchester, Va. They had twelve children. Source: Hallie Bottemiller, 670 Swain Woods Terrace, Sebastopol, CA 95472.

Shade, William R., was born on Oct. 5, 1831 and died on April 27, 1903. His wife, Jane, was born on March 19, 1831 and died on Oct. 9, 1893. Source: Tombstone inscriptions at the Timber Ridge Primitive Baptist Church, located in northern Frederick County, Va.

Shane, Benjamin Franklin, was killed by an anvil in his blacksmith/gunsmith shop at Cold Stream, Hampshire County, on April 17, 1861. Ben F. Shane inscribed his name on gun barrels made in his gunsmith shop. Some shipments added "Romney, W.Va." His wife was Catherine Virginia Gill. After his death, Catherine remarried to Gabriel McDonald II, in 1866, and immigrated to Cozad, Nebraska in 1883, where they died and were buried. I visited their graves, on the east side of town, in 1977. Source: *Coffin Book* of William Meade Edwards, and *Shanholtzer Family History*, pp. 197-198.

Shanholtz, Nancy, daughter of Samuel and Phebe (Iden) Shanholtz, was born in 1839 and died in 1907, in Hampshire County. Her husband, was Dorsey Whitacre, son of Aquilla and Rachel (Kerns) Whitacre. According to John W. Mellon's *Undertaker Book*, Dorsey Whitacre was buried on April 19, 1894. The funeral costs were $18.00. This notice is to correct an error in my *Shanholtzer History...*, on page 93.

Shanholtzer, John, son of Peter and Magdalena (Hott) Shanholtzer Jr., was born in 1795 and died in Taylor County, W.Va. on June 19, 1861. He married Abbylonia Foreman, daughter of David and Catherine Foreman, on Nov. 8, 1818 at Cold Stream, Hampshire County. Source: Tombstone inscription in Ford cemetery, Oak Grove, Taylor County, W.Va., according to Howard L. Hunt of Coraopolis, Penn.

Shanholtzer, Peter   Sr., was born in Chester County, Pennsylvania on April 1, 1753 and died in Capon Valley, Hampshire County, Va., in 1817. His wife was named Elizabeth, and they were progenitors of the Shanholtzer families in Hampshire and Frederick Counties, Va. Source: Birth record in Vincent Reformed Church register in Chester County, PA., and death year established from personal property tax records in the Virginia State Archives in Richmond.

Shanholtzer, Peter, Jr., was born in Chester County, PA on July 9, 1775 and died in January 1836 in Hampshire County. His first wife was Magdalena Hott, daughter of George and Eve Rebecca (Steidley) Hott, II. They were married on Jan. 10, 1795, in Frederick County. She was born at White Hall, Frederick County, Va. in 1775 and died in Hampshire County, Va. circa 1817, during the "plague." Peter, Jr. remarried to Charlotte Orr, daughter of Anthony Orr of the North River section of Hampshire County. Charlotte was born in 1797 and died in 1851, at Cold Stream, Hampshire County, Va.

Shanholtzer, Philip, son of Peter and Magdalena (Hott) Shanholtzer, Jr., died on March 22, 1870 at him farm near Slanesville, W.Va. He was born approximately, in 1802. Philip had made out his Will the previous week, on March 14, 1870. Source: April 1, 1870 issue of the *South Branch Intelligencer*.

Shannon, Andrew, was born in 1794 and died on Aug. 13, 1846. Source: Tombstone inscription, Springfield, W.Va.

Shannon, Mary G., was born in 1794 and died on Oct. 6, 1824. Source: Tombstone inscription, Springfield, W.Va.

Shannon, Rebecca H., was born on June 10, 1794 and died Sept. 16, 1854. Source: Tombstone inscription.

Shearwood (Sherwood), John W., (1828-1914) and wife, Frances, (1848-1935), were buried in the Ginevan Graveyard, at Okonoko, Hampshire County, W.Va. Source: Tombstone inscriptions.

Sheetz, Jacob, was born in 1812 and died in Hampshire County, W.Va. on June 26, 1885. He married Sarah Corbin, daughter of Isaiah and Nancy (French) Corbin. Jacob was listed as a gunsmith on the 1850 and 1870 censuses.

Sheetz, Zebulon, died on Nov. 9, 1868 near Monticello, Indiana, aged 75 years. He was born in Hampshire County. According to William H. Ansel, Jr., in West Virginia History: "Early Gunmakers of Hampshire County," Zebulon Sheets was a gunmaker, somewhere in the Cold Stream/Edwards Run area of Hampshire County, Va. Source: *South Branch Intelligencer.*

Sherrard, Martha, died in Winchester, Va. on July 8, 17__, in the "15th year of the Commonwealth of Virginia," "in a fit of lunacy died by means of a cord," at the house of Robert Sherrard. Edward Smith was the Cororner. The jury appointed to make an inquisition was composed of: Mahlon Smith, John Haymaker,

Abraham Neil, Lewis Wolf, Simon Lauch, Patrick Kirk, Jacob Sperry, and six other names illegible in German script. Source: Frederick County, Va., "Inquisition of Dead Bodies," Virginia State Archives.

Shinn, David, son of Clement and Elizabeth (Webb) Shinn, died near Capon Bridge, in 1815.

Short, Isaac, son of John and Mary (Miller) Short, was born in Ann Arundel County, MD on Feb. 15, 1739, and died in Hampshire County, Va. in 1826. His wife was named Martha. Contact: Mrs. Rosemary Dunne, 123 Corinne Ave., Santa Cruz, CA 95065.

Short, John W., born 1853, died 1936, according to tombstone inscription in "Noland's Graveyard" (Stump) at Little Capon, Hampshire County, W.Va. Buried in the Caudy/Stump graveyard near North River, near end of Hickory Corner Road, is Nannie V. (Stump) Short, "wife of J.W. Short," born April 5, 1853 and died on Nov. 14, 1894. I believe they are husband and wife, but have not yet proven it. A marriage record in the Hampshire County courthouse shows that one John William Short married Anna Dawson Moore, Jan. 31, 1881.

Short, Jacob, son of John and Mary (Miller) Short, was born May 5, 1741 in Ann Arundel County, MD and died in Hampshire County, Va., in 1791. His wife was named Mary. Source: Ann Arundel (MD) Parish records and Hampshire County, Va. court records.

Short, Jacob, died in Hampshire County, aged 76 years. Ed Short reported his death to the Hampshire County clerk. A tombstone inscription at Springfield, W.Va., shows one Jacob L. Short, born on Dec. 8, 1809 and died on Dec. 1, 1886. Source: Courthouse record and graveyard inscription.

Short, John, was born on March 8, 1810 and died on Aug. 27, 1886. His wife Sarah was born on May 3, 1817 and died on May 23, 1892. Source: Tombstone inscriptions in old, private, graveyard at North River Mills, Hampshire County, W.Va.

Short, Joseph, was born on Sept. 15, 1856 and died on June 27, 1894. His wife, Phebe J., died on Feb. 3, 1890, aged 44 years. Source: Tombstone inscriptions in the Frederick Kump graveyard at North River Mills, Hampshire County. The property is now owned by Mr. and Mrs. Paul Gilson.

Short, Sarah (wife of Jacob L.) died on Aug. 23, 1897. No other information was given. See entry for Jacob Short, above. Source: Tombstone inscription, Springfield, W.Va.

Shuler, William Cornelius, son of Cornelius and Harriett (Kerns) Shuler, was born circa 1839 in Frederick County, Virginia. On Dec. 6, 1860, he married Sarah Ann Abrell, daughter of Joseph and Lucinda (Oates) Abrell. He died sometime during the 1860's (possibly in Civil War?) because his widow, Sarah Ann Shuler, remarried to Walter Jefferson Leith, son of William P. and Mary (Powell) Leith, on Jan. 19, 1869. Sources: Marriage records in the Frederick County, Virginia courthouse.

Shultz, Anna, daughter of Jacob and Margaret (Huber) Schultz, was born in Switzerland on May 28, 1730 and died in Frederick County, Va. in January 1826. She married Casper Rinker on April 11, 1757 in Germantown, Penn. Source: cemetery inscription in Quaker Graveyard at Gainsboro, Frederick County, Va.

Shultz, Frederick, was born in Virginia in 1781, and died in Sept. 1869. Occupation: Farmer. Survived by spouse. Source: 1870 Mortality Schedule for Frederick County, Va.

Shultz, John, was born on Feb. 3, 1753 in Germantown, Penn. and died on Nov. 5, 1840 in Frederick County, Va. He was buried in the Old Lutheran cemetery in Winchester, Va.

Simmons, Charles, born in 1772 and died on Oct. 23, 1825 in Hampshire County, Va. His wife, Ann, was born in 1782 and died on Feb. 16, 1862. Source: Tombstone inscriptions at Capon Chapel cemetery, Hampshire County, W.Va.

Simmons, Mary, daughter of John and Mary Cooper, died on Nov. 3, 1875 at the age of 65 years, 4 months and 15 days. She was buried at Capon Chapel, Hampshire County, W.Va. Her husband, Aaron Simmons, was born on Dec. 28, 1809 and died on Dec. 25, 1893 in Lafayette County, Missouri. Source: Hampshire County Courthouse death record for Mary; and a tombstone inscription for Aaron, in Greenton cemetery (Baptist), Lafayette County, Missouri. He migrated from Hampshire County after his wife died.

Simmons, William, was born on Nov. 17, 1804 and died on Sept. 7, 1867. He was buried in the Greenton Cemetery (Baptist affiliation), Lafayette County, Missouri.

Sine, the Rev. Christy, son of William and Margaret (Christy) Sine, was born in York County, Pennsylvania, on July 5, 1798 and died in Frederick County, Virginia, on April 14, 1858. His first wife was Margaret Kackley, daughter of Abraham and Christina (Whissen) Kackley. Margaret was born on May 16, 1805 and died on Dec. 25, 1839. Both she and Christy were buried in the Timber Ridge Christian Church cemetery, on Timber Ridge, West Virginia side. Next, Christy married Nancy Murphy, daughter of Thomas Murphy, on June 25, 1840. She was born on March 11, 1815 and died on Nov. 15, 1851. His third wife was Cassandra Fletcher, daughter of James and Catherine (Ullery) Fletcher. She was born on June 29, 1823 and died on Dec. 27, 1914, and was buried at Ebenezer Christian Church at Gore, Va.

Sine, Margaret Christy, was born in Pennsylvania, and died in June 1850, aged 83 years, in Monogalia County, Va. Cause of death was "gastritis." Source: 1850 Mortality Schedule for Monogalia County, Va.

Sine, Mary, died in June 1860, aged 57 years. Born in Virginia. Was ill with "dropsy" for one month prior to her death. Source: 1860 Mortality Schedule for Shenandoah County, Va.

Singleton, Mary (widow of John Singleton), died in 82nd year of life, Dec. 24, 1869, at the home of her children in Iowa. She formerly lived at New Creek (now in Mineral County, W.Va.). Source: The *South Branch Intelligencer*, issue of January 7, 1870.

Sirbaugh, David, son of Henry Sirbaugh, was buried on Jan. 7, 1895. His age listed as 75 years. According to John W. Mellon's *Undertaker Book*, the funeral costs were $20.00. David was buried in Ebenezer Christian Church Cemetery, located between Whitacre and Gore, Va.

Sirbaugh, Harmon, son of Jacob and Elizabeth (Oates) Sirbaugh, Jr., was born on Aug. 2, 1853 and died on Oct. 21, 1942. His wife, Lucy J.Riley, daughter of Thomas B. and Mary Margaret (Kerns) Riley, Jr., was born on Jan. 25, 1855 and died on March 25, 1935. Source: Mrs. Daniel Harmison, Romney, W.Va.

Sirbaugh, George Lemuel, son of Jacob and Elizabeth (Oates) Sirbaugh, was born on Aug. 27, 1842 and died in 1924. He married: (1) Mary Elizabeth Keiter, on April 13, 1865. She was born on Jan. 23, 1848 and died on Oct. 27, 1908. (2) Alice Virginia Kerns, daughter of John Sanford and Mary (Allebaugh) Kerns, on Sept. 7, 1910, in Hampshire County. He had at least twelve children by his first wife. According to a Bible record they were: (a) Sarah Alice Sirbaugh was born on Sept. 7, 1867. It is believed that she married a Mr. Snyder. (b) Frances Ellen "Fannie" Sirbaugh was born on Jan. 27, 1869, (c) John Madison Sirbaugh was born on Dec. 2, 1870. He married Bernice ____. (d) Albertus Rena Sirbaugh was born on Dec. 24, 1872 and died on April 17, 1895. Sometimes she was called Irene or Irenia. John W. Mellon's *Undertaker Book* shows that she was buried on April 19, 1895, with funeral costs of $14.00. (e) Luther Josiah Sirbaugh was born on Aug. 4, 1873 and died on Jan. 23, 1902. (f) Bessie Sirbaugh was born on Jan. 2, 1875 and died on Jan. 3, 1875. (g) Laura Estelle Sirbaugh was born on Sept. 12, 1878 and died on April 19, 1921. She married Homer Bagaent (1877-1928), (h) Jacob Franklin Sirbaugh was born on Aug. 17, 1881 and died on Oct. 12, 1920. He married Myrtle Mae Bailey. (i) Ernest Lee Sirbaugh was born on Nov. 15, 1883 and died on Oct. 29, 1964. He married Agatha Mae Hogbin. (j) Bertha Edmonia Sirbaugh was born on Jan. 14, 1887 and died on Sept. 19, 1912. She married Henry Braithwaite. (k) Frederick Harrison Sirbaugh was born on April 28, 1889 and died in 1947. He married Dorothy Rankin. (l) Allegedly, a son was named Allen, who died young, but was alive in 1905. However, this "Allen Sirbaugh" may well have been Harry Allen Snyder, a grandson who was born in Nov. 1894, and raised by Lemuel and Mary E. Sirbaugh. This Sirbaugh family lived in Smokey Hollow, Hampshire County, W.Va. Source: Bible records in possession of Roger L. Sirbaugh, Rt. 1, Box 60, Paw Paw, W.Va. 25434. He would like to hear from Sirbaugh researchers.

Sirbaugh, Isaac, son of Jacob and Elizabeth (Oates) Sirbaugh, was born on March 1, 1837 and died on June 26, 1916. His wife, Sarah Mariah Riley, daughter of Thomas Butler and Mary Margaret (Kerns) Riley, Jr., was born on June 14, 1838 and died on Nov. 24, 1898. Source: Tombstone inscriptions in Evan Hiett graveyard, on Sandy Ridge, Hampshire County, W.Va.

Sirbaugh, James W., son of Jacob and Elizabeth (Oates) Sirbaugh, Jr., was born on Oct. 8, 1835 and died on June 1, 1862. James W. married Esther McDonald, daughter of George and

Mary (Miller) McDonald, on Sept. 10, 1857, by the Rev. Christy Sine. The marriage record is in the Virginia State Archives, under Hampshire County. Esther was born on July 16, 1838. His tombstone has been found under debris (composted matter and earth) in the Evan Hiett graveyard on Sandy Ridge, Hampshire County. His well-inscribed tombstone had been knocked over, and covered with 4 inches of dirt. I dug it out and identified it during a recent excursion of the graveyard. The graveyard is on land owned by Mr. John Whitacre. They were parents of two daughters. The oldest one was Mary E. Sirbaugh, born on July 2, 1858 and died on Sept. 24, 1907. Mary E. married Amos Wesley Miller, who was possibly a son of Stephen and Ann Miller, on March 24, 1878. This information comes from tombstone inscriptions, archived records and from Mrs. Delores Glass, 1036 Zuni Drive, Farmington, N.M. 87401.

Sirbaugh, Jacob, Jr., son of Jacob and Mary (Anderson) Sirbaugh, Sr., was born on May 11, 1808 in Frederick County, Va. and died on Nov. 22, 1868 in Hampshire County. His wife, Elizabeth Oates, daughter of John and Mary (Kerns) Oates, was born on March 11, 1815 in Hampshire County and died on Dec. 5, 1883. Source: Tombstone inscriptions in Fairview Lutheran Cemetery, Gore, Va.

Sirbaugh, John, a widower, died in February 1869, aged 80 years. He was a farmer, and the cause of death was "dropsy." Source: 1870 Mortality Schedule for Frederick County, Va.

Sirbaugh, Josiah, son of Jacob and Elizabeth (Oates) Sirbaugh,Jr., was born Aug. 28, 1851 and died in 1920. His wife, Harriett A. Harper, was born in 1855; died in 1952. Source: The Rev. Melvin L. Steadman, Jr., Falls Church, Va.

Sirbaugh, Mary Jane, daughter of William and Eliza (McDougan) Richmond, died on Dec. 13, 1888 at age 47 years. She married Aaron Sirbaugh, son of Henry and Nancy Sirbaugh, on Aug. 27, 1878. This was Aaron's second marriage, the first being to Emily Kerns, on Sept. 9, 1844, in Frederick County, Va. Aaron died on July 11, 1894. Source: Tombstone inscription (for Mary Jane) in the Foreman graveyard at Cold Stream, Hampshire County, W.Va.

Sirbaugh, Samuel, son of Jacob and Elizabeth (Oates) Sirbaugh, Jr., was born on Oct. 28, 1844 and died on Aug. 20,

1928. He married Rebecca Ann Lewis on March 12, 1868. She was born on April 20, 1840 and died on Feb. 8, 1917. Source: The Rev. Melvin L. Steadman, Jr., Falls Church, Va.

Sirbaugh, Sarah E., daughter of Jacob and Elizabeth (Oates) Sirbaugh, died on Sept. 7, 1871, age 24 years, 4 months, and 20 days. She was unmarried. Source: Death Record in Hampshire County Courthouse.

Slane, Benjamin, son of Daniel and Nancy Ann (McDonald) Slane, Sr., was born in Ireland in 1773 and died in Hampshire County on Sept. 29, 1842. He married Delilah Poston, daughter of Col Elias and Rebecca (Cheshire) Poston, on Nov. 8, 1801. She was born in 1783 in Hampshire County and died on March 31, 1850. The 1850 Mortality Schedule of the U.S. census stated that she died of chlorea. Major source of dates: Family Bible record.

Slane, Hugh, son of Daniel and Nancy Slane, was born circa 1771 in Ireland and died in 1835 in Licking County, Ohio. He married Mary Largent, daughter of James and Margaret Largent. They migrated from Hampshire County in 1811/12. See "Family History: More About the Slanes of the Region," *The West Virginia Advocate*, Capon Bridge, W.Va., Jan. 16, 1984.

Slane, James, son of Daniel and Nancy Ann (McDonald) Slane, was born circa 1763 in Ireland and died circa 1829 in Hampshire County, Va. He married Margaret Largent, daughter of James and Margaret Largent. He was a farmer and lawyer who resided in the North River area of Hampshire County, Va.

Slane, John, son of Daniel and Nancy Ann (McDonald) Slane, was born in Ireland circa 1765 and died circa 1834 in Hampshire County, Va. He married Phoebe Hiett, daughter of John and Margaret Hiett, Jr., on Feb. 19, 1786.

Slane, Nancy, daughter of Thomas and Margaret (Neilson) Slane, was born in 1795 and died on April 12, 1838. She married William French. Source: Tombstone inscription in Slane graveyard, behind the Elementary School, Slanesville, W.Va.

Slane, Nancy, was born circa 1799, in Hampshire County, Va., where she married Philip Winckleback, Dec. 25, 1826. He was listed on the Morgan County, Va. census in 1820, and they were on the 1830 Hampshire County census. The 1860 census for Pekin, Tazwell County, Ill., taken on June 19th, stated that she was a widow, aged 61 years (birth year 1799). It is believed that her parents were James and Margaret (Largent) Slane, but not proven. The children of Philip and Nancy: (1) Sarah Winckleback was born in 1828. (2) Sophia Winckleback was born Dec. 18, 1829. (3) Elias Winckleback was born in Ohio, on Feb. 5, 1832. (4) John Winckleback was born in Ohio, on Dec. 14, 1834. (5) Charles Winckleback was born Aug. 5, 1837, in Illinois. (6) Daniel Winckleback was born in Illinois, Sept. 20, 1840. (7) Warren Winckleback was born in Illinois, in 1849. Contact: Mrs. Elsie M. Larue, 3506 Northern, Independence, MO 64052.

Slane, Nancy Ann, was born in Hampshire County, Va., on May 24, 1790 and died at the home of her son, Jonah Nixon Jr., at Woodburn, Loudoun County, Va., on Feb. 22, 1885. Her first husband was Jonah Nixon of Hampshire County. After his death, Ann remarried to John Pyott, on March 28, 1839. They emigrated from Loudoun County to Tennessee, in 1840. John died and Ann returned to Loudoun County in 1864, to live with her son. She was a member of the Methodist Church. Source: March 5, 1885 issue of *The Mirror*, Leesburg, Va.

Slane, Thomas, son of Daniel and Nancy Ann (McDonald) Slane, died on Aug. 14, 1858, aged 89 years, 4 months and 19 days. He was born in Ireland. Margaret Nielson, his wife, died on May 4, 1842, aged 73 years, 2 months, and 9 days. Possibly Margaret was a daughter of Dr. John Nielson (Nelson), who practiced medicine in the Forks of Capon area of Hampshire County. Source: Tombstone inscriptions in Slane graveyard, behind the Slanesville Elementary School, Hampshire County, and death records in the Virginia State Archives.

Slane, William, son of Hugh and Mary (Largent) Slane, was born in Hampshire County in 1797 and died in Licking County, Ohio on June 27, 1879. His wife, Dorothea "Dolly" Smith, was born in "Va." in 1797 and died on Jan. 17, 1881. They were buried in the Swisher cemetery, Licking County, Ohio.

Sloan, George, an umarried son of Richard and Charlotte (Van Horn) Sloan, died in Mineral County, W.Va. on June 1, 1872, according to a tombstone inscription in the Sloan family graveyard and a notice in the *South Branch Intelligencer*. He was aged 77 years, 5 months, and 22 days.

Sloan, Isaac, unmarried son of Richard and Charlotte (Van Horn) Sloan, was born on June 16, 1798 and died in Oct. 1841.

Source: Tombstone inscription in Sloan Graveyard, west of Romney, W.Va., along U.S. Route 50.

Sloan, John, unmarried son of Richard and Charlotte (Van Horn) Sloan, was born on Dec. 6, 1790 and died on April 10, 1853. Source: Tombstone inscription in the Sloan graveyard, west of Romney. W.Va., on U.S. Route 50.

Sloan, John, "(brother?) of Richard Sloan," died on May 21, 1847, "about 86 years." Source: Tombstone inscription in the Sloan graveyard, west of Romney, W.Va., near the "Old Stone House" on U.S. Route 50.

Sloan, Mary, daughter of Richard and Charlotte (Van Horn) Sloan, was born in Hampshire County on June 16, 1801 and died on Jan. 21, 1871. She married David Arnold, son of Zachariah and Abigail (Miller) Arnold, on Oct. 17, 1822. He was born on Aug. 4, 1797 and died on Oct. 5, 1855. Source: Rev. Frank L. Baker, retired minister in United Methodist Church Conference of Virginia.

Sloan, Richard, was born in Ireland in 1757 and died in Hampshire County on June 6, 1831. He married Charlotte Van Horn, born in 1773 and died on June 17, 1837. This couple had 10 children; lived west of Romney, on Route 50 near Junction, W.Va. Sometimes this family has been confused in the records with the Slane family. Source: Information given to the Rev. Frank L. Baker by Ms. Ann Vandiver Stout, according to record passed on to me.

Sloan, Richard, Jr., an unmarried son of Richard and Charlotte (Van Horn) Sloan, was born on June 30, 1809 and died on Sept. 24, 1878.

Sloan, Thomas, unmarried son of Richard and Charlotte (Van Horn) Sloan, was born on March 15, 1796 and died on Sept. 12, 1863. Source: Tombstone inscriptions in the Sloan Graveyard, Hampshire County, W.Va.

Slonaker, David, son of Christopher and Mary (Stephens) Slonaker, Jr., was born in 1826 and died in 1864, of typhoid fever. His wife, Margaret Loy, daughter of Adam and Sarah (Hiett) Loy, was born in 1827 and died in 1903. Note: The 1900 census for Bloomery District shows Margaret living with her son, James A. Slonaker, and her birthdate being in July 1825. Source: Tombstone inscriptions in the Slonaker private graveyard on the western slope of Bear Garden Mountain, near the Little Cacapon River. Allegedly, Christopher Slonaker, Jr. and wife were buried in the same cemetery, but no tombstone has survived. From another source, Christopher, Jr. was born in 1799 and died on Dec. 24, 1863. His wife, Mary Stephens was born in 1798 and died on March 16, 1864. See the Jan. 3, 1983 issue of *The West Virginia Advocate*, "Family History: The Slonakers."

Slonaker, George H., was born in 1803 and died on Aug. 4, 1885. He married Leah Barrett (born in 1809), daughter of Joseph and Unity (Fulkamore) Barrett. After her death he married Kate Oates. The relationship between this George H. and the Christopher Slonaker branch has not been proven. Source: Mrs. Rosalie V. Flint, Quincy, WA 98848.

Slonaker, John, son of Christopher and Mary (Stephens) Slonaker, was born in 1828 and died on Nov. 22, 1912. His wife, Maggie Whitmire/Widemyer, was born in 1842 and died on Dec. 26, 1926. In same plot are buried: May Slonaker, born in 1882 and died in 1912; and Icie Slonaker, born in 1891 and died in 1907. Source: Tombstone inscriptions in the Christopher Slonaker, Jr. graveyard on west side of Bear Garden Mountain, near the Cacapon River.

Smaltz, William, was born on Oct. 21, 1830 and died on Feb. 7, 1909. His wife, Carolyn, was born on Aug. 6, 1842 and died on May 8, 1904. In the same graveyard, enclosed by a fence, are these tombstones: Ella M. Smaltz, born Nov. 20, 1876 and died on April 25, 1946; Emma Augusta Smaltz, daughter of William and Carolyn Smaltz, was born on May 28, 1872 and died on Jan. 28, 1899; Laura Virginia Smaltz, born on Sept. 13, 1869 and died on April 13, 1897; Minnie Smaltz, born on Nov. 6, 1866 and died on Sept. 22, 1882; and, William Henry Smaltz, born on June 2, 1868 and died on Sept. 2, 1937. Apparently this burial ground contains the graves of parents and five of their children. The graveyard is on a hill above North River, south of North River Mills, east side of river. The Smaltz farm is now owned by Mike Rose.

Smith, Anne, unmarried daughter of Timothy Smith, died on April 2, 1853 "on the Tearcoat," aged 53 years, 11 months and 2 days. Source: Death record in Virginia State Archives.

Smith, George, son of Capt. Jeremiah and Elizabeth Smith, was born in 1769 and died on Oct. 1, 1844 at Gore, Va. He married: (1) Frances Curlett, see data under Curlett (2) Margaret McDonald, and (3) Ann (Ellis) Albin on Nov. 26, 1819. Source: Mr. Ralph L. Triplett, Esq., Gore, Va. (Note: Mr. Triplett died on May 24, 1984, at his home in Gore, Va.).

Smith, Hannah, died in January 1860, aged 67 years, "of pneumonia." She was ill for 14 days prior to her death. Source: 1860 Mortality Schedule for Frederick County, Va.

Smith, Isaac, died in April 1860, aged 71 years, "of shingles." He was ill for 123 days prior to his death. Born in Virginia; occupation was farmer. His wife survived him. Source: 1860 Mortality Schedule for Frederick County, Va.

Smith, James, unmarried son of Timothy Smith, died on April 28, 1853, of "pneumonia," aged 55 years and 15 days. He was a farmer on the Smith homeplace "on the Tearcoat." Source: Death record in the Virginia State Archives.

Smith, James was born in 1732, in Trenton, Mercer County, New Jersey. He married: (1) Anna Park in 1750, in Frederick County, Va., and (2) Mary Capon in 1755, in Frederick County, Va. James came to Hampshire County during the Colonial period, settling in the vicinity of Parks' Valley, north of U.S. Route 50. His Will was filed on June 5, 1815, in Harrison County, Va. and probated on May 15, 1819. His son, Timothy Smith, appeared in the Hampshire County court on March 22, 1819. This James Smith died in Harrison County, Va. before March 22, 1819. Source: Mrs. Jesse Amalong, St. Rt., Box 377, Pearce, AZ 85625.

Smith, Capt. Jeremiah, was born in 1711 and died in 1787 at Back Creek, Frederick County, Va. He was an early settler and an Indian fighter in the area. The Smith graveyard was shown to me by Ralph L. Triplett, Esq. In 1989, Mr. Rual P. Anderson of Gore, Va., led a successful effort to clean the graveyard. Almost 200 old stones were found in the ground, most of them uninscribed. Allegedly, Smith was thrice married. Cartmell, in his *Shenandoah Valley Pioneers and Their Descendants*, stated that Smith and two other men settled at Back Creek, near the present town of Gore, in 1730; that they were the first settlers in the Shenandoah Valley of Virginia. However, land records reveal that Owen Thomas was the first settler on land that Smith later owned.

Smith, Jeremiah Jr., was a son of pioneer and French and Indian War hero, Capt. Jeremiah Smith. Junior was born circa

1756 and died in 1794, on his Back Creek farm in Frederick County. His wife was allegedly Elizabeth Snyder. Between Sept. 7, 1796 and Sept. 2, 1805, guardian bonds were taken for his four orphan children, whose names were: Samuel Smith, Sarah Smith, Thomas Smith, and Mary Smith. Persons who were "bound" by these court orders were: Jonathan Smith and James Lawrence, in 1801, for orphan Sarah; Morris Ellis and Joseph Gordon, in 1801, for orphans Thomas and Mary Smith; George Smith and Joseph Gordon, in 1805, for orphans Thomas and Mary Smith, and; Samuel Smith, Richard Taylor, Robert McKee, and Joseph Hayes, in 1796, for orphan Samuel Smith, son of Jeremiah Smith Jr. Source: Frederick County, Va. guardian bonds, Virginia State Archives, Richmond, Va.

Smith, Jonathan, died in October 1859, aged 67 years. He was ill 730 days with consumption. Occupation was miller. Source: 1860 Mortality Schedule for Frederick County, Va.

Smith, Joseph, son of Timothy and Anna Smith, was born on April 29, 1794 and died on June 11, 1880. Elizabeth Doran, his first wife, was born on May 29, 1796 and died on July 5, 1864. Both were buried in the "Smith and Doran Cemetery" near Sedan, W.Va. (just off North River Road). Joseph remarried to Mahala Bloxham on April 19, 1866. She was buried in the Doran cemetery. Source: Bible records in the possession of Iris Dale Kline, Augusta, W.Va.

Smith, Lewis, was born in Hampshire County, Va. on May 20, 1795. Source: *History of Lafayette County* (Missouri), St Louis: Missouri Historical Company, 1881, page 513.

Smith, Margaret, daughter of John and Anna (McBride) Smith, was born on Feb. 23, 1828 and died on Feb. 18, 1907. She married Isaac Haines on Feb. 11, 1847. He died on March 20, 1900. (Note: John Smith was born in Dec. 1796, and was possibly a son of Conrad Smith, the Hessian soldier. Anna McBride, daughter of John and Elizabeth (Stodoman) McBride, was born on May 12, 1799. These were Hampshire County families. Source: Bible records copied and mailed to the compiler by Mrs. Ethel O'Toole, Nevada, MO.

Smith, Maria, widow of James Smith, died "last Monday" in Cumberland, MD, aged 90 years. Source: *South Branch Intelligencer* newspaper, issue of Nov. 10, 1871.

Smith, Mary, daughter of Joseph and Elizabeth (Doran) Smith, was born on Jan. 1, 1820 and died on May 11, 1858. She married Adam Wolford on March 25, 1847 (officiated by the Rev. Stephen Smith). Source: Bible record.

Smith, Ruth, daughter of James and Mary (Capon) Smith, was born in Hampshire County circa 1767 and died on Jan. 28, 1845. She married James Moore. Source: Notation in a Bible record.

Smith, Sarah Ann, daughter of Joseph and Elizabeth (Doran) Smith, was born on Sept. 25, 1817 in Hampshire County and died on Sept. 9, 1874. She married George Emmart on Oct. 7, 1857. Source: Bible record provided by Iris Dale Kline, Augusta, W.Va.

Smith, the Rev. Stephen, died near Paw Paw on the Monday before Oct. 14th, 1871. He was in the ministry for over 50 years, according to the *South Branch Intelligencer*, issue of Oct. 20, 1871. He was buried in the Francis W. Heiskell graveyard, near the Cacapon River, near end of County Road 29/2. The farm is now owned by Edward Milburn. The inscriptions shows that the Rev. Stephen Smith was born on Nov. 1, 1802 and died on Oct. 9, 1873. "God was with him, Acts 7:9." Another grave next to him is marked only by an uninscribed slate stone.

Smith, Timothy, son of James and Mary (Capon) Smith, was born circa 1764 and died in April 1849, in Hampshire County, Va. His Will was filed on Jan. 21, 1848. Source: Iris Dale Kline of Augusta, W. Va.

Smoke, Henry, was born in 1787 and died on Aug. 2, 1827, in Frederick County, Virginia. Source: Tombstone inscription in Quaker graveyard at Gainsboro, Virginia.

Smoot, Ann, died a natural death at her home at Neff Town, Frederick County, Va., on Dec. 7, 1836. Source: Frederick County, Va., "Inquisition of Dead Bodies," Virginia State Archives.

Smoot, Barton, was deceased before Sept. 16, 1847, when a case was heard in chancery court. His wife was named Catherine, also deceased by Sept. 1848. Their children were: Silas Smoot; Elias Smoot; Susan Smoot married Eli D. Chadwick; and Maria Smoot married John Burkett. Source: Information in *Order Book II*, pages 231-232, in Circuit Court of Hampshire County, in Romney, W.Va.

Smoot, Josiah, was born on April 11, 1771 and died on April 14, 1847. He married Jane Riley, daughter of William and Isabella (McChesney) Riley. She was born on Nov. 13, 1785 and died on Feb. 28, 1858.

Snapp, George Jr., son of Hans George and Anna Margaretha (Lowenguth) Schnepp, was born in Bucks County, PA, in Feb. 1752, and died in 1843, in Knox County, IN. He married Margaret Rudolph, probably in Frederick County, Va. Source: Mrs. Leona Winemiller, 412 West Grantley Ave., Elmhurst, IL 60126.

Snapp, Hannah, daughter of Benjamin and P(hoebe?) Milleson, died in Hampshire County on March 14, 1876, age 76 years, 8 months, and 14 days. Her husband was John Snapp, according to the death record in the Courthouse. The March 31, 1876 issue of the *South Branch Intelligencer* stated that Hannah was born on July 30, 1799. In the same newspaper, in a Sept. 1879 issue, it stated that John Snapp, aged 88 years, died recently in Hampshire County. He was a veteran of the War of 1812.

Snapp, James, was born Feb. 2, 1813 and died May 11, 1886. Source: Tombstone inscription in Salem United Methodist cemetery, Slanesville, Hampshire County, W.Va.

Snapp, Joseph Sr., son of John and Anna Maria (Windel) Snapp, was born near Strasburg, Shenandoah County, Va. on June 17, 1771 (family Bible) and died in Hampshire County, Va., Dec. 12, 1847, aged 76 years, 6 months, 30 days. His wife, Margaret Cravens, was born Aug. 26, 1775 (family Bible) and died March 19, 1850, in Hampshire County, aged 74 years, 6 months, 21 days. They were married on Oct. 1, 1793, in Rockingham County, Va. Margaret was a daughter of John and Margaret (Hiett) Cravens. John Cravens was born in Delaware in 1722 and died in Rockingham County, Va., July 24, 1778. Children of Joseph and Margaret (Cravens) Snapp were: (1) John Snapp was born on July 30, 1794. He married Hannah Milleson. (2) Robert Snapp was born on June 24, 1796, and died in 1858 at Ft. Defiance, Augusta County, Va. (3) William Cravens Snapp was born Jan. 29, 1799. (4) Rhoda Snapp was born June 14, 1801. She first married Roswell Kilborne, and then John Cunningham. They immigrated to Ohio. (5) Mary Snapp was born April 19, 1803 and died Dec. 29, 1806. (6) Joseph Cravens Snapp was born

May 6, 1805, and died May 21, 1882. He married Eleanor Hiett. (7) Mariah Snapp was born Feb. 6, 1808 and died Sept. 26, 1834. She married Isaac Wolverton, May 16, 1826, in Hampshire County, Va. (8) Diana Snapp was born Dec. 31, 1810. (9) James Cravens Snapp was born Feb. 2, 1813 and died May 11, 1886. He married Malinda Monroe, daughter of Robert and Elizabeth Monroe. (10) Syntha Jane Snapp was born Nov. 30, 1815 and died June 10, 1855. He married Malinda Moore. (11) Cyrus Snapp was born Sept. 19, 1818 and died Sept. 13, 1836. Source: Tombstone inscriptions in Salem Methodist Cemetery, Slanesville, W.Va., and family Bible of Joseph Snapp Sr.

Snapp, Joseph, was born Jan. 30, 1761 and died Aug. 8, 1825, in Frederick County, Va. In same graveyard is another Joseph Snapp, born April 4, 1792 and died Oct. 16, 1832. Buried here, also, was Catherine Snapp, who married William Lupton. She was born Sept. 11, 1787 and died Jan. 26, 1812. Ralph L. Triplett Esq. reported that Catherine was a daughter of John and Sarah (Davis) Snapp. Source: Tombstone inscriptions in Wisecarver Graveyard, near State Route 622, Frederick County, Va., and records of Ralph L. Triplett, Esq.

Snapp, Joseph C. Jr., was born May 6, 1805 and died May 21, 1882. His wife, Eleanor Hiett, died Oct. 13, 1896, aged 85 years, 6 months, 15 days. Eleanor was a daughter of Joseph and Alice (Sutton) Hiett. Source: Tombstone inscriptions in Salem United Methodist cemetery, Slanesville, Hampshire County, W.Va.

Snapp, Margaret (Cravens), was born in 1775; died in March 1850, of "chlorea." Source: Mortality Census for Hampshire County, Va., in 1850.

Snapp, Sarah, daughter of George and Margaret (Rudolph) Snapp Jr. was born in Frederick County, Va., in 1787 and died in Knox County, IN, in 1860. She married Jacob Kackley in Frederick County, Va., on April 8, 1806. Source: Mrs. Leona Winemiller, 412 W. Grantley Ave., Elmhurst, IL 60126.

Sneathen, Samuel, age 67, died on April 27, 1875, in Hampshire County. His wife Elizabeth died on April 29, 1875. Source: *South Branch Intelligencer*, issue of May 14, 1875.

Snyder, Frederick, was born on July 22, 1828 and died on May 12, 1908. His wife Lydia A. died on Sept. 1, 1886, aged 50 years, 5 months, and 25 days. They were buried in the cemetery at Levels, Hampshire County, W.Va.

Snyder, Dr. John, was deceased prior to Sept. 15, 1845, when a chancery court case was heard. The records show that his wife was named Letitia, and these were their children: John Snyder; Charles Snyder; Harriett Snyder married Alonzo Welton; William Snyder; and Elizabeth Snyder married Jonathan Carlyle. Jonathan was deceased by 1845. Source: *Order Book II*, pages 118 and 139, Circuit Court of Hampshire County, West Virginia. The Jan. 13, 1860 issue of the *South Branch Intelligencer* stated that Dr. John Snyder was buried in the old Presbyterian cemetery, Lot 59, on the corner of High Street and Gravel Lane.

Sommerville, Alexander, was born March 2, 1823 and died Dec. 21, 1893, near San Antonio, Texas. His wife, Jemima H. Vanmeter, daughter of Garrett Vanmeter, was born Sept. 20, 1828 and died Aug. 8, 1886. Both were buried in Olivet Cemetery "on the hill" at Moorefield, W.Va. They were Presbyterians. Alexander was president of the South Branch Valley National Bank of Moorefield. Source: Graveyard inscriptions and local newspaper clipping (Moorefield, W.Va.).

Sommerville, Elizabeth (wife of William), was born on Jan. 12, 1788 and died on March 25, 1857. Source: Tombstone inscription, Springfield, Hampshire County, W.Va. The old graveyard is on top of a high hill overlooking the town.

Sommerville, James, was born on Feb. 27, 1793 (allegedly in Frederick County, Virginia) and died on Oct. 23, 1876 in Lafayette County, Missouri. He served in the War of 1812. James married Elizabeth Mauzy, daughter of Peter and Elizabeth (Buzzard) Mauzy II. She was born in 1793 in Smokey Hollow, Hampshire County, Va. and died on March 21, 1872, in Lexington, Missouri. They were married on April 17, 1817, and immigrated to Missouri in April 1849. Sources: Multiple, including The *South Branch Intelligencer*.

Sommerville, William, died in Berkeley County, Va., March 18, 1836. He served in the Revolutionary War, in the Pennsylvania Line. Source: Records in DAR Library.

Spaid, Frederick, died in Hampshire County, W.Va. on Dec. 15, 1871, age 86 years and 1 month. Source: Hampshire County courthouse death records. Note: This record is probably in error. See entry for Margaret (McVickers) Spaid.

Spaid, John, was deceased prior to 1868. A list of his heirs in chancery court, Circuit Court, Hampshire County, W.Va., found in **Order Book 4**, page 395:   (1) Enos Spaid, 1808-1886, married Elizabeth Brunner on Feb. 15, 1829 and Rose Ann Stripe, in July 1830.   (2) Hiram Spaid, 1811-1876, married Jemima LaFollette, in 1832.   (3) Mahala Spaid, 1806-1881, married William Arnold. He died in 1833.   (4) Christina Spaid married Joseph Secrest, son of Abraham and Katherine (Rudolph) Secrist   (5) Joseph Spaid, 1812-1900, married Elizabeth Leatherman   (6) Rachel Spaid, 1817-1899, married Amos LaFollette   (7) John W. Gardner, son of William Gardner who married Mary Spaid, 1817-1836.   (8) Amos Spaid, 1809-1871, married Marie Kackley   (9) Malinda Spaid (1826-1897) married Meredith Capper and (10) Michael Spaid, deceased, 1819-1868, married Mary Elizabeth Kline.   Listed also was Ann Jemima LaFollette who married James McCauley. Ann Jemima was a daughter of Elizabeth Spaid, 1828-1859, who married Silas LaFollette.   No dates were given in the document, but vital data were provided from miscellaneous other sources. The list of children is not complete. The name of John Spaid's wife was Hannah Anderson.

Springer, Dennis, son of Jacob Springer (1668-1738) of Burlington County, N.J., was born in 1712 and died in old Frederick County, Va., June 3, 1760. His wife, Ann Prickett, daughter of Jacob Prickett, died ca. 1790, in Fayette County, PA. They left many descendants.   Contact: Sara H. Rice, 4020 Southwest 77th Street, Gainesville, FL 32608-3604.

Starkey, Cassandra, wife of Joseph Starkey, was born on June 12, 1808 and died on Sept. 7, 1854. Source: Tombstone inscription at Asbury Cemetery near the Hampshire/Hardy County line.

Starkey, John was born in Hampshire County, Va. in 1804, between what is now Augusta and Rio, and was still living in the same neighborhood when he made a court deposition on Aug. 27, 1884. A tombstone inscription in Mountain Dale graveyard states that he was born June 19, 1804 and died April 23, 1894. His wife, Sarah, was born April 3, 1805 and died Feb. 24, 1875.

Sources: War of 1812 Pension Folder of William Loy, and tombstone inscriptions.

Starnes, Anna, daughter of Jacob and Catherine Starnes, was born on Jan. 20, 1792; died on May 4, 1873. Her husband was Alexander Patterson, son of Thomas and Anna (Mullen) Patterson. Source: Courthouse death record and family papers.

Statton, Jacob, died on April 5, 1855, aged 68 years, 10 months, 5 days. Source: Tombstone inscription in graveyard on Davy Road, Hampshire County, W.Va.

Stoker, Balzar, died Nov. ye 17, 1796, aged 73 years (born in 1723), according to a beautifully hand-hewn and inscribed field stone on a hillside, near the Little Cacapon River. He came to Hampshire County during colonial days, and lived in the Little Capon area, near what later became known as Okonoko (now a ghost town). His wife was named Eve, believed to be buried in adjacent grave with no inscription on slatestone. One source stated that Eve died on April 22, 1815. Source: Tombstone inscription in the "Ginevan Graveyard," at Okonoko, Hampshire County, W.Va.

Stoker, Critton, son of John and Elizabeth (Critton) Stoker, was born on Aug. 11, 1786 at Little Cacapon, Hampshire County, Va., and died on July 11, 1865, in Montgomery County, Ohio. His wife, Sarah Johnson, was born at Spring Gap Mountain, Hampshire County, Va. and died on Oct. 1, 1830, age 44 years. Source: Tombstone inscriptions in Old Johnson Graveyard, Wagner Ford Road, Wayne Township, Montgomery County, Ohio.

Stoker, John, son of Balzar and Eve Stoker, was born in Frederick County, Va. on April 3, 1754 and died on Nov. 7, 1833, in Montgomery County, Ohio. On Jan. 10, 1775, in Hampshire County, Va., he married Elizabeth Critton, who was born in Hampshire County, on May 18, 1757. She died in Montgomery County, Ohio, on Jan. 18, 1835. John Stoker was a veteran of the Revolutionary War, serving under Col. Alexander Spotswood.

Stone, the Rev. Benjamin, son of Thomas and Mary (Butler) Stone, was born in Virginia in 1743 and died at Beech Springs, Harrison County, Ohio, on June 4, 1832. His wife, Anna Asbury, was born in Stafford County, Va. on Oct. 6, 1747 and died in 1833. Her parents were George and Hannah (Hardwick) Asbury. Benjamin pastored several Baptist churches in eastern

Hampshire County, at least during the 1780s and 90s. Many members of his Hampshire County congregations (Crooked Run and North River) were emigrants from Fauquier County, Va.

Stotler, Elijah, son of Peter and Susannah (Shockey) Stotler, was born at Oakland, "Morgan County," Va. in 1817. and died in Clinton County, Ohio on Dec. 24, 1856. He married Evann Spillman, daughter of Peter and Susannah (Redman) Spillman. She was born in "Morgan County," Va. in 1816 and died on May 3, 1894. Source: *History of Clinton County, Ohio*: Indianapolis, B.F. Bowen & Co., Inc., by Albert J. Brown, 1915, pp. 600-602.

Stover, Catherine, died in August 1859, aged 63 years, of "consumption." Born in Virginia, she was survived by her spouse. Source: 1860 Mortality Schedule for Shenandoah County, Va.

Streit, Charles, son of William Streit Sr. of Bedford County, PA, was born in 1782 and died April 27, 1825 at Whitehall, Frederick County, Va. He married Catherine Fries, daughter of Martin and Catherine (Schaul) Fries, on Aug. 16, 1804, in Frederick County. She was born in 1785 and died on Jan. 12, 1861. They were buried at the Old Stone Church at Whitehall. Their children were: (1) George Streit was born Dec. 23, 1805 and died Oct. 3, 1872. He married Mary Manor, Dec. 1, 1831. (See *Will Book 31*, page 64.) (2) Elizabeth Streit was born Oct. 19, 1907 and died in 1837. She married Solomon Glaize, son of George and Catherine (Hetzel) Glaize. Solomon was born Jan. 12, 1796 and died March 11, 1878 (killed by a horse). After Elizabeth's death, he remarried to Elizabeth Fries, daughter of Michael Fries. (3) Margaret "Peggy" Ann Streit was born Oct. 16, 1810 and died Nov. 6, 1873. She married Isaac Shanholtz, daughter of Peter and Magdalena (Hott) Shanholtzer Jr., Sept. 8, 1835. He was born in 1808 and died April 18, 1885 at Cross Junction, Va. (4) Catherine Streit was born Feb. 21, 1813. She first married William Mincer, Oct. 14, 1844, and secondly to a Mr. Owens. (5) Mary Ann Streit was born Jan. 14, 1815 and she married William Lynn Jr., Oct. 19, 1835. (6) Susan Streit was born Oct. 13, 1816 and died Feb. 17, 1868. She married the Rev. James Carl Hott, son of John and Margaret Rebecca (Fries) Hott, Aug. 8, 1839. He was born on Nov. 4, 1817 and died on June 10, 1891. (7) Sarah Streit was born Oct. 13, 1818 and died July 17, 1852. She married Joel Barrett on Sept. 5, 1837. (8) Anna Streit was born Aug. 5, 1820 and died May 11, 1888. She married George Yeakley Fries, son of David and Mary (Hallihan) Fries, March 10, 1845, in Frederick County, Va. (9) Jane Streit was born June 20, 1822 and died March 13, 1905. She married the Rev. Jacob Fries Hott, Aug. 17, 1843. He was born Nov. 21, 1821 and died Aug. 31, 1884, in Frederick County. (10) John W. Streit was born July 22, 1824 and died Dec. 18, 1891. He married Elizabeth Fries on Feb. 8, 1848. Sources: Family Bible record of Charles Streit, and public records.

Streit, Charles W.P., died in February 1870, aged 34 years, "of consumption." His occupation was blacksmith. Source: 1870 Mortality Schedule for Frederick County, Va.

Streit, the Rev. Christian, son of John Leonard and Catherine Streit, was born on June 7, 1749 in Somerset County, New Jersey, and died at Winchester, Virginia on March 12, 1812. He was known as the "first Lutheran pastor born on American soil." Streit was thrice-married: (1) Anna Maria Christina Hoff, who was born on Feb. 6, 1760 and died on Aug. 20, 1782, (2) Salome Graef/Grove, on Feb. 19, 1783. She was born in 1765 and died on Jan. 6, 1788, and (3) Susannah Barr, on Oct. 15, 1789s. She was born on May 9, 1769. Source: For a more detailed discussion of this family, see "Family History: Focus on the Streit Family," *The West Virginia Advocate*, Feb. 7, 1983 issue, published at Capon Bridge, W.Va. 26711.

Streit, Frances Ann, daughter of the Rev. Christian and Susannah (Barr) Streit, was born in Winchester, Virginia on May 18, 1811 and died on Nov. 12, 1866. She married John Baker White of Romney, W.Va., the well-known Clerk of Court. During the Civil War they lived in Richmond, Virginia, where John Baker White died while allegedly serving in the Administration of Jefferson Davis. Frances was buried in the Indian Mound cemetery in Romney, W.Va.

Streit, Philip Barham, son of the Rev. Christian and Susannah (Barr) Streit, was born in Winchester, Va. on Sept. 3, 1804 and died on Oct. 9, 1860. His wife was Ann (McAllister) Glass. He was a prominent lawyer and manufacturer in Hampshire County, Va.

Strickler, Jacob, born in Pennsylvania in 1800, died in Mineral County, W.Va. in May 1870, of pneumonia. He was a plasterer. Source: Mortality Schedule of the U.S. Census.

Strickling, Joseph, son of John and Elizabeth (Timmons) Strickling, was born Nov. 28, 1790, in Hartford County, MD and died in Monroe County, Ohio, Dec. 18, 1874. His family moved to Frederick County, Va., circa 1802, where Joseph married Nancy Whitacre, daughter of Joshua and Rachel (Wilson) Whitacre, April 11, 1815. Nancy was born in Loudoun County, Va., Feb. 23, 1793, and died in Monroe County, Dec. 19, 1866. They raised a large family. Source: Family Bible record.

Strother, William, died on Dec. 24, 1816 in Frederick County, Va. After his body was found, a jury was appointed to determine the cause of death, and the ruling was "by natural causes." The jury consisted of: David Ridgeway, William Dillon, William Carr, John Pugh, Benjamin Sidwell, James Curl, Joseph Hackney, Daniel Wade, John Thompson, John Snider, George Swiers, and Daniel Royer. Source: Frederick County, Va., "Inquisition of Dead Bodies," Virginia State Archives, Richmond, Va.

Stuart/Stewart, John, died in Frederick County, Virginia circa 1750. His eldest son, James Stewart, was left an orphan, in care of James Caudy and Capt. Jeremiah Smith, who procured land for him on the Cacapon. Source: Notes in file of Abraham Fry, *Northern Neck Warrants and Surveys* for Fairfax grant on Hogue's Creek, issued in April 1751.

Stump, Benjamin, died on April 4, 1861, in his 76th year. Sarah Carlin, his wife, died on Dec. 29, 1861, aged 73 years. Her father was Andrew Carlin. Buried nearby: Sallie, daughter of Benjamin and Sarah Stump, was born on Dec. 20, 1819 and died on May 3, 1903. Source: Tombstone inscriptions in Little Cacapon Primitive Baptist Church Graveyard, Hampshire County, W.Va.

Stump, Benjamin D., was born on Feb. 14, 1814 and died on May 11, 1868. Source: Tombstone inscription in "Noland graveyard" at Little Capon, Hampshire County, W.Va.

Stump, Catherine, born on May 16, 1810, and died on Jan. 26, 1891, aged 80 years, 8 months, 10 days. Her husband, Jacob Shanholtzer, son of Jacob and Mary (Fahs) Shanholtzer Sr., was born on Feb. 12, 1816 and died on Feb. 5, 1887. Her parents were Benjamin and Sarah Stump. Source: Tombstone inscriptions in the Little Cacapon Primitive Baptist Graveyard, Hampshire County, W.Va.

Stump, Elizabeth, was born in 1779, nee Boggess, of Fauquier County, Va. and died in Dec. 1849 in Hampshire County, of "chlorea." She was married to Joseph Stump. Source: 1850 Mortality Census for Hampshire County.

Stump, George, son of Benjamin and Sarah (Carlin) Stump, died on Jan. 3, 1881, in 74th year. Source: Tombstone inscription, Little Cacapon Primitive Baptist Church, Hampshire County, W.Va.

Stump, Jacob, died on Oct. 23, 1890, aged 71 years, 11 days. His wife, Rhoda A. Huff, died on Sept. 7, 1871, aged 47 years, 7 months, and 7 days. Source: Court records.

Stump, Jacob, 1829-1909 and his wife Evaline Thompson, 1837-1926, were buried in the "Noland graveyard" at Little Capon, Hampshire County. Another source stated that Jacob was a son of William B. and Rebecca (Stump) Stump. Jacob was born on May 31, 1829 and died Nov. 24, 1909. Source: Tombstone inscriptions, and family records.

Stump, Mrs. James, age 49, died "last Monday" in Hampshire County. Source: *South Branch Intelligencer*, June 23, 1873 issue.

Stump, John, was born in 1774; died in April 1850, of "chlorea," in Hampshire County. His wife, Nancy Dawson, was born on June 25, 1774 and died on Sept. 7, 1846. Source: Mortality Census for 1850, and family records. See "History of the Peter Stump Family," *The West Virginia Advocate*, Feb. 1989.

Stump, John W., was born on Oct. 23, 1837 and died on June 9, 1885. His second wife, Jennie, was born on Dec. 23, 1847 and died on Aug. 10, 1908. They were buried together. His first wife was Rhoda Ann Catlett, daughter of Bailey and Elizabeth Catlett. Rhoda was born on Feb. 12, 1839 and died April 14, 1874. She was buried in the Huff graveyard at Largent, Morgan County, W.Va. Source: Tombstone inscriptions in "Noland cemetery," Little Capon, Hampshire County, and Huff graveyard, on the property of Marvin Keesecker, Largent, W.Va.

Stump, Joseph, died in an accident on Nov. 7, 1889, aged 80 years, 7 months. Nancy Hass, his wife, died on June 6, 1890, aged 83 years, 1 month, and 15 days. Source: Tombstone inscriptions in "Noland graveyard," Little Capon, Hampshire County, W.Va.

Stump, Peter, son of Jacob and Fannie (Moore) Stump, died on Nov. 6, 1838, aged 40 years. Peter's wife Margaret Caudy, daughter of John and Rebecca (McDonald) Caudy, died on May 12, 1880, aged 80 years. They were married on May 3, 1827. Source: Tombstone inscriptions in "Noland Graveyard" at Little Capon, Hampshire County, W.Va.

Stump, Rebecca, daughter of Jacob and Fannie (Moore) Stump, and wife of William Stump, died on Oct. 1, 1888, aged 90 years, 11 months, 5 days. Her son, J. Stump, reported her death to the courthouse in Romney.

Stump, Samuel J., son of John and Nancy (Dawson) Stump (1774-1850), died on March 30, 1869, age 64 years. He served as a Justice of the Peace in Hampshire County. His wife, Rebecca A. Caudy, daughter of John and Rebecca McDonald) Caudy, died on March 24, 1884, aged 80 years. In same graveyard, located near Hickory Corner Road and North River, Hampshire County, W.Va., were buried: Margaret E. Stump, born Nov. 16, 1832 and died May 4, 1915; Benjamin Stump, died aged 5 days; Ann R. Stump, 1834-1913. Source: Tombstone inscriptions in Caudy graveyard, now on property owned by a family named Frane.

Stump, William, son of Joseph and Elizabeth Stump, was born in Loudoun County, Va. on March 21, 1800 and died in Hampshire County, on Dec. 27, 1879, "of heart disease." His son, Jacob Stump, reported the death to the courthouse in Romney, W.Va.

Swartz, John W., son of George and Phoebe (Mercer) Swartz, died at Back Creek, Frederick County, Va. on June 17, 1854, aged 27 years, according to tombstone inscription in the Quaker cemetery in Gainsboro, Va. It is believed that he married Elvirah "Ellen" Harrison, daughter of Robert and Mary (Straynton) Harrison, on March 13, 1851 in Frederick County, Va., by the Rev. John Grove, a Methodist preacher on Timber Ridge. If this is the right person, Elvira was born on Dec. 5, 1831 in Hampshire County, Va. and died on April 6, 1860 in Capon Valley. See the Harrison family.

Swisher, Elizabeth Jane, daughter of Jacob Swisher, died in Hampshire County on April 20, 1870, aged 23 years. Source: *South Branch Intelligencer*, April 29, 1879 issue.

Swisher, Elizabeth, widow of John Swisher, died on Jan. 4, 1867, aged 79 years, 7 months. Source: Jan. 18, 1867 issue of the **South Branch Intelligencer**, Romney, W.Va.

Swisher, Henry, was born on Dec. 14, 1826 and died on Sept. 16, 1896. Source: Tombstone inscriptions in graveyard at Three Churches, W.Va.

Swisher, John, was deceased before April 12, 1849. His widow, Mary, was alive when a suit was filed in chancery court, naming these heirs: (1) Elizabeth Swisher married William Henderson (2) John Swisher, Jr. (3) Margaret Swisher married Stewart Bennett (4) Jacob Swisher married Sarah ____ (5) Henry Swisher (6) Samuel Swisher (7) Rebecca Swisher married John L. Parker (Note: See **Order Book 4**, page 175, Circuit Court of Hampshire County, W.Va.) (8) William Swisher (9) Daniel Swisher (10) James Swisher (11) Anna Swisher married Joseph Spohr and (12) Mary "Polly" Swisher married John Coiner.[47]

Swisher, John, died on Dec. 14, 1845, in his 69th year. Source: Tombstone inscription at Three Churches, Hampshire County, Va. Although I didn't retain my notes, I believe he was buried in the Primitive Baptist section.

Swisher, Capt. Simon W., was born in 1830, died in 1910. He served as a Captain in CSA, Co. K, 18th Regiment. His wife was Mary E. Hiett, daughter of John and Julia Ann (Stump) Hiett. Mary was born in 1837 and died in 1904. Source: Hiett graveyard near the Forks of Capon.

Tanquary, James, son of Abraham and Wilhelmineh (Whittington) Tanquary, was born in Calvert, Maryland, in 1770 and died in Frederick County, Va. in January 1825. He was buried at the Old Stone Church at Green Springs. His first wife, Rachel Royer was buried in the Old German cemetery in Martinsburg, W.Va. His second wife was named Hannah McClure. Their nine children intermarried with local families, such as the Hancher, Moss, Rust, Hackney, Duff, and Hughes. I have a copy of an unpublished "manuscript" on the Tanquary family, furnished to me by: Mr. Patrick G. Tanquary, P.O. Box 1063, Danville, Illinois 61832.

---

47. **Order Book II**, page 311, dated April 12, 1849, Hampshire County Circuit Court, Romney, W.Va. 26757.

Tarvin, George, II, son of George and Sarah (Bowel) Tarvin, I, was born circa 1740 in Charles County, Maryland and died in Bracken County, Kentucky, on Jan. 3, 1811. His wife was named Sarah Cracraft, born in Virginia circa 1747 and died in Kentucky (possibly Fleming County), on Aug. 10, 1806. After her death, he remarried to Mary Woods, on March 27, 1807. At least 12 of their 13 children were born in Hampshire County, Va., between the period of 1768-1795. The Tarvins and Cowgills intermarried, and emigrated from Hampshire County to Kentucky. George Tarvin, II, was a Dunkard preacher in Hampshire County. Further research shows that, if they were living here today, their land would be located in Morgan County, W.Va. William Bowel, who died circa 1772 in Hampshire County, was the father of Sarah Bowel, who married George Tarvin Sr. A descendant who is very knowledgeable about the Tarvin family history is: Mrs. Lillian Tarvin Williams, 3206 20th Street, Lubbock, Texas 79410.

Tasker, George G., aged 87 years, died on March 4, 1880, in Mineral County, West Virginia. Source: March 12, 1880 issue of the *South Branch Intelligencer*, Romney, W.Va.

Tate, Rachel, daughter of John and Hannah Tate, died April 16, 1876. aged 68 years. She was born in Berkeley County, Va. Source: Hampshire County courthouse death record.

Tate, Joseph, died on April 14, 1841, in Hampshire County, Va. He married Margaret Horn on Jan. 2, 1812. She died on April 30, 1883, in Palmyra, Ohio. Source: War of 1812 Pension records in the National Archives, Washington, D.C.

Tate, Samuel, born in Pennsylvania in 1777, and died in Frederick County, Va. in February 1850. Was ill for six days with "paralysis." Farmer. Survived by spouse. Source: 1850 Mortality Schedule for Frederick County, Va.

Taylor, Daniel, was born on Feb. 1, 1757 in Hunterdon County, New Jersey. He married: (1) Margaret Thatcher on Dec. 27, 1778. After her death on Sept. 2, 1804, Taylor remarried to Sarah Jane LaRue on Jan. 7, 1806. He died on May 3, 1844 at "Reese's Mill," in Mineral County, W.Va. Source: DAR records.

Taylor, Harrison, son of John and Hannah (Harrison) Taylor (1703-1740), was born in Rappahannock County, Va., Aug. 11, 1735, and died in Ohio County, KY, Nov. 22, 1811. He married Jane Curlett, born Sept. 5, 1742 and died Aug. 5, 1812. They were early settlers in Upper Back Creek Valley, Frederick County, Va., and immigrated to Kentucky during their later years. Harrison was a miller, and a close neighbor of Capt. Jeremiah Smith. The Taylors raised a large family. Contact: Douglas L. Foster, Route 2, Box 192, Calvert City, KY 42029.

Taylor, Mandly, of Warren County, Va., died on April 17, 1851. Five daughters were also taken in death. He was an Old School Baptist. Source: *Zion's Advocate*, Vol. I, No. 20, page 318, Saturday, Oct. 21, 1854.

Taylor, Simon, drowned in a milldam on the Plantation of William Taylor's in Frederick County, Va. on March 13, 1808. Source: Frederick County, Va., "Inquisition of Dead Bodies," Virginia State Archives, Richmond, Va.

Taylor, Simon, died on May 2, 1873 in Hampshire County, aged 57 years. Source: The June 6, 1873 issue of the *South Branch Intelligencer*, Romney, W.Va.

Taylor, Thomas, was born in Hunterdon County, N.J., in 1760 and died Sept. 14, 1851, about three miles southeast of Junction, Hampshire County. He first married Mary Thompson (according to tradition) and later married Grace Spencer in Oct. 1800. She was born in 1771 and died on Oct. 12, 1823. Taylor served in the Revolutionary War, entering in his 16th year. The family graveyard is located high on a hill of Mill Creek Mountain. This lovely mountain farm is used mostly for sheep and cattle raising. Other graves in the cemetery: Joseph Taylor was born on Jan. 4, 1813 and died on Jan. 15, 1893. His wife, Sarah, was born on Jan. 13, 1819 and died on July 30, 1901; John W. Taylor (1846-1915); John Taylor was born on Aug. 9, 1816 and died on April 5, 1905. Mary E, wife of John Taylor, died on Feb. 28, 1882, aged 52 years, and Sidona J., wife of John Taylor, died on Aug. 1, 1869, aged 44 years. Sources: Tombstone inscriptions and *Winchester Republican*, issue of Sept. 26, 1851.

Templer, John L., born on Jan. 19, 1809 and died Dec. 23, 1876. His wife was Esther Keiter, only child of John and Sarah (Beale) Keiter. She was born on Dec. 23, 1817. They were married in 1838. Source: Tombstone inscription in Buckwalter cemetery and family Bible. (Note: the death record in Frederick County, Va. courthouse is in error.)

Templer, Sarah, "our mother," died on June 22, 1899, aged 88 years. She was buried next to John L. Templer and Anthony Buckwalter. Source: Buckwalter cemetery, Bloomery District, Hampshire County, W.Va.

Templer, William, was born on Dec. 29, 1775 and died on Oct. 24, 1854. Source: Tombstone inscription in the Buckwalter cemetery in Bloomery District.

Thatcher, Thomas, was born on Aug. 23, 1774 in Frederick County, Va. and died on Jan. 25, 1867 at New Antioch, Ohio. His father died when he was two and one-half years old, and he was bound out to David Lupton until he was 21 years old. Then he married in Berkeley County, Va., where he lived for nine years before immigrating to Clinton County, Ohio in 1805. He remained a Quaker until 1812, when he developed a political difference. Source: *The Clinton Republican*, a newspaper printed in Wilmington, Ohio.

Thomas, Evan, was born in Wales circa 1685 and died in Frederick County, Va. on "the 4th day of the second month 1755, aged about seventy years." Born into the Church of England, Evan later became a Quaker convert and minister. His former house still stands along US Route 11, just north of Winchester, Va.

Thomas, Owen, was born Aug. 15, 1764 and died Sept. 30, 1838. Buried next to him was Sophia Thomas, born Oct. 11, 1779 and died Feb. 11, 1836, aged 56 years, 3 months, 28 days. In same graveyard was an old stone with initials W.T., no dates given; and James W. Thomas, born Feb. 27, 1842 and died Sept. 18, 1853, aged 11 years, 6 months, 22 days. Members of the Miles family were buried in this same mountain graveyard, located on Turkey Mountain Road (formerly the Morgantown Turnpike), above Kessel's Gap. The nearest community is Fisher, W.Va., in Hardy County. All stones in this old graveyard have been knocked over and they are in various stages of deterioration. Source: Tombstone inscriptions.

Thompson, John, was born in Belfast, Ireland in 1751. After serving in the Revolutionary War in this country, he married Martha Beard in 1789. She was born in Bucks County, Penn. on Feb. 6, 1773 and died in Hampshire County on Dec. 27, 1855.

Thompson died on Feb. 20, 1816 and they were buried on a farm near Three Churches, Va.

Thompson, Newton, died in Capon Valley on June 19, 1855. Source: Coffin-book of William Meade Edwards (mortician).

Thorndike, Jonathan, born in 1774 in Maryland and died in October 1859, in Frederick County, Va. "Paralysis, sudden-death." Source: 1850 Mortality Schedule for Frederick County, Va.

Throckmorton, Lewis, was born in 1743 in Freehold, New Jersey and died in Hampshire County in 1798. His wife was Rachel DeMoss, daughter of William and Rachel DeMoss. Source: DAR records.

Tilden, John Bell, was born in Philadelphia, Pennsylvania on Dec. 9, 1761, and died at Stephen City, Frederick County, on July 31, 1838. He married Jane Chambers, daughter of Joseph and Martha Chambers of York, Pennsylvania. Tilden, a Revolutionary War veteran was a practicing physician in Frederick County, Va. Ordained to the ministry of the Methodist Church in 1802, he was excommunicated in 1828 for heresy (advocating lay representation). He was instrumental in forming a splinter church called Methodist Union Society of Reformers.

Timbrook, Elizabeth, died on March 17, 1873 at the age of 40. She was a daughter of David and Malinda (Pyles) Hott. Her husband was Gibson Timbrook. Source: Hampshire County courthouse death record in Romney.

Timbrook, Gibson, son of John and Sarah (Haines) Timbrook, was born on July 21, 1829 in Hampshire County; died on Jan. 28, 1906. After his first wife, Elizabeth Hott died in 1873, he remarried to Mary Haines, daughter of William and Catherine (Mott) Haines, on March 18, 1875. Mary was born on Sept. 10, 1842. They moved to Carroll County, Missouri in 1880, and he returned to Hampshire County alone, several months prior to his death.

Timbrook, Henry, was born on Oct. 15, 1822 in Hampshire County and died on Sept. 1, 1905. He married Tabitha Wolverton, daughter of Joel and Susan (Paskell) Wolverton, in 1849.

Timbrook, Isaac, was born on Dec. 21, 1832 and died Feb. 22, 1919. He married Hannah Hott, daughter of David and Malinda

(Pyles) Hott. Source: Courthouse record and tombstone inscription.

Timbrook, Joseph, was born in 1836. He married Malinda Pyles on Sept. 4, 1867. Source: Hampshire County record and the U.S. Census.

Timbrook, William Jackson, was born on Dec. 30, 1820 and died on March 22, 1876. He married Susannah Ruckman. Source: Mrs. Terry D. Parks, Reseda, CA 91335.

Topper, Maria Ann, born on Jan. 27, 1807 and died Dec. 20, 1809. Source: Tombstone inscription in the Thomas Edwards cemetery, Cold Stream, Hampshire County, Va. It is believed that she was an infant daughter of Henry and Jemima (Powell) Topper. According to William H. Ansel Jr., author of a comprehensive article on "Early Gunsmiths in Hampshire County," Topper made guns in the Cacapon River area of Capon Bridge. Topper's tombstone inscriptions were very precise, carved on native stone. Ansel stated that Henry Topper died in Westmoreland County, PA, in 1840. His son, Josiah Topper, followed his father's footsteps in the gunsmith business.

Topper, Samuel L., born in "Gettysbury, Penn." on June 7, 1811 and died of diabetes on Dec. 17, 1882 in Hampshire County. His wife Julia Ann Spicer reported his death to the courthouse. The death record listed his parents as "H(enry) and M. Topper." Source: Courthouse record.

Topper, Susanna, born on Dec. 21, 1809 and died March 14, 1810. Source: Tombstone inscription in Thomas Edwards Jr. graveyard, Cold Stream, Hampshire County, Va. It is located along Edwards' Run, near its intersection with the Cacapon River.

Triplett, Ralph Lee Esq., son of Albertis and Maggie (Marple) Triplett, was born on March 27, 1898 and died on May 24, 1984. He was buried in the cemetery of the Trone United Methodist Church, on Timber Ridge, Frederick County, Va. Triplett was a collector of historical information, especially graveyard data, and he wrote *A History of Upper Back Creek Valley*, in 1983. He was one of my best friends; a man of sterling character, with a good sense of humor, and a perspective far beyond his time. His widow, Beulah Catherine Ritenour, is still living on the old homeplace on Upper Back Creek, Gore, Virginia (in January 1992).

Turner, Addison, son of John and Sarah (Evans) Turner, was born in Frederick County, Va., Dec. 1, 1813, and died Jan. 4, 1865. He married Harriett Orndorff, Sept. 14, 1837. They had four children: (1) Sarah Catherine Turner was born Aug. 28, 1839. She married Joseph Henry Peer, Feb. 20, 1868. He was born Feb. 20, 1834. (2) James Turner was born Feb. 12, 1841. (3) Martha Washington Turner was born Sept. 17, 1844. (4) Solomon T. Turner was born Aug. 16, 1846 and died Aug. 27, 1847. Source: Copied from Bible record in possession of Mrs. Wanda M. Riley, Capon Bridge, W.Va. 26711.

Turner, John, was born July 10, 1764 and died June 5, 1830. He married Sarah Evans, born Jan. 6, 1766, and died June 20, 1852. They lived near Philadelphia, PA, until 1798, when they immigrated to the Mt. Williams section of Frederick County, Va. Their children were: (1) Elizabeth Turner was born Aug. 29, 1795 and died at Capon Bridge, W.Va., May 8, 1867. She married Joseph Kackley. (2) Rebecca Evans Turner was born Sept. 21, 1797 and died May 2, 1868, unmarried. (3) James Turner was born Nov. 25, 1801 and died June 23, 1879. He married Judith Fry, Nov. 22, 1838, in Frederick County. (4) Mary Ann Turner was born Sept. 27, 1804. She married Isaac Hite, son of Jacob and Sarah (Piper) Hite, Jan. 6, 1827. (5) John Bailey Turner was born in Sept. 1806, and died unmarried. (6) Robert Turner was born Dec. 23, 1808, and he married Eliza Seibert. (7) Addison Turner was born Dec. 1, 1813, and died Jan. 4, 1865. He married Harriett Orndorff. Source: Turner Bible record in hands of Mrs. Wanda M. Riley, Capon Bridge, W.Va. 26711.

Tusing, Michael, died on May 9, 1872 in Hampshire County, W.Va., age 87 years. He was born in Rockingham County, Va. His second wife was Susan Rhinehart. Source: Death Record in Hampshire County Courthouse. [Comment: Michael Tusing was born on Jan. 8, 1794, according to Darrell D. Tussing, RR 1 Box 45E, 13210 Silver Street, Weston, Ohio 43569.]

Ullery, Henry, was born on May 5, 1788 and died on Aug. 7, 1849, in Frederick County, Virginia. Sometimes the name was spelled Woolery, Wolary, etc. in records. Source: Cemetery inscription, Quaker Graveyard (Back Creek Meeting) at Gainsboro, Virginia.

Ullery, Jacob, died July 11, 1862, aged 66 years, 10 months, 6 days. His wife, Mary Fletcher (daughter of George Fletcher), was buried by his side, no dates given. Source: Tombstone inscriptions in Salem Methodist graveyard, Slanesville, Hampshire County.

Vance, James, was born on Aug. 28, 1781 and died on Nov. 28, 1861. Source: Tombstone inscription in the Indian Mound cemetery, Romney, W.Va.

Vance, William, died on Feb. 11, 1863, aged 78 years. Margaret Vance, wife of William Vance, Esquire, died on Nov. 28, 1847, aged 63 years. Source: Tombstone inscriptions in Indian Mound Cemetery, Romney, W.Va.

Vanarsdall, Garret, was born in New Jersey on March 19, 1757. He moved to Berkeley County, where he joined the Revolutionary Army, after which he moved to Hampshire County, Va. His wife was named Amelia, based on an 1828 deed in Morgan County, Va. Possibly she was a second wife. When Garret Vanarsdale made his application for a military pension in 1834, he stated that his brother took his discharge papers down the Ohio many years ago, and he was not heard from since. It is believed that the brother's name was Cornelius.

Van Meter, Col. Garrett, was born in 1732 and died in 1788. Source: Tombstone inscription in field behindVanmeter house at Old Fields, Hardy County, W.Va.

Vanmeter, Isaac, was born Dec. 10, 1757 and died Dec. 13, 1837, in 87th year. His wife, Elizabeth, died ____ 20, 1827, 61 years, 7 months, 17 days. Source: Tombstone inscriptions at Methodist Church (Vanmeter's), Old Fields, Hardy County, W.Va.

Vanmeter, Jacob, (a Methodist) was born June 9, 1750 and died April 29, 1808. Source: Tombstone inscription in Vanmeter's graveyard, Old Fields, Hardy County, W.Va.

VanMeter, Jacob, son of Abraham VanMeter (son of explorer John VanMeter), died Oct. 22, 1800, aged 62 years. Source: VanMeter Graveyard, Arden District, Berkeley County, W.Va.

Vanmeter, Jacob, died Sept. 1, 1829 ("departed this life in the 65th year.) Tabitha, his wife, died Sept. 27, 1851, aged 84 years, 6 months, 16 days. Source: Vanmeter graveyard at Old Fields, Hardy County, W.Va.

Vanmeter, Joseph, born in April 1755 and died Sept. 30, 1834. Mary, his wife, was born July 25, 1761 and died Feb. 7, 1826. Source: Tombstone inscriptions in Vanmeter graveyard at Old Fields, W.Va., in Hardy County.

Vanorsdall, Abraham, was born in Somerset County, New Jersey on Oct. 27, 1765, and died in 1824 in Morgan County, Va. In 1794, he immigrated to Hampshire County, Va. where he settled at Great Cacapon. This section of Hampshire County fell into Morgan County when it was formed in 1820. He married Abigail Johnston, daughter of William and Elizabeth Johnston, circa 1799. Her Will was filed in 1849 and probated in 1850, in Morgan County, Va. Their children were: (1) The Rev. William Vanorsdall was born in 1800, and married Christina "Teena" Casler, daughter of John and Elizabeth Casler, on Feb. 9, 1820, (2) Garret Vanarsdall was born on June 29, 1801 and died on Aug. 14, 1876 in Fayette County, Ohio. He married Rosannah Gray, daughter of Michael Gray, of Morgan County. (3) Lemuel Vanorsdall was born on March 14, 1803 and died on May 30, 1875. He married Sarah Boyles, daughter of Henry and Mary Boyles. Lemuel represented Morgan County in the State Legislature. (4) Isaac Vanorsdall was born on Dec. 15, 1808 and died on Oct. 10, 1885, in Morgan County, W.Va. He married Frances Michael. (5) Anna M. (sometimes called Nancy) Vanorsdall was born Nov. 7, 1814 and died on Oct. 18, 1870. She married Mathias Ambrose and they had no children. (6) Abigail Vanarsdall was born on Jan. 15, 1817 and died on Sept. 28, 1893 in Madison County, Ohio. Her husband was named James Reed (1815-1899). They were buried in the Kirkwood cemetery near London, Ohio, and (7) Mariah Vanorsdall was born in 1820. She married Patrick Phillips on Oct. 18, 1843 and they had no children. [Note: it is believed that Abraham Vanorsdall was a son of Garret Van Arsdalen of New Jersey, a Justice of the Peace during the American Revolution.] Source: Research complied by Mr. Roy B. Fultz of Jeffersonville, Ohio and shared with me by Frederick T. Newbraugh of Berkeley Springs, W.Va.

Vanorsdall, Ann, daughter of Peter and Ellen Vanorsdall, was born on Nov. 29, 1787 and died on May 31, 1870. Peter Vanorsdall was born circa 1760. His wife Ellen was born in 1762, according to the 1850 census for Morgan County, Va. Ann married Thomas Alderton (1787-185_), who was a son of William and Margaret (Edwards) Alderton.

Vanorsdall, Cornelius, son of Garrett and Sarah Vanorsdall, died on Aug. 5, 1876, of "paralysis" at age 76 years, in Hampshire County, Va. His death was reported to the Hampshire County Courthouse by daughter Elizabeth Heiskell. The wife of Cornelius was named Catherine Huff, a daughter of William Cornelius and Elizabeth (Heironimus) Huff. The Vanorsdales were divorced on Sept. 4, 1866 in Hampshire County, W.Va.[48] Catherine died in Hampshire County, W.Va. on Aug. 8, 1874, at age 87 years, according to her son-in-law, Francis W. Heiskell, who reported her death to the Hampshire County courthouse. I found her grave near the Cacapon River, on a knoll close to the end of County Road 29/2. It is on the old Francis W. Heiskell place, now owned by Edward Milburn, not far from the Morgan County, W.Va. line. "Catherine, wife of Cornelius Van Arsdale, died Aug. 8, 1875, aged 89 years, 3 months, 13 days." Next to her was: Cornelius Van Arsdale, died Aug. 5, 1876, aged 49 years and 15 days. Was he a son? If so, why is his birth date the same as his father's?

Vanorsdall, Lemuel, died in Morgan County, W.Va. on May 30, 1875, aged 75 years, 2 months, 13 days. Nephew William H. Vanorsdall reported the death to the Clerk of the Court in Berkeley Springs, W.Va.

Vanorsdall, Margaret, died on June 6, 1883, aged 81 years, in Morgan County. Her husband was Richard Vanorsdall. Margaret's parents were William and Margaret (Edwards) Alderton. Richard Vanorsdale died on Aug. 18, 1889, aged 89 years. Source: Morgan County, W.Va. courthouse death records.

Vanorsdall, Nancy (nee Miller), died on Oct. 3, 1880, aged 73 years, in Hampshire County. Her husband was Isaac Vanorsdall [Note there were several Isaacs]. Nancy's parents were Conrad and Sarah Miller. Source: Mrs. Joanne Eustice, 1440 E. Campus, Redlands, CA. 92374.

Vause, William, son of Ephriam and Theodosia Vause, was born May 7, 1741. His wife, Rachel Hedges, was born Jan. 20, 1743 and died circa 1832. They lived in old Hampshire County, Va., and had these children: (1) Jemima Vause was born July 9,

---

48. See **Order Book 4,** page 235, Hampshire County Circuit Court.

1764. (2) Ephram Vause was born Aug. 14, 1766. (3) William Vause Jr. was born Aug. 30, 1769 and died July 29, 1852, in Ross County, Ohio. He married Rachel Inskeep, daughter of Abraham and Susan (Vause) Inskeep. Rachel was born Nov. 22, 1772 and died May 19, 1823. (4) Theodosia Vause was born Oct. 8, 1771. (5) Solomon Vause was born Nov. 7, 1774. He married Sarah Vanmeter, born Oct. 3, 1785 and died Aug. 18, 1810. (6) Rebecca Vause was born Oct. 19, 1779. (7) Abraham Vause was born Oct. 18, 1780. (8) Susannah Vause was born April 23, 1783. (9) Thomas Vause was born July 28, 1785 and died May 4, 1852. His wife was Elizabeth Decker. They went to Ohio in 1817. Source: "Copied from Prayer Book of Rachel (Hedges) Vause," and furnished by Joanne Eustice, 1534 N. Kelly, Redlands, CA 92374.

Wall, John, died in July 1849, aged 77 years. He was born in Pennsylvania. Occupation was bricklayer. Cause of death was asthma, folllowing an illness of 600 days. Source: 1850 Mortality Schedule of Frederick County, Va.

Waln, Samuel, was deceased before Oct. 29, 1829, when his estate was inventoried in Morgan County, Va. His estate included a library, desk, Dutch ovens, tools, furniture, grain, farm implements, etc. Source: *Will Book I*, page 266, Morgan County, W.Va. court, Berkeley Springs, W.Va. 25411. [Note: Samuel was a son of Joseph Waln of Frederick County, Va. According to deeds in the courthouse, the children of Joseph and Mary Waln were: Samuel Waln married Margaret Dick, daughter of Peter Dick; Joshua Waln married Catherine Null; Mary Waln married Leonard Keedick; John Waln married Martha Wilkinson; Elizabeth Waln married Randale Lockhart; Joseph Waln, Jr. married Eleanor Dick; William Waln married Mary Heironimus; Henry Waln married Elizabeth _____; and Nancy Waln married one John Grove. Several of the families named above emigrated from Frederick County to Ohio or Indiana.

Ward, James, died on Feb. 9, 1873 in Hampshire County, aged 87 years. Mrs. Mary Ward, widow of James Ward, died on Sept. 27, 1874, aged 79 years, at the home of her son-in-law, John W. Athey, in Mineral County, W.Va. Source: Feb. 14, 1873 issue of the *South Branch Intelligencer*, obit for James.

Ward, Joel was born in England in 1727, and died on Feb. 4, 1785. His wife, Eleanor, was born in Ireland in 1740 and died on Aug. 13, 1802. According to Mrs. Dorothy Becker, Fort Worth, Texas, the data were recorded in a "Sterritt Bible," and Joel was an immigrant ancestor for Wards who settled in Northern Virginia.

Ward, Joel, was born on Dec. 6, 1782 and died on Aug. 19, 1864. His wife, Hannah Cannon, was born on Jan. 10, 1785 and died on Feb. 15, 1862. Her coffin was made by William Meade Edwards, per his account book. Source: Tombstone inscriptions in Parks' Hollow.

Ward, Joel Nimrod, son of Joel and Hannah (Cannon) Ward, was born in Hampshire County, Va. on March 8, 1823 and died in Christian County, Illinois on Oct. 21, 1872. His wife, Rebecca Lupton died on Jan. 28, 1877. Their children (heirs) were: (1) Hannah E. Ward married Richard White   (2) Harriett E. Ward married James K. Luce on Sept. 2, 1869, and he died on May 14, 1874.   (3) Martha A. Ward married John E.P. Bell on Nov. 18, 1875. (4) James W. Ward and (5) Thomas A. Ward. This set of records stated that Rebecca Lupton had a sister who married John W. Russell of Clarke County, Va.   Source: Records in Box 221, Chancery Court of Law, Hampshire County, W.Va.

Ward, Simeon Cicero., son of Joel Ward, died on Aug. 17, 1870, aged 54 years. The cemetery inscription shows that he was on May 24, 1816. His wife, Emma E.O. Bennett, daughter of James and Mary (Brown) Bennett, was born on Oct. 13, 1826 and died on Feb. 22, 1900. Source: Death record in Hampshire County courthouse, and cemetery inscriptions in Quaker Graveyard, Parke's Hollow, Hampshire County, W.Va.

Ward, Simeon, was born in 1804 and died on Jan. 8, 1877. He was an Elder in the Christian Church, ordained by the Rev. Christy Sine in 1830 (according to Sine's *Journal*). Simeon was a son of Mary Ward, and a grandson of John Ward. This Mary Ward was born on March 6, 1784.   Simeon was a farmer, storekeeper, preacher and gunsmith, at various times.   Simion's first wife, Sarah, died on Dec. 21, 1857. She was nee Sarah Johnson, daughter of David and Catherine (Bruner) Johnson. On Jan. 31, 1869, he re-married to Sarah Racey (1815-1886), daughter of Thomas and Mary Racey.   According to the *Undertaker Book* of John W. Mellon, the second Sarah was buried on Sept. 4, 1886. All three were buried in the Timber Ridge Christian Graveyard. The death record reported to the Hampshire County Courthouse stated that #2 Sarah died in 1886, aged 71 years, 4 months, 6 days. Simion's first wife, was related to the Bruner family. They called "Uncle" and "Aunt" the children of George and Polly Bruner, based on an old letter written in 1844, to Bruner relatives in Illinois.

Warden, William, was born in 1748 and died in Sept. 1823, near Wardensville, Hardy County, W.Va. Source: Tombstone inscription in family graveyard.

Washington, Mariah, died in February 1860, aged 62 years. Cause of death was "consumption," following an illness of 548 days. Born in Virginia. Survived by her spouse. Source: 1860 Mortality Schedule for Frederick County, Va.

Watson, Walter, died in February 1860, aged 76 years. Cause of death was consumption, following a two-year illness. Survived by his spouse. Occupation was "day-laborer." Source: 1860 Mortality Schedule for Frederick County, Va.

Wayman, Edmund, was born on the "Western Shore of Maryland" in 1762 and died in Hampshire County on April 21, 1802. He had been a travelling Methodist preacher for the last five years of his life. Source: *A Short History of the Methodists: 1766-1809*, Magill and Clime, Baltimore, MD, by Jesse Lee, 1810.

Weaver, Abraham, born in 1762 in Penn. and died on June 28, 1831 in Greene County, Ohio. Source: Tombstone inscription in Loar Methodist cemetery, Caesar's Creek Township, per Joan G. Ellsworth.

Weaver, Joseph, son of Abraham and Magdalene (Senseny) Weaver, was born in Hampshire County on Jan. 2, 1794 and died circa 1862 in Wisconsin. He married Sarah Hedrick, believed to have been a daughter of Nicholas and Jane Hedrick (Jane died Aug. 6, 1836, aged 72 yrs., three months), ca. 1810, in Hampshire County. Source: Family Bible of David Ellis.

Weaver, Mary Magdalene (nee Senseny), was born on Oct. 12, 1766; died on June 15, 1827 in Bloomery District, Hampshire County. Her husband was Abraham Weaver. Source: Tombstone inscription in Buckwalter cemetery.

Weaver, Samuel, son of Abraham and Magdalene (Senseny) Weaver, was born in Hampshire County on July 14, 1809 and died on Sept. 19, 1884 in New Burlington, Clinton County, Ohio. He married Anna Ellis, daughter of Joel and Elizabeth (Schillinger) Ellis, on Feb. 19, 1834 in Greene County, Ohio. Anna was born on Feb. 25, 1814 (in Ohio?) and died on May 9, 1890. They had three children. Her grandfather Abraham Ellis (Alles in old German Bible) was born in Pennsylvania in 1750 and died in Clinton County, Ohio in 1837. He was a soldier in the Revolution. Abraham Ellis married Catherine Joel. Source: History of Greene County, Ohio, and tombstone inscriptions in the New Burlington cemetery, Clinton/Greene County, Ohio.

Westfall, Abel, son of Johannes and Maritie (Cool) Westfall, was baptized Feb. 9, 1696, in the Dutch Reformed Church, Kingston, New York, and died in old Frederick County, Va. (Hampshire County), in 1755. He married Antje Bogart, daughter of Cornelius Bogard, Feb. 25, 1717. They were early Dutch settlers along the South Branch of the Potomac River, about 1740. In 1748, Abel Westfall received a 400-acre grant from Lord Fairfax.

Westfall, Johannes, son of Abel and Antje Westfall, was baptized Oct. 25, 1724 in New York, and died in 1789 in Hardy County, Va.

Whitacre/Whitaker family: I have a comprehensive, national, database on the Whitacre family in the USA, most of which is unpublished. Information is still being collected for exchange and possible publication.   Write to: Dr. Wilmer L. Kerns, 4715 North 38th Place, Arlington, Va. 22207.

Whitacre, Addison, son of Washington and Elizabeth (Oates) Whitacre, was born on March 28, 1842 and died on Dec. 21, 1919. His wife, Ruth E. Miller, was born on July 18, 1848, and died on Dec. 5, 1893. They were married on April 9, 1866, and lived in the Timber Ridge area. Children of Addison and Ruth Whitacre: (1) Carl R.R. Whitacre was born July 9, 1867 and died March 5, 1869. (2) Arthur C. Whitacre was born Nov. 9, 1868. (3) Benton W. Whitacre was born March 8, 1870 and died Aug. 25, 1896. (4) Harrison R. Whitacre was born Dec. 3, 1871. (5) William W. Whitacre was born Feb. 26, 1873. (6) Vossie E. Whitacre was born April 28, 1878. (7) Clarence E. Whitacre was born Sept. 26, 1879. (8) Debourney Whitacre was born April 16, 1883. He married Anna Stewart on April 12, 1912. Source: Family Bible, in possession of Cletus Whitacre, Park's Valley, Hampshire County. The Bible record was copied by Dan P. Oates of Romney, W.Va., and given to me.

Whitacre, Aquilla, son of George and Rachel (Tumbleston) Whitacre, was born in 1808, near Paris, Fauquier County, Va. and was buried on Sept. 18, 1886, according to the *Undertaker Book* of John W. Mellon. Aquilla married Rachel Kerns, daughter of Nathan and Sarah (Whitacre) Kerns. Rachel was born in Frederick County, Va., on Dec. 25, 1810 and died on Feb. 13, 1898, in Hampshire County, W.Va. Her death record was recorded in the Hampshire County Court. Tradition says they were buried in the Bloomery Presbyterian Cemetery, Bloomery, W.Va., but there are no inscribed tombstones.

Whitacre, Caroline, died in October 1869, aged 27 years, of "consumption." Survived by spouse. Source: 1870 Mortality Schedule for Frederick County, Va.

Whitacre, Dorsey, son of Aquilla and Rachel (Kerns) Whitacre, was born in 1830. According to the *Undertaker Book* of John W. Mellon, Dorsey was buried on April 19, 1894. Apparently he died from pneumonia. One source says that he was buried in the Foreman graveyard at Cold Stream. His wife, Nancy Shanholtz (1839-1907), was a daughter of Samuel and Phoebe (Iden) Shanholtz. They were married on April 27, 1856, in Hampshire County, Va. Note: This corrects an error in the *Shanholtzer Family History*, which gave a death year of 1883, for Dorsey Whitacre.

Whitacre, George, II, son of George and Ruth Whitacre, was born in 1778 in western Loudoun County, Virginia and died in Hampshire County, Va. circa 1855. He married Rachel Tumbleston, daughter of Nathaniel Tumbleston, on Feb. 16, 1807, in Fauquier County, Va. They raised a large family- at least 10 children. Most genealogists have "missed" this very important branch of the Whitacre family. It was George's brother Joshua Whitacre (1768-1814) who settled on the opposite side of Timber Ridge in Frederick County. My data collection on the Whitacre family is extensive.

Whitacre, George, died on June 1, 1911, age 72 years. He died of "Bright's disease," and was "single." George was born at Bloomery, Virginia, probably a son of Aquilla and Rachel (Kerns)

Whitacre. Source: Hampshire County death record in courthouse, Romney, W.Va.

Whitacre, John W., son of Jonas (of George Whitaker Jr.) and Mary Whitacre, was born on Feb. 2, 1837 and died on Dec. 18, 1911, at Levels, Hampshire County, W.Va. His death record in the Hampshire County courthouse in Romney, W.Va. states that he was born in the Gore District of Hampshire County, Va. A second death record was reported to the court for a William Whitacre, with almost the same dates, believed to be the same person. This record stated that he was born in Bloomery, Va. He married Mary Catherine Sirbaugh, daughter of Jacob and Elizabeth (Oates) Sirbaugh Jr., on Dec. 31, 1857, by the Rev. Christy Sine. Rev. Sine stated that John W. was a son of Jonas and Mary Whitacre. At first this caused some consternation, but further research revealed that this Jonas Whitacre was a son of George and Rachel (Tumbleston) Whitacre; that he was a cooper on the north side of the Potomac in Maryland. This has opened the door to a new branch of the family, now being researched. They had ten children and numerous descendants entered the ministry in the Church of the Brethren. Mary was born on March 1, 1838 and died on May 19, 1922. Both were buried in the cemetery at Levels, W.Va.

Whitacre, Jonah, died Dec. 3, 1912, "of heart failure,", aged 40 years. Born in Hampshire County; farmer. Source: Hampshire County courthouse death record.

Whitacre, Jonas, son of Joshua and Rachel (Wilson) Whitacre, was born in 1794 and died in Frederick County, Va. on Nov. 8, 1836. He was a constable for Frederick County. He married Mary Kerns, daughter of Nathan and Rachel (Reid) Kerns, Sr., on April 22, 1818. They were early supporters of the Rev. Christy Sine, pioneer preacher in the Christian Church. Mary was buried at Chestnut Grove in Frederick County, Va., but believed to have died in Illinois. Source: Extensive research and multiple sources.

Whitacre, Jonas, son of John W. and Mary C. (Sirbaugh) Whitacre, was born on Jan. 16, 1873 and died on Dec. 3, 1912. He was buried in the cemetery at Levels, Hampshire County, W.Va. Source: Tombstone inscriptions.

Whitacre, Joshua, Jr., son of Joshua and Rachel (Wilson) Whitacre, Sr., was born in Frederick County, Va. on Jan. 8, 1811 and died in Hickory County, Missouri on April 9, 1869. He married Ann Nesmith in Frederick County on Sept. 12, 1833. Source: Bruce Whitacre, Winchester, Va.

Whitacre, Mahlon, son of Jonas and Mary (Kerns) Whitacre, was born in 1829 in Frederick County, Va. and died on Dec. 23, 1887 in Olathe Kansas. On Dec. 19, 1852, Mahlon married Sarah J. Shane, daughter of Andrew and Rebecca (DeHaven) Shane. She was born circa 1836. Source: Mrs. Helene M. Whitaker, 328 South Violet Lane, Orange, CA 92669.

Whitacre, Meredith, son of Wilson and Rachel (Kerns) Whitacre, was born in Frederick County, Va. in 1833 and died in Kosciusko County, Indiana on Nov. 6, 1899. He lived in Tippecanoe Township. He married Rachel Noel, daughter of Nicholas and Nancy (Kerns) Noel, on April 27, 1857, in Frederick County, Va. Source: Courthouse records in Warsaw, Indiana.

Whitacre, Minnie, died (typhoid fever) on Oct. 8, 1914, aged 40 years. She left a widower, not named in Hardy County, W.Va. courthouse death record. Residence was Rio, W.Va.

Whitacre, Snowden, son of George and Rachel (Tumbleston) Whitacre, was born in Hampshire County, Va. on Jan. 10, 1828 and died April 14, 1904 at Zepp, Shenandoah County, Va. According to his obituary these children survived him: (1) Thomas Whitaker of Berryville, Va. (2) Mrs. Emma Virginia (Whitaker) Wood (1858-1936), and (3) George Whitaker of Saumsville, Va. Snowden married Sarah Elizabeth Orndorff (ca. 1833-1905). Source: Cemetery inscriptions.

Whitacre, Wilson, son of Joshua and Rachel (Wilson) Whitacre, was born in 1800 and died "of gavel" in February 1880, in Frederick County, Va. His attending physician was Dr. John C. Janney. His wife preceded him in death. He married Rachel Kerns, daughter of Jacob and Rachel (Cowgill) Kerns II, Dec. 27, 1821, in Frederick County, Va. They had at least 10 children. Source: See *Shanholtzer Family History and Allied Family Roots*, 1980, by Wilmer L. Kerns, Ph.D. See also *Deed Book 33*, page 500; *Deed Book 34*, page 472, Frederick County Courthouse, Winchester, Va.; and the 1880 Mortality Schedule for Frederick County, Va.

White, Alexander, son of John and Ann (Patton) White, was born in 1735 and died in 1805. He lived in Frederick and

Hampshire Counties, Va. He served as a Delegate in the Virginia State Assembly, representing both Hampshire and Frederick County at various times and he served as a Delegate to ratify the Constitution in 1788 in Richmond, Va. Alexander White left no offspring, although he was twice-married: (1) Elizabeth Wood and (2) Mrs. Sarah Hite.

White, Christian Streit, son of John Baker White, died on Jan. 28, 1917, of pneumonia. He was a widower. Retired clerk of court and attorney, aged 77 years, 10 months, 18 days. Hampshire County courthouse death record.

White, Elizabeth died in July 1869, aged 72 years, "of cancer." She was born in Virginia. Her husband preceded her in death. Source: 1870 Mortality Schedule for Frederick County, Va.

White, Francis, son of Dr. Robert and Elizabeth White, died on Oct. 6, 1826, aged 65 years. He married a cousin, Margaret White, Dec. 5, 1787, in Frederick County, Va. Francis was formerly a Sheriff and landowner in Hampshire County, Va. Source: Tombstone inscription in the White family graveyard, near Hayfield, Frederick County, Virginia. In the Hampshire County Circuit Court, *Order Book II*, page 133, it lists the heirs of Francis White, deceased: Robert N. and Elizabeth White; Evan and Mary (White) McDonald; Thomas B. White; Francis M. White; John A. White. It mentions, also, Ann P. Keyes, widow and devisee of Francis Keyes. The document was dated Sept. 13, 1845.

White, Francis, Jr., son of Francis White Sr., died on Sept. 8, 1868, aged 68 years, at Cold Stream, Hampshire County. He was the last surviving child of Francis and Margaret White Sr. Francis Jr. was a miller, and his wife was named Elizabeth, possibly nee Stewart (not yet proven) Source: *South Branch Intelligencer*, published in Romney, W.Va.

White, Jacob, was born in 1789 and died Nov. 13, 1862. His wife, Elizabeth, was born in 1792, and died on Aug. 2, 1870. Source: Tombstone inscriptions in Fairview Lutheran Church cemetery, Gore, Frederick County, Va.

White, John, son of Dr. Robert and Elizabeth White, died on June 13, 1848, in his 80th year. His wife, Elizabeth, died in 1836, aged 65 years. Source: Tombstone inscription in White Family Graveyard, near Hayfield, Virginia.

White, John Baker, son of Robert and Arabella (Baker) White, was born on Aug. 4, 1794 and died in Richmond, Va. on Oct. 9, 1862. He served as Clerk of the County and Circuit Courts from 1815 to 1862. He was driven from his home in Romney by Union soldiers. His second wife was Frances Ann Streit, daughter of the Rev. Christian Streit. They had a son named Christian Streit White, the confederate soldier who helped protect the Hampshire County court records from being totally destroyed. C. S. White was born on March 10, 1839 and died on Jan. 28, 1917. He served as the Hampshire County Court clerk from 1873 to 1902.

White, Mary M., daughter of Francis White, of Hampshire County, Va., died Thursday the 7th of Feb., 1839, aged 28 years. She married Evan McDonald. Source: The *South Branch Intelligencer*, issue of Feb. 14, 1839, Romney, Va.

White, Robert, son of Dr. John White of Paisley, Scotland, was born in 1681 and died in Frederick County, Virginia on Feb. 11, 1742. He was one of the first settlers near North Mountain, west of Winchester. Robert was a surgeon in the British Navy; then came to America where he married Margaret Hogue, daughter of William and Barbara (Hume) Hoge Sr.. He was the first White immigrant to Frederick County, and he established White's Fort at North Mountain, used during the French and Indian War.

White, Robert, M.D., was born on March 8, 1734 and died in Frederick County, Virginia, on Aug. 5, 1815. His wife, Elizabeth, died on July 17, 1811, aged 72 years. Source: Tombstone inscriptions in White Graveyard, near Hayfield, Frederick County, Virginia.

White, Robert, son of Judge John and Ann (Patton) White, was born in Frederick County, Va. on March 29, 1759 and died in Winchester on March 16, 1831. Robert served as a Judge of the General Court of Virginia. He married Arabella Baker, daughter of John and Judith (Wood) Baker of Frederick County, MD. Robert was a grandson of immigrants Robert and Margaret (Hoge) White.

White, Robert, was born on Oct. 2, 1804 and died on Jan. 9, 1896. His wife, Frances, was born on Jan. 13, 1812 and died on Feb. 3, 1887. Source: Tombstone inscriptions from the Powell cemetery, Forks of Capon, Hampshire County, W.Va.

Whiting, Anna Eliza, wife of Alfred Whiting, was born on Oct. 7, 1836 and died on April 26, 1900. Source: Tombstone inscription along roadside, just below (and outside) the Indian Mound cemetery, Romney, W.Va., which probably means they were black Americans.

Wiley, Elizabeth, was born in 1794; died in Nov. 1849 in Hampshire County, of "lung inflammation." Source: Mortality records from 1850 census, Hampshire County, Va.

Wiley, Laban was deceased before April 13, 1847, according to *Order Book i*, page 201, Circuit Court, Hampshire County, Va. His widow, Elizabeth, received one-third of his estate. Five equal shares were given to: John Reiley and Elizabeth his wife; Benjamin Wiley; Zail Wiley; Naomi Wiley married William House; and Elizabeth Wiley married Richard Madden. Mentioned, also, in the document were: Benjamin Reiley, Thomas Reiley, and Louise Reiley. This was copied hurriedly, and I suggest that a more detailed study be given to the document.

Williams, Daniel, was born near Philadelphia, PA, on April 28, 1792, and died near Hoy, Hampshire County. He married Sarah Grapes on Jan. 13, 1814. She was born on Nov. 11, 1792, in Frederick County, Va.

Williams, Col. Edward, son of Vincent and Mary (Harness) Williams, born in 1756, almost 3 three months after his father was killed by Indians. He married, in 1788, Elizabeth Neville, daughter of Joseph and Nancy (Brown) Neville Sr. She was born on Jan. 15, 1769 and died in 1812 in Moorefield, Hardy County, Va. Source: Compilation by Mrs. Luke Hodges, Wichita Falls, TX.

Williams, George S., died on March 20, 1856, aged 38 years, 9 months, 22 days. He was buried on a high bank of North River, on southwest side of North River Mills, Hampshire County, on property now owned by Kenny Baker. I have not been able to identify this person. There was one George Tharp Williams, who was a son of Daniel and Sarah (Grapes) Williams, who was born on May 29, 1817, according to a Bible record. The dates don't quite match, but I still wonder whether or not these two Georges are the same person.

Williams, Thomas, was born circa 1734 and died in Hampshire County, Va. in November 1816. He received a Fairfax grant in 1754, believed to have been in present-day Morgan County,

W.Va. Isaac married Elizabeth Dawson (ca 1740-1821). After his death, Elizabeth remarried to John Hartley. Children: (1) Isaac Williams was born and died in Hampshire County. His wife was named Nancy. (2) Benjamin Williams was born in Hampshire County and died in Fleming County, KY. (3) John Williams was born circa 1780 and died on July 17, 1833, in Mercer County, PA. He married Sarah Wright (1791-1878). (4) Thomas Williams Jr. was born circa 1779 and died after 1850 in Lawrence County, PA. (5) William Williams died circa 1818. (6) Zedekiah Williams married Margaret Hillery on Oct. 14, 1808, and they moved to Ross County, Ohio. (7) Rachel Williams was born Dec. 30, 1784 in Hampshire County. She married Capt. James Smith. (8) Leah Williams was born Dec. 30, 1784 and died Dec. 22, 1845 in Green County, IL. She married Middleton Smith (1788-1849), on Dec. 13, 1808. (9) Syche Williams was born May 9, 1776 and died in Vigo County, IN. She married Isaac Dawson (1773-1824). (10) Abigail Williams married Thomas Bennet. (11) Eleanor Williams married Anthony Snyder. Source: Charles X McCalla III, M.D., PO Box 151, 307 West Main, Paoli, IN 47454.

Williams, Vincent, was killed by the Indians on July 16, 1756. His wife was Mary Harness. Source: Oaths of David Cosner and Simon Wykoff, to Clerk of Court.

Wills, Benjamin, son of Deskin Wills, was born on Aug. 4, 1839 and died on Dec. 23, 1861. Source: Tombstone inscription in Wills graveyard, on North River, Hampshire County, W.Va.

Wills, Benjamin F. was born on Dec. 24, 1787 and died in 1849. His wife Charity Furr, daughter of Enoch and Sarah (Clawson) Furr, was born in 1796 in Loudoun County, Va. and died on May 1, 1868, in Hampshire County, W.Va., according to testimony given in Chancery Court, "William Wills vs Mary Francis Alkire," Box 238, Hampshire County Circuit Court, Romney, W.Va. It is not clear why they were buried in the Kump graveyard. At the time of their death, the graveyard was owned by Frederick Kump, from 1847 to 1891, and prior to that it was owned by the Basil, Richard, and George Moreland families, respectively, going back to 1802. Frederick Kump's first wife was Elizabeth Furr, who died during the early 1840's Probably the basic link between these families was the Furr connection. Source: Tombstone inscription in old private graveyard at North River Mills, Hampshire County.

Wills, Deskin, was born on Jan. 31, 1813 and died on Feb. 12, 1884. He married Ann Carmichael, who died on April 15, 1882, aged 76 years, 6 months, 2 days. Nearby is a stone which says, Benjamin Wills, son of D. & S. Wills, was born on Aug. 4, 1839 and died on Dec. 23, 1861. The Wills log house is now vacant. Source: The Deskin Wills family Graveyard, on east side of North River, between North River Mills and the Forks of Capon, Hampshire County, W.Va.

Wills, Thomas, son of Benjamin F. and Charity (Furr) Wills, was born in Hampshire County, Virginia and died in Oklahoma. His wife, Rebecca Milleson, daughter of Silas and Harriett (Slane) Milleson, died on March 5, 1876, near Higginsville, W.Va., according to the March 17, 1876 issue of the *South Branch Intelligencer*. A death record in the Hampshire County courthouse, states that Rebecca was 49 years and 9 days old when she died.

Wills, William. was born April 7, 1837, in Hampshire County, Va. and died on Sept. 24, 1912. He married Mary Frances Alkire, daughter of Peter Alkire Jr.. They were divorced and he remarried to Amanda C. Milleson, daughter of George Milleson. He was survived by these daughters: Sallie Wills who married Thompson Powers; Lillie Wills who married Robert Grapes; Minnie Wills who married Ferman Wolfe, of Delray, W.Va.; Mrs. Sude Largent of Slanesville; Mrs. Bertha Dalton of Morgantown, and; Mrs. Mayme Arnold of Elkins, W.Va. Source: Family records and obituary published in *The Hampshire Review*.

Wilson, Isaac N., was born on Oct. 20, 1794 and died on Feb. 15, 1856. His wife, Rachel, was born on Jan. 30, 1794 and died on March 22, 1874. Other nearby burials were: Mary A., daughter of Isaac N. Wilson, was born on March 2, 1816 and died on March 28, 1850. Lucinda A.H., daughter of Isaac N. Wilson, was born on June 6, 1818 and died on April 3, 1873. Source: Tombstone inscriptions in the Baker Graveyard, on bank of North River, near Delray, Hampshire County, W.Va.

Wilson, Thomas, died in July 1859, aged 87 years, of "paralysis," after a five-day illness. Born in Virginia. Farmer. Survived by spouse. Source: 1860 Mortality Schedule for Frederick County, Va.

Wilson, William, was born in Ulster, Ireland on Nov. 16, 1722 and died in Hardy County, Va. in 1801. His wife was Elizabeth Blackburn, born on Feb. 25, 1725. It is believed that they were settlers in old Frederick and Hampshire Counties, Va. circa 1742. The lived near Trout Run near Wardensville, in what is now Hardy County, W.Va. Their Bible record lists eleven children. A book of tremendous importance, on William Wilson and his descendants, was published in 1977 by Mr. Roy Wilson, 1258 Greenwood Avenue, Zanesville, Ohio. See also, *Descendants of William Wilson (1722-1801) and Elizabeth Blackburn*, compiled by C.J. Maxwell, Dallas, Texas, 1943.

Windle, Rebecca, a "widow," died in August 1859, aged 74 years. Born in Virginia, she was ill for three months prior to her death (of unknown cause). Source: 1860 Mortality Schedule for Shenandoah County, Va.

Wolford, David was born on Sept. 23, 1823 in Hampshire County (per court deposition re William Loy's wife Magdalene for widow's pension), and died on Nov. 7, 1890. His wife was named Mary, died on Nov. 24, 1905, aged 78 years and 17 days. Both were buried at the Mt. Zion Lutheran cemetery between Augusta and Rio, W.Va.

Wolford, Elijah, son of , was born on April 1, 1825 and died on June 14, 1884. His wife, Lucinda, died on Feb. 21, 1907, aged 68 years, 10 months and 3 days. Source: Tombstone inscriptions in the John Wolford graveyard, Hoy, Hampshire County, W.Va. See accompanying photos of this historic graveyard.

Wolford, George, son of Henry and Elizabeth (Kidwell) Wolford, was born in Hampshire County, Virginia on Dec. 1, 1815, according to a Bible record. He died during the 1890's in Peoria, Illinois, according to Russell Wolford of Brimfield, Illinois. George married Nancy Loy on Thursday Dec. 24, 1840, according to a letter written by Benjamin McDonald, II, of North River Mills, Va. to Samuel Farmer of New Hope, Lincoln County, Missouri. Nancy was a daughter of Adam and Sarah (Hiett) Loy. She was born on June 3, 1810 in Hampshire County, Va. and died on Dec. 18, 1881, in Peoria County, Illinois. Source: Bible record in possession of Mrs. Leatha Taylor.

Wolford, Henry, son of John and Catherine (Sidener) Wolford, was born on Oct. 20, 1789, according to a family Bible. His wife was Elizabeth Kidwell, daughter of John and Ellen (Hayes) Kidwell, of Sandy Ridge, Hampshire County, Va. Apparently Elizabeth died relatively young, during the early 1820's. They had three proven children: George Wolford married Nancy Loy; John Wolford; Lucinda Wolford married John Stewart. After Elizabeth's death, Henry Wolford married Margaret Rhinehart, daughter of Abraham and Margaret Rhinehart.

Wolford, Isabella, daughter of John and Catherine Sidener) Wolford, was born on April 10, 1805 and died on Jan. 4, 1870 in Hampshire County. She married William Bennett on Oct. 24, 1827. He was born on July 25, 1805 and died on Dec. 25, 1841. Source: Oscar L. Bennett, Bethel Park, PA, who wrote a pamphlet on their descendants.

Wolford, Jacob, son of John and Catherine (Sidener) Wolford, died on July 10, 1874, aged 74 years, 4 months and 4 days. He was born on March 6, 1800. His wife was named Catherine Grapes. They lived in Hoy section of Hampshire County. Source: Courthouse death record, et al.

Wolford, John, was born on Aug. 11, 1763 in "Washington County, MD" and died in mid-Nov. 1849, near Augusta, Hampshire County. He was buried on one of his Hampshire County farms, now located on the property of Stanley Haines, adjoining an apple orchard owned by Kenneth Grapes, at Hoy. He was a soldier in the Revolutionary War. According to a family Bible record, his wife was Catherine Sidner, born on Feb. 8, 1764. Source: Hampshire County Courthouse records (Will, deeds,etc.) and U.S. Mortality Census for 1850; pension application, in National Archives, and family Bible page.

Wolford, Josiah, died on July 8, 1874, in Hampshire County, aged 47 years. He left a widow and five children. Source: Aug. 6, 1874 issue of the *South Branch Intelligencer*. It is believed that his parents were Henry and Margaret (Rhinehart) Wolford.

Wolford, Martin, son of John and Catherine (Sidener) Wolford, died on May 17, 1872, in Hampshire County, West Virginia. He married Mary Crim, on Aug. 3, 1815, in Berkeley County, Va. Martin's Will stated that he wanted to be buried in the Malick cemetery, but I have not been able to locate the grave. The assumption is that descendants did not erect a tombstone.

Source: Hampshire County death record and Berkeley County, Va. marriage records.

Wolford, Phebe Jane, daughter of George and Nancy (Loy) Wolford, was born on Sept. 5, 1851 and died on Sept. 22, 1863, aged 12 years, 17 days. This is from a tombstone inscription in the Evan Hiett graveyard on Sandy Ridge. The Wolford family moved to Peoria, Illinois about 1876. The Bible record states that Phebe Jane died in 1864, but the other dates are in agreement. I'm inclined to go with the information on the tombstone, assuming that the Bible was filled in later.

Wood, James Sr., was born in England, in 1705 and died in Winchester, Va. on Nov. 6, 1759. His wife was named Mary Rutherford. Wood was a surveyor for old Orange County, Va. and he founded the town of Winchester, Va. Source: *Winchester, Virginia and Its Beginnings*, Shenandoah Publishing House: Strasburg, Va., 1926, by Katherine Glass Greene, page 108.

Wood, Lydia, born circa 1775, and died in April 1860, "of typhoid pneumonia," after a 4-day illness. Born in Virginia Weaver. Source: 1860 Mortality Schedule for Frederick County, Va.

Woodrow, Andrew Sr., died in 1814, when his Will was probated in Hampshire County, Va. The Will suggests that he was twice-married, his second wife being Mary Harrison. Three children of this marriage were: Andrew Woodrow Jr., William Craig Woodrow and Emily Jean Woodrow, who married Samuel Kercheval Jr. By his first marriage, Andrew Woodrow Sr. had Elizabeth Woodrow who married James Dailey, a Romney merchant, and Matilda Woodrow, who married John McDowell. Andrew Woodrow Sr. served as Clerk of the Hampshire County Court from 1782-1814. He served as a captain in the Revolutionary War, but did not receive a pension.

Woolary, Michael, died on Nov. 2, 1857, aged 72 years. His wife Elizabeth died on April 25, 1858, aged 65 years. It's possible that this is was a Quaker couple with roots in Frederick County, Va. (no proof, yet). They were buried in the Center Friends Burying Ground, Clinton County, Ohio. In this same cemetery was buried one Henry Babb. At the Quaker Cemetery in Gainsboro, Va., also, were buried members of the Babb and Woolary (sometimes spelled Woolery or Ullery).

Wright, James, was born in 1676 and died on the 15th day, 5th month, 1759, in Frederick County, Va., according to Quaker records. James was a Quaker minister. His wife was named Mary, maiden name not proven. They were among the first settlers to settle in the "Opeckon settlement," in 1735, in old Orange County, Va. A history of this family will appear in a forthcoming book, titled *Settlements and Settlers in Old Frederick County, Va.*

Wright, Lydia, was born on the 31st day, 8th month, 1730, in Monocacy Valley, Prince George County, MD, and died on June 27, 1778, in Hampshire County, Va. Lydia was the youngest child of James and Mary Wright, first settlers in "old Frederick County, Va.." She married Owen Rogers. They resided at Bear Garden Mountain, where they raised eleven children, in what is now the Bloomery District of Hampshire County. After Lydia's death, Owen remarried to Mary Roach, on Nov. 29, 1780, at Fairfax Meeting, Va. Source: Quaker records.

Wright, Rebecca, wife of John Wright, died on Dec. 24, 1817, aged 31 years, 3 months, 17 days. Source: Tombstone inscription, Indian Mound Cemetery, Romney, W.Va.

Wright, Sidney, daughter of John and Phebe Wright, was born in Frederick County, Va. on Oct. 18, 1791 and died July 12, 1871. She first married William Mercer. Their only child, Phebe Mercer, was born Feb. 11, 1815. After William's untimely death, Sidney remarried to Abraham Grove, son of John and Mary Grove. Their family burial ground was in the Heironimus graveyard at Whitacre, Frederick County, Va. Source: *Grove Fractur Book*, possessed by Joan Powell of Martinsburg, W.Va.

Yonley, Rebecca, (nee Lupton) died in Hampshire County, age 83, on Aug. 13, 1876. Source: *South Branch Intelligencer*, issue of Aug. 25, 1876. Her husband, Thomas Yonley, was deceased before April 13, 1849. In *Order Book II*, pages 314-315, Circuit Court of Hampshire County, these children of Thomas and Rebecca Yonley are listed: (1) Samuel Yonley married Maria Rogers, daughter of Robert and Mercy Rogers, Hampshire County (2) Maria Yonley married Samuel Slane (3) Louisa Yonley married Michael C. Wolford (4) Jane Yonley (5) Thomas Yonley, Jr. (6) Julianne Yonley.

Yost, Daniel, son of Peter and Elizabeth (Caw) Yost, was born on Feb. 27, 1817 and died on June 24, 1871. He was a mechanic. Wife was named Hannah. Lived entire life in the area. Source: Morgan County, W.Va. death record in courthouse.

Yost, Henry, died on Feb. 14, 1892, aged 76 years. Source: Tombstone inscription at Three Churches, Hampshire County.

Yost, Michael, son of a Revolutionary soldier (John Yost), was born on Nov. 3, 1766 in Frederick County, Va. and died on Feb. 2, 1849 in Harrison County, Ohio. His wife was nee Rachel Kackley, daughter of John and Elizabeth (Whiteman) Kackley, also a Revolutionary War veteran. She was born near Winchester, Va. (at North Mountain) on March 28, 1770 and died on Feb. 19, 1849 in Harrison County, Ohio. Sources: Historical Collections of Harrison County, by Charles A. Hanna, 1900, page 584.

Yost, Peter, son of John and Elizabeth Yost, died in Morgan County, W.Va. on March 8, 1872, aged 76 years, 7 months, 8 days. He was a farmer. His wife, Elizabeth Caw, daughter of Joseph and Evy Caw, died on Nov. 29, 1875, aged 72 years. Source: Death records in the Morgan County, W.Va. courthouse.

Yost, Peter, filed a Will[49] in Morgan County, Va. on Dec. 22, 1855. It named: wife Catherine to receive 200-acre farm; (1) daughter Elizabeth Yost married John Spriggs (2) Rosannah Yost married Henry Kerns (3) John Yost (4) Mary Yost married Abner Batt (5) William Yost (6) George B. Yost and (7) Amanda Yost married John Henry. [Comment: A tombstone at Ambrose Chapel shows that Peter Yost was born in 1777 and died in 1856, and that Catherine Bohrer his wife was born on May 20, 1776 and died on May 26, 1856, aged 80 years, 6 days. See Graveyard History of Morgan County, W.Va., published by the Morgan County Historical and Genealogical Society, Berkeley Springs, W.Va. 25411.]

Yost, William, filed his Will in Morgan County, Va. on Jan. 5, 1824 and he was deceased before Oct. 31, 1825. Named were: wife Elizabeth; sons John Peter, and William; and daughters Mary Catherine, and Elizabeth. Mathias Ambrose and Peter Michael were named executors of his estate. Bondsmen were: Adam Hinkle, Sarah Miller, and James H. Brewer.

---

49. See **Will Book 3**, Morgan County, W.Va.

Index

Index

Index